*f*P

Also by James P. Womack and Daniel T. Jones

The Machine That Changed the World
(with Daniel Roos)

The Future of the Automobile
(with Alan Altshuler, Martin Anderson, and Daniel Roos)

Seeing the Whole: Mapping the Extended Value Stream

LEAN THINKING

BANISH WASTE AND CREATE WEALTH IN YOUR CORPORATION

Revised and Updated

James P. Womack
and Daniel T. Jones

FREE PRESS
New York   London   Toronto   Sydney

For Anne
Both necessary and sufficient;
my picture of perfection
J.P.W.

and

for Pat
My patient and wise counselor
D.T.J.

ƒP

FREE PRESS
A Division of Simon & Schuster, Inc.
1230 Avenue of the Americas
New York, NY 10020

Copyright © 1996, 2003 by James Womack and Daniel Jones
All rights reserved,
including the right of reproduction
in whole or in part in any form.

First Free Press Edition 2003

FREE PRESS and colophon are trademarks
of Simon & Schuster, Inc.

For information regarding special discounts for bulk purchases,
please contact Simon & Schuster Special Sales at 1-800-456-6798
or business@simonandschuster.com

Designed by Irving Perkins Associates

Manufactured in the United States of America

20 19 18 17 16 15 14 13

Library of Congress Cataloging-in-Publication Data is available.

ISBN 0-7432-4927-5

Preface to the 2003 Edition

Lean Thinking was first published in the fall of 1996, just in time—we thought—for the recession of 1997 and the financial meltdown of 1998. The book's mission was to explain how to get beyond the financial games of the 1990s to create real, lasting value in any business. Toward this end, it demonstrated how a range of firms in North America, Europe, and Japan took advantage of the recession of 1991 to rethink their strategies and embark on a new path.

In our presentations to industrial audiences, we often point out that the only sure thing about forecasts is that they are wrong. (Which is why lean thinkers strive to reduce order-to-delivery times to such an extent that most products can be made to order and always try to add or subtract capacity in small increments.) Instead of a recession in 1997, the most ebullient economy of the entire twentieth century charged ahead for five more years, into 2001, extending a remarkable era in which practically anyone could succeed in business.

Given that the book was published years before our ideas were most needed, it's surprising how many readers took the advice in *Lean Thinking* seriously during the best of times. More than 300,000 copies have been sold in English, and it's been translated into German, French, Italian, Portuguese, Polish, Turkish, Korean, Japanese, and Chinese. We have heard from readers across the world about their successes in applying its principles.

Once reality caught up with our forecast, and the recession of 2001 gave way to the financial meltdown of 2002, reader interest surged. Indeed, *Lean Thinking* reappeared on the *Business Week* business-books bestseller list in 2001—nearly five years after its launch and with no publicity campaign—an unprecedented event, according to our publishers.

Given clear evidence that readers are now finding *Lean Thinking* even more relevant in their business lives than when it was first published, we have decided to expand and reissue the book. In Part I we explain some simple, actionable principles for creating lasting value in any business during any business conditions. We then show in Part II how to apply these principles, step by step, in real businesses, from large to small. In Part III, we show how a relentless focus on the *value stream* for every product—from concept to launch and order to delivery, and from the upstream headwaters of the supply base all the way downstream into the arms of the customer—can create a true *lean enterprise* that optimizes the value created for the customer while minimizing time, cost, and errors.

In the two new chapters of Part IV, we bring the story of the continuing advance of lean thinking up-to-date. We track the trend in inventory turns—the lean metric that cannot lie—across all industries, singling out one industry for special praise. We also track the progress of our profiled companies. We discover that as economies have gyrated, stock markets have crashed, and the poster companies of the 1990s hailed in other business books have flown a ballistic trajectory, our lean exemplars—led by Toyota—have defied the fate of most firms featured in successful business books. They have continued their methodical march from success to success and have done it the hard way by creating real and truly sustainable value for their customers, their employees, and their owners.

Finally, in the concluding chapter, we share what we have ourselves learned since 1996 about lean thinking and its successful application by describing a range of new implementation tools. These begin with the concept of value stream mapping, which we have found to be a remarkable way to raise consciousness about value and its components, leading to action.

In revising the book we have corrected a few minor errors and omissions in the original text. However, we have been careful not to change the pagination. We know that many organizations use *Lean Thinking* as a text to guide their change process, distributing copies widely and often including their distributors and suppliers. Thus we wanted to ensure that there will be no difficulty in interchanging the two editions.

Today, nearly seven years after its publication, we are even more certain that lean thinking, as explained in *Lean Thinking*, is the single most powerful tool available for creating value while eliminating waste in any organization. We hope that previous readers will use this new edition as an opportunity to renew their commitment to lean principles. And we especially hope that many new readers will discover a whole new world of opportunity.

Jim Womack and Dan Jones
Brookline, Massachusetts, and Ross-on-Wye, Herefordshire, U.K.
February 2003

Contents

Preface to the 2003 Edition ... 5
Preface to the First Edition: From Lean Production to Lean Enterprise ... 9

PART I: LEAN PRINCIPLES
Introduction: Lean Thinking versus *Muda* ... 15
  1. Value ... 29
  2. The Value Stream ... 37
  3. Flow ... 50
  4. Pull ... 67
  5. Perfection ... 90

PART II: FROM THINKING TO ACTION: THE LEAN LEAP
  6. The Simple Case ... 102
  7. A Harder Case ... 125
  8. The Acid Test ... 151
  9. Lean Thinking versus German *Technik* ... 189
 10. Mighty Toyota; Tiny Showa ... 219
 11. An Action Plan ... 247

PART III: LEAN ENTERPRISE
 12. A Channel for the Stream; a Valley for the Channel ... 275
 13. Dreaming About Perfection ... 286

PART IV: EPILOGUE
 14. The Steady Advance of Lean Thinking ... 299
 15. Institutionalizing the Revolution ... 313

Afterword: The Lean Network	338
Appendix: Individuals and Organizations Who Helped	341
Glossary	347
Notes	355
Bibliography	377
Index	379

PREFACE TO THE FIRST EDITION

From Lean Production to Lean Enterprise

In the fall of 1990, we set out on a trip around the world to launch our previous book, *The Machine That Changed the World*. Our objective was to send a wake-up message to organizations, managers, employees, and investors stuck in the old-fashioned world of mass production. *Machine* presented a wealth of benchmarking data to show that there is a better way to organize and manage customer relations, the supply chain, product development, and production operations, an approach pioneered by the Toyota company after World War II. We labeled this new way *lean production* because it does more and more with less and less.

As we started our travels across North America, then to Japan (where many mass producers still reside) and Korea, and on through Europe, we were greatly concerned that no one would listen. Perhaps the slumber of mass production was too deep to disturb? In fact, *The Machine That Changed the World* found an overwhelming response. More than 400,000 copies have been sold so far in eleven languages (not counting the pirated Chinese translation).[1] Far from ignoring our findings or resisting our advice, many audiences during that inaugural trip and many readers in subsequent forums told us that they were anxious to give lean production a try. Their question was seemingly a simple one: How do we do it?

In posing this question, they were not asking about specific techniques—how to organize teams, how to use Quality Function Deployment in product development, or how to *poka-yoke* (mistake-proof) production processes. After all, there is a plethora of very good books on each of these topics. Rather, they were asking: What are the key principles to guide our actions? and How do we as managers, employees, investors, suppliers, and customers take stuck-in-the-mud mass production organizations and make them lean? A few thoughtful respondents asked an even more difficult question: What comes next? What's the next leap, once you become a Toyota yourself?

The fact was, we didn't know the answers. We had been busy benchmarking industrial performance across the world for fifteen years, but *Machine* focused on aggregated processes—product development, sales, production—rather than broad principles, and we had never ourselves tried to convert a mass-production organization into a lean one. What was more, we had been so busy thinking through the initial leap from mass to lean production that we had not had time to think much about next steps for firms like Toyota.

The idea for this book emerged directly from these questions. First, we realized that we needed to concisely summarize the principles of "lean thinking" to provide a sort of North Star, a dependable guide for action for managers striving to transcend the day-to-day chaos of mass production. This summary was hard for most readers to construct because the Japanese originators of lean techniques worked from the bottom up. They talked and thought mostly about specific methods applied to specific activities in engineering offices, purchasing departments, sales groups, and factories: dedicated product development teams, target pricing, level scheduling, cellular manufacturing. Although they wrote whole books describing specific techniques and a few high-level philosophic reflections as well (such as the memoirs of Taiichi Ohno),[2] the thought process needed to tie all the methods together into a complete system was left largely implicit. As a result, we met many managers who had drowned in techniques as they tried to implement isolated bits of a lean system without understanding the whole.

After interactions with many audiences and considerable reflection, we concluded that lean thinking can be summarized in five principles: precisely specify *value* by specific product, identify the *value stream* for each product, make value *flow* without interruptions, let the customer *pull* value from the producer, and pursue *perfection*. By clearly understanding these principles, and then tying them all together, managers can make full use of lean techniques and maintain a steady course. These principles and their application are the subject of Part I of this book.

With regard to the conversion process, we knew of one heroic example—the original lean leap by Toyota immediately after World War II—but only in sketchy outline. What was more, our most striking benchmark examples in *Machine* were the "greenfield" plants started from scratch by Japanese auto firms in the West in the 1980s. These were critical achievements because they blew away all the claims, so prevalent up to that time, that, to work, lean production somehow depended on Japanese cultural institutions. Greenfields, however—with new bricks and mortar, new employees, and new tools—bore little resemblance to the long-established "brownfields" most managers were struggling to fix. Our readers wanted a detailed plan of march suited to their reality, and one that would apply in any industry.

We therefore resolved to identify firms in a range of industries in the leading industrial countries that had created or were creating lean organizations from mass-production brownfields. Observing what they had done seemed to be our best hope of discovering the common methods of becoming lean. In doing this, we did not want a survey to discover average practice but rather to concentrate on the outliers—those organizations recently moving far beyond convention to make a true leap into leanness.

But where to find them? We knew the motor vehicle industry well, but we wanted examples from across the industrial landscape, including service organizations. In addition, we wanted examples of small firms to complement household-name giants, low-volume producers to contrast with high-volume automakers, and "high-tech" firms to compare against those with mature technologies.

In the end, through a lot of hard digging and some good fortune, we tapped into networks of lean thinking executives in North America, Europe, and Japan, and gained hands-on experience from a personal investment in a small manufacturing company. Over a four-year period, we interacted with more than fifty firms in a wide range of industries and gained a deep understanding of the human exertions needed to convert mass-production organizations to leanness. We describe our findings and prescribe a practical plan of action in Part II of this book.

To our delight, as we began to find our key examples, this book became an intensive collaboration between a group of like-minded people across the world. They believe passionately in a set of ideas, have made great progress in introducing them, and want to see lean thinking universally embraced. At the end of this volume we list the firms and executives we have worked with and describe ways for you to join them. Here let us simply express our profound appreciation for the hours, days, and even weeks many of them took with us.

Because we needed to look at the entire firm, indeed at the whole *value stream* for specific products, running from raw material to finished good, order to delivery, and concept to launch, and because we needed to examine many things which would rightly be considered proprietary, we proposed an unusual way of working together. In return for access to every aspect of the firm, including interviews with suppliers, customers, and unions, we offered to share our drafts with our respondents, asking for criticism and corrections. We stated in advance that any material our example firms could not bear seeing in the public domain would be deleted, but if the need to protect proprietary interests (or self-esteem) required deletion of those details which made the story "true," we would simply leave the firm in question out of the book. In the end we didn't lose anyone.

Our method of working as outsider-insiders, perhaps first used fifty years ago by Peter Drucker for his landmark study of General Motors, *The Concept of the Corporation*,[3] placed special demands for "transparency" on the authors. There is today a profound and warranted skepticism about "business" books, both because they promise instant cures and because their authors—especially consultants but sometimes academics as well—have financial links to the firms they write about. We therefore need to assure you that we have no financial or consulting relationship of any sort to any of the individuals or firms we write about in these pages.[4] We need to further assure you that we have verified all the performance data presented. Indeed, in most cases we have verified it with our own eyes by walking the production floor and spending extended periods in the engineering, marketing, sales, customer support, and purchasing functions and with product development teams.

In order to maintain complete independence in our search for leanness, we financed our efforts over four years with an advance from Simon & Schuster and from our personal savings.

As we began to write up our findings on how to make a lean leap in traditional, mass-production organizations, we began to realize that it is both possible and necessary to go even farther than any firms have done to date. A wholly new way of thinking about the roles of firms, functions, and careers to channel the flow of value from concept to launch, order to delivery, and raw material into the arms of the customer is now needed in order to achieve a further "leap." A new concept—the *lean enterprise*—can move the whole "value stream" for products dramatically in the direction of perfection. We introduce this concept briefly in Part I and then look carefully at the challenge of lean enterprise in Part III. There we also dream a bit about the next "leap." No one has made it yet. Perhaps some reader will be the first.

After four years of exhaustive study of organizations around the world who are actually doing it, we now know how to succeed at leanness. As the examples will show, we know how to apply lean thinking, techniques, and organization to practically any activity, whether a good or a service. What's more, we now have a glimmering of the next leap beyond today's best practice. In the pages ahead we'll explain in detail what to do and why. Your job, therefore, is simple: Just do it!

PART I
LEAN PRINCIPLES

INTRODUCTION
Lean Thinking versus Muda

Muda. It's the one word of Japanese you really must know. It sounds awful as it rolls off your tongue and it should, because *muda* means "waste," specifically any human activity which absorbs resources but creates no *value:* mistakes which require rectification, production of items no one wants so that inventories and remaindered goods pile up, processing steps which aren't actually needed, movement of employees and transport of goods from one place to another without any purpose, groups of people in a downstream activity standing around waiting because an upstream activity has not delivered on time, and goods and services which don't meet the needs of the customer.

Taiichi Ohno (1912–1990), the Toyota executive who was the most ferocious foe of waste human history has produced, identified the first seven types of *muda* described above and we've added the final one.[1] Perhaps there are even more. But however many varieties of *muda* there may be, it's hard to dispute—from even the most casual observation of what gets done in an average day in the average organization—that *muda* is everywhere. What's more, as you learn to see *muda* in the pages ahead, you will discover that there is even more around than you ever dreamed.

Fortunately, there is a powerful antidote to *muda: lean thinking.* It provides a way to specify value, line up value-creating actions in the best sequence, conduct these activities without interruption whenever someone requests them, and perform them more and more effectively. In short, lean thinking is *lean* because it provides a way to do more and more with less and less—less human effort, less equipment, less time, and less space—while coming closer and closer to providing customers with exactly what they want.

Lean thinking also provides a way to make work more satisfying by providing immediate feedback on efforts to convert *muda* into value. And, in striking contrast with the recent craze for process reengineering, it provides a way to create new work rather than simply destroying jobs in the name of efficiency.

Specify Value

The critical starting point for lean thinking is *value*. Value can only be defined by the ultimate customer. And it's only meaningful when expressed in terms of a specific product (a good or a service, and often both at once) which meets the customer's needs at a specific price at a specific time.

Value is created by the producer. From the customer's standpoint, this is why producers exist. Yet for a host of reasons value is very hard for producers to accurately define. Business school–trained senior executives of American firms routinely greet us when we visit with a slick presentation about their organization, their technology, their core competencies, and their strategic intentions. Then, over lunch, they tell us about their short-term competitive problems (specifically their need to garner adequate profits in the next quarter) and the consequent cost-cutting initiatives. These often involve clever ways to eliminate jobs, divert revenues from their downstream customers, and extract profits from their upstream suppliers. (Because we are associated with the concept of lean production, they are usually eager to label these programs "lean," although often they are only "mean.") By dessert, we may be hearing about their personal career issues in the current age of "downsizing."

What only comes up when we push it to the foreground is the specific products the firm expects specific customers to purchase at a specific price to keep the company in business and how the performance and delivered quality of these products can be improved while their fundamental costs are pushed steadily down. In raising this issue it's often revealing to ask these executives a simple question: Can you put yourself in the position of a design as it progresses from concept to launch, an order as information flows from initial request to delivered product, and the physical product as it progresses from raw material to the customer, and describe what will happen to you at each step along the way? Usually there is an awkward silence, and then, if we aren't persistent, these issues quickly slip out of sight to be replaced once more by aggregated financial considerations. In short, the immediate needs of the shareholder and the financial mind-set of the senior managers have taken precedence over the day-to-day realities of specifying and creating value for the customer.

When we've gone to Germany, until very recently, we've found a reverse distortion of value specification. For much of the post–World War II era, executives of private or bank-controlled companies could ignore the need for short-term financial performance and were eager to tell us all about their products and process technologies. Even the most senior executives could go into great detail about product features and new processing methods which had taken years to perfect.

But who specified their value? The engineers running the companies! Designs with more complexity produced with ever more complex machinery were asserted to be just what the customer wanted and just what the production process needed. But where was the evidence?

In pressing this point, it often became apparent that the strong technical functions and highly trained technical experts leading German firms obtained their sense of worth—their conviction that they were doing a first-rate job—by pushing ahead with refinements and complexities that were of little interest to anyone but the experts themselves. Our doubts about proposed products were often countered with claims that "the customer will want it once we explain it," while recent product failures were often explained away as instances where "the customers weren't sophisticated enough to grasp the merits of the product."

A central feature of the crisis of German industry in the period since the end of the cold war has been the dawning perception that the complex, customized designs and sophisticated processing technologies favored by German engineers are too expensive for customers to afford and often irrelevant to their real desires.

When we have traveled to Japan, also until very recently, we have encountered yet a third distortion. What's been really important for Japanese firms as they have defined value is *where* value is created. Most executives, even at firms like Toyota which pioneered lean thinking, have begun their value definition process by asking how they can design and make their product at home—to satisfy societal expectations about long-term employment and stable supplier relations. Yet most customers across the world like products designed with an eye to local needs, which is hard to do from a distant home office. And they like products made to their precise order to be delivered immediately, which ocean shipping from a Japanese production base makes impossible. They certainly do not define the value of a product primarily in terms of where it was designed or made.

What's more, the stay-at-home-at-all-costs thinking of Japanese senior managers, even as the yen steadily strengthened, depleted the financial resources these firms needed to do new things in the future. The immediate needs of employees and suppliers took precedence over the needs of the customer, which must sustain any firm in the long term.

Moving beyond these national distortions in the world's three most important industrial systems (and every country probably has its own unique set),[2] we are repeatedly struck how the definition of value is skewed everywhere by the power of preexisting organizations, technologies, and undepreciated assets, along with outdated thinking about economies of scale. Managers around the world tend to say, "This product is what we know how to produce using assets we've already bought, so if customers don't respond we'll adjust the price or add bells and whistles." What they should be doing instead is fundamentally rethinking value from the perspective of the customer.

One of the best (and most exasperating) illustrations of this backwards thought-process is the current-day airline industry. As frequent users of this service we have long been keeping detailed notes on our experiences and contrasting our own definition of value with that proposed by most companies in this industry. Our value equation is very simple: to get from where we are to where we want to be safely with the least hassle at a reasonable price. By contrast, the airline's definition seems to involve using their existing assets in the most "efficient" manner, even if we have to visit Timbuktu to get anywhere. They then throw in added features—like executive lounges in their hubs and elaborate entertainment systems in every seat—in hopes the inconvenience will be tolerable.

Just today, as this is written, one of us has traveled the 350 miles from his summer home in Jamestown in western New York State, across Lake Erie, to Holland, Michigan, in order to make a presentation on lean thinking to an industrial audience. What was needed was a way to fly from Jamestown directly to Holland (both of which have small airports) at an affordable cost. What was available was either an absurdly priced charter service from Jamestown to Holland (total door-to-door travel time of about two hours) or an eighty-mile drive to the Buffalo, New York, airport, a flight on a large jet to the Detroit sortation center of Northwest Airlines (where the self-sorting human cargo finds its way through a massive terminal from one plane to the next), another flight on a large jet to Grand Rapids, Michigan, and a forty-mile drive to the ultimate destination. (The lower-cost option required a total travel time of seven hours.)

Why aren't airlines like Northwest (and its global partner KLM) and airframe builders like Boeing and Airbus working on low-cost, point-to-point services using smaller jets instead of developing ever-larger aircraft? And why aren't they developing quick turnaround systems for small jets at small airports instead of constructing Taj Mahal terminals at the absurd "hubs" created in America after airline deregulation—and long present in Europe and East Asia due to the politically motivated practice of routing most flights of state-controlled airlines through national capitals? (One hour of the seven hours spent on the trip just cited was taxiing time in the Detroit hub and a second was occupied with self-sortation inside the terminal.)

Few firms are aggressively promoting this definition of value because the airlines and airframe builders start their thinking with extraordinarily costly assets in the form of large aircraft; the engineering knowledge, tooling, and production facilities to make more large aircraft; and massive airport complexes. Old-fashioned "efficiency" thinking suggests that the best way to make use of these assets and technologies is to get larger batches of people on larger planes and to do this by sending ever more passengers through the expensive sorting centers. This type of efficiency calculation, focused on the airplane and the hub—only two of the many elements in the total trip—loses sight of the whole. Much worse from the standpoint of value for the passenger, it simply misses the point.

The end result of fifteen years of this type of thinking in the United States is that passengers are miserable (this is not what they meant by value!), the aircraft producers make little money (because the airlines can't afford new planes), and the airlines (excepting Southwest and a few other start-ups pursuing the more sensible strategy of flying point-to-point, although still using large aircraft) have flown a decade-long holding pattern in the vicinity of bankruptcy. Europe and parts of East Asia are not far behind.

Lean thinking therefore must start with a conscious attempt to precisely define value in terms of specific products with specific capabilities offered at specific prices through a dialogue with specific customers. The way to do this is to ignore existing assets and technologies and to rethink firms on a product-line basis with strong, dedicated product teams. This also requires redefining the role for a firm's technical experts (like the inward-looking German engineers we just cited) and rethinking just where in the world to create value. Realistically, no manager can actually implement all of these changes instantly, but it's essential to form a clear view of what's really needed. Otherwise the definition of value is almost certain to be skewed.

In summary, specifying value accurately is the critical first step in lean thinking. Providing the wrong good or service the right way is *muda*.

Identify the Value Stream

The *value stream* is the set of all the specific actions required to bring a specific product (whether a good, a service, or, increasingly, a combination of the two) through the three critical management tasks of any business: the *problem-solving task* running from concept through detailed design and engineering to production launch, the *information management task* running from order-taking through detailed scheduling to delivery, and the *physical transformation task* proceeding from raw materials to a finished product in the hands of the customer.[3] Identifying the *entire* value stream for each product (or in some cases for each product family) is the next step in lean thinking, a step which firms have rarely attempted but which almost always exposes enormous, indeed staggering, amounts of *muda*.

Specifically, value stream analysis will almost always show that three types of actions are occurring along the value stream: (1) Many steps will be found to unambiguously create value: welding the tubes of a bicycle frame together or flying a passenger from Dayton to Des Moines. (2) Many other steps will be found to create no value but to be unavoidable with current technologies and production assets: inspecting welds to ensure quality and the extra step of flying large planes through the Detroit hub en route from Dayton to Des Moines (we'll term these Type One *muda*). And (3) many additional steps will be found to create no value and to be immediately avoidable (Type Two *muda*).

For example, when Pratt & Whitney, the world's largest manufacturer of aircraft jet engines, recently started to map its value streams for its three families of jet engines, it discovered that activities undertaken by its raw materials suppliers to produce ultrapure metals were duplicated at great cost by the next firms downstream, the forgers who converted metal ingots into near-net shapes suitable for machining. At the same time, the initial ingot of material—for example, titanium or nickel—was ten times the weight of the machined parts eventually fashioned from it. Ninety percent of the very expensive metals were being scrapped because the initial ingot was poured in a massive size—the melters were certain that this was efficient—without much attention to the shape of the finished parts. And finally, the melters were preparing several different ingots—at great cost—in order to meet Pratt's precise technical requirements for each engine, which varied only marginally from those of other engine families and from the needs of competitors. Many of these activities could be eliminated almost immediately with dramatic cost savings.

How could so much waste go unnoticed for decades in the supposedly sophisticated aerospace industry? Very simply: None of the four firms involved in this tributary value stream for a jet engine—the melter, the forger, the machiner, and the final assembler—had ever fully explained its activities to the other three. Partly, this was a matter of confidentiality—each firm feared that those upstream and downstream would use any information revealed to drive a harder bargain. And partly, it was a matter of obliviousness. The four firms were accustomed to looking carefully at their own affairs but had simply never taken the time to look at the whole value stream, including the consequences of their internal activities for other firms along the stream. When they did, within the past year, they discovered massive waste.

So lean thinking must go beyond the firm, the standard unit of scorekeeping in businesses across the world, to look at the whole: the entire set of activities entailed in creating and producing a specific product, from concept through detailed design to actual availability, from the initial sale through order entry and production scheduling to delivery, and from raw materials produced far away and out of sight right into the hands of the customer. The organizational mechanism for doing this is what we call the *lean enterprise*, a continuing conference of all the concerned parties to create a channel for the entire value stream, dredging away all the *muda*.

Whenever we present this idea for the first time, audiences tend to assume that a new legal entity is needed, some formalized successor to the "virtual corporation" which in reality becomes a new form of vertical integration. In fact, what is needed is the exact opposite. In an age when individual firms are outsourcing more and themselves doing less, the actual need is for a voluntary alliance of all the interested parties to oversee the disintegrated value stream, an alliance which examines every value-creating step and lasts as long as the product lasts. For products like automobiles in a specific size class, which go through successive generations of development, this might be decades; for short-lived products like software for a specific application, it might be less than a year.

Creating lean enterprises *does* require a new way to think about firm-to-firm relations, some simple principles for regulating behavior between firms, and *transparency* regarding all the steps taken along the value stream so each participant can verify that the other firms are behaving in accord with the agreed principles. These issues are the subject of Part III of this book.

Flow

Once value has been precisely specified, the value stream for a specific product fully mapped by the lean enterprise, and obviously wasteful steps eliminated, it's time for the next step in lean thinking—a truly breathtaking one: Make the remaining, value-creating steps *flow*. However, please be warned that this step requires a complete rearrangement of your mental furniture.

We are all born into a mental world of "functions" and "departments," a commonsense conviction that activities ought to be grouped by type so they can be performed more efficiently and managed more easily. In addition, to get tasks done efficiently within departments, it seems like further common sense to perform like activities in batches: "In the Claims Department, process all of the Claim As, then the Claim Bs, and then the Claim Cs. In the Paint Department, paint all of the green parts, then shift over and paint all the red parts, then do the purple ones." Batches, as it turns out, always mean long waits as the product sits patiently awaiting the department's changeover to the type of activity the product needs next. But this approach keeps the members of the department busy, all the equipment running hard, and justifies dedicated, high-speed equipment. So, it must be "efficient," right? Actually, it's dead wrong, but hard or impossible for most of us to see.

Recently, one of us performed a simple experiment with his daughters, ages six and nine: They were asked the best way to fold, address, seal, stamp, and mail the monthly issue of their mother's newsletter. After a bit of thought their answer was emphatic: "Daddy, first, you should fold all of the newsletters. Then you should put on all the address labels. Then you should attach the seal to stick the upper and lower parts together [to secure the newsletter for mailing]. Then you should put on the stamps." "But why not fold one newsletter, then seal it, then attach the address label, and then put on the stamp? Wouldn't that avoid the wasted effort of picking up and putting down every newsletter four times? Why don't we look at the problem from the standpoint of the newsletter which wants to get mailed in the quickest way with the least effort?" Their emphatic answer: "Because that wouldn't be efficient!"

What was striking was their profound conviction that performing tasks in batches is best—sending the newsletters from "department" to "department" around the kitchen table—and their failure to consider that a rethink of the task might permit continuous flow and more efficient work. What's equally striking when looked at this way is that most of the world conducts its affairs in accord with the thought processes of six- and nine-year-olds!

Taiichi Ohno blamed this batch-and-queue mode of thinking on civilization's first farmers, who he claimed lost the one-thing-at-a-time wisdom of the hunter as they became obsessed with batches (the once-a-year harvest) and inventories (the grain depository).[4] Or perhaps we're simply born with batching thinking in our heads, along with many other "common sense" illusions—for example, that time is constant rather than relative or that space is straight rather than curved. But we all need to fight departmentalized, batch thinking because tasks can almost always be accomplished much more efficiently and accurately when the product is worked on continuously from raw material to finished good. In short, things work better when you focus on the product and its needs, rather than the organization or the equipment, so that all the activities needed to design, order, and provide a product occur in continuous flow.

Henry Ford and his associates were the first people to fully realize the potential of flow. Ford reduced the amount of effort required to assemble a Model T Ford by 90 percent during the fall of 1913 by switching to continuous flow in final assembly. Subsequently, he lined up all the machines needed to produce the parts for the Model T in the correct sequence and tried to achieve flow all the way from raw materials to shipment of the finished car, achieving a similar productivity leap. But he only discovered the *special case*. His method only worked when production volumes were high enough to justify high-speed assembly lines, when every product used exactly the same parts, and when the same model was produced for many years (nineteen in the case of the Model T). In the early 1920s, when Ford towered above the rest of the industrial world, his company was assembling more than two million Model Ts at dozens of assembly plants around the world, every one of them exactly alike.

After World War II, Taiichi Ohno and his technical collaborators, including Shigeo Shingo,[5] concluded that the real challenge was to create continuous flow in small-lot production when dozens or hundreds of copies of a product were needed, not millions. This is the *general case* because these humble streams, not the few mighty rivers, account for the great bulk of human needs. Ohno and his associates achieved continuous flow in low-volume production, in most cases without assembly lines, by learning to quickly change over tools from one product to the next and by "right-sizing" (miniaturizing) machines so that processing steps of different types (say, molding, painting, and assembly) could be conducted immediately adjacent to each other with the object undergoing manufacture being kept in continuous flow.

The benefits of doing things this way are easy to demonstrate. We've recently watched with our own eyes, in plants in North America and Europe, as lean thinkers practiced *kaikaku* (roughly translatable as "radical improvement," in contrast with *kaizen*, or "continuous incremental improvement"). Production activities for a specific product were rearranged in a day from departments and batches to continuous flow, with a doubling of productivity and a dramatic reduction in errors and scrap. We'll report later in this book on the revolutionary rearrangement of product development and order-scheduling activities for these same products to produce the same magnitude of effect in only a slightly longer adjustment period. Yet the great bulk of activities across the world are still conducted in departmentalized, batch-and-queue fashion fifty years after a dramatically superior way was discovered. Why?

The most basic problem is that flow thinking is counterintuitive; it seems obvious to most people that work should be organized by departments in batches. Then, once departments and specialized equipment for making batches at high speeds are put in place, both the career aspirations of employees within departments and the calculations of the corporate accountant (who wants to keep expensive assets fully utilized) work powerfully against switching over to flow.

The reengineering movement has recognized that departmentalized thinking is suboptimal and has tried to shift the focus from organizational categories (departments) to value-creating "processes"—credit checking or claims adjusting or the handling of accounts receivable.[6] The problem is that the reengineers haven't gone far enough conceptually—they are still dealing with disconnected and aggregated *processes* (for example, order-taking for a whole range of products) rather than the entire *flow of value-creating activities for specific products*. In addition, they often stop at the boundaries of the firm paying their fees, whereas major breakthroughs come from looking at the whole value stream. What's more, they treat departments and employees as the enemy, using outside SWAT teams to blast both aside. The frequent result is a collapse of morale among those who survive being reengineered and a regression of the organization to the mean as soon as the reengineers are gone.

The lean alternative is to redefine the work of functions, departments, and firms so they can make a positive contribution to value creation and to speak to the real needs of employees at every point along the stream *so it is actually in their interest to make value flow*. This requires not just the creation of a *lean enterprise* for each product but also the rethinking of conventional firms, functions, and careers, and the development of a lean strategy, as explained in Part III.

Pull

The first visible effect of converting from departments and batches to product teams and flow is that the time required to go from concept to launch, sale to delivery, and raw material to the customer falls dramatically. When flow is introduced, products requiring years to design are done in months, orders taking days to process are completed in hours, and the weeks or months of throughput time for conventional physical production are reduced to minutes or days. Indeed, if you can't quickly take throughput times down by half in product development, 75 percent in order processing, and 90 percent in physical production, you are doing something wrong. What's more, lean systems can make any product currently in production in any combination, so that shifting demand can be accommodated immediately.

So what? This produces a onetime cash windfall from inventory reduction and speeds return on investment, but is it really a revolutionary achievement? In fact, it is because the ability to design, schedule, and make exactly what the customer wants just when the customer wants it means you can throw away the sales forecast and simply make what customers actually tell you they need. That is, you can let the customer *pull* the product from you as needed rather than pushing products, often unwanted, onto the customer. What's more, as explained in Chapter 4, the demands of customers become much more stable when they know they can get what they want right away and when producers stop periodic price discounting campaigns designed to move goods already made which no one wants.

Let's take a practical example: the book you hold in your hand. In fact, your copy is lucky. One half of the books printed in the United States each year are shredded without ever finding a reader! How can this be? Because publishers and the printing and distribution firms they work with along the value stream have never learned about flow, so the customer can't pull. It takes many weeks to reorder books if the bookseller or warehouse runs out of stock, yet the shelf life of most books is very short. Publishers must either sell the book at the peak of reader interest or forgo many sales. Because the publisher can't accurately predict demand in advance, the only solution is to print thousands of copies to "fill the channel" when the book is launched even though only a few thousand copies of the average book will be sold. The rest are then returned to the publisher and scrapped when the selling season is over.

The solution to this problem will probably emerge in phases. In the next few years, printing firms can learn to quickly print up small lots of books and distribution warehouses can learn to replenish bookstore shelves frequently (using a method described in Chapter 4). Eventually, new "right-sized" book-printing technologies may make it possible to simply print out the books the customer wants at the moment the customer asks for them, either in a bookstore or, even better, in the customer's office or home. And some customers may not want a physical copy of their "book" at all. Instead, they will request the electronic transfer of the text from the "publisher" to their own computer, printing out an old-fashioned paper version only if they happen to need it. The appropriate solution will be found once the members of the publishing value stream embrace the fourth principle of lean thinking: *pull*.

Perfection

As organizations begin to accurately specify *value*, identify the entire *value stream*, make the value-creating steps for specific products *flow* continuously, and let customers *pull* value from the enterprise, something very odd begins to happen. It dawns on those involved that there is no end to the process of reducing effort, time, space, cost, and mistakes while offering a product which is ever more nearly what the customer actually wants. Suddenly *perfection*, the fifth and final principle of lean thinking, doesn't seem like a crazy idea.

Why should this be? Because the four initial principles interact with each other in a virtuous circle. Getting value to flow faster always exposes hidden *muda* in the value stream. And the harder you pull, the more the impediments to flow are revealed so they can be removed. Dedicated product teams in direct dialogue with customers always find ways to specify value more accurately and often learn of ways to enhance flow and pull as well.

In addition, although the elimination of *muda* sometimes requires new process technologies and new product concepts, the technologies and concepts are usually surprisingly simple and ready for implementation right now. For example, we recently watched while Pratt & Whitney replaced a totally automated grinding system for turbine blades with a U-shaped cell designed and installed by its own engineers in a short time and at a quarter of the capital cost of the automated system being replaced. The new system cuts production costs by half while reducing throughput times by 99 percent and slashing changeover time from hours to seconds so Pratt can make exactly what the customer wants upon receiving the order. The conversion to lean thinking will pay for itself within a year, even if Pratt receives nothing more than scrap value for the automated system being junked.

Perhaps the most important spur to perfection is *transparency*, the fact that in a lean system everyone—subcontractors, first-tier suppliers, system integrators (often called assemblers), distributors, customers, employees—can see everything, and so it's easy to discover better ways to create value. What's more, there is nearly instant and highly positive feedback for employees making improvements, a key feature of lean work and a powerful spur to continuing efforts to improve, as explained in Chapter 3.

Readers familiar with the "open-book management" movement in the United States[7] will recall that financial transparency and immediate feedback on results, in the form of monetary bonuses for employees, are its central elements. Thus, there is a broad consistency between our approach and theirs. However, a major question emerges for open-book managers as finances are made transparent and employees are rewarded for performance. How can performance be improved? Sweat and longer hours are not the answer but will be employed if no one knows how to work smarter. The techniques for flow and pull that we will be describing in the pages ahead are the answer. What's more, when employees begin to feel the immediate feedback from making product development, order-taking, and production flow and are able to see the customer's satisfaction, much of the carrot-and-stick apparatus of open-book management's financial reward system becomes unnecessary.

The Prize We Can Grasp Now

Dreaming about perfection is fun. It's also useful, because it shows what is possible and helps us to achieve more than we would otherwise. However, even if lean thinking makes perfection seem plausible in the long term, most of us live and work in the short term. What are the benefits of lean thinking which we can grasp right away?

Based on years of benchmarking and observation in organizations around the world, we have developed the following simple rules of thumb: Converting a classic batch-and-queue production system to continuous flow with effective pull by the customer will double labor productivity all the way through the system (for direct, managerial, and technical workers, from raw materials to delivered product) while cutting production throughput times by 90 percent and reducing inventories in the system by 90 percent as well. Errors reaching the customer and scrap within the production process are typically cut in half, as are job-related injuries. Time-to-market for new products will be halved and a wider variety of products, within product families, can be offered at very modest additional cost. What's more, the capital investments required will be very modest, even negative, if facilities and equipment can be freed up and sold.

And this is just to get started. This is the *kaikaku* bonus released by the initial, radical realignment of the value stream. What follows is continuous improvements by means of *kaizen* en route to perfection. Firms having completed the radical realignment can typically double productivity again through incremental improvements within two to three years and halve again inventories, errors, and lead times during this period. And then the combination of *kaikaku* and *kaizen* can produce endless improvements.

Performance leaps of this magnitude are surely a bit hard to accept, particularly when accompanied by the claim that no dramatically new technologies are required. We've therefore worked for several years to carefully document specific instances of lean transformations in a wide range of firms in the leading industrial economies. In the chapters ahead, we provide a series of "box scores" on precisely what can be achieved and describe the specific methods to use.

The Antidote to Stagnation

Lean thinking is not just the antidote to *muda* in some abstract sense; the performance leap just described is also the answer to the prolonged economic stagnation in Europe, Japan, and North America. Conventional thinking about economic growth focuses on new technologies and additional training and education as the keys. Thus the overwhelming emphasis of current-day popular writing on the economy is on falling computing costs and the growing ease of moving data around the planet, as exemplified by the World Wide Web. Coupling low-cost, easily accessible data with interactive educational software for knowledge workers will surely produce a great leap in productivity and well-being, right?

The record is not promising. During the past twenty years we've seen the robotics revolution, the materials revolution (remember when cars would have ceramic engines and airplanes would be built entirely of plastic?), the microprocessor and personal computer revolution, and the biotechnology revolution, yet domestic product per capita (that is, the average amount of value created per person) in all the developed countries has been firmly stuck.

The problem is not with the new technologies themselves but instead with the fact that they initially affect only a small part of the economy. A few companies like Microsoft grow from infants to giants overnight, but the great bulk of economic activity—construction and housing, transport, the food supply system, manufacturing, and personal services—is only affected over a long period. What's more, these activities may not be affected at all unless new ways are found for people to work together to create value using the new technologies. Yet these traditional tasks comprise 95 percent or more of day-to-day production and consumption.

Stated another way, most of the economic world, at any given time, is a brownfield of traditional activities performed in traditional ways. New technologies and augmented human capital may generate growth over the long term, but only lean thinking has the demonstrated power to produce green shoots of growth all across this landscape within a few years. (And, as we will see, lean thinking may make some new technologies unnecessary.)

The continuing stagnation in developed countries has recently led to ugly scapegoating in the political world, as segments of the population in each country push and shove to redivide a fixed economic pie. Stagnation has also led to a frenzy of cost cutting in the business world (led by the reengineers), which removes the incentive for employees to make any positive contribution to their firms and swells the unemployment ranks. Lean thinking and the lean enterprise is the solution immediately available that can produce results on the scale required. This book explains how to do it.

Getting Started

Because lean thinking is counterintuitive and a bit difficult to grasp on first encounter (but then blindingly obvious once "the light comes on"), it's very useful to examine the actual application of the five lean principles in real organizations. The material in the remainder of Part I, therefore, provides real instances of lean principles banishing *muda*. The place to start, as always, is with *value* as defined by the customer.

CHAPTER 1

Value

A House or a Hassle-Free Experience?

Doyle Wilson of Austin, Texas, had been building homes for fifteen years before he got serious about quality. "In October of 1991 I just got disgusted. Such a large part of my business was waiting and rework, with expensive warranty claims and friction with customers, that I knew there must be a better way. Then I stumbled across the quality movement."

He read Carl Sewell's book on car dealing, *Customers for Life*,[1] and decided to test his claims by buying a car at Sewell's Dallas dealership. ("I thought that if even a car dealer could make a customer feel good, it should be easy for a homebuilder!") His purchase was such a positive experience that he asked Sewell for advice on quality in home building and was told to read the works of W. Edwards Deming.

Doyle Wilson is the archetypical Texan and never does things halfway. By February of 1992 he had launched a wall-to-wall Total Quality Management campaign at Doyle Wilson Homebuilder. Over the next three years he personally taught his workforce the principles of TQM, began to collect and analyze enormous amounts of data on every aspect of his business, got rid of individual sales commissions ("which destroy quality consciousness"), eliminated the traditional "builder bonus" for his construction superintendents (who were qualifying for the "on-time completion" bonus by making side deals with customers on a "to-be-done-later" list), reduced his contractor corps by two thirds, and required the remaining contractors to attend (and pay for) his monthly quality seminars.

Customer surveys showed a steady rise in satisfaction with the homebuilding experience and sales grew steadily even in a flat market as Wilson took sales from his competitors. In 1995, Doyle Wilson Homebuilder won the National Housing Quality Award (often called the Baldrige Award for quality of the construction industry), and Wilson set a goal of winning the Baldrige Award itself by 1998. Yet he was not satisfied.

"I knew I was making progress in competing with other builders for the new-home buyer, but a simple fact, once it lodged in my mind, wouldn't go away: 78 percent of the homes bought in central Texas each year are 'used' or older homes. I've been making progress in increasing my share of the 22 percent seeking a new home, but what about the 78 percent who bought older homes? Obviously, these buyers are the real market opportunity."

So instead of surveying people who were buying new homes, Wilson began to talk with people who were buying older homes. What he discovered was obvious in retrospect but has required a complete rethinking of his business. Specifically, he found that many buyers of older homes hated the "hassle factor" in negotiating for new construction, the long lead times to get the job done and move in, the inevitable "to-be-done" list after moving in, and the "phony choices" available from builders who promise custom homes but then load on as "standard equipment" many features of little interest to buyers.

Wilson soon realized that that was exactly what he had been asking his customers to go through. By contrast, older-home customers could clearly see what they were getting, buy only what they wanted, and, often, move in immediately. "No wonder I was losing 78 percent of my potential customers!"

To create a hassle-free experience to go with the house itself (these together constituting Wilson's "product"), it was necessary to rethink every step in the process. He has recently opened a one-stop sales center where the customer can see and decide on every option available in a house (for example, the forty different varieties of brick, the three thousand varieties of wallpaper, the four styles of built-in home office), customize a basic design with the help of an Auto-Cad computer system, select features beyond the standard level (for example, extra-thick carpet pads, additional outdoor lighting, and heavier-duty wiring), determine the exact price, work out the mortgage, arrange for insurance, and arrange for the title search. For customers truly in a hurry this can be done during one walk-through of the sales center.

To shrink the lead time from contract signing to moving in from six months to a target of thirty days, he has reorganized his contract-writing and job-release process and is developing a system of pull scheduling for contractors who are assigned new jobs as downstream jobs are completed. He is also introducing standardized work statements, parts lists, and tool kits for every job. Eventually these steps will eliminate the "to-do" list because the new system does not allow the next task to start until the previous task is certified as complete with perfect quality.[2]

Finally, Wilson has created a wide range of basic house designs with a minimum construction standard and asks the customer to specify all materials and systems upgrades (using the computer design system) to a selected base design so the customer only pays for exactly what she or he feels is really needed.

Doing all of this will not be easy, as we'll see when we return to this example in Chapter 3 on flow, but Doyle Wilson has already made the key leap. Instead of concentrating on conventional markets and what he and his contractors were accustomed to making in a conventional way, he has looked hard at *value* as defined by his customers and set off down a new path.

Start by Challenging Traditional Definitions of "Value"

Why is it so hard to start at the right place, to correctly define value? Partly because most producers want to make what they are already making and partly because many customers only know how to ask for some variant of what they are already getting. They simply start in the wrong place and end up at the wrong destination. Then, when providers or customers do decide to rethink value, they often fall back on simple formulas—lower cost, increased product variety through customization, instant delivery—rather than jointly analyzing value and challenging old definitions to see what's really needed.

Steve Maynard, vice president for engineering and product development at the Wiremold Company in West Hartford, Connecticut, was trying to deal with these very problems when he reorganized Wiremold's product development system in 1992. For many years previously, Wiremold had developed new products—consisting of wire guides for office and industrial users and surge protectors for PCs and other business electronics—through a conventional departmentalized process. It started with marketing, which commissioned surveys comparing Wiremold's products with the offerings of competitors. When an "opportunity" was identified, usually a gap in the market or a reported weakness in a competitor's offering, a design was developed by product engineering, then tested by the prototype group. If it worked according to specification, the design proceeded to the engineers designing the machines to make the products and eventually went into production.

This system produced designs which lacked imagination and which customers often ignored. (The designs also took too much time and effort to develop and cost too much to make, but these are a different type of problem we'll discuss in Chapter 3.) Simply speeding up this process through simultaneous engineering and then broadening product variety would just have brought more bad designs to market faster. Pure *muda*.

Steve Maynard's solution was to form a team for each product to stick with that product during its entire production life. This team—consisting of a marketer, a product engineer, and a tooling/process engineer—proceeded to enter into a *dialogue* with leading customers (major contractors) in which all of the old products and solutions were ignored. Instead, the customer and the producer (Wiremold) focused on the value the customer really needed.

For example, traditional Wiremold wire guides (which channel wiring through hostile factory environments and provide complex arrays of outlets in high-use areas like laboratories and hospitals) had been designed almost entirely with regard to their ruggedness, safety, and cost per foot as delivered to the construction site. This approach nicely matched the mentality of Wiremold's product engineers, who dominated the development process and who found a narrow, "specification" focus very reassuring.

As the new dialogue began, it quickly developed that what customers also wanted was a product that "looked nice" and could be installed at the construction site very quickly. (Wiremold had never employed a stylist and knew relatively little about trends in the construction process.) Customers were willing to make substantial trades on cost per foot to get better appearance (which increased the bid price of construction jobs) and quicker installation (which reduced total cost).

Within two years, as all of Wiremold's product families were given the team treatment, sales for these very conventional products increased by more than 40 percent and gross margins soared. Starting over with a joint customer-producer dialogue on value paid a major dividend for Wiremold quite aside from savings in product development and production costs.

While Wiremold and Doyle Wilson Homebuilder and every other firm needs to be searching for fundamentally new capabilities that will permit them to create value in unimagined dimensions, most firms can substantially boost sales immediately if they find a mechanism for rethinking the value of their core products to their customers.

Define Value in Terms of the Whole Product

Another reason firms find it hard to get value right is that while value creation often flows through many firms, each one tends to define value in a different way to suit its own needs. When these differing definitions are added up, they often don't add up. Let's take another nightmarish (but completely typical) travel example.

One of us (Jones) recently took his family on an Easter holiday in Crete from his home in Herefordshire in the United Kingdom. What was wanted was a total, hassle-free package of transport to the airport, a flight to Crete, transport to the villa in Crete, and the villa itself. What was available instead was a product pieced together by the user and involving nineteen different operating organizations:

The *travel company* (to book the air tickets and the villa), the *taxi firm* (which doesn't deal with the travel company) handling the long trip from Hereford to London Gatwick—no airline flies nonstop between Birmingham (the nearest airport) and Crete at Easter time, the *ground staffs* at both airports (independent contractors to the airline), the *security staffs* at both airports (more independent contractors), the two *customs staffs* (to check your documents at both ends and to keep themselves occupied doing so), the two *airport authorities* (who love long layovers because spending per passenger goes up), the *airline* (which has been deintegrating and performs less of the support activities for its operations itself), the *air-traffic authorities* in five countries along the route of flight (who follow the standard form for governments by being undercapitalized and optimized for delays), the *bank* exchanging currency at Gatwick airport, the *bus company* to convey the family to the villa in Crete, and the *villa*.

The trip was reasonably routine but look at what the Jones family did to "process" itself through the system:

1. Call the travel company to make the booking.
2. Receive the tickets by mail.
3. Call the taxi company to make the booking.
4. Wait for the taxi.
5. Load the luggage (8:00 A.M. GMT).
6. Drive to the airport (three and a quarter hours), arriving two hours before the scheduled flight time as required by the airline.
7. Unload the luggage.
8. Wait in the currency exchange queue (to change English pounds into Greek drachma).
9. Wait in the check-in line.
10. Wait in the security line.
11. Wait in the customs line.
12. Wait in the departure lounge.
13. Wait in the boarding line.
14. Wait in the airplane (two-hour air-traffic delay).
15. Taxi to the runway.
16. Fly to Crete (three hours).
17. Wait in the airplane (taxi and deboarding).
18. Wait in the baggage-claim line.
19. Wait in the immigration line.
21. Wait in the customs line.
22. Load luggage onto the bus.
23. Wait in the bus.

24. Travel by bus to the villa (almost forty-five minutes).
25. Unload luggage and carry to villa.
26. Wait to check in at the villa (9:00 P.M. GMT).

The box score:

Total travel time: 13 hours
Time actually going somewhere: 7 hours (54 percent of the total)[3]
Queuing and wait time: 6 hours
Number of lines: 10
Number of times luggage was picked up and put down: 7
Number of inspections (all asking the same questions): 8
Total processing steps: 23

The problem here is not that there were too many firms involved. Each was appropriately specialized for its current task. The problem instead is that each firm was providing a partial product, often only looking inward toward its own operational "efficiency" while no one was looking at the whole product through the eyes of the customer. The minute the focus is shifted to the whole as seen by the customer, obvious questions emerge:

Could one person at check-in handle the security, customs, and check-in tasks? (Letting you walk past them into the boarding area or even onto the plane.) Better yet, could the ticket sent by your travel agent include your baggage tags, boarding passes, taxi voucher, bus tickets, and villa registration, so you just drop these off as you walk through each point? (Or perhaps travelers could create their own ticket using their personal computer linked to reservations systems. They could simply swipe their credit card through a card reader at each point, eliminating paperwork altogether along with the travel agent.) Could the customs authorities in Crete have your passport scanned at check-in in London and use the hours you are en route to figure out whether you ought to be admitted? (Then, unless there is a problem, you could just walk off the plane without visiting immigration and customs at all.) And why (does *anyone* know?) do you need to arrive at the airport two hours before departure? In short, the appropriate definition of the product changes as soon as you begin to look at the whole through the eyes of the customer.

The Critical Need for Lean Firms to Rethink Value

If you take a few moments to reflect on almost any "product"—a good, a service, or more likely both in combination—you will begin to see the same issue of the appropriate way to define it. Doing this will generally require producers to talk to customers in new ways and for the many firms along a value stream to talk to each other in new ways. (We'll see many more examples of this need in the pages ahead—for example, the need for car companies to stop selling a product and car dealers to stop selling services, both to be replaced by a new product [personal mobility] provided jointly to the user.)

It's vital that producers accept the challenge of redefinition, because this is often the key to finding more customers, and the ability to find more customers and sales very quickly is critical to the success of lean thinking. This is because lean organizations, as we will demonstrate shortly, are always freeing up substantial amounts of resources. If they are to defend their employees and find the best economic use for their assets as they strike out on a new path, they need to find more sales right now. Beginning with a better specification of value can often provide the means.

Then, once the initial rethinking of value is done (in what might be called *kaikaku* for value), lean enterprises must continually revisit the value question with their product teams to ask if they have really got the best answer. This is the value specification analog of *kaizen* which seeks to continually improve product development, order-taking, and production activities. It produces steady results along the path to perfection.

The Final Element in Value Definition: The Target Cost

The most important task in specifying value, once the product is defined, is to determine a *target cost* based on the amount of resources and effort required to make a product of given specification and capabilities *if* all the currently visible *muda* were removed from the process. Doing this is the key to squeezing out the waste.

Conventional firms set target selling prices based on what they believe the market will bear. They then work backwards to determine acceptable costs to ensure an adequate profit margin, and they must do this any time they begin to develop a new product. So what's different here? Lean enterprises look at the current bundles of pricing and features being offered customers by conventional firms and then ask how much cost they can take out by full application of lean methods. They effectively ask, What is the *muda*-free cost of this product, once unnecessary steps are removed and value is made to flow? This becomes the target cost for the development, order-taking, and production activities necessary for this product.[4]

Because the target is certain to be far below the costs borne by competitors, the lean enterprise has choices: reduce prices (another way to increase sales volume and utilize freed-up resources); add features or capabilities to the product (which should also increase sales); add services to the physical product to create additional value (and jobs); expand the distribution and service network (again increasing sales, although with a time lag); or take profits to underwrite new products (which will increase sales in the longer term).

Once the target cost is set for a specific product, it becomes the lens for examining every step in the value stream for product development, order-taking, and production (this latter being called operations in the case of a service like insurance or transportation). As we will see in the next chapter, the relentless scrutiny of every activity along the value stream—that is, asking whether a specific activity really creates any value for the customer—becomes the key to meeting the aggressive cost target.

CHAPTER 2
The Value Stream*

The View from the Aisle

An excellent spot for observing the value stream is the aisle of the supermarket, for it is here that a thousand streams empty into the arms of the customer. Not only does the flow of the physical product culminate in the supermarket aisle, as pulled forward by the decisions of the shopper, but also the process of product development as new products are launched. Indeed, Taiichi Ohno found this vantage point in the modern supermarket so stimulating that it inspired him in 1950 to invent the new system of flow management we now call Just-in-Time (JIT).[1]

In the past two years we have been putting ourselves in the aisle, in collaboration with the British grocery chain Tesco[2] and a number of its suppliers, to think through the value stream for specific products in a search for *muda*. To do this we have started to map out every step—each individual action—involved in the process of physical production and order-taking for specific products. Recently we have started to think about product development as well.

Our method is based on a simple premise. Just as activities that can't be measured can't be properly managed, the activities necessary to create, order, and produce a specific product which can't be precisely identified, analyzed, and linked together cannot be challenged, improved (or eliminated altogether), and, eventually, perfected. The great majority of management attention has historically gone to managing aggregates—processes, departments, firms—overseeing many products at once. Yet what's really needed is to manage whole value streams for specific goods and services.

Our initial objective in creating a value stream "map" identifying every

---
* This chapter is based largely on a case study developed by Nick Rich of the Lean Enterprise Research Centre, Cardiff Business School. We are grateful for his help.

action required to design, order, and make a specific product is to sort these actions into three categories: (1) those which actually create value as perceived by the customer; (2) those which create no value but are currently required by the product development, order filling, or production systems (Type One *muda*) and so can't be eliminated just yet; and (3) those actions which don't create value as perceived by the customer (Type Two *muda*) and so can be eliminated immediately. Once this third set has been removed, the way is clear to go to work on the remaining non-value-creating steps through use of the flow, pull, and perfection techniques described in the chapters ahead.

The Value Stream for a Carton[3] of Cola

The only way to make this method clear is to describe a typical value stream analysis.[4] We'll use a product chosen more or less at random in the beverages aisle at Tesco, a cardboard carton of eight cans of cola. We should, however, tell you at the outset that what we will find is fairly horrific—a lengthy set of actions extending over three hundred days, most of which consume resources but create no value and are therefore *muda*. You should understand that looking at any of the thirty thousand other items in the typical Tesco store would produce very much the same result. The cola example is neither better nor worse than the norm.

You should also bear in mind that the firms arrayed along the cola value stream are all competently managed in terms of mass-production thinking. The problem is not the competence of managers operating the system in accord with an agreed logic. The problem is the logic itself.

Producing Cola

Even the mightiest river has modest headwaters. For cola one of these is literally water, supplied in the United Kingdom by the local Water Authorities. Other basic ingredients are the "essence" (in plain language, the taste) used in tiny amounts and supplied as a concentrate by the parent cola company,[5] beets for sugar, corn for caramels (to provide the "cola" color and additional taste), fir trees for cardboard to make the carton, and bauxite or recycled cans to create aluminum for the can.[6]

Because the can rather than the actual beverage is by far the most complex aspect of a carton of cola[7]—and the one with the longest production lead time—we'll initially focus our analysis on the flow of aluminum for the can, treating sugar, caramels, essences, and cartons as tributaries joining the stream farther down the valley.

As shown in the value stream map in Figure 2.1, the first step is to mine bauxite in Australia. Although the ore could in principle be mined in small amounts and sent along to the next step within a few minutes of the receipt of an order, the mining machinery is truly massive and the actual process involves scooping out millions of tons of bauxite at a go in accord with a long-term production forecast. The mountain of ore is then transferred to massive trucks for shipment to a nearby chemical reduction mill where the bauxite is reduced to powdery alumina.

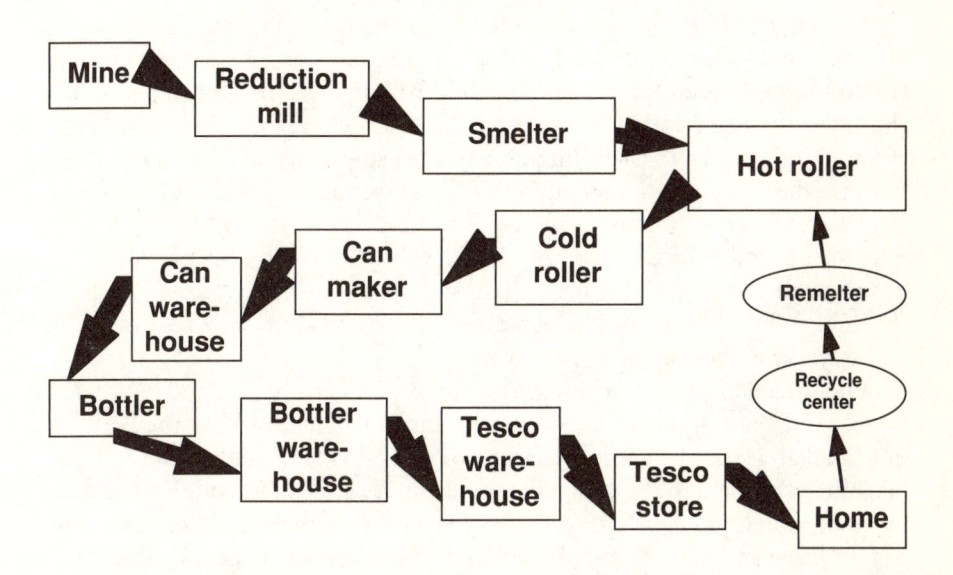

FIGURE 2.1: VALUE STREAM FOR COLA CANS

This process, which turns four tons of bauxite into two tons of alumina, requires about thirty minutes. When enough alumina is accumulated to fill an ultralarge ore carrier (over two weeks or so; about 500,000 tons or enough for 10 million cans), it is shipped by sea—a four-week trip—to Norway or Sweden, countries with cheap hydroelectric power, for smelting.

After about a two-month wait at the smelter, the application of an enormous amount of energy (twenty times that needed to melt down and recycle old cans) reduces two tons of alumina to one ton of aluminum in about two hours. Again, scale in smelting dictates that large amounts of aluminum be created in each batch, with the molten aluminum poured into dozens of ingots one meter on each side and ten meters long. These are then carefully cooled and stored for about two weeks before shipment by truck, boat, and truck to a hot rolling mill in Germany or Sweden.

After about two weeks of storage at the hot rolling mill, the ingot is heated to five hundred degrees centigrade and run through a set of heavy rollers three times to reduce the thickness from one meter to three millimeters. The actual rolling process takes about one minute, but the machinery is extremely complex and difficult to change from one specification of product to another, so management has found it best to wait until there are orders in hand for a large amount of material of a given specification and then to process these orders all at once. When this is done for the specification of aluminum needed for cola cans, the aluminum sheet emerging from the rolling mill is wound onto a ten-ton coil and taken to a storage area, where it sits for about four weeks.

When needed for the next step, the coil is taken from storage and shipped by truck to a cold rolling mill, either in Germany or Sweden, where it is stored for about another two weeks. Cold rolling (at 2100 feet of aluminum sheet per minute—about 25 miles an hour) squeezes the aluminum sheet from 3 millimeters to .3 millimeter, the thickness needed by can makers. Because the cold rolling equipment is also extremely expensive and difficult to change over to the next product, the managers of the cold rolling mills have also found it most economical to accumulate orders for products of a given specification and do them all at once. The thin sheet emerging from the cold roller is then slit into narrower widths, wound onto ten-ton coils, and stored for about a month on average.

When needed for can making, the aluminum coils are shipped by truck, by sea, and again by truck to the can maker in England, where the coils are unloaded and stored, again for about two weeks. When needed, the coils are taken from storage to the can making machinery and run through a blanking machine which punches circular discs out of the aluminum sheet at the rate of four thousand per minute. The discs are then fed automatically into "wall drawing" machines, which punch the disc three times in succession to create a can without a top, at the rate of three hundred cans per minute per machine. (Thirteen forming machines are downstream from each blanking machine.)

From the forming machines, the cans travel by conveyor through a washer, a dryer, and a paint booth applying a base coat and then a top coat consisting of the cola color scheme plus consumer information in different languages and varying promotional messages. The cans then travel through lacquering, necking and flanging (to prepare the cans to receive their tops after filling), bottom and inside spraying (to prevent discoloration and any aluminum taste from getting into the cola), and on to final inspection.

The can making machinery just described (really just one big interconnected machine) is a technical marvel capable of converting a sheet of aluminum into a finished, painted can—with no human intervention—in less than ten seconds of actual processing time. However, it is also extremely expensive to change over from one type of can to the next and one paint scheme to the next, so management tries to produce large lots of each type. From the can maker's standpoint this is clearly the most economical approach, and it also meshes with the practice of the smelter, hot roller, and cold roller of processing specific types of aluminum in large batches.

After inspection, the cans proceed to an automated palletizing machine which loads the empty cans on pallets, eight thousand to each pallet, and sends them to a massive warehouse for storage until needed, usually four weeks. In the warehouse, they are stored by type of can because the bottling firm eventually filling the cola cans needs a variety of cans with different labels for beverages besides plain cola (for example, diet cola, caffeine-free cola, cherry cola). And even for plain cola, the bottler must support many different packaging configurations and promotional campaigns. Each package and many marketing campaigns require different information to be painted on the cans.[8]

From the can maker's warehouse, the cans are trucked to the bottler's warehouse, where they are stored again, although this time only for about four days. They are then depalletized and loaded into massive can filling machines, where they are washed and filled. It is at this point that the major tributary streams converge in a massive tank adjacent to the filling machine.

In this step, water, caramels, sugar, and essence are carefully mixed, and carbon dioxide (the fizz) is added to create cola. (Figure 2.2 shows the confluence of the tributaries.) The value streams for these items also require detailed analysis by Tesco, the bottler, and their suppliers, but the method for value stream analysis is best illustrated by sticking to the longest stream.

After the cola is poured into the cans (at the rate of fifteen hundred cans per minute), the cans are sealed with an aluminum can end containing the familiar "pop top," supplied through a separate but very similar process by the can maker. The cans are then date stamped and packed into cartons of varying numbers of cans, eight in the present case. Each type of carton has its own paint scheme and promotional information.

The mixing and filling process, which brings all of the tributary value streams together, requires only one minute to proceed from washing to packing, but it is expensive and time-consuming to change over. In addition, putting cola in a few cans and then a clear soda in the next can requires purging the whole fill system, so the bottler has found it most economical to run large lots of each type of beverage through its complex equipment.[9]

At the end of the filling/packing line, the cartons are palletized, stretch-wrapped (using equipment you will learn a bit more about in Chapter 6), and taken to the bottler's central warehouse serving all customers in the U.K. Storage time for the pallets of cola is about five weeks.

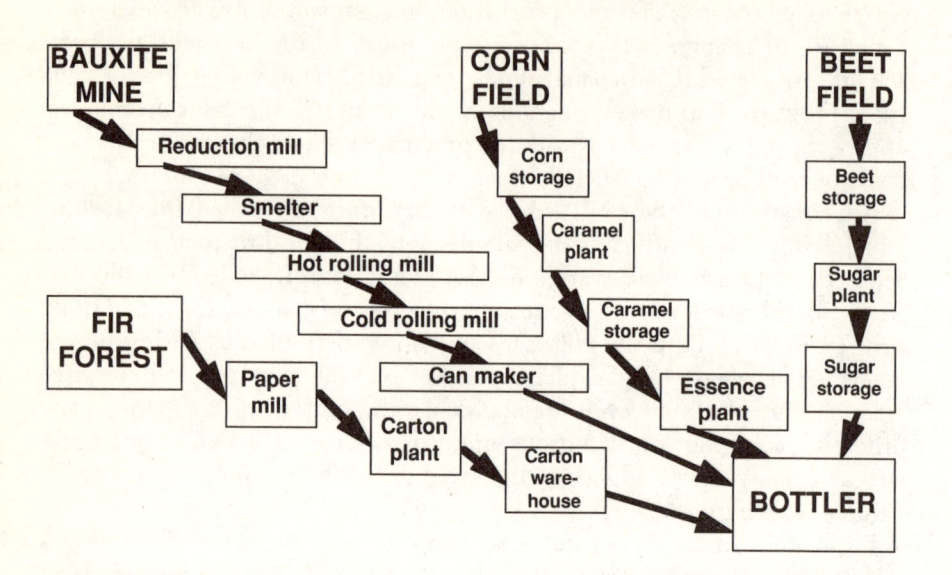

FIGURE 2.2: CONFLUENCE OF COLA VALUE STREAMS

```
BAUXITE MINE → Reduction mill → Smelter → Hot rolling mill → Cold rolling mill → Can maker
CORN FIELD → Corn storage → Caramel plant → Caramel storage → Essence plant
BEET FIELD → Beet storage → Sugar plant → Sugar storage
FIR FOREST → Paper mill → Carton plant → Carton warehouse
→ BOTTLER
```

At the warehouse, the pallets are sorted and placed in designated areas by type. (A process called "stocking.") They are then "picked" as needed and loaded onto one of the bottler's trucks for conveying to one of Tesco's regional distribution warehouses around the U.K.

Once at the Tesco warehouse things move much faster. Incoming pallets are stored for about three days before cases are taken from the pallets and placed in roll cages going overnight to each store. Once at the retail store, the roll cages are taken from the receiving dock to a storage area in the rear or directly to the shelves, and the cola is sold in about two days.

When the cola is taken home it is typically stored again, at least for a few days, perhaps in the basement if the shopper has bought a number of cartons to take advantage of a special promotional offer. Then it's chilled and, finally, consumed. The last step probably requires about five minutes, after nearly a year along the stream.

A final important step, also shown in Figure 2.1, is recycling the can to reintroduce it into the production process at the smelting stage. Currently, only 16 percent of aluminum cans in the U.K. are recycled (and shipped back to Norway), but the percentage is rising. If the percentage of cans recycled moved toward 100 percent, interesting possibilities would emerge for the whole value stream. Mini-smelters with integrated mini-rolling mills might be located near the can makers in England, eliminating in a flash most of the time, storage, and distances involved today in the steps above the can maker. (These activities would suddenly convert from type 1 in our typology—*muda* but unavoidable—to type 2—*muda* that can be completely eliminated right away.) The slow acceptance of recycling is surely due in part to the failure to analyze costs in the whole system rather than just for the recycling step in isolation.

When laid out this way, action by action, so it's possible to see every step for a specific product, the value stream for physical production is highly thought-provoking. First, as shown in Table 2.1, the amount of time when value is actually being created (3 hours) is infinitesimal in relation to the total time (319 days) from bauxite to recycling bin. More than 99 percent of the time the value stream is not flowing at all: the *muda* of waiting. Second, the can and the aluminum going into it are picked up and put down thirty times. From the customer's standpoint none of this adds any value: the *muda* of transport. Similarly, the aluminum and cans are moved through fourteen storage lots and warehouses, many of them vast, and the cans are palletized and unpalletized four times: the *muda* of inventories and excess processing. Finally, fully 24 percent of the energy-intensive, expensive aluminum coming out of the smelter never makes it to the customer: the *muda* of defects (causing scrap).

TABLE 2.1: THE VALUE STREAM OF A CARTON OF COLA

	INCOMING STORAGE*	PROCESSING TIME	FINISHED STORAGE	PROCESS RATE	CUM. DAYS	CUM.† SCRAP
Mine	0	20 min	2 weeks	1000 t/hr	319	0
Reduction mill	2 weeks	30 min	2 weeks		305	0
Smelter	3 months	2 hrs	2 weeks		277	2
Hot rolling mill	2 weeks	1 min	4 weeks	10 ft/min	173	4
Cold rolling mill	2 weeks	<1 min	4 weeks	2100 ft/min	131	6
Can maker	2 weeks	1 min	4 weeks	2000/min	89	20
Bottler	4 days	1 min	5 weeks	1500/min	47	24
Tesco RDC	0	0	3 days	—	8	24
Tesco store	0	0	2 days	—	5	24
Home storage	3 days	5 min	—	—	3	[90]
Totals	5 months	3 hours	6 months		319	24

* Includes transport time from previous step.

† Cumulative scrap is the percentage of the original aluminum scrapped. The jump in scrap at the can maker is due to the loss of about 14 percent of the material in the punch. The loss at the bottler is mainly from damaged cans rejected as they are loaded in the filling machinery. Because the cans are stored empty with no internal pressure, they are easy to damage in handling.

The jump in scrap rate at the home of the customer, shown in brackets, is the consequence of recycling only 16 percent of the 76 percent of the original aluminum which reaches the customer.

The Root Cause of *Muda*

The simplest way to think about this situation is that a can of cola is very small and cola is consumed by the individual customer in small amounts, yet all of the apparatus used to make cola and get it to the customer is very large, very hard to change over, and designed to operate efficiently at very high speeds. The boats, warehouses, and processing machines we have been describing are truly massive and we can see that the primary objective of technologists in the beverage industry has been to scale up and speed up this equipment while removing direct labor, in a classic application of the ideas of mass production.[10]

However, what appears to be efficient to individual companies along the stream—for example, purchase of one of the world's fastest canning machines, operating at fifteen hundred cans per minute, to yield the world's lowest fill cost per can—may be far from efficient when indirect labor (for technical support), upstream and downstream inventories, handling charges, and storage costs are included. Indeed, this machine may be much more expensive than a smaller, simpler, slower one able to make just what the next firm down the stream needs (Tesco in this case) and to produce it immediately upon receipt of the order rather than shipping from a large inventory.

For the moment, let's just reemphasize the critical leap in embracing value stream thinking: Stop looking at aggregated activities and isolated machines—the smelter, the rolling mill, the warehouse, and the can filling machine. Start looking at all the specific actions required to produce specific products to see how they interact with each other. Then start to challenge those actions which singly and in combination don't actually create or optimize value for the customer.

Ordering Cola

If it takes 319 days to bring a cola from bauxite to Tesco (and a similar amount of time to make most of the other items along Tesco's aisles), there is a clear problem in ordering. Either orders must be completely uniform over time so the producers all along the stream can operate stable schedules with little inventory, or the upstream producers must maintain large inventories at every stage to deal with shifts in demand, or Tesco's customers must learn to live with shortages. None of these is desirable because all create *muda*.

In fact, we encountered Tesco because this firm has made remarkable progress in recent years in streamlining its own ordering system to avoid these choices. It has dramatically reduced "stock-outs" (a situation of not having a product the customer wants) while also slashing its own in-store and warehouse inventories by more than half. Because Tesco was already one of the most efficient grocers in the world when it started this process, it appears that its current inventories are only half the U.K. average, a quarter the European average, and an eighth the North American average.

However, Tesco has recently realized that to move even further in reducing inventories, stock-outs, and costs on a total system basis (where more than 85 percent of the costs of a typical product like cola are outside Tesco's corporate control), it will need to improve responsiveness and ordering accuracy all the way up its value stream, running across seven firms in this particular case.[11]

To understand why Tesco reached this conclusion, let's look at their current order-taking system, which is probably the most advanced in the world. Tesco installed a Point-of-Sale (POS) bar-code scanning system in the checkout lanes of all of its stores in the mid-1980s. This permitted each store to maintain a "perpetual inventory" of exactly how much of every item it had on hand and to make more accurate orders to suppliers. This was possible because every time a customer in the aisle took a carton of cola past the checkout, the system noted this fact along with the recent rate of sales and the number of cartons remaining. Replenishment orders could be automatically generated.

A few years later, Tesco transferred decision making on what each store would purchase and when from the store manager, who had been ordering direct from each supplier, to a centralized system where Tesco placed orders combined from all stores to suppliers. At the same time, it opened a dozen Regional Distribution Centers (RDCs) in England so that suppliers for more than 95 percent of all sales volume (the exceptions being milk, sugar, and bread) would ship to the RDC rather than the store. Instead of sending a small truck, partially loaded, to each store, each supplier could send a large truck to each RDC and Tesco could send another large truck to the retail store each night.

In 1989, Tesco took a revolutionary step for the grocery industry by moving toward daily orders (rather than weekly or even monthly) for all fresh products and for many long-shelf-life items. Today, when each store takes inventory at the end of each day, the Tesco ordering system calculates the quantity needed to restore normal stocks plus any special demand likely to be caused by the day of the week, the time of year, the weather, or a sales promotion. After a quick review by the store manger, to check for glitches in the assumptions, this information is dispatched to Tesco's central computer. There, the requirements from all stores in each region are accumulated and orders are dispatched electronically to each supplier during the night.[12] The suppliers are given a precise time (within fifteen minutes) on a precise day[13] to have the precise amount of goods delivered to a specific receiving dock in each RDC.

When the goods arrive at the RDC, they are taken to an area on the floor assigned to each store and consolidated as a load to be taken that night from the RDC to the store, arriving early in the morning. Thus, orders made by each Tesco store on Monday night result in replenishment goods from suppliers reaching each store before it opens on Wednesday morning,[14] effectively creating a twenty-four-hour continuous replenishment system. (The system is shown in Figure 2.3.)

FIGURE 2.3: TESCO REORDER SYSTEM

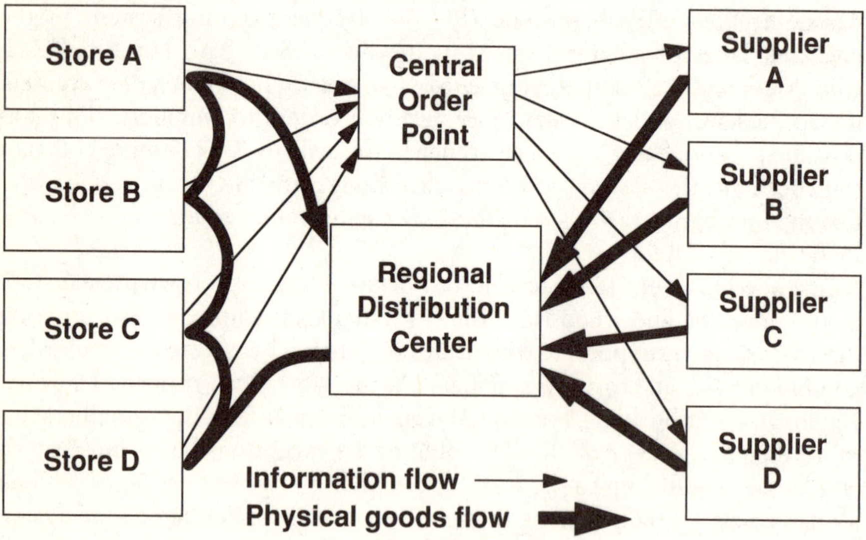

As a result of this system of daily replenishment, Tesco has increased the "service level" to its retail stores (the percentage of supplier shipments which arrive exactly on time in good condition in exactly the right amount) from 92 to 98.5 percent. At the same time, the stocks on hand of the average good (in the retail stores plus the RDCs) fell from 21 to 12.8 days. For "fast movers" like cola, accounting for more than half of Tesco's total sales, inventories at the RDC and the retail store combined are now only 3 to 5 days.

However, as Tesco did this, they learned the limits of what can be accomplished by one firm alone. Specifically, first-tier suppliers like its bottlers have been fulfilling Tesco orders nightly, just-in-time, but from massive finished goods inventories. Their production methods—with high-speed machines, long changeover times, and large batches—have given them no real choice.[15] Meanwhile, the firms farther up the value stream from the bottler, also using massive high-speed machines with long changeovers to produce large batches, have not yet even taken the step of delivering just-in-time from finished goods inventories. Because the bottler cannot get rapid response from its upstream suppliers to changing levels of demand, it continues to order batches of goods at weekly, monthly, or even quarterly intervals (in the case of some raw materials).

If Tesco wants to shrink costs and improve the reliability of the 85 percent of the value stream it does not directly control, it's obvious that the upstream firms must collectively rethink their operating methods, and this is how Tesco and the Lean Enterprise Research Centre joined forces. While it is still in the early stages, the process of jointly conducting the analysis just described should gradually change Tesco, the bottler, the can maker, the cold roller, the hot roller, the smelter, and the bauxite miner from seven isolated adversaries into a team of collaborators, indeed into a *lean enterprise*.

Creating Cola

The final element in the cola story is the value stream for product development. Historically, in the grocery business, first-tier suppliers like the bottler or the branded purveyor of goods have been responsible for the great bulk of product innovations and introductions. Yet only a brief effort to list the activities in the value stream culminating in the launch of a new product raises many questions.

Typically, a firm like the bottler is continually looking for new products to defend its current market share, to expand its scope of offerings (and justify more shelf space at Tesco), and to substitute products with higher margins for old standbys like cola. In the industry, the typical product development cycle is about one year and consists of a number of product clinics followed by larger product trials culminating in the decision for a full-scale launch.

Although the actual steps involved are very simple and typically involve very little true "research and development," they are conducted sequentially so that if one looks down on a product concept from a bird's-eye view it is quickly apparent that during most of the development period the concept is sitting still, awaiting feedback from the group which conducts the clinics on all of the firm's products or awaiting its place on the schedule of the department which conducts small-scale market trials for all products. Then, when the decision to launch is made, there is more waiting while the production system is adapted to accept the new product, new packaging materials are developed, and the marketing campaign is planned.

The end result of this system is that new products—which are often "new" only in the sense of having reformulated ingredients (for example, caffeine-free and cherry cola)—cost an average of $15 million to launch (half of this going to advertising) and . . . usually fail in the marketplace.[16]

The result for Tesco is large amounts of shelf space tied up with "new" products that don't sell and are launched at the same time in the stores of its direct competitors. The obvious question is: How can it take a year's development time and a $15 million expenditure to introduce a "new" product which isn't new and which no one wants?

Simply reducing development time and expense, while highly desirable, will not be enough to have much effect on this value stream, so Tesco has started to rethink the product development process on a more fundamental level in terms of value. Perhaps, just as the individual steps in the value stream are incomprehensible in isolation, customers do not really want to shop for isolated items. Would it perhaps be better for Tesco and its bottler to jointly undertake the development of the full complement of beverages necessary to keep Tesco customers happy, and for Tesco to develop longer-term relations with its customers so they would not be strangers? Toward this end Tesco has just launched a frequent-shopper program that will gather purchase pattern data on every regular customer and should permit a more coherent value stream in product development.

Putting Value Stream Analysis to Work

Having looked at the specific steps involved in the value stream for one specific product, we are ready to put our findings to work more broadly. In the cola case, unlike the Pratt & Whitney example cited in the Introduction, we do not see any steps in the third category which can be immediately eliminated because they are simply redundant. Instead, we see a large number of steps in the second category. They clearly add no value—they're *muda*—and they therefore become targets for elimination by application of lean techniques.

Note that in performing this analysis we are not "benchmarking" by comparing Tesco's cola value stream with those of its competitors. Although we gave a boost to the benchmarking industry with our previous book, *The Machine That Changed the World*, which described the most comprehensive benchmarking ever attempted in a gigantic global industry, we now feel that benchmarking is a waste of time for managers that understand lean thinking.[17]

Lean benchmarkers who discover their performance is superior to their competitors' have a natural tendency to relax (the risk Tesco would run today in benchmarking its internal operations) while mass producers discovering that their performance is inferior often have a hard time understanding exactly why (for example, General Motors and Volkswagen in the 1980s). They tend to get distracted by easy-to-measure or impossible-to-emulate differences in factor costs, scale, or "culture," when the really important differences lie in the harder-to-see ways value-creating activities are organized.

Our earnest advice to lean firms today is simple: To hell with your competitors; compete against *perfection* by identifying all activities that are *muda* and eliminating them. This is an absolute rather than a relative standard which can provide the essential North Star for any organization. (In its most spectacular application, it has kept the Toyota organization in the lead for forty years.) However, to put this admonition to work you must master the key techniques for eliminating *muda*. It all begins with flow.

CHAPTER 3

Flow

The World of Batch-and-Queue

What happens when you go to your doctor? Usually, you make an appointment some days ahead, then arrive at the appointed time and sit in a waiting room. When the doctor sees you—usually behind schedule—she or he makes a judgment about what your problem is likely to be. You are then routed to the appropriate specialist, quite possibly on another day, certainly after sitting in another waiting room. Your specialist will need to order tests using large, dedicated laboratory equipment, requiring another wait and then another visit to review the results. Then, if the nature of the problem is clear, it's time for the appropriate treatment, perhaps involving a trip to the pharmacy (and another line), perhaps a trip back to the specialist for a complex procedure (complete with wait). If you are unlucky and require hospital treatment, you enter a whole new world of specialized functions, disconnected processes, and waiting.

If you take a moment to reflect on your experience, you discover that the amount of time actually spent on your treatment was a tiny fraction of the time you spent going through the "process." Mostly you were sitting and waiting ("patient" is clearly the right word), or moving about to the next step in the diagnosis and treatment. You put up with this because you've been told that all this stopping and starting and being handed off to strangers is the price of "efficiency" in receiving the highest-quality care.

We've already looked briefly at another service, a trip involving an airline. And most of the time the experience is even worse than the Joneses' family trip to Crete because rather than taking a direct flight you must go through a hub for sortation. In the end, the time you spend actually moving along the most direct route is likely to be little more than half the total time required to get from door to door. Yet most travelers put up with this system without dreaming of anything better. After all, it's extremely safe, and travelers are told that it's highly efficient because it fully utilizes expensive airplanes and airports.

Health care and travel are usually called "personal services," in contrast with "products" like VCRs, washing machines, Wiremold's wire guides, and Tesco's beverages. Actually, the major difference is that in the case of health care and travel, you the customer are being acted upon—you are necessarily part of the production process. With goods, by contrast, you wait at the end of the process, seemingly beyond harm's reach. However, there is no escaping the consequences of the way the job gets done even if you are not directly involved.

Let's take just one example for a common good, the single-family home. Henry Ford dreamed about mass-producing homes using standard but modularized designs with the modules built in factories to slash design and production costs while still providing variety. A number of entrepreneurs actually created modular designs and briefly set up production lines in the United States to make the modules for prefabricated houses immediately after World War II.[1] And Toyota has had modest success in Japan since the 1960s in offering a wide range of floor plans and exterior appearances using a few basic modules fabricated on a production line and assembled almost instantly at the construction site.

Yet, almost all of the world's new single-family homes are still built largely at the construction site by cutting and fastening a welter of materials to create the basic structure and then installing thousands of individual components, from plumbing fixtures to kitchen appliances to wall sockets.

If you go to your home builder and then to the construction site and take a seat to watch the action, you will mostly note inaction. For example, when Doyle Wilson started to measure what occurred in his office and at the work site as part of his TQM effort, he discovered that five-sixths of the typical construction schedule for a custom-built home was occupied with two activities: *waiting* for the next set of specialists (architects, cost estimators, bill-of-material drafters, landscape architects, roofers, sheetrockers, plumbers, electricians, landscapers) to work a particular job into their complex schedules, and *rework* to rip out and correct the work just done that was either incorrect from a technical standpoint or failed to meet the needs and expectations of the home buyer.

As the buyer at the end of the process, you pay for all the waiting and rework—grumbling, of course—but it is a custom product, after all, and you've heard many stories from your friends about even worse problems with their homes, so you tend to accept the predominant system and its problems as unavoidable and inherent to the nature of the activity.

In fact, all of these activities—the creation, ordering, and provision of any good or any service—can be made to flow. And when we start thinking about ways to line up all of the essential steps needed to get a job done into a steady, continuous flow, with no wasted motions, no interruptions, no batches, and no queues, it changes everything: how we work together, the kinds of tools we devise to help with our work, the organizations we create to facilitate the flow, the kinds of careers we pursue, the nature of business firms (including nonprofit service providers) and their linkages to each other and society.

Applying flow to the full range of human activities will not be easy or automatic. For starters, it's hard for most managers to even see the flow of value and, therefore, to grasp the value of flow. Then, once managers begin to see, many practical problems must be overcome to fully introduce and sustain flow. However, we do insist that flow principles can be applied to any activity and that the consequences are always dramatic. Indeed, the amount of human effort, time, space, tools, and inventories needed to design and provide a given service or good can typically be *cut in half* very quickly, and steady progress can be maintained from this point onward to cut inputs in half again within a few years.

The Techniques of Flow

So, how do you make value flow? The first step, once value is defined and the entire value stream is identified, is to focus on the actual object—the specific design, the specific order, and the product itself (a "cure," a trip, a house, a bicycle)—and never let it out of sight from beginning to completion. The second step, which makes the first step possible, is to ignore the traditional boundaries of jobs, careers, functions (often organized into departments), and firms to form a lean enterprise removing all impediments to the continuous flow of the specific product or product family. The third step is to rethink specific work practices and tools to eliminate backflows, scrap, and stoppages of all sorts so that the design, order, and production of the specific product can proceed continuously.

In fact, these three steps must be taken together. Most managers imagine that the requirements of efficiency dictate that designs, orders, and products go "through the system" and that good management consists of avoiding variances in the performance of the complex system handling a wide variety of products. The real need is to get rid of the system and start over, on a new basis. To make this approach clear and specific, let's take as a concrete example the design, ordering, and production of a bicycle.

From Batch to Flow in Bicycles

We've chosen this example partly because the bicycle itself is simple and lacks glamour. You will not be distracted by novel product designs or exotic technologies. We've also chosen it because we happen to know something about the bicycle industry, one of us having resolved to test the methods we describe in this book by taking an ownership position in a real bicycle company. Finally, we have chosen bicycle manufacture because it is a deeply disintegrated industry, with most final-assembler firms making only the frame while buying the components—wheels, brakes, gears, seats, handlebars, plus raw materials in the form of frame tubing—from a long list of supplier companies, many larger than the final assemblers themselves. The problems of value stream integration are present in abundance.

Design

Product design in the bicycle industry was historically a classic batch-and-queue affair in which the marketing department determined a "need," the product engineers then designed a product to serve the need, the prototype department built a prototype to test the design, the tooling department designed tools to make a high-volume version of the approved prototype, and the production engineering group in the manufacturing department figured out how to use the tools to fabricate the frame and then assemble the component parts into a completed bike. Meanwhile, the purchasing department, once the design was finalized, arranged to buy the necessary component parts for delivery to the assembly hall.

A design for a new product, usually only one of many under development at a given time, moved from department to department, waiting in the queue in each department. Frequently it went back for rework to a previous department or was secretly reengineered at a point downstream to deal with incompatibilities between the perspectives of, say, the tool designers and the product designers who handled the design in the previous step. There was no flow.

In the late 1980s and early 1990s, most firms switched to "heavyweight" program management with a strong team leader and a few dedicated team members, but without changing the rest of the system. The product "team" was really just a committee with a staff that sent the great bulk of the actual development work back to the departments, where it still waited in queues. What's more, there was no effective methodology for carrying designs through the system without lots of rework and backflows. Even worse, no one was really responsible for the final results of development efforts because the accounting and reward systems never linked the success of a product through its production life with the original efforts of the design team. There was, therefore, a bias toward ingenious designs with admirable technical features which customers liked but which failed to return a profit due to excess costs and launch delays.

The lean approach is to create truly dedicated product teams with all the skills needed to conduct value specification, general design, detailed engineering, purchasing, tooling, and production planning in one room in a short period of time using a proved team decision-making methodology commonly called Quality Function Deployment (QFD).[2] This method permits development teams to *standardize work* so that a team follows the same approach every time. Because every team in a firm also follows this approach, it's possible to accurately measure throughput time and to continually improve the design methodology itself.

With a truly dedicated team in place, rigorously using QFD to correctly specify value and then eliminate rework and backflows, the design never stops moving forward until it's fully in production. The result, as we will demonstrate in the examples in Part II, is to reduce development time by more than half and the amount of effort needed by more than half while getting a much higher "hit rate" of products which actually speak to the needs of customers.

In our experience, dedicated product teams do not need to be nearly as large as traditional managers would predict, and the smaller they can be kept the better all around. A host of narrowly skilled specialists are not needed because most marketing, engineering, purchasing, and production professionals actually have much broader skills than they have (1) ever realized, (2) ever admitted, or (3) ever been allowed to use. When a small team is given the mandate to "just do it," we always find that the professionals suddenly discover that each can successfully cover a much broader scope of tasks than they have ever been allowed to previously. They do the job well and they enjoy it.

Moving most of the employees formerly in marketing, engineering, and production groups into dedicated teams for specific products does create problems for the functional needs of each firm along the value stream, a point we will address in Part III. Similarly, the need to include employees of key component and material supply firms as dedicated members of the product team raises difficult questions of where one firm stops and the next begins, the second major topic of Part III.

ORDER-TAKING

The historic practice in the bicycle industry has been to task the Sales Department with obtaining orders from retailers. In the United States, these range from the giant mass-marketers like Wal-Mart at one extreme to thousands of tiny independent bicycle shops at the other. When the orders are fully processed—to make sure that they are internally consistent and that the buyer is credit-worthy—they are sent to the Scheduling Department in Operations or Manufacturing to work into the complex production algorithm for a firm's many products. A shipment date is then set for communication back to Sales and on to the customer.

To check on the progress of orders, particularly in the event of late delivery, the customer calls Sales, which then calls Scheduling. When orders are really late and important customers threaten to cancel, Sales and Scheduling undertake some form of expediting by going directly into the physical production system in both the assembler firm and the supply base to move laggard orders forward. This is done by jumping them to the head of each queue in physical production.

Under the influence of the reengineering movement in the early 1990s, a number of firms integrated Sales and Scheduling into a single department so that the orders themselves can be processed much more quickly—often by one person tied in to the firm's electronic information management system so that orders never need to be handed off, placed in waiting lines, or put down. (They now flow.) As a result, orders can be scheduled for production in a few minutes rather than the days or even weeks previously required; at the same time, order information can be transmitted electronically to suppliers. Similarly, expediting procedures are tightened up to eliminate the confusion which often arose between Sales and Scheduling.

These innovations certainly helped, but a fully implemented lean approach can go much further. In the lean enterprise, Sales and Production Scheduling are core members of the product team, in a position to plan the sales campaign as the product design is being developed and to sell with a clear eye to the capabilities of the production system so that both orders and the product can flow smoothly from sale to delivery. And because there are no stoppages in the production system and products are built to order, with only a few hours elapsed between the first operation on raw materials and shipment of the finished item, orders can be sought and accepted with a clear and precise knowledge of the system's capabilities. *There is no expediting*.

A key technique in implementing this approach is the concept of *takt* time,[3] which precisely synchronizes the rate of production to the rate of sales to customers. For example, for a bicycle firm's high-end titanium-framed bike, let's assume that customers are placing orders at the rate of forty-eight per day. Let's also assume that the bike factory works a single eight-hour shift. Dividing the number of bikes by the available hours of production tells the production time per bicycle, the *takt* time, which is ten minutes. (Sixty minutes in an hour divided by demand of six bikes per hour.)

Obviously, the aggregate volume of orders may increase or decrease over time and *takt* time will need to be adjusted so that production is always precisely synchronized with demand. The point is always to define *takt* time precisely at a given point in time in relation to demand and to run the whole production sequence precisely to *takt* time.

In the lean enterprise, the production slots created by the *takt* time calculation—perhaps ten per hour for high-end bicycles (for a *takt* time of six minutes) and one per minute for low-end models (for a *takt* time of sixty seconds)—are clearly posted. This can be done with a simple whiteboard in the product team area at the final assembler but will probably also involve electronic displays (often called *andon* boards) in the assembler firm and electronic transmission for display in supplier and customer facilities as well. Complete display, so everyone can see where production stands at every moment, is an excellent example of another critical lean technique, *transparency* or *visual control*.[4] Transparency facilitates consistently producing to *takt* time and alerts the whole team immediately to the need either for additional orders or to think of ways to remove waste if *takt* time needs to be reduced to accommodate an increase in orders.[5]

Raising awareness of the tight connection between sales and production also helps guard against one of the great evils of traditional selling and order-taking systems, namely the resort to bonus systems to motivate a sales force working with no real knowledge of or concern about the capabilities of the production system. These methods produce periodic surges in orders at the end of each bonus period (even though underlying demand hasn't changed) and an occasional "order of the century" drummed up by a bonus-hungry sales staff, which the production system can't possibly accommodate. Both lead to late deliveries and bad will from the customer. In other words, they magically generate *muda*.

PRODUCTION

The historic practice in the bicycle industry was to differentiate production activities by type and to create departments for each type of activity: tube cutting, tube bending, mitering, welding, washing and painting for the frame and handle bars, and final assembly of the complete bike. Over time, higher-speed machines with higher levels of automation were developed for tasks ranging from cutting and bending to welding and painting. Assembly lines were also installed to assemble a mix of high-volume models in dedicated assembly halls.

All bike makers produced a wide range of models using the same production equipment, and part fabrication tools typically ran at much higher speeds (expressed as pieces per minute) than the final assembly line. Because changing over part fabrication tools to make a different part was typically quite time-consuming, it made sense to make large batches of each part before changing over to run the next part. The typical final assembly plant layout and materials flow looked as shown in Figure 3.1.

FIGURE 3.1: BICYCLE PLANT LAYOUT AND FLOW

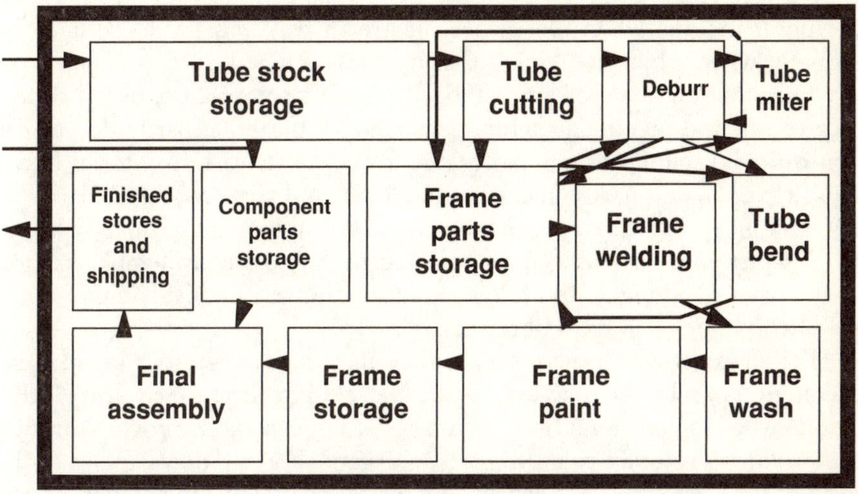

As batches of parts were created, an obvious problem arose: how to keep track of the inventory and make sure that the right parts were sent to the right operation at the right time. In the early days of the bicycle industry—an activity dating back to the 1880s and a key precursor to the auto industry—scheduling was handled by means of a master schedule and daily handwritten orders to each department to make the parts final assembly would need.

After nearly a hundred years, these manual scheduling methods were replaced in the 1970s by computerized Material Requirements Planning systems, or MRPs. A good MRP system was at least 99 percent accurate in keeping track of inventory, ordering materials, and sending instructions to each department on what to make next. As a group, these systems were a clear improvement on older manual systems for controlling batch-and-queue operations and became progressively more complex over time. Eventually capacity planning tools were added to evaluate the capacity of machines at every step in the production process and to guard against the emergence of bottlenecks and capacity constraints.

MRP, however, had a number of problems. If even one part was not properly logged into the system as it proceeded from one production stage to the next, errors began to accumulate that played havoc with the reorder "triggers" telling a department when to switch over to the next type of part. As a result, downstream manufacturing operations often had too many parts (the *muda* of overproduction) or too few parts to meet the production schedule (producing the *muda* of waiting).

A worse problem was that total lead times in batch-and-queue systems were usually quite lengthy—typically a few weeks to a few months between the point in time when the earliest upstream part was produced and the moment when a bike containing that part was shipped to the retailer. This would have been fine if orders had been perfectly smooth, but in fact orders received by the bike manufacturer changed all the time, partly due to the bonus-driven selling system, partly due to the substantial inventories in the retail channel, and partly due to seasonal demand patterns, particularly for low-end bikes. What's more, there were often engineering changes in bicycle designs, even for mature products, meaning that a considerable fraction of the parts piled up alongside the value stream were suddenly either completely obsolete or in need of rework.[6]

MRP systems which were very simple in concept therefore became exceedingly complex in practice. In the bicycle industry, every firm's MRP system was supplemented by a backup system of expediters moving through the production system to move parts in urgent shortage downstream to the head of the queue in every department and at every machine. Their efforts, while essential to avoiding cancellations or large penalties on overdue orders, played havoc with the internal logic of the MRP system—often causing it to generate absurd orders—and with inventory accuracy as well. In the end, most MRP applications were better than manual systems, but they operated day to day at a level of performance far below what was theoretically possible and what had been widely expected when MRP was first introduced.

Just-in-Time, an innovation pioneered at Toyota in the 1950s and first embraced by Western firms in the early 1980s, was designed to deal with many of these problems. This technique was envisioned by Taiichi Ohno as a method for facilitating smooth flow, but JIT can only work effectively if machine changeovers are dramatically slashed so that upstream manufacturing operations produce tiny amounts of each part and then produce another tiny amount as soon as the amount already produced is summoned by the next process downstream. JIT is also helpless unless downstream production steps practice level scheduling (*heijunka* in Toyota-speak) to smooth out the perturbations in day-to-day order flow unrelated to actual customer demand. Otherwise, bottlenecks will quickly emerge upstream and buffers ("safety stocks") will be introduced everywhere to prevent them.

The actual application of JIT in the bicycle industry largely ignored the need to reduce setup times and smooth the schedule. Instead, it concentrated on suppliers, making sure that they only delivered parts to the final assemblers "just in time" to meet the erratic production schedule. In practice, most suppliers did this by shipping small amounts daily or even several times a day from a vast inventory of finished goods they kept near their shipping docks. Some final assemblers even specified the existence of these safety stocks and periodically sent around their purchasing staffs to inspect them. In the end, "just in time" was little more than a once-and-for-all shift of massive amounts of work-in-process from the final assembler to the first-tier supplier and, in turn, from first-tier supplier to firms farther upstream.

To get manufactured goods to flow, the lean enterprise takes the critical concepts of JIT and level scheduling and carries them all the way to their logical conclusion by putting products into continuous flow wherever possible. For example, in the case of the bicycle plant shown in Figure 3.1, flow thinking calls for the creation of production areas by product family, which includes every fabrication and assembly step. (Product families can be defined in various ways, but in this industry they would logically be defined by the base material used for the frame, specifically titanium, aluminum, steel, or carbon-fiber. This classification makes sense because the fabrication steps and processing techniques are quite different in each case.)

Better yet, if noise problems can be managed, the lean enterprise groups the product manager, the parts buyer, the manufacturing engineer, and the production scheduler in the team area immediately next to the actual production equipment and in close contact with the product and tool engineers in the nearby design area dedicated to that product family. The old-fashioned and destructive distinction between the office (where people work with their minds) and the plant (where people work with their hands) is eliminated.

(We're often struck that in the old world of mass production, the factory workforce really had no need to talk to each other. They were supposed to keep their heads down and keep working and professionals rarely went near the scene of the action. So production machinery could make a lot of noise. The isolated workers simply donned their ear protection and shut out the world. In the lean enterprise, however, the workforce on the plant floor needs to talk constantly to solve production problems and implement improvements in the process. What's more, they need to have their professional support staff right by their side and everyone needs to be able to see the status of the entire production system. Many machine builders are still oblivious to the fact that a lean machine needs to be a quiet machine.)

In the continuous-flow layout, the production steps are arranged in a sequence, usually within a single cell, and the product moves from one step to the next, one bike at a time, with *no* buffer of work-in-process in between, using a range of techniques generically labeled "single-piece flow." To achieve single-piece flow in the normal situation when each product family includes many product variants—in this case, touring and mountain bike designs in a wide range of sizes—it is essential that each machine can be converted almost instantly from one product specification to the next. It's also essential that many traditionally massive machines—paint systems being the most critical in the bike case—be "right-sized" to fit directly into the production process. This, in turn, often means using machines which are simpler, less automated, and slower (but perhaps even more accurate and "repeatable") than traditional designs. We will look in detail in Chapter 8 at the Pratt & Whitney example of simplified blade grinding machinery that we mentioned in the Introduction.

This approach seems completely backward to traditional managers who have been told all their lives that competitive advantage in manufacture is obtained from automating, linking, and speeding up massive machinery to increase throughput and remove direct labor. It also seems like common sense that good production management involves keeping every employee busy and every machine fully utilized, to justify the capital invested in the expensive machines. What traditional managers fail to grasp is the cost of maintaining and coordinating a complicated network of high-speed machines making batches. This is the *muda* of complexity.

Because conventional "standard-cost" accounting systems make machine utilization and employee utilization their key performance measures while treating in-process inventories as an asset—even if no one will ever want them—it's not surprising that managers also fail to grasp that machines rapidly making unwanted parts during 100 percent of their available hours and employees earnestly performing unneeded tasks during every available minute are only producing *muda*.

To get continuous-flow systems to flow for more than a minute or two at a time, every machine and every worker must be completely "capable." That is, they must always be in proper condition to run precisely when needed and every part made must be exactly right. By design, flow systems have an everything-works-or-nothing-works quality which must be respected and anticipated. This means that the production team must be cross-skilled in every task (in case someone is absent or needed for another task) and that the machinery must be made 100 percent available and accurate through a series of techniques called Total Productive Maintenance (TPM). It also means that work must be rigorously *standardized* (by the work team, not by some remote industrial engineering group) and that employees and machines must be taught to monitor their own work through a series of techniques commonly called *poka-yoke*, or mistake-proofing, which make it impossible for even one defective part to be sent ahead to the next step.[7]

A simple example of a *poka-yoke* is installing photo cells across the opening of each parts bin at a workstation. When a product of a given description enters the area the worker must reach into the boxes to get parts, breaking the light beam from the photo cells on each box. If the worker attempts to move the product on to the next station without obtaining the right parts, a light flashes to indicate that a part has been left out.

These techniques need to be coupled with *visual controls,* as mentioned earlier, ranging from the 5Ss[8] (where all debris and unnecessary items are removed and every tool has a clearly marked storage place visible from the work area) to status indicators (often in the form of *andon* boards), and from clearly posted, up-to-date standard work charts to displays of key measurables and financial information on the costs of the process. The precise techniques will vary with the application, but the key principle does not: Everyone involved must be able to see and must understand every aspect of the operation and its status at all times.

Once the commitment is made to convert to a flow system, striking progress can be made very quickly in the initial *kaikaku* exercise. However, some tools (for example, massive paint booths with elaborate emission control equipment) will be unsuited for continuous-flow production and won't be easy to modify quickly. It will be necessary to operate them for an extended period in a batch mode, with intermediate buffers of parts between the previous and the next production step. The key technique here is to think through tool changes to reduce changeover times and batch sizes to the absolute minimum that existing machinery will permit.[9] This typically can be done very quickly and almost never requires major capital investments. Indeed, if you think you need to spend large sums to convert equipment from large batches to small batches or single pieces, you don't yet understand lean thinking.

The original small-lot, quick-change techniques pioneered at Toyota in the 1960s are a striking achievement, but we caution readers not to take quick-change machines still producing batches, however small, as an end in themselves. Any changeover requiring any loss in production time and any machine which must run at a rate far out of step with the rest of the production sequence can still create *muda*. The end objective of flow thinking is to totally eliminate all stoppages in an entire production process and not to rest in the area of tool design until this has been achieved.

Let's tie all of these techniques together by showing what a lean bicycle production process looks like, as shown in Figure 3.2. First, note that the same number of bikes are being produced but that the plant is more than half empty, in large part because all of the in-process storage areas have disappeared. Although the diagram cannot show this, the human effort needed to produce a bicycle has been cut in half as well, and time through the system has been reduced from four weeks to four hours. (We'll talk in Part II about what to do with people no longer needed for their traditional tasks as *muda* is eliminated. Protecting their jobs by finding them other productive tasks is a central part of any successful lean transition.)

FIGURE 3.2: LEAN BICYCLE PLANT LAYOUT AND FLOW

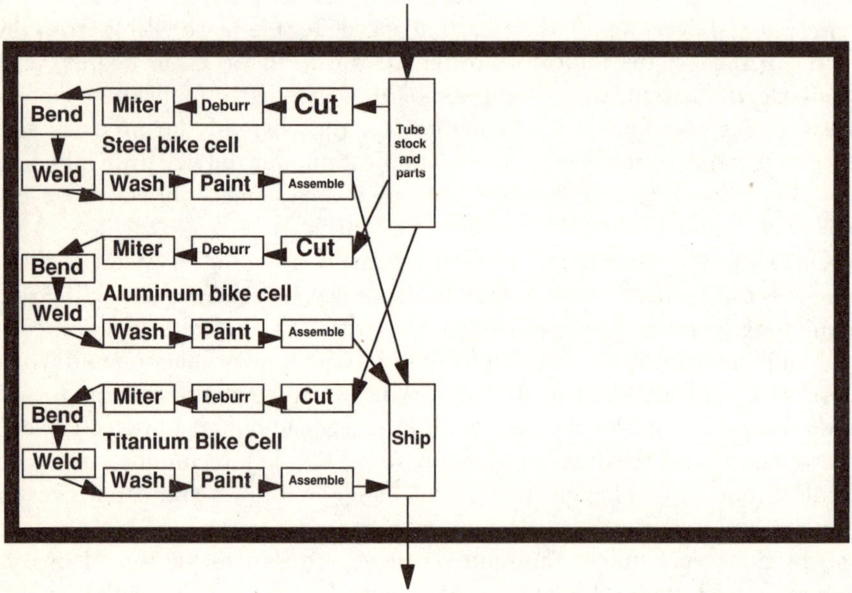
Bend
Miter
Deburr
Cut
Tube stock and parts
Steel bike cell
Weld
Wash
Paint
Assemble
Bend
Miter
Deburr
Cut
Aluminum bike cell
Weld
Wash
Paint
Assemble
Bend
Miter
Deburr
Cut
Titanium Bike Cell
Weld
Wash
Paint
Assemble
Ship

The diagram does show that single large machines have been broken down into multiple small machines, in particular the washing systems and paint booths, so that bikes can proceed continuously, one at a time, from tube cutting to mitering to bending to welding to washing to painting to final assembly without ever stopping. In this arrangement the inventory between workstations can be zero and the size of the work team can be geared to the production volume of the cell, with high-volume cells having more workers than low-volume cells. Finally, note that the track assembly operations have been eliminated. When production is broken into product families, it is often the case that no family accounts for the kind of volume needed for track assembly. Remarkably, manual advancing of the product through assembly is often cheaper.

Because the work flow has been so drastically simplified, the MRP system and the accompanying expediters are no longer needed to get parts from step to step. (MRP still has a use for long-term capacity planning for the assembler firm and its suppliers.) When the sequence is initiated at the end of final assembly, work progresses from each station to the next in accordance with *takt* time and at the same rate as final assembly.

The entire product team including the team leader, the production engineer, the planner/buyer, the TPM/maintenance expert, and the operators (collectively the heart of the lean enterprise) can be located immediately adjacent to the machinery for each product cell. Because the process machinery currently available for these operations in the bicycle industry either makes very little noise inherently—for example, paint—or can be shielded so that very little noise escapes into the team area—the mitering step—it's possible to lay out activities so everyone can see the whole operation and its status at a quick glance.

A final point about the cells which is hard to illustrate with a diagram is that the work in each step has been very carefully balanced with the work in every other step so that everyone is working to a cycle time equal to *takt* time. When it's necessary to speed up or slow down production, the size of the team may be increased or shrunk (contracting or expanding job scope), but the actual pace of physical effort is never changed. And when the specification of the product changes, the right-sized machines can be added or subtracted and adjusted or rearranged so that continuous flow is always maintained.

Right Location

Only one more flow technique needs mentioning, which is to locate both design and physical production in the appropriate place to serve the customer. Just as many manufacturers have concentrated on installing larger and faster machines to eliminate direct labor, they've also gone toward massive centralized facilities for product families (sometimes called "focused factories") while outsourcing more and more of the actual component part making to other centralized facilities serving many final assemblers. To make matters worse, these are often located on the wrong side of the world from both their engineering operations and their customers (Taiwan in the bicycle case) to reduce the cost per hour of labor.

The production process in these remotely located, high-scale facilities may even be in some form of flow, but launching products and improving the process machinery is much harder (because the core engineering skills are on the other side of the world), and the flow of the product stops at the end of the plant. In the case of bikes, it's a matter of letting the finished product sit while a whole sea container for a given final assembler's warehouse in North America is filled, then sending the filled containers to the port, where they sit some more while waiting for a giant container ship. After a few weeks on the ocean, the containers go by truck to one of the bike firm's regional warehouses, where the bikes wait until a specific customer order needs filling, often followed by shipment to the customer's warehouse for more waiting. In other words, there's no flow except along a tiny stretch of the total value stream inside one isolated plant.

The result is high logistics costs and massive finished unit inventories in transit and at retailer warehouses. Another consequence is obsolete goods, eventually sold at large discounts, created by the need to place orders based on forecasts months in advance of demonstrated demand. When carefully analyzed, these costs and revenue losses are often found to more than offset the savings in production costs from low wages, savings which can be obtained in any case by locating smaller flow facilities incorporating more of the total production steps much closer to the customer. (We'll return to this point in Chapter 10 on Japan, because wrong location, rather than high wages, lies at the heart of Japan's current competitive dilemma.)

Applying Flow Thinking to Any Activity

Flow thinking is easiest to see in conventional, discrete-product manufacturing, which is where flow techniques were pioneered. However, once managers learn to see it, it's possible to introduce flow in any activity and the principles are in every case the same: Concentrate on managing the value stream for the specific service or good, eliminate organizational barriers by creating a lean enterprise, relocate and right-size tools, and apply the full complement of lean techniques so that value can flow continuously. At the end of this volume, in Chapter 13, we'll apply lean thinking to a wide range of activities besides traditional manufacturing.

Flow in Work; Work as Flow

So far, we have been talking about the flow of value as if the needs of the customer and the investor are the only ones which count. However, we all know from our daily lives that our experience as producers (that is, as employees and workers) is often far more significant than our activities as consumers or investors. What does the transition to flow mean for the experience of work?

Let's begin with a brief look at the recent research findings of the Polish-born psychologist Mihaly Csikszentmihalyi, now at the University of Chicago. He has spent the last twenty-five years reversing the usual focus of psychology. Instead of asking what makes people feel bad (and how to change it) he has explored what makes people feel good, so that positive attributes of experience can be built into daily life.

His method has been to attach beepers, which sound at random intervals, to his research subjects. When the beeper sounds, the subject is asked to record in a notebook what she or he was doing and how they were feeling. After sifting decades of notebook data from thousands of subjects around the world, he has reached some very simple conclusions.

The types of activities which people all over the world consistently report as most rewarding—that is, which make them feel best—involve a clear objective, a need for concentration so intense that no attention is left over, a lack of interruptions and distractions, clear and immediate feedback on progress toward the objective, and a sense of challenge—the perception that one's skills are adequate, but just adequate, to cope with the task at hand.

When people find themselves in these conditions they lose their self-consciousness and sense of time. They report that the task itself becomes the end rather than a means to something more satisfying, like money or prestige. Indeed, and very conveniently for us, Csikszentmihalyi reports that people experiencing these conditions are in a highly satisfying psychological state of *flow*.[10]

Csikszentmihalyi's classic flow experience is rock climbing, where the need for concentration is obvious and the task itself is clearly the end, not a means. Participation sports less dangerous than rock climbing, interactive games, and focused intellectual tasks (such as writing books!) are often mentioned by Csikszentmihalyi's respondents as flow experiences. However, traditional work-related tasks are only rarely mentioned despite the fact that work is rated the most important overall life activity. This is for a good reason. Classic batch-and-queue work conditions are hardly conducive to psychological flow. The worker can see only a small part of the task, there is often no feedback (much less immediate feedback), the task requires only a small portion of one's concentration and skills, and there are constant interruptions to deal with other tasks in one's area of responsibility.

By contrast, work in an organization where value is made to flow continuously also creates the conditions for psychological flow. Every employee has immediate knowledge of whether the job has been done right and can see the status of the entire system. Keeping the system flowing smoothly with no interruptions is a constant challenge, and a very difficult one, but the product team has the skills and a way of thinking which is equal to the challenge. And because of the focus on perfection, to be further explored in

Chapter 5, the whole system is maintained in a permanent creative tension which demands concentration.

Flow Is Not Enough

We've now seen striking examples of what happens when the value stream flows smoothly. What's more, there is absolutely no magic involved. Any organization can introduce flow in any activity. However, if an organization uses lean techniques only to make unwanted goods flow faster, nothing but *muda* results. How can you be sure you are providing the services and goods people really want when they really want them? And how can you tie all the parts of a whole value stream together when they can't be conducted in one continuous-flow cell in one room? Next you need to learn how to *pull*.

CHAPTER 4
Pull

Pull in simplest terms means that no one upstream should produce a good or service until the customer downstream asks for it, but actually following this rule in practice is a bit more complicated. The best way to understand the logic and challenge of pull thinking is to start with a real customer expressing a demand for a real product and to work backwards through all the steps required to bring the desired product to the customer. Bob Scott's bumper for his out-of-production 1990 Toyota pickup truck provides a mundane but perfectly typical example.

In August 1995, Bob Scott backed his pickup into a pole near Glenside, Pennsylvania, and bent his rear bumper to a point where it couldn't be straightened. He was determined that his truck look sharp—it was originally ordered with the "deluxe" chrome bumper at extra cost—and the severity of the dent also meant that the trailer hitch on the bumper was no longer safe to use. He needed a new bumper.

When Bob Scott took his pickup to Sloane Toyota in Glenside to get a new bumper installed, he touched off a pull sequence just at the point Toyota was taking a major step in its decade-long effort to synchronize the effort of its dealers, its parts distribution system, and its suppliers so customers could truly pull the flow of value all the way through a highly complex production and service system.

The Bad Old Days of Production

If Bob Scott had wrecked his bumper a year or two earlier, nothing would have happened immediately. When he tried to pull, Sloane Toyota wouldn't have had the right bumper on hand for his out-of-production vehicle. Using a traditional stocking system, it's simply impractical for a car dealer to keep on hand a wide range of replacement parts for older vehicles. With about ten thousand part numbers per vehicle, the carrying cost of the inventory would be staggering.

Instead, Sloane Toyota would have needed several days to get a bumper shipped by truck from a Toyota parts warehouse or used expensive overnight freight in order to get it delivered the next day. Bob Scott would have lost the use of his vehicle for some period of time or paid a premium if he wanted it the next day, and in either case would have been an unhappy customer.

Yet even as he waited, there would have been stacks of the precise bumper needed, indeed mountains of them, in Toyota's parts warehouses and at the bumper maker because no satisfactory method was in place for pulling. To see why this was so and to understand what is being done to implement a true pull system all the way along the value stream, let's go back in time and very nearly to the headwaters of the stream, to the Bumper Works factory in Danville, Illinois, which made the bumper Bob Scott cracked.

Shahid Khan, the president of Bumper Works's parent firm, Flex-N-Gate Corporation, is practically a cliché of the American dream. He came to the United States from Pakistan when he was sixteen to go to engineering school at the University of Illinois in Urbana. To put himself through school, he got a job running a massive stamping press in the down-and-out Bumper Works factory in nearby Danville. When he graduated he became the engineering director of Bumper Works and then, by the time he was twenty-eight, he had raised the funds to buy the company.

When Khan entered Bumper Works in 1970, he also entered the world of batch-and-queue. Bumper Works made chromed and painted steel bumpers in a variety of styles for customizing pickup trucks at the car dealership. It made large batches of each type of bumper—typically a month's worth—before shifting production to the next model and sold the bumpers to new-car dealers and crash-repair body shops through a complex wholesale distribution system.

Because large batches were considered normal in this world, it was not important that it took sixteen hours to change over Bumper Works's stamping presses. Because large batches of raw materials were considered unavoidable, Bumper Works had a warehouse at the end of its plant to receive flat sheets of steel by the ton from the steel company. And because the chroming company performing the key step in the middle of the production process also worked in a batch mode, Bumper Works piled up partially made bumpers in its intermediate goods warehouse until there was an enormous batch and then shipped them to the chromer all at once.

When the chromer shipped them back, all in a batch, they were run through a final assembly operation (to install inner reinforcing bars, attachment brackets, and cosmetic coverings), stored once more in a finished goods warehouse, and sent in a batch to the customer according to a predetermined schedule.

As Shahid Khan grew his business in the 1980s, he began to supply replacement bumpers to the service parts organizations of the American Big Three auto companies and he did very well. His batch thinking and their batch thinking were a match. However, Kahn had always set his standards very high, so in 1984 he approached Toyota about supplying bumpers for the pickups they were importing from Japan. This would give him their "crash" parts business as well.

In 1985, Bumper Works was signed on as a supplier for a small volume of Toyota business, and in 1987 won a sole-source contract for the bumpers on the new version of Toyota's small pickup (the model Bob Scott bought). By 1989, Bumper Works was Toyota's sole bumper supplier for North American needs.

There was only one problem: Bumper Works's production system was still a classic case of batch-and-queue. Toyota took Shahid Khan and his senior managers on their first trip to Japan late in 1989 and walked them through showcase lean suppliers, but as Khan remembers, "The light didn't come on; I really couldn't figure out how they could stay in business using the strange practices I saw." So in May 1990, Toyota told Khan they were dispatching a lean *sensei*,[1] a master of the Toyota system, as Khan's personal tutor.

In fact, Toyota sent a number of *sensei* from its Operations Management Consulting Division, the group established in 1969 by Taiichi Ohno to promote lean thinking within Toyota and in the firms in its supplier group.[2] They stayed for months at a time, and by the end of 1992, they had totally transformed Bumper Works—a unionized, grimy operation using old tools in old facilities—into one of the best examples of lean production in North America.

Lean Production for Pull

The first thing the Toyota *sensei* noted at Bumper Works was the massive inventories and batches. Nothing flowed. Immediately right-sizing the massive stamping presses to permit single-piece flow was not possible, so the only solution was to drastically reduce their changeover times and shrink batch sizes. Changeover times were already down from sixteen hours in the mid-1980s to around two hours, but this was not nearly enough.

The Toyota *sensei* applied their standard formula that machines should be available for production about 90 percent of the time and down for changeovers about 10 percent of the time. Then they looked at the range of products Bumper Works would need to make every day. They concluded that the large presses would need to be changed over in twenty-two minutes or less and the small presses in ten minutes or less. (In fact, the numbers were soon down to sixteen minutes and five minutes, respectively.)

Next, the plant was physically reorganized so flat sheets flowed directly from the receiving dock to the blanking machine, which cut the steel into rectangular shapes just larger than a bumper. The blanks then went immediately to the adjacent cell of three stamping presses, where they were given their shape. Next, they were shipped at frequent intervals to the outside-the-plant chroming operation and returned to the welding shop adjacent to the stamping presses. There, the inner and outer parts of the bumper plus the brackets for attaching the bumper to the vehicle were welded together. Finally, the bumpers went straight to the shipping dock just in time for scheduled shipment. *But they flowed only when pulled by the next step.* That is, the blanking machine did nothing until it received a signal from the stamping machines and the stamping machines made nothing until instructed to do so by the welding booth. Each activity pulled the next. The shipping schedule and *takt* time became the pacemaker for the entire operation.

Because most of Bumper Works's customers, as of 1992, were still ordering massive batches—one-month lots to be delivered by the last day of the month—Bumper Works decided to prepare for the future by creating its own daily schedule using a technique Toyota calls *level scheduling*. Shahid Khan's production manager would take the orders for the next month, let's say 8,000 of Bumper A, 6,000 of Bumper B, 4,000 of Bumper C, and 2,000 of Bumper D. She would add them up (to get 20,000) and divide by the number of working days in the month (say, twenty) to discover that Bumper Works would need each day to make 400 of Bumper A, 300 of Bumper B, 200 of Bumper C, and 100 of Bumper D (with a *takt* time of .96 minutes). This would require four changeovers of the blanking and stamping machines, totaling 88 minutes (9 percent of the 960 minutes of two-shift working time) at the maximum allowable changeover speed of 22 minutes.

The daily schedule was given to the welding booth to start the process. As the booth used up its reserve of inner and outer panels and brackets for Bumper A, the welders would slide the empty parts tub and its associated *kanban*, or signal card, down the short slide to the stamping machines. This provided the only signal needed to stamp more parts for Bumper A. Then, as the stamping press used up its blanks for Bumper A, the empty parts tub was sent back down the slide to the blanking machine, providing the only signal needed to make more blanks for Bumper A.

The in-plant MRP system that had been sending orders to every machine —but which never quite worked right so that expediting was always necessary to keep production going—was no longer needed. The new, simple system of pull and visual control always worked once the inevitable start-up problems were resolved. Bumper Works's new operating doctrine could be summarized simply as "Don't make anything until it is needed; then make it very quickly."

But there was a problem right in the heart of the new system. The steel bumpers once welded required a coat of chrome before they could go to final assembly. This was a complex process conducted by specialist firms operating in batch mode. Shahid Khan's chromer, Chrome Craft in Highland Park, Michigan (near Detroit), was the best supplier Bumper Works had found but was not in step with the new approach. Bumpers disappeared into Chrome Craft and didn't reappear for weeks. What was more, getting a rapid turnaround on expedited orders was impossible.

Khan and the Toyota *sensei* were soon on their way to Chrome Craft, where president and owner Richard Barnett watched with some amazement as rapid changeovers were implemented on Barnett's bumper polishing machines so that small lots could be pulled from the loading dock, taken through the necessary polishing process, and run through the long line of chroming tanks. (Chrome Craft was doing bumpers for other manufacturers and had dozens of bumper types going through its plant.)

By arranging for quick unloading and loading of the Bumper Works truck, it became possible to bring a load of bumpers in at 7:00 A.M. while picking up the load just completed, then to return at 3:00 P.M. to pick up the freshly chromed versions of the bumpers dropped off at 7:00 A.M. By 1995, a bumper's time in the Chrome Craft plant had fallen from fifteen days, on average, to less than a day. What was more, at the end of every shift the entire output of Toyota bumpers was being trucked out of the plant, leaving zero in-process inventories. Chrome Craft's inventory "turns" on Toyota bumpers had zoomed from about twenty to about five hundred per year.

Even this achievement is by no means the limit. In mid-1995, Chrome Craft helped install a right-sized chroming operation in a new Flex-N-Gate plant in Indiana making bumpers for the American Big Three. This brings time-in-process down from twenty-four hours (consisting of two eight-hour truck rides from Bumper Works to Chrome Craft and back, plus eight hours at Chrome Craft) to about eight hours.

As Bumper Works learned how to pull value through its system, it became capable of responding practically instantly to customer orders. Because of its quick changeover ability, Bumper Works could start welding a given type of bumper within about twenty minutes of receiving an order and it could easily vary its entire production as demand changed. All that was needed was to drop off a new set of order cards at the welding booth. Similarly, the time elapsed between the arrival of a flat sheet of steel on Bumper Works's loading dock and the shipment of a finished bumper to the customer fell from an average of four weeks to forty-eight hours. Quality also zoomed, as it always does when flow and pull thinking are put in place together. As of mid-1995, Bumper Works hadn't shipped a bad bumper to Toyota in five years.

The new system gave Bumper Works and Chrome Craft the ability to make small lots of bumpers at short notice—for example, a few replacement bumpers of the type Bob Scott needed—but Khan's customers did not know how to take advantage of his new capabilities. Until very recently, even Toyota was still ordering large batches, then erratically changing its orders as shortages developed in the distribution system. Another step was needed to create a smoothly pulling value stream.

The Bad Old Days of Distribution

When Toyota introduced its Corona model in America in 1965, it suddenly began to sell large numbers of cars. These needed service parts, everything from new bumpers to replace those crumpled in accidents (like Bob Scott's) to oil filters and spark plugs for periodic maintenance. Because of the long shipping time from Japan, Toyota needed large stocks of parts in North America and soon built a network of warehouses—called Parts Distribution Centers, or PDCs—stretching from Los Angeles to Boston.

In 1965, the Toyota Production System (TPS) was just being implemented in Toyota's supplier plants in Toyota City. No one had given any thought to applying TPS principles to Toyota's Japanese service parts warehouses, much less in faraway American warehouses. As a result, the eleven PDCs Toyota built in the United States were laid out like every warehouse in America. Each had vast bins stacked to a high ceiling, thousands and thousands of them, one for each type of part. The bins were lined up in long rows to create endless aisles in a massive square of a building.

The PDCs received parts from Japan in sealed containers, typically in large batches coming off massive container ships at weekly intervals. When the containers arrived at the PDC, they were opened in the receiving area and the parts were given to "stockers" with carts who walked up and down the aisles placing the parts in the proper bin. Because fifteen days were required back in Japan to assemble an order, another thirty-eight days were required for ocean shipping, and five days were needed at the PDC to bin the parts, the PDC needed to order parts at least fifty-eight days ahead of probable need to ensure uninterrupted supplies to Toyota dealers.

Toyota dealers, like Sloane Toyota, placed orders for parts once a week, by estimating likely increases or decreases in demand before the next weekly order. Because these forecasts were often wrong, they produced what Toyota calls "created demand"; that is, dramatic waves of orders traveling back up the value stream that are unrelated to actual demand expressed by real customers like Bob Scott. When the weekly orders were received at the PDC, a "picker" was dispatched to collect the appropriate parts from the appropriate bins in the appropriate aisles and take them to shipping. The parts were then delivered to the dealer by common carrier truck service the next day.

Because Toyota accepted the notion that large batches, expressed as "economic order quantities," were efficient due to savings in shipping costs, and because overnight shipment of parts was expensive, it encouraged its dealers to order large amounts of each part whenever they replenished. To make this attractive, Toyota paid the freight for the large weekly batches and allowed dealers to send back up to 5 percent of the value of a weekly order for a credit if they ordered too many parts of a certain type—for example, for a special service promotion which failed to meet its target.

In the event that the dealer didn't have a part in stock—for example, a bumper for Bob Scott's pickup—a VOR or "vehicle off road" order system was able to locate and deliver the exact part needed to the dealership before noon the next day. This system looked electronically into the inventory at the nearest PDC; then, at all PDCs; and finally, at Toyota's national warehouse in Torrance, California, to find the part, print a shipping order, get the order to the pickers in the appropriate warehouse, and get it shipped. To cover the cost of this premium service, Toyota required the dealers or the customer, like Bob Scott, to pay the express freight charge for getting the parts there quickly. In this way dealers could keep large numbers of the most frequently used parts on hand while ordering special needs overnight.

At the PDC, the bins for each type of part were large and the shipping containers were larger. And the container ships were truly massive. Air freight to supply parts in the event of a shortage was very expensive, so it seemed like common sense to order large batches of a given part whenever stocks at the PDC began to run low. In addition, Toyota's scheduling computer, reaching all the way back to the factories in Japan, was programmed to anticipate certain events—the onset of winter, when more bumpers are crumpled, or sales promotions, when a large number of oil filters and spark plugs are needed in a short time as dealers offer a "special" on routine service. Extra orders were added to ensure adequate supplies for these predictable surges in demand.

By the time Toyota's warehouse network was fully in place in the early 1970s, the typical PDC had a six-month supply of the typical part. In addition, a special area of the national warehouse in Torrance housed very low-volume, rarely ordered parts, often for very old Toyotas. The months of supply on hand in this warehouse was difficult to calculate because some parts might never be ordered. Shortages still occurred, for reasons which always seemed mysterious, and some air freight across the Pacific was still necessary, but in general the system ran pretty well and permitted Toyota to achieve the highest "fill rate" (or percentage of parts available from the PDCs on demand) in the North American auto industry, at 98 percent. For fifteen years, it was "good enough."

Lean Distribution for Pull

When Toyota began to assemble cars in the United States at the Fremont, California, joint venture with General Motors (NUMMI) in 1984, it began to develop a network of suppliers for bulky and "commodity" items—tires, batteries, and seats. Then, when Toyota opened its mammoth Georgetown, Kentucky, plant in 1988, it needed a comprehensive network of suppliers for a wide variety of parts.

These same parts were needed for routine service and body-shop work at Toyota dealers; so in 1986, Toyota had opened a receiving warehouse for American-made service parts in Toledo, Ohio. This Parts Redistribution Center, or PRC, was where Shahid Khan shipped his bumpers once he started producing for Toyota.

A major mission for this facility was to reduce shipping costs per part by consolidating the less than truckload shipments of parts received from suppliers into fully loaded trucks for onward shipment to each PDC. However, this focus on low freight cost per part created a classic batch-and-queue operation in which a month's worth of parts were queued up at each supplier before shipment to the PRC. Upon arrival, the parts were queued again for quality inspection and then delayed one more time in a staging area awaiting a full truckload before shipment to each PDC.

As the yen strengthened at the end of the 1980s, and American competitors like Ford began to implement some aspects of the Toyota Production System, Toyota executives started to wonder how they could sustain their competitive advantage. In addition, Toyota's four-year replacement cycle for every model, its steadily expanding range of models on offer in the United States,[3] and the tendency of Americans to drive their cars longer and longer,[4] meant rapid growth in "active" part numbers which Toyota needed to stock as replacement parts to keep its customers happy. This seemed to require larger and larger inventories of parts and ever-growing distribution costs.

As Toyota executives pondered this situation, it occurred to them that they had never applied any of Toyota's lean thinking to their North American warehousing and distribution system. As they thought about this, it quickly became apparent that startling advantages could be gained if they did.

The Toyota warehouses at that time were run in the familiar batch-and-queue mode we described in the Introduction and again in Chapter 3. Supervisors directed hourly workers to haul large carts or forklift loads of incoming parts from the receiving area down endless aisles for binning. The supervisors tried to ensure that the "stockers" were working hard when they were out of sight by giving each worker the same number of "lines" to stock during each shift. A "line" was a specific part number—for example, Bob Scott's deluxe chrome bumper carries Toyota corporate part number 00228-35911-13—with a varying quantity of that part, perhaps only one but sometimes hundreds.

Each "line" could therefore involve a very different amount of work. Putting one hundred spark plugs on a low shelf was a lot easier and could be completed much faster than hoisting one heavy bumper into an upper bin, yet both counted as one stocking line. Because each supervisor gave each stocker the same number of lines to complete during the shift, there were endless claims of favoritism or punitive assignments. "You're giving me all the heavy bumpers because I refused to go on the night shift when you were shorthanded," etcetera. What was more, it was practically impossible for supervisors to determine the cause when stockers failed to complete their runs in the allotted time. Was it because bins were too full to hold more parts or because of a faulty forklift, or was it simply a matter of unsupervised workers relaxing on the job? Without accurate identification of causes it was hard to implement remedies and improve practices.

The same organization and logic regulated "picking" parts for the weekly shipments to the dealers. In addition, there was an expediting system in place for the "hot list" VOR parts which were needed the next day by dealers. Unfortunately, the VOR orders often caused chaos among the pickers and slowed down the routine picks for weekly dealer orders, and it's easy to see why. A picker would be told at the last minute to run all the way across the warehouse to get a single part to meet the air freight pickup deadline. If this need had been anticipated, the pick could have been part of a complete circuit of the warehouse for many parts and would have been much more efficient.

But perhaps the worst features of the warehouse system in the late 1980s were the size of the bins, the inefficient use of storage space, and the size of the batches ordered as replenishments. Both the bins and reorder quantities were massive, involving hundreds or thousands of parts of a given type and number. This inevitably meant months of spare parts on hand and large facilities to hold all of them. Large facilities, in turn, were time-consuming for stockers and pickers to work their way around.

As Toyota executives thought about this situation, the solution to the stocking half of the problem became obvious: Toyota should dramatically shrink the size of the storage bins, and reduce the lot size for reorders. Instead of ordering from suppliers on a weekly or monthly basis, why not order *daily* and order *just the amount shipped to the dealers that day?* This was much more practical for domestic parts obtained from suppliers, like Bumper Works, who had mastered lean techniques and could respond to requests for small amounts. Fortunately, Toyota was rapidly transferring production of its parts from Japan to North America, and many suppliers were starting down the path pioneered by Bumper Works.

The other half of the problem, the picking, could be solved with an equally dramatic rethinking of relations with the dealers. Instead of asking dealers to order large batches weekly and then make special requests each night for missing parts, why not have the dealers order *daily* and order *just the amount sold to customers that day?*

Toyota knew that its dealers would strenuously object, unless the company offered to pay the freight for the daily shipments. Yet, a bit of analysis showed that if Toyota shipped parts from its eleven PDCs to the dealers in each of its eleven sales regions every night, the extra costs of the trucks would be offset by the simplification of the picking process, savings on inventory carrying costs, and the elimination of express delivery charges. In addition, day-to-day consistency in orders, with no sudden waves, would allow consolidation of some truck routes.

There was one last problem to solve. This was the crisis at the dealer when a customer like Bob Scott came in with a request for a part not normally carried in the dealer's parts inventory. Of course, the part could be supplied overnight by the new system, as it always had been, but the customer would be unhappy. Customers want their cars fixed *right now!*

Toyota realized that if dealers ordered every part *daily* to replace the exact number sold that day, dealer inventories of parts could be reduced dramatically. As dealers reduced their average stock of each part number, they could afford to increase the range of part numbers on hand. Instead of having hundreds of the most common parts requested and none of those requested less frequently, dealers could have a small number of each part across a very wide range. In this way they would be more likely to have a low-volume item like a bumper for an older vehicle when a customer like Bob Scott asked for one.

From Theory into Practice

The logic just described for introducing a pull system in warehousing that responds faithfully to actual customer demand was understood by Toyota's North American executives by the late 1980s. Getting it fully in place, however, has required years, even in a supremely lean organization like Toyota, and the final steps needed are just now being taken. The translation of lean concepts into the warehouse has required considerable getting used to, for managers as well as employees, and Toyota has had to convince its employees that the new way of thinking would not cause anyone to lose his or her job.

The first step along the path, beginning in 1989, was to reduce bin sizes and to relocate parts by size and by frequency of demand. Trying to stock or pick a truck fender along with a spark plug on the same run was causing lost parts and the use of grossly oversized equipment, so it was important to segregate parts into small, medium, and large categories with their own sections of the warehouse. As this was done, those parts most frequently demanded were moved closest to the start of the sorting and picking runs and the length of the aisles was reduced markedly. The consequences of these steps for the layout of a typical PDC are shown in Figures 4.1 and 4.2. Note that a typical picking route was much shorter after downsizing and reorganization of bin locations. However, it's also important to note that because the batch size of replenishment orders was not changed, the total amount of a given part on hand remained the same. The extra stocks were stored in the "Reserves" area of the warehouse and moved to the "Active" bins as required.

The next step, beginning at the end of 1990, was to introduce the con-

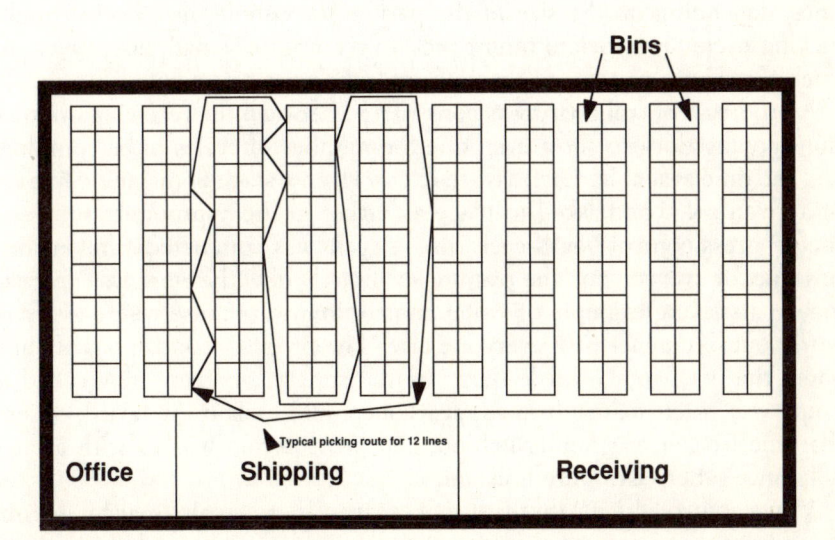

FIGURE 4.1: TOYOTA PDC BEFORE LEAN THINKING

FIGURE 4.2: TOYOTA PDC AFTER DOWNSIZING

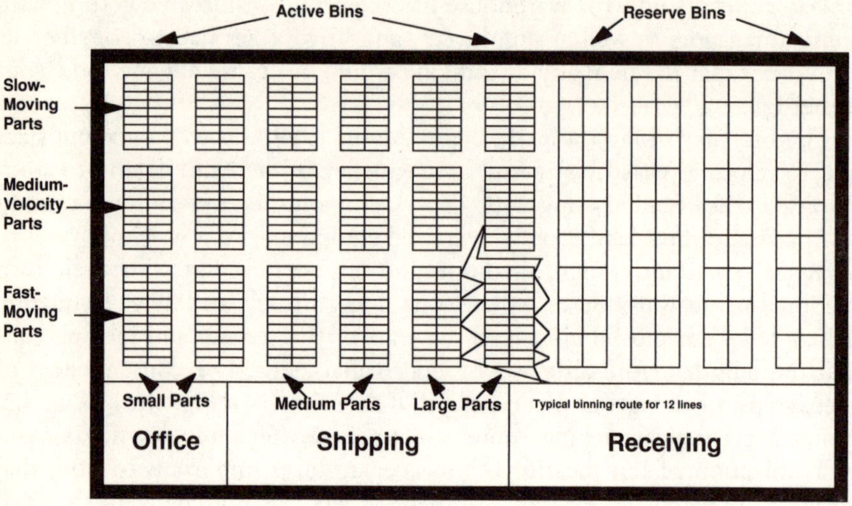

cepts of standard work and visual control by dividing the workday into twelve-minute cycles. An interval of this length was found to be the best compromise between walking distance and cart size in making a round of the bins to load or unload a cart. During each cycle an "associate," as hourly workers were now called, was expected to pick or bin a different number of lines, depending on the size of the part. For example, in a twelve-minute picking cycle an associate might pick thirty lines of small parts or twenty lines of medium parts or twelve lines of large parts.

A progress control board was constructed between the receiving dock and the shipping dock to show everyone the number of cycles to be completed and the time available. Each associate was given a stack of magnetic markers of a given color and asked to place a marker in the appropriate square on the progress control board each time a cycle was completed. This made it possible for everyone on the team to see exactly how the work was proceeding, in a striking example of visual control in a warehouse where everyone works out of contact with everyone else. The progress control board eliminated the need for "team leaders," as the supervisors were now called, to "supervise" their teams. Instead, everyone could look at the board, observe that one worker was falling behind, and provide that worker with a bit of help once other tasks were finished.

Visual control along with the use of exact work cycles also made it possible to address the causes of disruptions in work flow. The right side of the progress control board provided a blank area beside each cycle for associates to write in the reason that a cycle could not be completed on time. These reasons, when summarized, became the raw materials for directing work team *kaizen* activities when these were introduced in 1992.

One of the first *kaizen* activities was for the teams to build new work carts, using scrap materials and parts from local building supply stores, so the carts were right-sized for each type of picking or binning task. The carts were also designed to hold just the right number of parts—for example, with thirty part holding cubicles for routes for small parts—to provide another form of visual control.

At the same time the precise picking cycles were being introduced, Toyota's master computer back in Torrance was being reprogrammed to group orders from dealers by bin location in each PDC so that a set of picking labels in precise bin order was printed out at the beginning of each shift at each PDC. The picking labels were divided into twelve-minute cycles—based on the size of the parts and the knowledge of the team leader about current conditions in the PDC—and placed in pigeonholes in a dispatch box. The pickers obtained their jobs of exactly twelve minutes duration from the dispatch box, always taking labels from the next available slot so there could be no possibility of favoritism in work assignments. In this way, each associate was given five assignments per hour and the work could proceed in a smooth flow from the shelves to the shipping dock. Posting start times above the slots and visually controlling completion times also eliminated another traditional warehousing problem of working ahead to "beat the system." This practice invariably led to quality problems as associates in their haste picked the wrong part or put parts in the wrong bins.

After six years of work Toyota was ready in August 1995 to transition from weekly to daily orders from its dealers and to do this without the need for an additional headcount at the PDCs. Indeed, at the end of 1995, the twenty-two pickers at the Toyota PDC near Boston were picking 5,300 lines per day while the hundred pickers at the Chrysler parts warehouse across the road were picking 9,500 lines per day using traditional methods, a productivity difference of 2.5 to 1.

When the new Toyota Daily Ordering System (TDOS) is combined with the relocation of the PRC for Japanese-sourced parts from Japan to Ontario, California, in October 1996 and the replenishment time to the PDCs from the PRCs is reduced from forty to seven days, it will be possible to dramatically reduce the stocks in the PDCs by eliminating the reserve stocks, as shown in Figure 4.3. The ability to get parts resupplied very quickly from the next level of the system, and therefore the ability to reorder in small amounts, is always the secret to reducing total inventories in a complex production and supply stream.

Technology for Lean Distribution

It is important to note that the Toyota PDCs are dramatically boosting productivity and reducing space requirements without resort to any spending for new technology. Indeed, the company has recently conducted its own test of the most appropriate technology for lean distribution by automating the Chicago PDC while converting the other ten PDCs in accord with the methods just described.

FIGURE 4.3: TOYOTA PDC AFTER DOWNSIZING, TDOS, AND RAPID REPLENISHMENT FROM PRCs

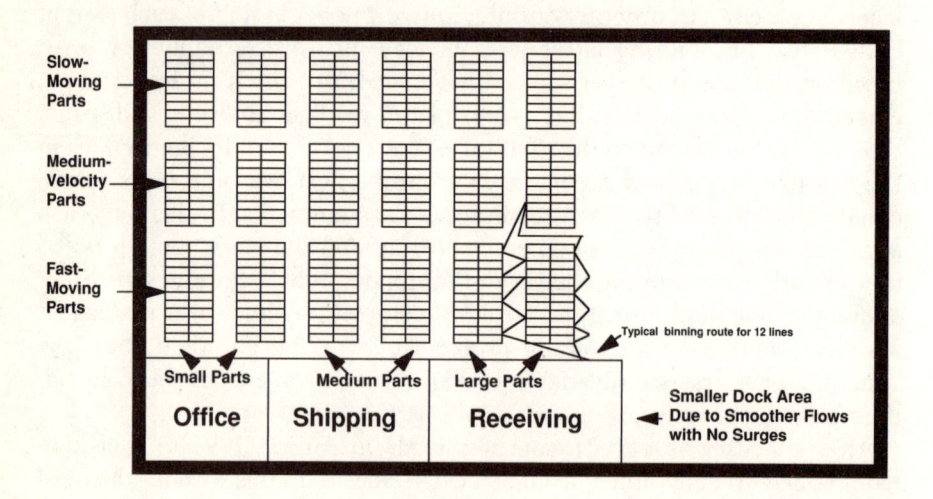

The Chicago experiment was undertaken at the end of the 1980s when Toyota back in Japan was obsessed with a shortage of workers during the Bubble Economy and was pressing ahead with much higher levels of assembly automation at its new Tahara plant near Toyota City. It seemed appropriate to try a high level of warehouse automation as well and the objective in Chicago was to completely automate the actual stocking and picking of parts.

By 1994, after much effort and enormous cost, the Chicago PDC was fully automated but productivity per employee lagged behind the other PDCs implementing standard work, visual control, and efficient bin size and location. While some direct effort was saved in Chicago, the amount of technical support needed to maintain the complex system offset the gains in direct labor and the capital costs made the whole approach uneconomic.

We'll have more to say in Chapter 10 about "appropriate" technology for a lean system and how to select it.

Level Scheduling Needs Level Selling

As Toyota thought more about installing a pull system in service parts production and distribution, another benefit emerged. If inventories and handling costs for service and crash parts could be slashed dramatically as the North American suppliers and warehouses implemented lean techniques and if production of more parts could be transferred from high-yen Japan to North America, it should be possible to offer the highest-quality and lowest-cost service and crash parts to Toyota dealers. If this were possible, special promotions to temporarily lower prices and boost sales—the bane of every distribution and production system in every industry—could be eliminated. Toyota dealers would always have the best deal for their customers.

In 1994, Toyota and its dealers together spent $32 million in the United States on direct mail, print, and broadcast advertising for "specials," offers by dealers to Toyota owners to perform anything from oil changes to complete maintenance programs at far below the "normal" price. They made these offers because the cost of "genuine" Toyota parts and dealer service was at best equal to—but often much higher—than the customer's best alternative, the independent garage or mass merchandiser. So promotions were conducted to bring in more service customers for limited periods, partly to support customer retention, partly in hopes owners could be enticed into looking at new Toyotas while at the dealer to service their current model.

The problem with promotions was very simple. They required the production of large amounts of parts in advance, yet it was never possible to predict how many would actually be needed. When not all of the parts made were actually needed, dealers shipped them back to the PDC and the PDC temporarily stopped ordering from suppliers until the excess inventory was consumed. Here we see one of the mechanisms of the familiar "pogo stick" phenomenon of "chaotic" orders coming into production facilities when the end market itself is actually quite stable, a tendency we'll examine further in a moment.

The net result was a temporary increase in Toyota orders to suppliers to a level far above long-term average demand (in order to build stocks for the promotion), followed by a dramatic drop in orders to far below long-term average demand. This was costly in both directions, requiring overtime in parts plants during the upswing and causing excess capacity during the downswing. It also created costs in the distribution channel to ship excess parts back from the dealers and for the excess stocking and picking costs of running the same parts through the warehouse system twice. The solution was to concentrate on "level selling" by keeping prices constant and making replacement parts at the exact rate parts were being sold.[5]

As Toyota executives thought about applying pull to the entire value stream, from the dealer service bay all the way back to the bumper chromer and similar "second-tier" suppliers, the more advantages they could see. But they knew it would be very hard to persuade the dealers to go along. They come from generations of batch-and-queue thinking.

The Bad Old Days of Car Service

Whenever we drive by a car dealer our first thought is always the same: "Look at all that *muda*, the vast lot of cars already made which no one wants." Similarly, when we see the large banner out in front offering "rebates" off list prices and "specials" on service and parts, we wonder, "Why did the dealer order cars and service parts which aren't needed, and why did the factory build cars and parts in advance of customer pull?"

The answer lies partly in the unresponsiveness of mass-production car makers. Chrysler in the United States is currently trying to reduce the wait for a specially ordered car from sixty-eight to sixteen days, yet for a generation, already, Toyota's lean production system has been able to build and deliver cars to order in Japan in about a week. Out of fear of losing sales to "impulse purchasers," mass producers create vast seas of cars on dealer lots, one of practically every specification, so no buyer need walk away unsatisfied. (Converting all factories to flow systems can deal with this problem, as we have already shown.)

But the answer also lies in the mentality of retailers and customers across the world. Dealers love to "deal" and the public loves a "sale." (One of us took a trip to France some years ago and discovered that the only phrase of high school French our wife could remember was "on sale"!) Changing the way retailers and consumers think about the process of ordering goods and making transactions may be difficult, but as we will see, it is essential to doing things a better way.

Pulling from the Service Bay

Most readers, we hope, have never been into the parts storage area of a car dealership. It's generally a horrible sight. When we first visited the Parts

Department at Bob Sloane's Toyota near Philadelphia in 1994, we found a rabbit warren of rickety shelves, meandering aisles, and dim lighting in two separate buildings. Clearly, the physical flow of parts was an orphan activity compared with the income-producing service bays for car repairs and the showroom where cars are sold.

When we first visited Sloane Toyota, the dealership had about a three-month supply of the average part, creating an inventory of about $580,000 in service and crash parts. When a car was driven into Sloane for repairs, it was taken to a service bay where the technician evaluated the problem and determined what parts would be needed. The technician then went to the parts window, requested the necessary parts, and waited for the counter person to go and get them somewhere in the labyrinth of bins and aisles.

Because Sloane received most parts in weekly batches, the workload of the parts stockers who took the parts from the receiving area and put them in the proper bin was very erratic. It generally took three days to get all of the parts from the receiving area into the bins, with the result that the counter person would often find empty bins when the computer showed the parts were in stock. Indeed they were, but they were "missing in action" somewhere between the receiving area and the proper bin. This knowledge touched off "treasure hunts," which are the distribution equivalent of the expediting always necessary in batch-and-queue production operations. Good counter staff would generally find their part, but the whole exercise was inherently wasteful. (The highly skilled technician, meanwhile, was standing idly at the window all the time the counter person was treasure-hunting.)

In 1995, when Sloane Toyota joined Toyota's campaign to introduce pull in the whole parts distribution and manufacturing system, it reorganized its parts storage area just the way Toyota reorganized its PDCs. By cutting the size of the bins dramatically, generally by three quarters, and reorganizing all parts storage into one building, Sloane found it possible to increase part numbers on hand by 25 percent (including Bob Scott's bumper) while cutting its storage area in half and reducing its parts inventory from $580,000 to $290,000. While freeing up $290,000 in cash from inventory Sloane was able to add four new revenue-producing service bays, created with practically no capital investment, in the empty second parts warehouse.

Sloane Toyota found that the number of cars which could receive "same-day service" went up substantially (reducing the number of cars in its overnight "loaner" fleet) even as its inventory generated cash and the number of parts the average picker could gather in a given period of time more than doubled. Most important, customers were happier because their cars were more likely to get fixed right away and the total cost of service had fallen dramatically. Indeed, Bob Scott was able to get his truck's bumper replaced the same day.

Pulling from Service Bay to Raw Materials

We can see the full magnitude of what is happening by "pulling" together all the pieces of the service value stream. By the end of 1996, when Toyota's new pull system will be in place throughout North America, the request of the customer arriving in a Toyota dealer service bay will become the trigger for pulling parts through four replenishment loops going all the way back to steel blanks, as shown in Figure 4.4.

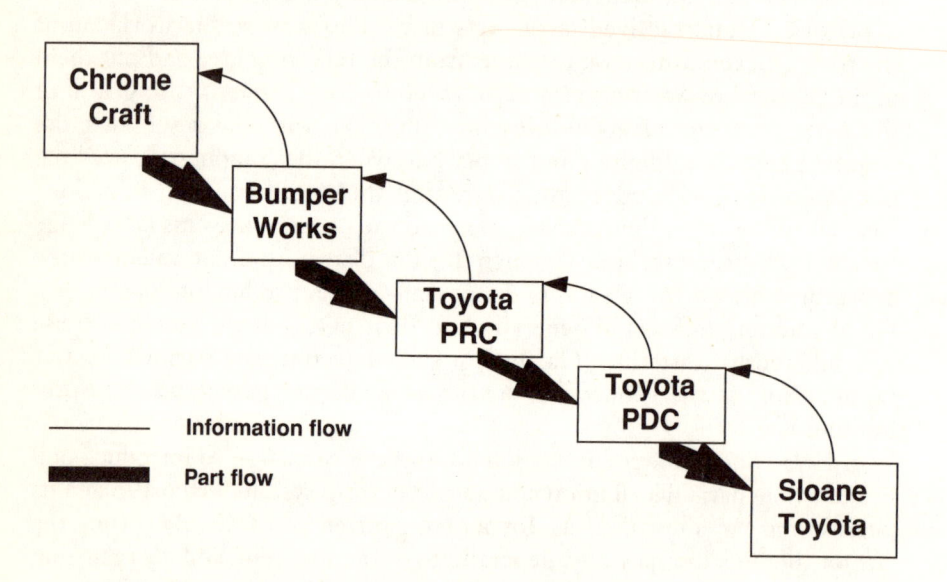

FIGURE 4.4: PULL THROUGH FOUR LOOPS

Toyota dealers and parts suppliers will still rely on Toyota's computerized macroforecast for capacity planning to answer questions about the size of manufacturing plants and the number of warehouses that would be needed in the future. However, day-to-day part replenishment will now be handled in a radically different way: Each time a customer requests a part at the service bay, a series of replenishment loops will result eventually in more parts being made by the supplier in a situation which might be called "sell one; buy one" or "ship one; make one."

To see what this means, let's follow the bumper example all the way through the value stream. Before lean techniques were applied to any aspect of the system—that is, prior to 1989—the elapsed time from the arrival of steel blanks at Bumper Works until the bumper made from those blanks was actually installed on a truck was nearly eleven months. Four weeks in

Bumper Works, two weeks at Chrome Craft, a few days at the Toledo PRC, six months at the PDC, and three months in Bob Sloane's parts inventory. (Lead time of this magnitude was the norm, not the exception, for the entire automotive parts industry in North America.)

By the end of 1995, the elapsed time had fallen to four months: forty-eight hours in Bumper Works and Chrome Craft, a few days in the Toledo warehouse, two months in the PDC, and one and a half months in Bob Sloane's inventory. And by the end of 1996, elapsed time should fall further to about 2.5 months as both the PDC and Bob Sloane shrink their inventories in response to falling resupply times. At the same time, the percentage of vehicles fixed the same day is increasing substantially, and costs—inventory, warehouse space, and direct labor—are falling dramatically.

Note that practically no capital equipment has been required. The tool modifications to permit quick changeovers and the specialized stocking carts in the factories and warehouses were created by production workers as part of *kaizen* activities, and the elaborate MRP systems formerly regulating activities inside the Bumper Works and Chrome Craft plants are no longer needed.

Just the Beginning

The savings we describe are just the beginning. Sloane Toyota, Toyota Motor Sales, Bumper Works, and Chrome Craft are now working on the value stream for service and crash parts as a lean enterprise under Toyota's leadership and are deeply committed to the concept of *perfection*, which we will discuss in the next chapter. They all expect to steadily reduce the elapsed time and cost of service parts. (Superlative quality is taken as a given, but quality will improve as well, as a natural complement to flow and pull.) One approach will be to extend the smooth-flowing value stream all the way to raw materials by helping the steel maker and steel fabricator overcome their current batch-and-queue thinking. At the other end of the stream, with encouragement and help from the dealer, customers may be able to schedule many of their service requirements in advance so the need for parts can be precisely predicted.

The parent Toyota company began to pursue this latter approach in Japan shortly after the 1982 merger of Toyota Motor Sales and the Toyota Motor Company, which formed the current-day Toyota Motor Corporation. Between 1982 and 1990, Toyota reorganized its service and crash parts business in a manner identical to the new North American pattern, except that it took two additional steps. It created Local Distribution Centers (LDCs) in each metropolitan area (jointly owned with the dealers) and took practically all of the parts stock out of dealerships with the result that Toyota dealers in Japan now carry only a three-day supply of forty commodity parts like windshield wiper blades. It then encouraged dealers to work intensively with every customer to preschedule maintenance so that parts needs could be precisely predicted in advance.

Because the Local Distribution Centers are only a short drive from each dealer, a "milk run" parts delivery vehicle can circulate from the LDC to every dealer every two hours, very much the way parts are sent from suppliers to lean assembly plants. And because the LDCs are large enough to stock a few of every active part, practically every car can be repaired the same day with no need for express freight from the Parts Distribution Center at the next level up the system.[6]

When the customer first schedules service for a given day, a preliminary order for the necessary parts is prepared. Then, the day before the scheduled visit, when the dealer calls the customer to be sure that the repairs will be conducted the next day, firm orders for parts are placed with the LDC for delivery on the next milk run. Finally, on the morning of the service visit, the dealer technicians examine the car to see if any additional parts will be needed and place orders for these extra parts, to be supplied in two to four hours from the LDC.

While some features of this system may work only in regions with a very high population density—for example, Japan and many areas of Western Europe—the additional gain in parts system efficiency and level of service for the customer is striking, as shown in Table 4.1.

Service parts warehouses are, of course, Type-One *muda*, being necessary to run service systems at the present time but not actually creating any value. However, as stock levels fall and replenishment orders grow smaller and more frequent, PDCs will look less and less like warehouses and more

TABLE 4.1: PARTS DISTRIBUTION EFFICIENCY AND LEVEL OF SERVICE, TOYOTA U.S.A. and JAPAN

	U.S.A. 1994 Parts/Days	U.S.A. 1996 Parts/Days	JAPAN 1990 Parts/Days
Parts Distribution Center	50,000　120	65,000　30	60,000　18
Local Distribution Center	—　—	—　—　15,000　9	
Dealer	4,000　90	6,000　21	40　3
Stock Level Index	100	33	19
Service Rate	98% in 7 days	98% in 1 day	98% in 2 hours

Note: Toyota U.S.A. has eleven regional PDCs, serving 1,400 dealers; Toyota Japan has thirty-three regional PDCs, serving 273 DCs who in turn serve 4,700 dealers. (In the U.S.A., Toyota dealers also act as local wholesalers.) Each has on average the above days' worth of that number of parts in stock. The Stock Level Index is the total sum of the days times the part numbers in each system, with U.S.A. 1994 = 100.

like cross-docking points. Many parts on their way to a dealer will simply be moved from the incoming container to a roll-cage containing the dealer's order, without ever being binned. Instead of a series of deep lakes with little flow, the PDCs will gradually become wide spots in the channel where tributaries come together and parts are speeded to the required destination.

Perhaps at some completely lean point in the distant future it will be possible to use stereolithography and other emerging technologies to actually make parts at the dealership one by one as they are needed. However, the improvements instituted by Toyota in Japan and the United States in the past few years are available to any service business in any industry right now and constitute a remarkable leap compared with most current practice.

Is Chaos Real?

The introduction of pull in the Toyota service value stream, even to the partial extent achieved to date, raises profound questions going far beyond this particular value stream. Specifically, what happens to the "chaos" that observers have detected in many product markets when customers can pull value practically instantly from raw materials into reality? And what happens to the macroeconomy when lead times and inventories largely disappear?

Since James Gleick published his fascinating book *Chaos*[7] in 1987, it has become fashionable for business writers to talk about chaotic markets and the need for organizations to be able to instantly respond. Much of the writing on reconfigurable "virtual" corporations (whatever those are) and chaos management stems from this new perception of reality. Indeed, to apply to business MIT meteorologist Edward Lorenz's original metaphor for a chaotic system—the world's weather where the nonlinear nature of forces potentially makes it possible for a butterfly in Beijing to affect the weather a few days later in New York—managers today seem to be living in fear of butterflies.

In our view, this new way of thinking is appropriate for purely physical phenomena like the weather but miscomprehends the nature of customer-producer relations. Indeed, in looking at the great bulk of the world's industrial economy, the most striking feature of this decade is the relative stagnation and predictability of most product markets. In activities ranging from motor vehicles to aircraft to industrial machinery to personal computers to home building, the trajectory of product technology is quite predictable. What's more, the end-use demand of customers is inherently quite stable and largely for replacement. We believe that the volatility—the perceived marketplace chaos—in these industrial activities is in fact self-induced, the inevitable consequence of the long lead times and large inventories in the traditional world of batch-and-queue overlaid with relatively flat demand and promotional activities—like specials on auto service—which producers employ in response.[8]

One solution—as recently proposed by Peter Senge[9]—is the creation of learning organizations which can reflect upon these phenomena and respond to them. One might think of a learning organization as a sort of intellectual MRP to take the kinks out of production and consumption.

We have a radically different proposal: Get rid of lead times and inventories so that demand is instantly reflected in new supply rather than the current situation of misjudged supply perennially searching for demand and creating chaos in the process. We are confident that the pattern of demand will suddenly be seen for what it is: remarkably stable except for a few new products—like multimedia—whose value and final form are being determined in real time.

Do We Really *Need* a Business Cycle?

If we can get rid of lead times and inventories to give people what they want when they want it, we believe that demand will stabilize for another reason: the damping effect on the traditional business cycle.

Conventional wisdom among economists is that about half of the downswing of economic activity in business cycles is due to consumers and producers working off the inventories built up toward the top of the cycle. Similarly, about half the upswing is due to building up new inventories in expectation of higher upstream prices ("buy raw materials now to get a bargain before prices go up") and to the expectation of greater downstream sales that require plenty of product in the distribution channel to supply, but which never quite materialize).[10] And no amount of government fine-tuning and countercyclical intervention has been able to damp the amplitude or frequency of the cycle during the fifty years since World War II.[11]

Unfortunately, our hypothesis that largely eliminating inventories will greatly damp the cycle can't be tested just yet, despite several decades of lean thinking in Japan and a decade of awareness about JIT in the United States and Europe. When one looks at the data on inventories, the amount associated with any given level of economic activity (normalizing for the business cycle) hasn't budged in America, Europe, or Japan. The reason, we believe, is that most applications of JIT, even in Japan, have involved Just-in-Time *supply*, not Just-in-Time *production*, and batch sizes have not been reduced by much. Thus, nothing has happened except to push inventories of the same magnitude one step back up the value stream toward raw materials, and one of the great prizes of the lean leap is still waiting to be claimed.

Pulling Value in Pursuit of Perfection

We hope you can now see the need to precisely specify value and to identify every step in the value stream for specific products, then to introduce flow, and next to let the ultimate customer pull value from its source. However, much of the potential of lean thinking is lost unless you take the final principle to heart. We'll end Part I of this book with some thoughts on *perfection*.

CHAPTER 5

Perfection

The Incremental Path

When Joe Day, the president of Freudenberg-NOK General Partnership (FNGP) of Plymouth, Michigan, began in 1992 to introduce lean thinking in the North American alliance between the world's largest seal and gasket makers,[1] he noticed something very curious. No matter how many times his employees improved a given activity to make it leaner, they could always find more ways to remove *muda* by eliminating effort, time, space, and errors. What's more, the activity became progressively more flexible and responsive to customer pull.

For example, when Freudenberg-NOK set out to reorganize the manufacture of vibration dampers in its Ligonier, Indiana, facility, an initial *kaizen* event achieved a 56 percent increase in labor productivity and a 13 percent reduction in the amount of factory space needed. However, in revisiting this activity in five additional three-day *kaizen* events over the next three years, it was gradually possible to boost productivity by 991 percent while reducing the amount of space needed by 48 percent, as shown in Table 5.1. What's more, additional improvements are possible and planned for the future.

This seems to defy all logic. After all, there *are* diminishing returns to any type of effort, aren't there? *Kaizen* activities are not free, and perfection — meaning the complete elimination of *muda*—is surely impossible. So, shouldn't managers eventually stop efforts to improve the process and simply manage it in a steady state, avoiding variances from "normal" performance?

As we have reviewed data similar to those in Table 5.1 with senior managers in many firms around the world, we have found two prevalent reactions. One is that steady-state management—management of variances—really is the cost-effective approach once an activity has been "fixed." The other was summarized by a senior manager of an English firm, which had done nothing to fix its product development, scheduling, and production systems but was *planning* to do something. "Why didn't FNGP get the job done the first

Table 5.1: Repeat *Kaizens* on Same Part Number, FNGP Ligonier, Indiana, Factory, 1992–94

	February 1992*	April 1992	May 1992	November 1992	January 1993	January 1994	August 1995
Number of associates	21	18	15	12	6	3	3
Pieces made per associate	55	86	112	140	225	450	600
Space utilized (square feet)	2,300	2,000	1,850	1,662	1,360	1,200	1,200

* Baseline performance before start of lean initiative on this three-shift operation with seven associates per shift.
NOTE: During this period OSHA reportable accidents and Workers' Compensation costs both declined by more than 92 percent. Total capital spending over this period was less than $1,000, for a right-sized, in-line painting system permitting single-piece flow.

time! Why didn't they conduct a thorough planning exercise to identify the perfect process at the outset so they wouldn't waste three years before finally getting it 'right'?"

Both reactions show how traditional management fails to grasp the concept of *perfection* through endless steps, which is a fundamental principle of lean thinking. Because FNGP is one of the most relentless pursuers of perfection we have found, their approach makes an excellent illustration of what perfection means in practice and how to pursue it.

The Radical Path

There is an alternative, radical path to perfection, a total value stream *kaikaku* involving all the firms from start to finish. Glassmaking for the automotive industry provides an interesting example. Currently in North America, Japan, and Europe, manufacture of the fixed glass for cars and trucks (excluding the glass mounted in doors which moves up and down) involves very similar steps no matter which companies perform them. (These are shown in Figure 5.1.)

The first step is the glass float, a vast device in which silica is melted and floated on a reservoir of liquid tin. Sheets of glass are pulled off the float, cut into rectangular shapes, and carefully cooled. Because of the size of the typical float and the problem of getting batch-to-batch consistency, large batches are produced and stored for considerable periods before shipment to the glass fabricator.

FIGURE 5.1: AUTO GLASS TODAY

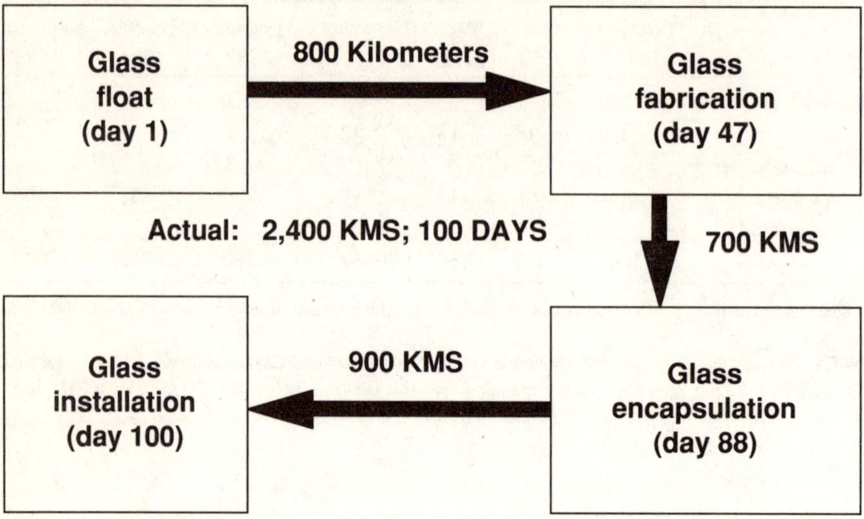

```
┌─────────────┐   800 Kilometers    ┌─────────────┐
│   Glass     │ ──────────────────▶ │   Glass     │
│   float     │                     │ fabrication │
│  (day 1)    │                     │  (day 47)   │
└─────────────┘                     └─────────────┘
                                           │
     Actual: 2,400 KMS; 100 DAYS           │ 700 KMS
                                           ▼
┌─────────────┐      900 KMS        ┌─────────────┐
│   Glass     │ ◀────────────────── │   Glass     │
│ installation│                     │encapsulation│
│  (day 100)  │                     │  (day 88)   │
└─────────────┘                     └─────────────┘
```

The glass fabricator cuts the glass to net shapes (discarding about 25 percent in the process). The net shapes are then heated to just below the melting point and positioned in dies of the desired shape, where they are "drooped" (without any pressure) or "pressed" (using an upper die to stamp them into shape) into the final geometry needed to precisely fit the frame of the car. Again, the complexity of changing the dies and the problems of achieving batch-to-batch consistency have caused glass fabricators to manufacture enormous batches of a given part number and to store them before shipment to the glass encapsulator.

The encapsulator takes the glass from its own incoming storage and inserts each piece in a molding machine which injects some form of rubber or plastic (most commonly polyvinyl chloride) into a channel around the perimeter of the glass to create a waterproof seal and an expansion joint for attaching the glass to the steel auto body.

After some additional storage at the encapsulator, the glass is shipped to the auto assembly plant, where it is installed in the car.

Clearly, there would be substantial gains from incrementally improving each step in this process. For example, pull systems like those described in the last chapter could be introduced for each replenishment loop and tool changes could be speeded up, particularly by the glass presser, to make smaller batches. However, there would still be enormous amounts of *muda* due to the distant location of the four plants involved and the large amounts of time-consuming, expensive transport. What's more, quality problems causing high levels of scrap would still be difficult to address because of the long time lags between the pressing, encapsulation, and installation steps, where problems with the previous step are most likely to be discovered.

A radical leap toward perfection in this process would involve right-sizing the glass float for the amount of product needed by a specific customer, dramatically reducing batch sizes in the pressing step and conducting it at the end of the float to save the energy required to reheat the glass, then conducting the encapsulation step in continuous flow at the next workstation from the pressing step, and finally locating this whole activity across the road from the auto assembly plant so the pull of the plant could be answered instantly (as shown in Figure 5.2).

FIGURE 5.2: AUTO GLASS AFTER RADICAL REALIGNMENT

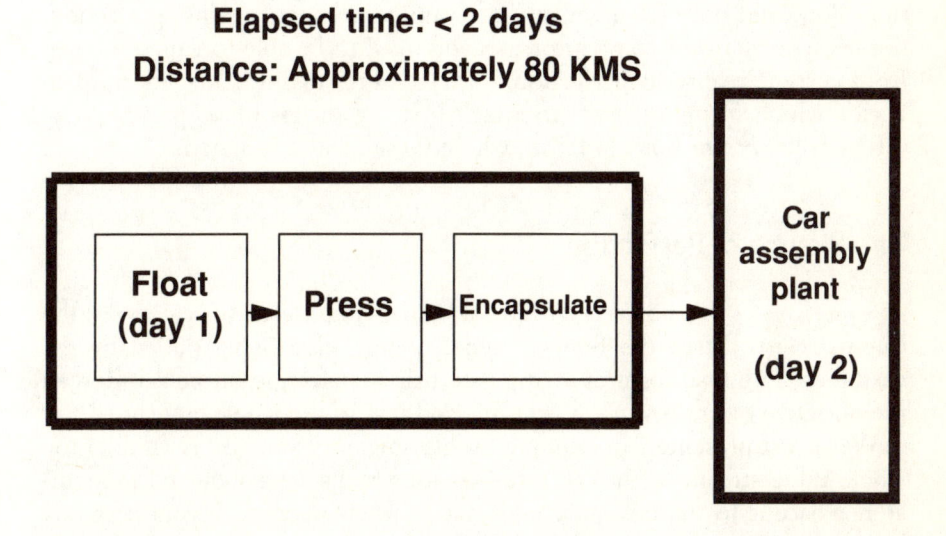

Elapsed time: < 2 days
Distance: Approximately 80 KMS

Float (day 1) → Press → Encapsulate → Car assembly plant (day 2)

No one has pursued this approach because, like most truly radical rethinks of a value stream, a number of firms (four in this case) would need to cooperate in changing their methods by forming a lean enterprise for this product (which might best be defined as all of the fixed glass needed for a specific auto assembly plant). However, if a lean enterprise were formed to rethink the whole value stream, additional radical reconfigurations would no doubt follow as the enterprise asked: What is the real value here for the customer and how do we create it? At a minimum, it would be necessary to rethink the proper location for product design (the auto company, the glass presser, the glass encapsulator, or some alliance of all three?) and the flow of service and crash parts.

Continuous Radical *and* Incremental Improvement

In fact, every enterprise needs both approaches to pursue perfection. Every step in a value stream can be improved in isolation to good effect. And there is rarely any ground for concern about investing to improve an activity which will soon be replaced altogether. To repeat the lesson from Chapter 3: If you are spending significant amounts of capital to improve specific activities, you are usually pursuing perfection the wrong way. Going further, most value streams can be radically improved as a whole if the right mechanisms for analysis can be put in place.

However, to effectively pursue both radical and incremental improvement, two final lean techniques are needed. First, in order to form a view in their minds of what perfection would be, value stream managers need to apply the four lean principles of value specification, value stream identification, flow, and pull. (Remember, you want to compete against perfection, not just your current competitors, so you need to be able to gauge the gap from current reality to perfection.) Then, value stream managers need to decide which forms of *muda* to attack first, by means of *policy deployment* (often called *hoshin kanri* in Japan, where these ideas originated).

The Picture of Perfection

At every step we've noted the need for managers to learn to see: to see the value stream, to see the flow of value, to see value being pulled by the customer. The final form of seeing is to bring perfection into clear view so the objective of improvement is visible and real to the whole enterprise.

We've just presented an example for glassmaking: a radical rethink of the whole value stream so that all value-creating steps are conducted immediately adjacent to the customer and exactly when needed. Toyota certainly had a picture of perfection—derived from its mastery of lean principles—when it set out in 1982 to rethink its Japanese service parts business, and then in 1989 when it began to apply the same concepts in North America. And Tesco needs a vision of perfection for the value and value stream of its beverage lines, as described in Chapter 2.

Paradoxically, no picture of perfection can be perfect. If the value stream for automotive glass could be reconfigured as we suggest, it would then be time (immediately!) to imagine a new perfection which goes even further. Perfection is like infinity. Trying to envision it (and to get there) is actually impossible, but *the effort to do so provides inspiration and direction essential to making progress along the path*. We'll return to this theme in Part III.

One of the most important things to envision is the type of product designs and operating technologies needed to take the next steps along the path. As we have seen repeatedly in the preceding chapters, one of the greatest impediments to rapid progress is the inappropriateness of most existing processing technology—and many product designs as well—to the needs of the lean enterprise. A clear sense of direction—the knowledge that products must be manufactured more flexibly in smaller volumes in continuous flow—provides critical guidance to technologists in the functions developing generic designs and tools.

In addition to forming a picture of perfection with the appropriate technologies, managers need to set a stringent timetable for steps along the path. As we will see in the examples in Part II, the greatest difference between those organizations that have done a lot and those that have accomplished little or nothing is that the high achievers set specific timetables to accomplish seemingly impossible tasks and then routinely met or exceeded them. The low achievers, by contrast, asked what would be reasonable for their current organization and disconnected value streams to accomplish, and generally defeated themselves before they ever set out.

Focusing Energy to Banish *Muda*

Firms which never start down the path because of a lack of vision obviously fail. Sadly, we've watched other firms set off full of vision, energy, and high hopes, but make very little progress because they went tearing off after perfection in a thousand directions and never had the resources to get very far along any path. What's needed instead is to form a vision, select the two or three most important steps to get you there, and defer the other steps until later. It's not that these will never be tackled, only that the general principle of doing one thing at a time and working on it continuously until completion applies to improvement activities with the same force as it applies to design, order-taking, and production activities.

What's critically needed is the last lean technique of *policy deployment*. The idea is for top management to agree on a few simple goals for transitioning from mass to lean, to select a few projects to achieve these goals, to designate the people and resources for getting the projects done, and, finally, to establish numerical improvement targets to be achieved by a given point in time.

For example, a firm might adopt the goal of converting the entire organization to continuous flow with all internal order management by means of a pull system. The projects required to do this might consist of: (1) reorganizing by product families, with product teams taking on many of the jobs of the traditional functions, (2) creating a "lean function" to assemble the expertise to assist the product teams in the conversion, and (3) commencing a systematic set of improvement activities to convert batches and rework into continuous flow. The targets would set numerical improvement goals and time frames for the projects—for example: Convert to dedicated product teams within six months, conduct improvement activities on six major activities each month and at least once on every activity within the first year, reduce the total amount of inventories on hand by 25 percent in the first year, reduce the number of defects escaping to customers by 50 percent in the first year, and reduce the amount of effort required to produce a given amount of each product by 20 percent in the first year.

Most organizations trying to do this find it easiest to construct an annual policy deployment matrix, as shown in Figure 5.3, which summarizes the goals, the projects for that year, and the targets for these projects so everyone in the entire organization can see them. In doing this, it's essential to openly discuss the amount of resources available in relation to the targets so that everyone agrees as the process begins that it is actually doable.

FIGURE 5.3: LEAN POLICY DEPLOYMENT MATRIX

						Improvement teams					
*		Reorganize by product families		*	*						
	*	Create productivity and quality improvement function	*			*					
*	*	*	Create lean enterprises with suppliers		*			*	*	*	*	*
Identify value stream by product	Introduce continuous flow and pull	Dramatically improve quality	Selected projects / Objectives × Improvement targets / Target dollar results (current year)	Perform six major improvement activities/month	Form product teams within six months	Form lean enterprises within one year	Product line reorganization	Improvement function team	Product family A team	Product family B team	Product family C team	Product family D team	Product family E team
*			Reduce inventory by $30M	*								
	*		Reduce cost of quality $15M	*								
*			Reduce labor costs by $30M	*								

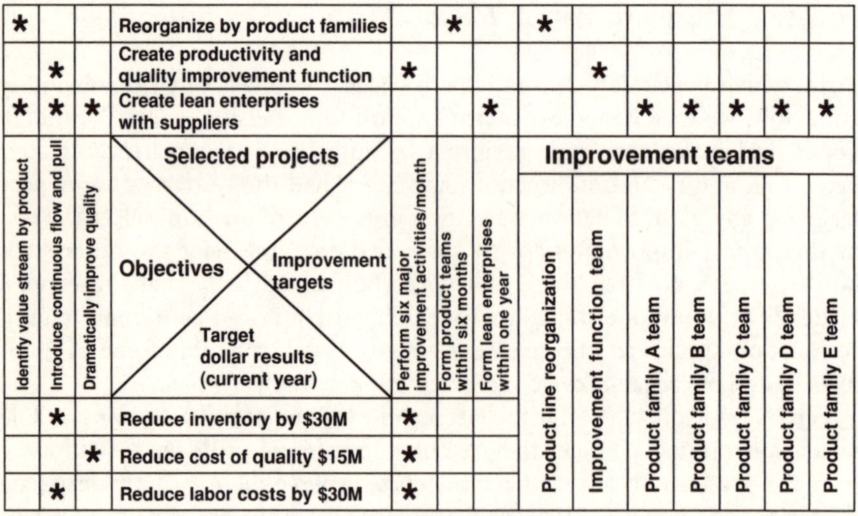

It's also important to note that the process is top-down in the first step of setting goals but top-down/bottom-up in subsequent steps. For example, once the specific projects are agreed on, it's essential to consult with the project teams about the amount of resources and time available to ensure that the projects are realistic. The teams are collectively responsible for getting the job done and must have both the authority and resources from the outset.

As the concept of making a dramatic transition begins to take hold, we often observe that everyone in an organization wants to get involved and that the number of projects tends to multiply. This is exhilarating but is actually the danger signal that too much is being taken on. The most successful firms we've found have learned how to "deselect" projects,[2] despite the enthusiasm of parts of the organization, in order to bring the number of projects into line with the available resources. This is the critical final step before launching the lean crusade.

Smashing Inertia to Get Started

We've now reviewed the basic lean principles, the five powerful ideas in the lean tool kit needed to convert firms and value streams from a meandering morass of *muda* to fast-flowing value, defined and then pulled by the customer. However, there's a final and very serious paradox inherent in introducing thinking in real organizations to pursue perfection.

The techniques themselves and the philosophy are inherently egalitarian and open. Transparency in everything is a key principle. Policy deployment operates as an open process to align people and resources with improvement tasks. And massive and continuing amounts of problem solving are conducted by teams of employees who historically have not even talked to each other, much less treated each other as equals.

Yet the catalytic force moving firms and value streams out of the world of inward-looking batch-and-queue is generally applied by an outsider who breaks all the traditional rules, often in a moment of profound crisis. We call this individual the *change agent*.

In fact, there is no way to reconcile this paradox, no way to square the circle. The change agent is typically something of a tyrant—what one of our most thoughtful research subjects calls a "Conan the Barbarian"—hell-bent on imposing a profoundly egalitarian system in profoundly inegalitarian organizations.

Yet there are tyrants and there are tyrants. Those who succeed in creating lean systems over the long term are clearly understood by the participants in the firm and along the value stream to be promoting a set of ideas which have enormous potential for benefiting everyone. Those who fail (like many of the failed leaders of reengineering campaigns) are either identified as narrow technocrats with no concern for the very real human issues inherent in the transition, or they are dismissed by the organization as self-promoters who are simply seeking to advance their own position by riding the wave of the next "program." Both quickly fall victim to organizational lassitude, if not to active sabotage.

Because lean systems can only flourish if everyone along the value stream believes the new system being created treats everyone fairly and goes the extra mile to deal with human dilemmas, only beneficent despots can succeed. We hope that many readers of this book will take up the mantle of the change agent. And we are equally hopeful that self-promoters and cold-blooded technocrats will look elsewhere.

For those of you with the right spirit and a willingness to invest five years in gaining the full benefits, the examples in Part II are designed to show you how to succeed.

PART II
FROM THINKING TO ACTION: THE LEAN LEAP

Even once you begin to see the importance of the five lean principles, it's often hard to imagine how to install them in your own organization without a clear example of successful practice to follow, a template for action. This needs to be specific enough to show the real nuts and bolts, but broad enough to keep the big picture in view. What's more, the example needs to share enough of the characteristics of your situation that extrapolation is possible with confidence about the results.

We've therefore provided a series of examples selected from two dimensions—size and complexity, and nationality. We will begin with three American examples which progress from a small, family-owned firm with a simple product range and only a limited past to overcome, to a massive, publicly traded organization with highly complex product and process technologies, a complex supply and distribution chain, a culturally diverse, unionized workforce, and a long history to overcome of conflictual relations with its employees, customers, and suppliers.

Then we switch our focus to the three great national industrial systems by comparing the installation of lean principles in a leading German firm and in two Japanese firms of broadly varying degrees of complexity.

Your own organization is probably different from any of these in some important ways and some customization will be required. However, the examples are sufficiently broad and the results so startling that no manager can any longer claim that lean principles cannot be applied to their situation.

CHAPTER 6

The Simple Case

Pat Lancaster of Louisville, Kentucky, is a heroic American type, the stand-alone inventor-industrialist often found at the heart of capitalist lore. He grew up tinkering in the family workshop, convinced from an early age that he could be an inventor. After college, he tried the family business of selling packaging materials to industrial firms and then life in the product development group of a large chemical company. "But it just wasn't satisfying. From my earliest memories I wanted to be an independent inventor, manufacturer, and entrepreneur." When he was twenty-nine (in 1972), he had his big idea, a new way for manufacturers to wrap their products for shipment. He and his brother invested $300 in simple metalworking tools to build their first machine, rented a small warehouse, and went to work under the corporate name of Lantech, a contraction of Lancaster Technologies.

Lancaster's big idea was for a device to "stretch-wrap" pallets of goods (for example, the cases of cola we examined in Chapter 2) with plastic film so they could be shipped easily from plant to plant within a manufacturing system and then onward, as finished products, to the wholesaler and retailer. Traditional "shrink-wrapping" was then in wide use by manufacturers and distributors who laid plastic bags loosely around large pallet loads of goods that were then run through an oven to shrink the plastic and give a tight fit.

Stretch-wrapping, by contrast, pulled the plastic wrap tightly around the pallet load as it rotated on a turntable. As the plastic was stretched taut, it rebounded slightly to give a snug fit while eliminating the energy, equipment, effort, and time required for heat treating. In addition, stretching the wrap practically halved the amount of plastic required to secure a pallet load for shipment.

Lancaster's next invention was the key complement to his fundamental insight that the plastic should be stretched rather than shrunk. He discovered that a complex set of precision rollers (collectively termed the roll carriage) could exert a smooth force on the plastic to stretch it dramatically before it was wound around the pallet. Eventually, he found ways to decrease the amount of plastic needed to hold a pallet load together by a factor of 7.5 compared with shrink-wrapping.

When Lancaster obtained patents for his concepts at the beginning of the 1970s, they were so general and broad that he could easily fend off competitors for years. All he needed was a market. This was supplied by the world energy crisis of 1973, which unfolded just as he completed his first, handmade stretch-wrapping machine. As energy prices zoomed, the amount of process energy and plastic (made from natural gas) which his new technique could save created an overwhelming advantage for stretch-wrapping in the contest with traditional shrink-wrapping.

Suddenly he had a real business and needed to think about how to make his product in volume. He had created his initial design and his first machine in a continuous flow of activities, so Lantech, like most start-up businesses, was born lean. However, it didn't seem plausible to run an established business this way.

In reconstructing his thought process during the transition from start-up to established firm, Lancaster recollects that "I had no production experience—remember, I was an inventor—so I decided I should get myself an experienced operations manager. What's more, I knew I would need to engineer a variety of configurations of my basic concept for different wrapping tasks, so I got an engineering manager. Finally, I had a complex product which needed explanation to the customer, so I got a sales manager. I knew instinctively about the division of labor and returns to scale, so it seemed natural that my operations, sales, and engineering managers should organize my rapidly growing firm into a series of departments, each with a specialized task, and each operating in batch mode."

The operations manager created a series of departments in the manufacturing plant, one for each of the basic steps in building a Lantech stretch-wrapper. The Sawing Department used metal saws to fashion frame members from steel beams. The Machining Department drilled and punched holes in the steel to create attachment points for component systems. The Welding Department welded the frame members together to form the completed frame for the machine. The Painting Department applied a corrosion-inhibiting base coat and a cosmetic finish coat to the completed frame. Component systems—notably the roll carriage, the turntable, and the control module—were assembled in the Sub-Assembly Department from parts purchased from suppliers. These were attached to the frame in the Final Assembly Department.

Final Assembly was not the end of the line for products making their way from department to department and storage area to storage area. Because it was thought to be efficient, Lantech built its four basic types of machines in batches. Ten or fifteen machines of a type would be fabricated and assembled at a go. The nature of the product, however, meant that individual customers usually bought only one. Therefore, it was necessary to store many machines in a finished goods area for some time before they could be matched up with customers.

When it was time for shipment, it was often necessary to remove grime and to paint over nicks caused by moving machines from department to department. This meant a journey to a Touch-Up Department. Often the machine had to be sent back to Final Assembly as well to change its mix of optional features in order to accommodate changing customer desires. Finally, the machine was sent to the Crating Department for actual shipment.

The progression of a stretch-wrapper through Lantech is shown in Figure 6.1, often called a "Spaghetti Chart" by firms who have mastered lean thinking.

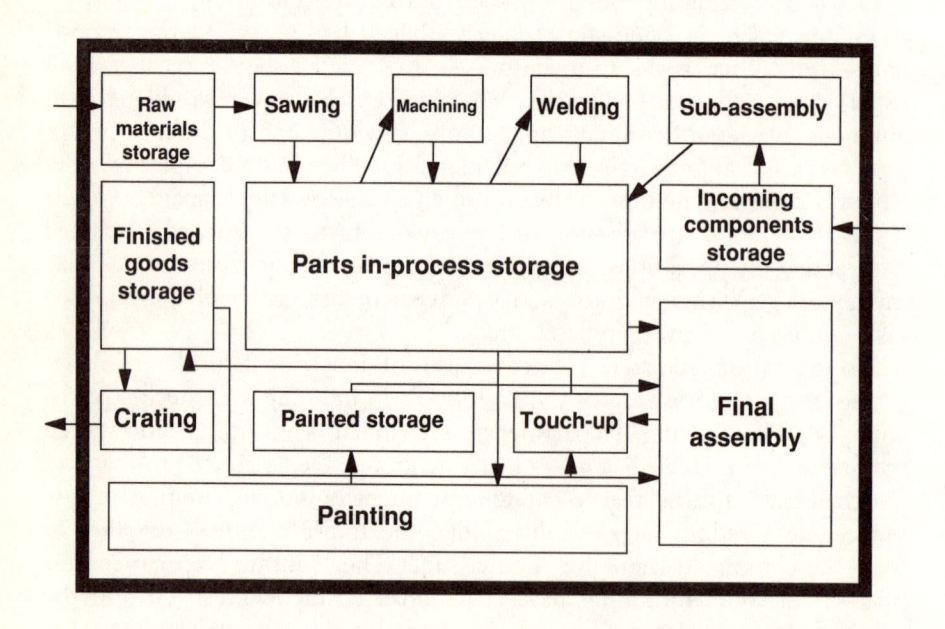

FIGURE 6.1: PHYSICAL PRODUCTION AT LANTECH

Physical production of the machine was not the only process to manage. The real complexity in volume production began to emerge as Lantech tried to move the orders gathered by the sales force (a group of about fifty independent firms distributing industrial machinery) through the office and into the plant.

Because the machines were often customized and cost from $10,000 to $50,000 apiece, it was decided that a standard price list would not work.

Instead the sales force contacted Lantech for authorization before quoting a price on any machine with special features. The proposal was sent to the Engineering Applications Department within Sales for cost analysis. After analysis, the "right number" was sent back to the sales force. Then, once the offer was accepted (with the distributor negotiating a final price with the customer which included the distributor's margin), the order was sent back to Lantech for production scheduling.

Upon arriving back at Lantech, the order proceeded from the Order Entry Department to the Credit Checking Department to the Engineering Applications Department (for its second visit). There, a Bill of Materials (BOM) was generated for the order. This was the precise list of every part which would be needed to manufacture a specific machine. Because every department had a waiting list of orders, there were usually delays. Typically, an order took twelve to fourteen working days to travel from the Entry Department to the Scheduling Department, while the actual processing time—what we will call "continuous flow time"—was less than two days.

The order with the BOM was then taken to the Scheduling Department inside Production Operations to work into the master schedule. Because it became apparent immediately that the flow of production through the plant would be very erratic, a separate Order Management Department was created in Sales to maintain liaison between the independent sales force and the plant on just where the machine was in the production process and to initiate expediting (using a technique we will examine in a moment) if the customer was getting restless. Information progressed through the system as shown in Figure 6.2.

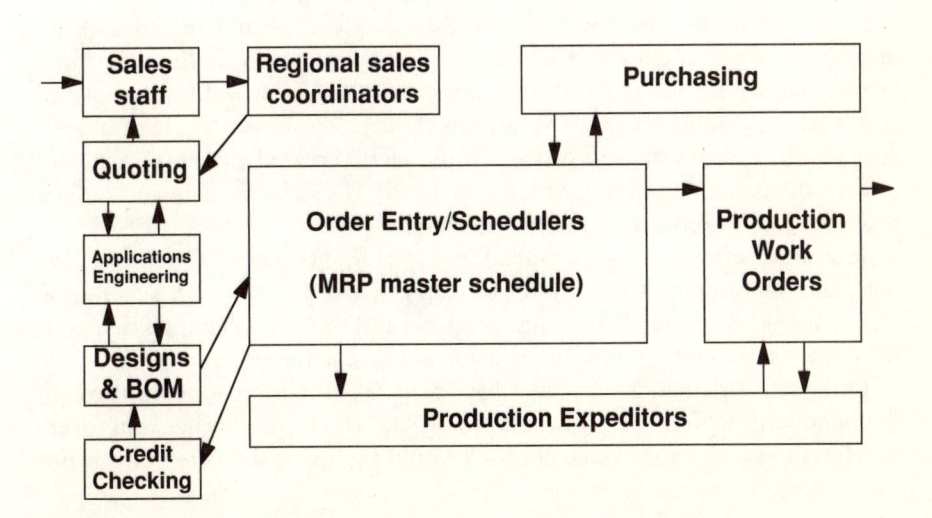

FIGURE 6.2: LANTECH ORDER FLOW

The master schedule itself resided in the Scheduling Department inside Production Operations in the form of a computerized Material Requirements Planning system. The MRP melded a long-term forecast for orders with actual orders as they were received to create a daily production schedule assigning tasks to each department in the plant. Each morning, workers in each department—sawing, machining, welding, paint, sub-assemblies, final assembly, touch-up, and crating—would pick up a printout with their tasks for the day. At the end of each day, each department would report its progress back to the computerized Scheduling Department.

This system was fine in plan, but always a mess in practice because of the conflict between changing customer desires and the logic driving the production system. In order to gain scale economies, Pat Lancaster and his operations manager decided from the beginning that each department should do its work in batches: ten frames welded for the E model, then twenty frames welded for the T, then twenty-five welded for the V. This minimized the time Lantech's machinery was idle during the changeover to a new part. In addition, running long batches was thought to improve quality by minimizing opportunities to misset machines and by keeping operators focused on the operation itself rather than changeovers.

Separate departments for each production step, batches of parts run through the departments, and waiting time at the entrance to each department inherently meant long lead times. Typically, it took sixteen weeks to turn the incoming steel for the frame into a completed machine on the shipping dock. Most of this time was spent waiting as batches of parts were built in each department and then sent to storage to await the next fabrication step in the next department. The actual amount of time needed to complete the physical transformation of raw materials into a stretch-wrapper—the "continuous flow time"—was only three days.

Long lead times meant in turn that the sales force distributing Lantech's machines to the end user tried to figure out how to beat the system. A favorite approach was to order machines on speculation and then, as a real customer was found, to alter the options requested (or even the base model) very late in the production process. This tactic created the need either to rework the machine initially ordered or to slip the delivery date and build a properly configured machine from scratch.

Soon the factory was being pulled in opposite directions by two conflicting planning systems—the master schedule worked out by the Scheduling Department based mostly on sales forecasts, and the ever-changing demands from the Sales Group intent on pleasing actual customers.

These latter demands were met by a team of expediters moving through the plant with a "hot list." These were orders which were either long overdue for shipment or in which the sale would be lost if the product was not reconfigured to the new specification. The expediters visited departments in sequence and ordered the workforce to make just one item of a batch—a "partial"—so they could take that part immediately to the next department and move it to the head of the line in that department. In an extreme situation, when Pat Lancaster agreed that an order absolutely had to be expedited all the way through the company, it was possible to get a machine built in less than four weeks. However, when this was done, the schedule of every other machine in the plant slipped, creating the need for more expediting.

This system of order-taking and production sounds chaotic—and it was. But it was and is the standard method in most of the industrial world for making products when there is considerable product variety, long lead times, and a complex production process. To make matters worse, the production and sales technique of batch-and-queue soon had an exact analog in product development in Lantech's departmentalized engineering process.

To create a new design, it was necessary for the marketing staff, engineers skilled in several specialties, the purchasing staff, and operations planners to work together. The marketing group determined what the customer wanted. ("A machine able to wrap forty four-thousand-pound pallet loads per hour in a fifteen-by-fifteen-foot work area at a cost of fifty cents per pallet.") The chief engineer then translated these desires into engineering specifications. ("A turntable able to support a four-thousand-pound pallet load, a turntable motor of x horsepower capable of y rotation speed, a control system able to direct the wrapping procedure automatically, etcetera.")

Next, a mechanical engineer designed the moving mechanical parts, notably the roll carriage and the turntable. Another mechanical engineer then designed the frame and an electrical engineer designed the control system to meet the engineering specification. The manufacturing engineer then designed the fabrication tools. Once the product design and tools were finalized, an industrial engineer from the Production Department figured out how to get the product to progress by steps through the plant.

The Engineering Department was initially quite small, with only a half dozen engineers, but even then the communication barriers between the one-person "departments" were substantial as the design was moved from marketing group to chief engineer to mechanical engineer to electrical engineer to industrial engineer. A considerable amount of rework and backtracking was required to get from the initial concept to a complete, production-ready design. (The prime cause of the backtracking was that the design didn't fit the needs of the next specialist in the line—"there's not enough room for my control panel," etcetera—and was sent back for modification. A frequently employed alternative to sending the design back was to secretly redesign it.) As Lantech grew and more engineers were added, these communication problems got worse.

What was more, each engineer typically had a stack of projects on her or his desk, so that expediters soon appeared in engineering as well as in the plant to get "rush" projects through the system. In practice, it typically took a year to introduce a minor improvement in a family of machines and three or four years to introduce a new family suited to a different task, such as wrapping small bundles. The "continuous flow time," by contrast, was only a few weeks for minor improvements and six months for a new family of machines. The progression of a design through the design and engineering system is shown in Figure 6.3.

FIGURE 6.3: LANTECH PRODUCT DEVELOPMENT SYSTEM

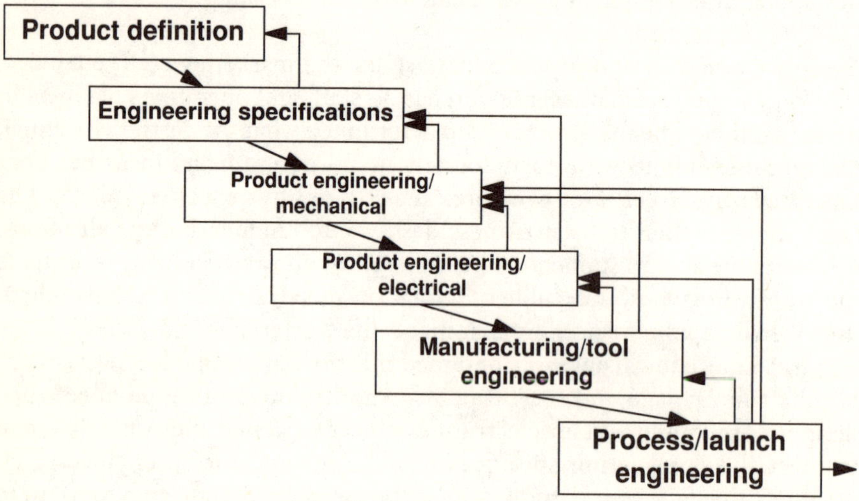

```
Product definition
    ↓
Engineering specifications
    ↓
Product engineering/mechanical
    ↓
Product engineering/electrical
    ↓
Manufacturing/tool engineering
    ↓
Process/launch engineering
```

The three major activities undertaken in Pat Lancaster's new company—development of new designs, management of information on what to make, and physical production of the machines—were all conducted in a classic batch-and-queue manner. And they were conducted with great success.

Looking back, Pat Lancaster summarized his dream of becoming a highly successful inventor, manufacturer, and entrepreneur. "After 1973, we were selling a top-priced product which had major performance advantages over competitor products due to my patent position. Over the next fifteen years Lantech grew to 266 employees and $43 million in sales. We could and did deliver late because of conflicting demands for efficiency versus speed within the production process. We offered so-so quality in terms of manufacturing defects in machines delivered to customers. We took more than a year to develop 'new' machines which differed only in very minor ways from previous models. But we were way ahead of the competition and we made tons of money. For fifteen years my dream came true."

Then, on June 26, 1989, Lantech lost a patent infringement suit against a competitor offering lower-priced clones of Lantech machines. (The suit concerned a new generation of patents Lantech had obtained in the mid-1980s as follow-ons to its original patents obtained in the early 1970s.) This threw open the market to every packaging machinery firm. "By the end of 1989, clones with roughly comparable performance started to appear everywhere and the bottom fell out of my pricing. I was still turning a small profit but I knew worse was coming as soon as the business cycle turned down. In my heart I knew that Lantech was 'walking dead.' "

Pat Lancaster is by nature a highly dynamic individual. So he had plenty of ideas on what to do. In fact, he tried many of the remedies popular in the American business community at that time. His first approach was to reorganize the firm into profit centers for "standard products" and "specials" (those requiring extensive customization). This was to increase accountability and to move the highly customized products out of the path of easier-to-make "mass-production" machines. Then, as sales flattened, he considered laying off employees and shrinking Lantech—what we now call "downsizing." However, Lancaster was convinced that no firm had ever been saved by cost cutting and retrenchment alone.

He needed a new way to think about his business and sought it in the Total Quality Management (TQM) movement. After a visit to Milliken, the South Carolina textile giant, he came back to Louisville with plans for putting the voice of the customer first and foremost. The old "good enough" standard for delivered defects and customer service was quickly replaced with talk about perfection.

Over the next few years this focus was supplemented with a process of "value-driven culture change" to create an empowered organization, build trust, and knock down departmental barriers. The original senior management team, which had been composed of hierarchical personalities accustomed to a top-down, command-control style, was replaced by a new group of managers willing to work in a team-based organization. (Lancaster is the only senior manager remaining from the 1970s.) In addition, extensive training was conducted in team processes, team leadership, and individual interaction.

These programs were an essential start, but they lacked a direct link to Lantech's core activities. As Bob Underwood, a longtime production worker, put it in retrospect: "We learned to respect each other and wanted to work together in teams, but we were all revved up with nowhere to go." The factory was still a mess. Product development was still too slow. The sales force was still playing games to beat the lead-time problem.

The third approach to the crisis was a new production method called "Max-Flex." The idea was to dramatically reduce lead times by building inventories of major components—machine frames, roll carriages, turntables, control modules—far in advance and then mixing and matching the components to build complete machines to customer specification very quickly once orders were confirmed. The objective was to overcome Lantech's pricing disadvantage by promising more rapid delivery of machines with customer-specified features.

On one level the performance of the new Max-Flex concept was impressive—lead times fell from sixteen weeks to four. But the costs were enormous. Engineering change orders were frequent in Lantech's business now that it had become highly competitive. These changes were both to add product features to keep up with the competition and to rectify defects discovered in service. Therefore, it was often necessary to work backwards, "retrofitting" changes into the mountain of components built in advance. Obviously, the cost of carrying this mountain of "just in case" components was substantial, and Lantech began looking for a new warehouse to store components as storage space in its plant was exhausted. But most exasperating, despite Lantech's best efforts at planning production, cases quickly arose where one critical component needed to complete a machine was lacking. (Taiichi Ohno noted long ago that the more inventory you have, the less likely you are to have the one part you actually need.) The solution was a new team of expediters to move the missing component through the production system.

Yet a fourth approach to the crisis was better technology. A new scheduling system, based on the next generation of MRP, was installed in 1990. It permitted every worker to have direct access to the status of every machine in production and to input their own data as they moved a part or a whole machine ahead. This permitted every worker to get work orders from a terminal at his workstation and, in theory, to feel full "control" over his activities. (As Pat Lancaster noted: "It seemed to be a wonderful marriage of technology and democracy. Everyone could look into the computer to see what was going on all over the plant and get their work orders immediately. Our slogan was 'Data to the people.'")

The new system required a new computer, a new Management Information System Department with four people on the day shift and three more on the night shift to keep all of the data current, and direct inputting of every work task by workers on the plant floor as they completed it. As Jose

Zabaneh, Lantech's manufacturing director, noted, "Pretty soon workers were fully in 'control,' yet the system was wildly inaccurate because many items simply never got entered and there was no means of catching errors. The old MRP system was slow but 99 percent accurate. Our new 'democratic' MRP system was a complete catastrophe; instead of information we had given *muda* to the people." To compound the situation, the magnitude of inputs and changes was causing the computer to run very slowly. Lantech's information technology consultant recommended that the best solution would be a much more powerful and expensive computer.

By the end of 1991, Lantech's orders began to fall for the first time, despite price reductions, and the factory was finding it nearly impossible to respond to continuous shifts in demand. As Pat Lancaster summarized the situation later, "We began losing money for the first time and our fundamental ideas on how to run the business were in a meltdown." Then he discovered lean thinking.

The Lean Revolution

Ron Hicks does not look like a revolutionary. He looks like an accountant (although he was trained as an industrial engineer) and talks in dispassionate tones. But he brought a revolution when he came to work at Lantech as vice president of operations in March of 1992.

He had learned how to be a revolutionary while working at the Danaher Corporation, a collection of fifteen manufacturing companies collected by Steve and Mitchell Rales in the 1980s. Quite improbably, these two youthful entrepreneurs from Washington, D.C., had become acquainted with the lean concepts pioneered by Taiichi Ohno, and the firm had convinced some of Ohno's Japanese disciples to establish operations in the United States in 1987 to support Danaher's conversion effort. They grasped that lean thinking could revolutionize their firms, which had initially been bought because they were attractively priced, as part of their effort to diversify out of their core real estate business. One of these firms was Hennessy Industries of Nashville, Tennessee, a manufacturer of automotive repair tools and garage lifts. Ron Hicks was working there as vice president of operations.

Ron Hicks remembers the day in 1989 when "the light went on." "I went to visit the Jacobs Brake Company in Bloomfield, Connecticut, another Danaher company, and discovered they had followed Ohno's advice by completely eliminating their traditional production departments. They had installed work cells in which all of their machines were realigned into the actual processing sequence needed to make specific product families of truck engine components. Each part was then manufactured in a continuous flow with absolutely no buffer stocks between steps using a concept they called 'single-piece flow.'

"What really amazed me was that on the day of my visit they were conducting an improvement exercise and had decided that the work flow for a particular item would be much smoother if they moved a massive machine from one position to another. They decided to do it early in the morning, got the moving team together almost instantly, moved the machine, and were back in production in a few hours.

"In my fourteen years as an operations manager at the General Electric Company, where I worked before moving to Hennessy, it would have taken an act of Congress to move such a large machine. But these guys just did it, and it worked. I suddenly realized I was living in a different world."

By March 1992, when Hicks received a phone call from Pat Lancaster, he had transformed himself from a "concrete head" into a lean thinker and was ready for a new challenge. Lancaster had screened hundreds of applicants in his search for a new operations vice president and was sure that Ron Hicks had the ability to transform a manufacturing operation. The question was exactly how and how fast.

In the newly empowered spirit of Lantech, Ron was invited to Louisville and interviewed by those he would manage. His simple proposal came as a revelation: Lantech would immediately form teams to rethink the value stream and flow of value for every product in the plant, and then every step in order-taking and product development. Lantech would line up the essential activities required to design, order, and manufacture a stretch-wrapping machine and perform them in sequence, one machine, one design, one order at a time. Batches, queues, backflows, and waste—*muda* of all sorts—would be banished. The *value stream*—the irreducible minimum set of activities needed to design, order, and make a stretch-wrapper—would flow smoothly, continuously, and rapidly.

Ron Hicks was hired and immediately went to work with a simple plan: Disaggregate the four basic types of machines flowing through Lantech's departmentalized, batch-and-queue production system; eliminate all of the production departments; create a production cell—four in total—for each type of machine; and then line up all of the activities required to make each machine within a cell and perform them in a continuous flow. This was the *kaikaku* phase in the Lantech plant, the time to completely tear things apart and recombine them in a totally different way.

The T/V model, which was soon replaced by the new Q model, was the acid test. A team of Lantech's best workers was selected to rethink the flow and quickly, in only one week, devise and put into production the plan—shown in Figure 6.4.

The sawing operation was located immediately adjacent to the machining

FIGURE 6.4: FLOW OF Q LINE

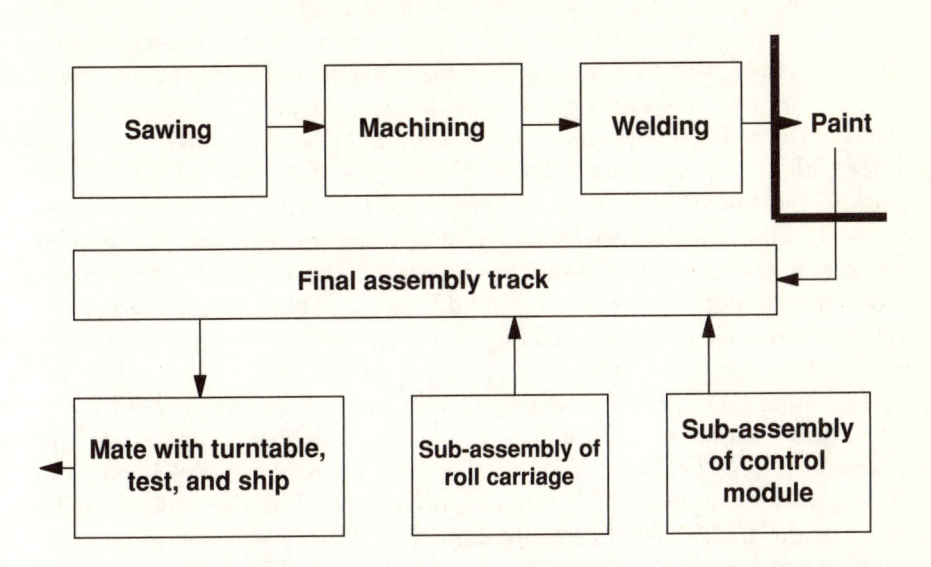

```
Sawing → Machining → Welding → Paint
                                  ↓
        Final assembly track ←————┘
         ↓            ↑            ↑
  Mate with      Sub-assembly   Sub-assembly
  turntable,     of roll         of control
  test, and ship carriage        module
```

operation, which was only a few steps from the welding operation. Although it was still necessary for all four models to share a massive, centralized paint booth, continuous flow picked up again with sub-assembly and final assembly. Testing and crating were placed at the end of the line and conducted by the work team. Even though only eight machines were made each day—one per hour—an imperceptibly moving track was installed in final assembly as a pacing device.

Each morning the saw operator would start production of a new machine on the hour. A kit of all the frame parts required for the machine was prepared by the saw operator by the end of the hour and rolled about three feet to the machining station. From there it would proceed about four feet to welding. Fourteen hours later—about half of this due to the curing time required by the paint booth—a completed machine was ready for shipping.

To make this simple system work, Lantech had to change a generation of industrial thinking about how to do work and how to work together. Because all of the jobs were directly linked, with no buffers, it was necessary that everyone think about *standard work*, which is to say the best way to get the job done in the amount of time available and how to get the job done right the first time, every time. (By design, either the whole cell is working or nothing is working.) Every step of every job was soon charted by the work team and posted for everyone to see.

Similarly, because in this new system machines are only made when ordered—remember that production lead time has fallen from sixteen *weeks* to fourteen *hours* so there is no need to build machines ahead of time on speculation in order to permit rapid deliveries—it was important to introduce the concept of *takt* time. This is the number of machines to be made each day to meet the orders in hand divided into the number of hours in the day. (With production at eight machines per eight-hour day, *takt* time is one hour.) The important point about *takt* time was that when orders did not require the full utilization of equipment and workers, *takt* time was increased. The machinery was slowed down and each of the multiskilled workers in the Q cell performed several of the jobs in the cell while excess workers were put on other tasks around Lantech. This reversed the age-old tendency to work ahead and build inventories if no orders were immediately on hand.

Two other concepts were needed as well. Lantech had to *right-size* many of its tools and devise a number of new tools so that smaller saws and machining tools could be fitted in the work cells. (As it turned out, the excess workers freed up by rethinking production flow were able to make most of the tools needed.) Finally, Lantech had to learn how to perform *quick changeovers* on all of its tools so it could make all of the parts for each machine and a variety of product options for successive machines with very little downtime.

When the new cell concept was proposed, many of the production workers were baffled or dismayed. As Bob Underwood, one of the most skilled workers on the floor, noted: "We were used to a system in which each of us had a set of hard-earned skills—welding, machining, and, in my case, the ability to adjust nonconforming parts so they would fit. We were used to doing our own work as we saw fit at our own pace in our own department. As long as we met our daily production quota we were left alone. What's more, the real kick in the work was 'fire fighting,' in which the Lantech Volunteer Fire Department went into crisis mode to get an emergency order through the system or eliminate a sudden production bottleneck. I was one of the best fire fighters at Lantech and I loved it."

Ron Hicks was proposing a new system of standard work and *takt* time that sounded like oversight by the industrial engineer, which every skilled tradesman hates. (The difference, of course, was that the work team would standardize its own work.) What was more, he was proposing making complete machines one at a time. Finally, he claimed that if the work was standardized by the work team, the machines were realigned to permit single-piece flow, and *takt* time was adhered to with no working ahead, there would be no more fires to fight. As Underwood remembers, "It didn't sound like much fun and I thought it would never work."

When the conversion week was completed and the new cell was ready to go . . . it didn't work. All kinds of problems, long submerged in Lantech's massive inventories and closely held work practices, suddenly emerged. Some steps had not been included in the standard work charts. Poor tool maintenance—easily tolerated in the old batch system—repeatedly stopped the whole cell. The supply of components to the cell was not dependable. The widespread feeling was that Ron Hicks was pushing a novel concept that would never work at Lantech.

At this point Jose Zabaneh, the production manager, played the key role: "I was so fed up with our failures and so taken with the logic of the new system that I threw my heart into it. I called a meeting of the workforce and announced that I would stay all night and all weekend to work hands-on on fixes to the problems we were encountering with the new cell, but that I would not spend one second discussing the possibility of going back to the old batch-and-queue system."

Pat Lancaster gave unfaltering support to the new system, Ron Hicks (along with his consultant, Anand Sharma, who had advised him earlier on the conversion of Hennessey) had the technical skills to work the bugs out, and Jose Zabaneh was "our spark plug." Gradually, it all began to come together.

(We'll see that these three attributes—taking the long view, technical virtuosity, and a passionate will to succeed—are essential for any organization making the lean transition. Sometimes they are possessed by a single individual, sometimes, as at Lantech, they are shared by a group of leaders. However initially distributed, they are all necessary and eventually they must be shared by the whole organization.)

By the fall of 1992, the whole Lantech production system had been converted from batches to single-piece flow, including the cell for the largest Lantech machine—the $50,000 H model—made at the rate of only one per week. The plant now looked as shown in Figure 6.5.

The consequences for performance were truly staggering. Although Lantech's headcount stayed constant at three hundred, the number of machines shipped doubled between 1991 and 1995. (The sales growth was due to a general recovery in the market, aggressive pricing by Lantech to capture share, and a host of new products, to be described in a moment.) The plant, which had been bulging at the seams with inventory, now had 30 percent excess space despite the doubling of output. The number of defects reported by customers fell from 8 per machine in 1991 to .8 per machine in 1995. Production throughput time, as we have noted, fell from sixteen weeks to fourteen hours. The percentage of machines shipped on the date agreed with the customer went from 20 to 90 percent.

To speed this remarkable transition, Pat Lancaster made two promises to his workforce. These seemed almost quixotic in 1992, given the financial

FIGURE 6.5: NEW LANTECH PRODUCTION FLOW

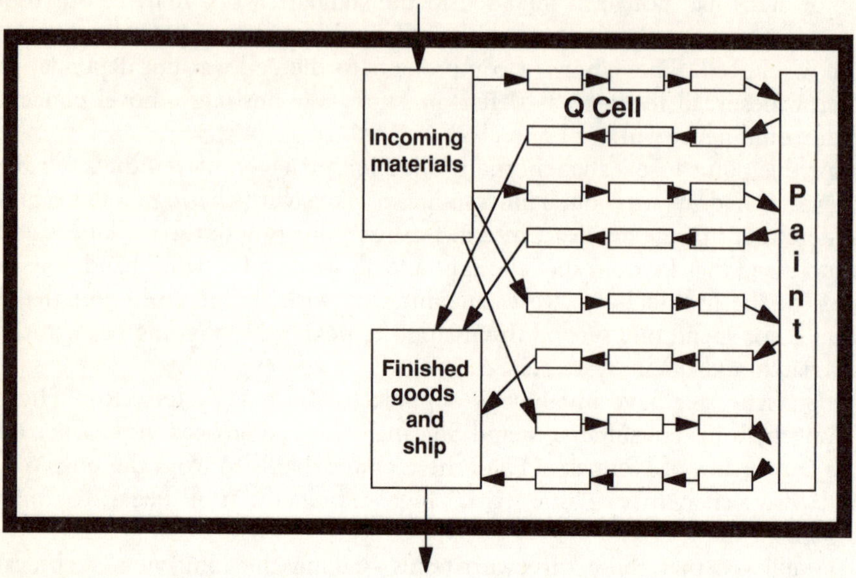

condition of the firm, but have proved critical to success. First, he promised that no one would be let go because of the lean conversion. Instead, a *kaizen* team was created from freed-up workers who were deployed to plan the improvement of other activities. Bob Underwood, the original skeptic and chief "fireman," was made head of this team. After every improvement, the best (not the worst) workers in the revamped process are transferred to the *kaizen* team, making clear that this is a promotion, not a punishment. The steady growth in output of the newly competitive Lantech has meant that within a short period these workers have been needed again for production work.

At the same time, Lancaster reviewed Lantech's wage policy and adjusted the base wage upward from about $7.00 to about $8.50 per hour. As Ron Hicks noted, "We had been running unskilled employees through like McDonald's, with a sharp premium for our small core of skilled workers. It quickly became apparent that all workers in the new Lantech would be skilled workers, but with a very different type of skills. So we had to pay all of them a better wage. As a result, turnover quickly fell to just about zero." (Note that because each machine is now being made with one half of the formerly needed hours of human effort, a 25 percent wage increase is easily affordable.)

• • •

As the lean revolution gained momentum in the plant, it was time to turn to the office and in particular the order-taking process. As Pat Lancaster put it, "We wanted the goodness of the plant to suck the badness out of the office. If we could make a machine in fourteen hours, how could we live with an order-taking process which required three weeks?" In one notable case, Lantech made and delivered a machine in four days—long before the credit check could be completed—only to discover that the buyer was insolvent.

The technique employed to transform the office was exactly the same. Lantech set up a *kaizen* team to collectively rethink the process. It included all the workers involved in a specific process, the firm's technical experts—including production workers from the plant *kaizen* team and one outside consultant (Sharma). The group mapped the entire value flow and looked for wasted time and effort. As each process was rethought and turned from batch-and-queue into flow, the best of the workforce was assigned to the *kaizen* team to lay the groundwork for the next process review. No one was laid off and the move to the *kaizen* team was clearly an acknowledgment of superior performance.

When these techniques were applied to the entire order-taking and plant-scheduling system, the results were truly astounding. Because Lantech now understood its costs much better, it was possible to publish fixed prices on all but truly custom-built machines and to eliminate the haggling step between Lantech and the distributor. The order itself, once at Lantech, could be inserted into the production schedule in only two days.

Perhaps most remarkably, most of the computerized scheduling system was no longer needed. MRP was retained for long-term materials ordering from suppliers, but day-to-day scheduling is now run off a large white board in the sales office. The production day is divided into slots by *takt* times and orders are written on the board as they are confirmed. At the times we have visited Lantech, the white board slots have been filled anywhere from three days to two weeks ahead of the current date and no machine will be made except in response to a confirmed order.

A large white board easily visible to everyone in the firm has proved to be a remarkable spur to the sales force, particularly as the amount of filled space gets smaller and the amount of empty space gets larger. This is an excellent example of yet another lean technique, *visual control*, in which the status of an activity is displayed so every employee can see it and take appropriate action.

The final step in this process is to copy down each evening the roster of machines to be made the next day and to take this list to the four production cells. For each machine, the cell is given the name of the actual customer and the promised delivery date, typically two days from the start of the build sequence for high-volume machines and ten days for the lowest-volume, large machine. The former Management Information System Department with its seven full-time workers has been eliminated because the parts within the plant are pulled along to the next workstation automatically. Information flows that had been automated have now been completely eliminated because product and information have been combined into one. The full results, as shown in Figure 6.6, can be contrasted with the labyrinthine order process shown in Figure 6.2.

FIGURE 6.6: NEW LANTECH ORDER FLOW

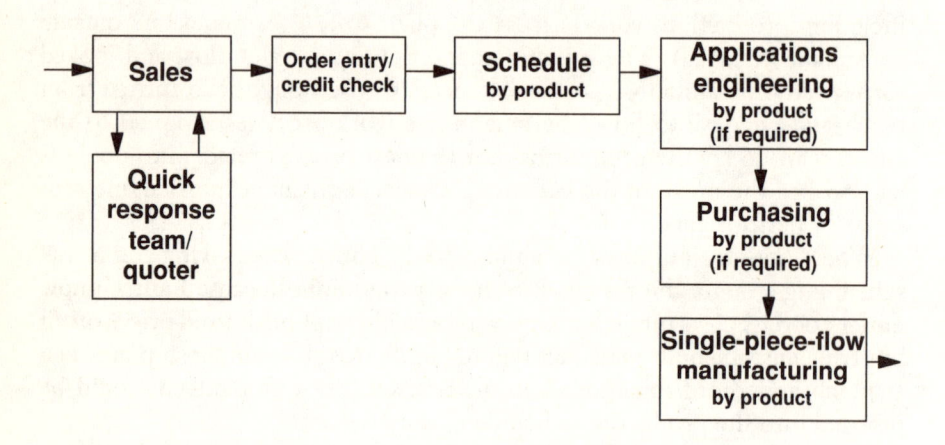

```
Sales → Order entry/credit check → Schedule by product → Applications engineering by product (if required)
  ↕                                                              ↓
Quick response team/quoter                                 Purchasing by product (if required)
                                                                 ↓
                                                          Single-piece-flow manufacturing by product →
```

The main transitional problem has been that the distributors and buyers of industrial equipment are unaccustomed to getting rapid and on-schedule deliveries. Orders have often been "guesstimated" on the presumption that many weeks were available to firm up the precise specification, notify the manufacturer of changes, and plan for the machine's installation. In one notable case, Lantech made and delivered a machine within one week of the order, just as promised, to find the customer quite upset: "You've sent us our machine before we've given any thought to how to use it. We thought we were placing an order simply to guarantee ourselves a place in the production line, that we would have time to respecify the options, and that you would deliver late as usual. Now, you've gone and made it already!"

The final step in transforming Lantech has been to rethink the product development process. Pat Lancaster knew from the early days of the plant conversion that he would need to grow his business dramatically in order to keep everyone busy, as he promised, while productivity zoomed. This meant turning strategic thinking on its head: "I didn't have time to find a brand-new business to go into and I didn't have the money to buy out any of my major competitors. Instead, I needed to revitalize and expand my product range so I could sell more in an established market I knew well. At the same time, I knew that a total redesign of my products to make manufacturability a key consideration would slash my costs even further and dramatically improve quality and flexibility for the customer."

He also knew that his batch-and-queue product development system would take years to come up with market-expanding products if not given the same treatment as the plant and the office. He wanted to put new product designs into single-piece flow, just like orders and machines. "We needed the design to move continuously from the initial concept to the launch of production. This meant no stopping due to the bureaucratic needs of our organization, no backflows to correct mistakes, and no hitches during production ramp-up."

Lantech had experimented with development teams in the late 1980s and early 1990s but without much success. A few "bet the company" projects were pushed through by a designated "dictator" who was effectively a new type of expediter (slowing down all other projects to get his project through). Otherwise, weak "team leaders" tried to coordinate the activities of the numerous technical specialists needed to develop a complete product, each with their own priority list. In no case was the team leader—dictator or weak coordinator—responsible for the end results of the project: Did the product please the customer and make money for Lantech during its production life? No one was really in charge and not much had changed despite the new "team" terminology.

In 1993, Lantech went to a new system of dedicated teams led by a Directly Responsible Individual (DRI) clearly charged with the success of the product during its lifetime. The corporate annual planning process identified the major projects to be developed that year and ranked them. A team of dedicated specialists was designated for the two top-ranking projects. This consisted of marketing, mechanical engineering, electrical engineering, manufacturing engineering, purchasing, and production (including hourly workers from the plant *kaizen* team who would actually build the machine once launched). These teams were co-located and told to work nonstop on the designated project and to do nothing else until it was done. The welter of minor projects which formerly cluttered up the Engineering Department were simply dropped (or "deselected" in Lantech-speak). As the engineering director noted, "We never would have finished them anyway!"

A *kaizen* of Lantech's prototyping process showed that if all of the needed skills were available, a working prototype for the top-ranked project could be put together in a week, a process which formerly would have taken three months. And the presence of the actual production staff on the team quickly identified manufacturing problems which the mechanical and electrical engineers had never imagined.

The major objections to dedicated teams—that work flow is uneven, so some team members will be underutilized some of the time and teams will be in conflict for scarce skills needed at specific points in development—were overcome in two ways. First, it developed that team members actually had much broader skills than they had ever been asked to use. (After all, they had been reengineering each other's designs in secret for years!) They could quickly develop additional, narrow skills to address specific problems. Mechanical engineers could actually help manufacturing engineers with their work and the reverse. This meant that the uneven work flow problem could be largely corrected within the team.

Second, it turned out that a bit of careful scheduling could identify conflicts in requirements for skilled personnel far ahead of time. Moving a few specialists from one team to the other and back, as needed, could solve the problem.

Under the new Lantech product development system, the progression of the design looks as shown in Figure 6.7, in contrast with the maze shown in Figure 6.3:

FIGURE 6.7: NEW LANTECH PRODUCT DESIGN FLOW

Co-located, dedicated product team A

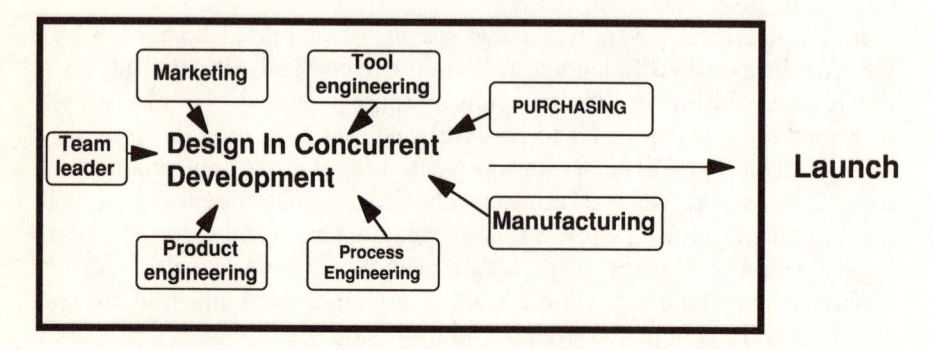

The first product to come through the new system showed its dramatic potential. The new S series, launched in mid-1994, was developed in one year (compared with four years for its predecessor) with about half the effort previously thought to be required. (Remember: There were no delays for lack of personnel or queue time, no backtracking, and no secret rework.) Then, the launch was much smoother than in the past and the number of defects reported by customers was a tiny fraction of the rate experienced with previous new products.

The Bottom Line

The conversion of Lantech from classic batch-and-queue to lean thinking has produced a dramatic box score of performance improvements (see Table 6.1).

TABLE 6.1: THE LEAN TRANSFORMATION AT LANTECH

	BATCH-AND-QUEUE/1991	FLOW/1995
Development time for a New Product Family	3–4 years	1 year
Employee hours per machine	160	80
Manufacturing space per machine	100 square feet	55 square feet
Delivered defects per machine	8	.8
Dollar value of in-process and finished goods inventory*	$2.6 million	$1.9 million
Production throughput time	16 weeks	14 hours–5 days
Product delivery lead time †	4–20 weeks	1–4 weeks

*Note that sales doubled during this period. If Lantech's traditional sales-to-inventory ratio had held constant, $5.2 million in inventory would have been needed to support 1995 sales volume.

† Product delivery lead time is the period customers must wait before their product can be delivered. In 1991, most of this time was in-process time in the production system. In 1995 most of this time was wait time for a production slot as Lantech's sales zoomed.

However, the result by which any business in a market economy must be measured is the ability to make enough profit to renew itself. If the transition at Lantech cost a fortune in new investment or disrupted the firm's ability to satisfy customers it would be an interesting technical exercise rather than a revolution in business practice.

In fact, the amount of investment required was substantially zero. The tools were moved and reconfigured, for the most part, by workers freed up from inefficient production tasks. The reconfiguration of the office and the development process were performed much the same way. Fewer computers, less space, and less expensive tooling were needed at every step. And the effect on customers was dramatic: Lantech's share of the stretch-wrapping market zoomed from 38 percent in 1991 to 50 percent in 1994. As a result, the large operating losses of 1991 were turned into solid profits by 1993 and an industry-leading financial performance by 1994.

Work as "Flow"

As noted in Chapter 3, the rethinking of work in accord with lean principles produces the potential for greatly expanded experiences of psychological "flow." Workers in the Lantech manufacturing cells can now see the entire work flow from raw materials to completed machine. *Takt* time, standard work, and visual control (including posted work charts for all tasks) give an immediate sense of how the work is proceeding. Multiskilling and job rotation make full use of each worker's skills and the frequent repetition of *kaizen* events (as described in Chapter 5 on perfection) gives an opportunity to participate actively in work design. The constant elimination of *muda* and the movement of workers out of work cells as more efficient methods are discovered mean that the work is a constant challenge. Finally, there are few interruptions in the form of line stoppages and sudden demands to shift to a completely different task to deal with a crisis.

The situation in the office is very similar. Visual control in order-taking makes it clear to everyone where Lantech stands and the new order entry system in which one employee can perform the whole task makes it possible to get immediate results. The *kaizen* process in the office melds thinking and doing, planning and acting, just as it does in the plant.

Finally, the rethinking of development work gives a true sense of feedback as everyone involved in a project works in the same space and projects move rapidly to completion. (Formerly, the majority of Lantech's development activities were *never* completed because market conditions changed before the cumbersome development process could be concluded. We have found this same phenomenon in a wide range of firms over many years.) Employees respond positively to gaining new skills and being encouraged to use all the skills they've always had. The lack of interruptions and conflict over which task to work on next has come as a great relief.

As Bob Underwood characterizes the situation now compared to the recent past, "We were living in darkness and now we have come into the light."

Yet it would be inaccurate to characterize Lantech as some sort of paradise. Indeed, coming out into the light can be painful to your eyes. The reorganization of work tasks into a continuous flow seems to have produced widespread psychological satisfaction in daily tasks, but it is also producing the need for constant change. "We just get something working smoothly when it's time to improve it again" is a common refrain, and it's clear that each change, at least subliminally, carries risks: "Will Lantech really honor its commitment to retain excess workers? Will my contribution to improvement activities be recognized and rewarded?" Perhaps most important, many employees ask, "What will change mean for my career? Am I going anywhere or just flying a holding pattern while Lantech prospers?"

These are all important questions which firms must face once they make the initial leap to lean thinking. We will return to them in Part III on the challenge of building a lean enterprise.

The Last Step

One last step in the conversion of Lantech from a batch-and-queue to a flow organization remains to be discussed. In April 1995, Pat Lancaster promoted himself to the new position of chairman (at age fifty-two) and stepped down from day-to-day operations, turning the CEO job over to his son, Jim. Now he is starting a new creative process by thinking again about the value of his products to the customer.

As it happened, the lean transformation at Lantech was easy in one important respect because customers were quite satisfied with current-generation stretch-wrapping equipment in terms of its performance, price, and service support. That is, its *value* to them was not in question, and Lantech could safely skip the first step of lean thinking described in Chapter 1.

However, in a supremely ironic twist, Lantech has revitalized itself by banishing batches and their associated *muda* from the design and production of a product whose sole use is to wrap.... batches! Stretch-wrapping machinery exists for the purpose of quickly and efficiently packaging large pallet loads of goods which are shipped from firm to firm within complex production and distribution chains.

Pat Lancaster has therefore embarked on a new strategic exercise to think through the nature of packaging his customers will need in the emerging world of small-lot production, single-piece flow, and right-located facilities. Lantech needs to be ready with the right-sized, right-tasked process machinery likely to be needed in the future in order to provide the desired value for the customer.

Beyond the Simple Case

Lantech is a striking example of what happens when a small American firm makes the value stream flow smoothly as pulled by the customer in pursuit of perfection. What's more, there is absolutely no magic involved. Any small firm can follow the conversion steps just described.

However, Lantech is a simple case. Pat Lancaster is a patient investor, not beholden to the impatient stock market. He had the authority as a change agent to "make it happen." Lantech has only one plant, and it is still possible for senior management to know everyone's name. The product range is relatively simple, really just four variants of one basic concept. The workforce is relatively young and has never shown an interest in joining a union to square off against management.

While the world is full of small firms like Lantech (which can make excellent investments for an individual or small group with the skills and energy to make the lean conversion), the majority of industrial activity in almost all countries is accounted for by much larger firms with much more complexity. What does it take to carry through a lean revolution in a larger and more traditional company?

CHAPTER 7
A Harder Case

Art Byrne of West Hartford, Connecticut, presides daily over his own United Nations. Within the main plant of the Wiremold Company, of which he is president and CEO, are representatives of twenty-four nationalities. A substantial fraction of the workforce is foreign born and 30 percent list a language other than English as their original tongue.

Wiremold's polyglot workforce produces a set of objects which Art Byrne describes as "splendidly mundane": wire management systems that route complex combinations of power, voice, and data wiring through buildings, and power protection devices such as surge protectors and line conditioners, which protect sensitive electronic equipment from voltage fluctuations.

Wiremold employees use simple production machinery—plastic injection molding machines, stamping presses, and rolling mills—to make products for mature and highly competitive markets. The workforce is organized by the International Brotherhood of Electrical Workers, one of the most traditional unions in the United States. The main plant was built in the 1920s and has been expanded over the years by hodgepodge additions of one small annex after another, making continuous flow and transparency difficult to achieve.

In short, Wiremold is the typical instance of "smokestack" America: a "low-tech" product made with "low-tech" tools by a unionized, immigrant, aging workforce with limited skills, working in an ancient facility; the type of firm which has had great difficulty in world competition in the past twenty years.

When Art Byrne arrived in September 1991, Wiremold was in a profound crisis, with declining sales, deteriorating production assets, and practically no profits. Four years later, the company has more than doubled its sales with the same workforce, increased wages, upgraded its physical plant, entered into a permanent growth trajectory, and become outstandingly profitable. How this happened is an object lesson in leaning American industry.

"We Nearly JITd Ourselves to Death"

In the late 1970s, family-owned Wiremold, which had been a successful manufacturer of wire raceways since 1900, switched from family to professional management and, in the words of Orrie Fiume, its longtime vice president for finance, "asked what we wanted to be when we grew up." The wire raceway business seemed to have practically no growth potential, so Wiremold decided to enter the surge protector business. These are the ubiquitous devices, generally found on the floor under your desk, which protect your personal computer from the electric company.

The easiest route seemed to be through an acquisition, and after some searching, Brooks Electronics of North Philadelphia, Pennsylvania, was acquired in 1988. Brooks brought with it not only an established market position but also a close acquaintance with W. Edwards Deming. President Gary Brooks had embraced Deming's Total Quality Management (TQM) in the early 1980s, struck up an acquaintance with Deming, and taken not only his entire management but half of his total workforce to Deming's weeklong seminars.

When Brooks was acquired, TQM was embraced by Wiremold as well, and the management of Wiremold was soon enrolled in the Deming seminars. As Orrie Fiume notes, "Deming's Fourteen Points were a perfect fit with our values and we all loved the principles. There was only one problem: Deming teaches what he called the 'Theory of Management,' or what I call a philosophy of change. But like a lot of good management theories, it was critically short on implementation details."

By 1989, Wiremold was ready to try harder at implementation, and sent its vice president for operations to visit Japanese factories. He came back praising the concept of Just-in-Time (JIT) and immediately set about pulling down inventories and reducing lot sizes. What he could not do, because no one knew how, was introduce flow and pull by reducing changeover times for Wiremold's tools and building to a level schedule.

As Orrie Fiume remembers, "Our customer service went *completely* to hell! We soon discovered that our MRP had years earlier had a 50 percent extra margin added to the safety stock calculation. We also discovered that our reliance on enormous batches and mountainous inventories meant not only that we could tolerate slow tool changes but that we could skimp on tool maintenance. If a tool was installed in a machine and found to be defective, there was plenty of time to send it out for maintenance and get it back before we actually ran out of parts. Our tools had deteriorated to a shocking extent without the management ever realizing what was happening."

Between 1989 and 1991, Wiremold slid steadily from record profits toward breakeven. Some of the problem was lost sales when Wiremold couldn't deliver, but total sales went down only a few percent. The real problem was costs, as Wiremold paid express freight, added a whole customer service staff to explain why deliveries would be late, and paid to fix its tools. As Fiume notes wryly, "We nearly JITd ourselves to death by doing it the wrong way."

By 1991, Wiremold's longtime president was ready to retire, creating the opportunity to find a chief executive who could actually implement a lean system. As Fiume recalls, "You might think we would have simply gone backward to large batches and massive inventories, but something had permanently switched over in our minds as a result of exposure to Deming and the rudiments of lean thinking. We gave no thought to going back to the old way, but instead set out to find someone who could implement the new way."

The Change Agent

For Art Byrne, the "light went on" in 1982 when he was general manager of a small business unit, the High Intensity and Quartz Lamp Division, within the vast General Electric Corporation. One of his manufacturing managers had gone on a study trip to Toyota and had come back with amazing stories about inventory reductions due to JIT. Byrne began to read the available literature, then took his own trip, and was soon ready to give JIT a try. In one of the first JIT applications in GE, Byrne and his colleagues were able to reduce in-process inventories in his business unit from forty days down to three. He remembers, "It seemed like a miracle."

Art Byrne's problem was not with JIT but with GE. "I hated the 'make-the-month' mentality where everything was evaluated on the basis of short-term financial performance, and I became convinced that I would never be allowed to take the more difficult next steps in creating a lean organization. I already knew that when you try to create continuous flow there is going to be a step backward for every two steps forward, and I doubted that GE's instant-results management culture could deal with it."

So Byrne left to become a group executive of the Chicago Pneumatic Tool Company, a manufacturer of small air-driven tools for industrial users. However, he had hardly arrived at Chicago Pneumatic in 1986 when it was taken over by the Danaher Corporation (which we heard about in Chapter 6), and Art Byrne was soon put in charge of eight Danaher companies.

The Knowledge

One of the Danaher firms in Byrne's portfolio was the Jacobs Equipment Company (commonly known as Jake Brake) of Bloomfield, Connecticut. The sales and marketing vice president of this firm was George Koenigsaecker,[1] a particularly eager advocate of lean ideas who had made numerous study trips to Japan, including to Toyota, and read every book and article he could find on lean production.

When he was promoted to president of Jake Brake at the end of 1987, Koenigsaecker and his new operations vice president, Bob Pentland,[2] began moving machinery from process villages, tearing out conveyors (which are really moving warehouses), and setting up their first cells to make truck engine components in single-piece flow. They began to get dramatic results, but neither Koenigsaecker nor Pentland felt they knew as much as they needed to know, and they were constantly looking for ways to learn more.

Early in 1988, Koenigsaecker noticed that a weeklong seminar and *kaizen* event on the Toyota Production System was being held at the Hartford Graduate Center and in the plant of a nearby firm. He, Pentland, and Byrne decided to attend. The organizer of the course was Masaaki Imai, then becoming well known for his book, *Kaizen*. The other instructors were Yoshiki Iwata, Akira Takenaka, and Chihiro Nakao of the Shingijutsu consulting group in Japan, whom none of the Danaher group had ever heard of.

After the Danaher delegation had listened to the first day of the Shingijutsu presentation on TPS and discovered that they had worked for years as pupils of Taiichi Ohno in his efforts to spread lean thinking through Toyota's supplier group and beyond, they thought they were on to something. Koenigsaecker approached the instructors about visiting Jake Brake.

As Bob Pentland remembers, "We had never met a Japanese-style teacher, or *sensei*, and we weren't prepared for being turned down cold. Iwata simply said 'no' and stalked away. However, George is a uniquely persistent person and kept approaching Iwata, first at lunch, then at the afternoon coffee break, then at the end of the day. Every time he posed the question through Iwata's translator, the answer was a brusque 'no.' The next day George was at it again, before class, at lunch, and during coffee breaks. Finally, at the end of the second day, Iwata and his colleagues agreed to go to dinner, probably so George would stop asking.

"The minute we sat down to dinner, I pulled out a layout of our plant with the new single-piece-flow cell [identical to the Lantech cells described in Chapter 6] which we had just created. I laid it on the table in front of Iwata, and asked him whether we were doing the right thing. There was a long, frosty silence. Finally, Iwata said, 'If I come to your plant, will you do *whatever* I tell you to do?' George and I said, 'Of course.' Iwata responded, 'If this is true, roll up the drawing, let me eat my dinner in *peace*, and I will come to your plant this evening.'"

When they arrived at the plant around 10:00 P.M., the Japanese team took one look at the new cell and pronounced it all "no good." They explained that among other problems it was laid out backwards (the work should have been flowing counterclockwise) and it would be necessary to move all the machines immediately. Koenigsaecker and Pentland had done no preparation for the visit and they knew their union leaders would be upset about the abrupt changes (which they were), but it was also clear that this was the test: "Would we do immediately exactly what they told us?" So everyone pitched in to reconfigure the cell and by 2:00 A.M. it was running again, with results far better than before.

With this introduction to the "just-do-it" mind-set of the lean *sensei*, Koenigsaecker knew he had entered a new world. "My whole notion of how much improvement was possible in a given period of time was fundamentally and permanently altered. I also realized that these guys could be a gold mine for the Danaher group."

Koenigsaecker and Pentland assumed that they had passed the critical test and that arranging a consulting relationship would be easy. So they were dismayed when Iwata abruptly headed out of the plant once the cell was running, explaining that he had done what he could but that Jake Brake managers were hopeless "concrete heads" beyond his ability to help further.

Fortuitously, the *kaizen* event held during the rest of the week at another Hartford area firm ran into the entrenched resistance of the firm's management, which refused to do any of the things the *sensei* requested. By Friday, the Danaher delegation was ready to ask for help again. This time Iwata responded that Danaher managers seemed to have no idea how to operate their business but that compared with the other American managers he had just met, there was at least some hope. However, he and his colleagues also said they were too old to learn English and that America was too far away.

Art Byrne was determined not to give up and arranged to meet them in Japan a short time later. There, after asking for help a third time, he finally got an agreement for a one-week trial to see if Danaher was truly serious.

The first day of the trial was conducted at the Jacobs Chuck Company, another Danaher subsidiary, in Charleston, South Carolina, which manufactures drill chucks for small electric drills of the type most of us have in our home tool kit and for industrial models as well. Byrne and Jacobs president Dennis Claramunt thought they would start with a one-hour plant tour and go from there. However, after five minutes, Iwata, Takenaka, and Nakao announced they had seen enough. "Everything is no good," they announced through their translator. "Will you fix it now?"

Two teams were formed immediately, one with Iwata to work on final assembly and the other with Takenaka and Nakao to work on machining the steel bodies for Jacobs's industrial drill chucks. Byrne and Claramunt followed Iwata but were soon interrupted by Jacobs's manufacturing engineers, who were upset that Takenaka and Nakao were demanding to move all of the heavy machinery used for machining the chucks during the lunch hour.

Claramunt told the engineers to let Takenaka and Nakao do whatever they wanted and then went to the machining area with Byrne after lunch to see what was happening. With their sleeves rolled up and pry bars in hand, Takenaka and Nakao were working furiously to move the massive machines out of their departments and into the proper sequence for single-piece flow while Jacobs engineers and the rest of the workforce stood with their mouths hanging open.

On one level it was pure theater; the Japanese visitors surely understood what an extraordinary scene they were causing. But on another level, they were prying Jacobs loose from their bureaucratic, departmentalized, batch-and-queue past. As Byrne remembers, "By moving those machines themselves in only a few minutes—when many hadn't been moved in years and Jacobs executives would never have dreamed of touching any machinery themselves—they demonstrated how to create flow and what a few determined individuals can do. Neither Dennis nor the rest of the Jacobs workforce was ever the same again. They all threw away their reservations and got to work."

So Danaher passed the test and Japanese advisers agreed to work intensively for Danaher as their exclusive North American client. "With our *sensei* on board and with the full backing of the Rales brothers as they began to grasp these ideas in mid-1989, we had the knowledge and the authority to push lean thinking faster and faster."

By 1991, Art Byrne had introduced lean thinking all the way across the eight companies in his group, with spectacular results. He was also instrumental in spreading lean thinking in the five other Danaher companies, led by John Cosentino, who became a true believer. The transmission device was Byrne's innovation of the "presidents' *kaizen*" in which the presidents of all of the Danaher companies and their operations vice presidents were required to participate hands-on every six weeks in a three-day *kaizen* event in a Danaher plant. They moved machines themselves and in many cases learned the realities of the shop floor and the ordering and scheduling system for the first time. (One of these companies was Hennessy Industries, where Ron Hicks, whom we met in the last chapter, made the transition from "concrete head" to lean thinker through his experiences in presidents' *kaizen*.)

However, Byrne was growing restless. Like most change agents, he wanted to run his own show, but the top jobs at family-controlled Danaher were unavailable. Wiremold, on the other side of Hartford, had heard about Byrne's work at Danaher, and a match was made.

The Leaning of Wiremold

When Art Byrne arrived at Wiremold in September 1991, he found about what he expected, a classic batch-and-queue system in production operations, order-taking, and product development. Products took four to six weeks to go from raw materials to finished goods. Orders took up to a week to process. New products, even when they were nothing more than a reshuffling of existing parts, required two and a half to three years to progress from concept to launch. As a result, only two or three new products were being launched each year. Thick departmental and functional walls were everywhere, damming up the flow of value and making it impossible to see.

Byrne quickly realized that by applying lean techniques he could run the company at its current sales volume with half the people and half the floor space. Given the financial situation, he had to take immediate action. So, as his first step, he tackled the excess-people problem.

Dealing Up Front with Extra People and Anchor-Draggers

In November 1991, Art Byrne announced that the crew was too large to keep the ship afloat and offered a generous early retirement package to the aging workforce in the plants and to the office staff. Although he believed that only half the workforce was needed, he set the headcount reduction goal at 30 percent, knowing that as soon as he got the product development system working right, sales growth would absorb the remaining excess people.

Almost all of the eligible hourly workers took the retirement offer, but only a small fraction of the office staff accepted. Art and Judy Seyler, his vice president for human resources, therefore conducted a "de-layering." They classified every job in management as either:

- value creating (defined as the ability of Wiremold to pass the costs of the job along to the customer),
- nonvalue creating (from the standpoint of the customer) but currently necessary to run the business (for example, the environmental expert helping the company meet government regulations, Type One *muda*), or
- nonvalue creating and unnecessary (Type Two *muda*)

132 LEAN THINKING

They then classified each manager as either:

- able to create value,
- able to create value with some development of skills, or
- unable to create value, even with development (usually due to unwillingness to change their attitudes about the organization of work)

After years of creating lean organizations, Art had concluded that about 10 percent of existing management will not embrace the new system. "Lean thinking is profoundly corrosive of hierarchy and some people just don't seem to be able to make the adjustment. It's essential that these anchor-draggers find some other place to work—after all, there's still plenty of hierarchy out in the world—or the whole campaign will fail."

The people in the first two categories were therefore matched up with jobs in the first two categories to create a new organization structure (compare Figure 7.1 with 7.2) with a new roster of players. Employees not finding useful jobs were given a generous severance and within thirty days of Art's arrival the new structure and player roster was in place. Only one outsider was recruited, Frank Giannattasio, the new vice president for operations.

As Judy Seyler looks back on this event, she notes that it was terribly traumatic in a hierarchical, paternalistic organization in which no one had ever been asked to leave. "Even though the financial cost was very large,

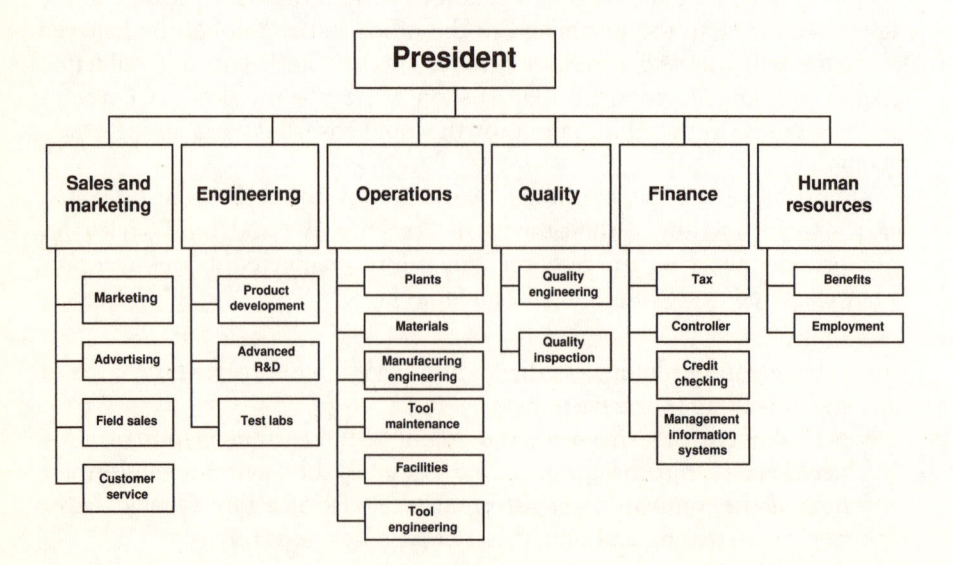

FIGURE 7.1: OLD WIREMOLD ORGANIZATION

FIGURE 7.2: NEW WIREMOLD ORGANIZATION

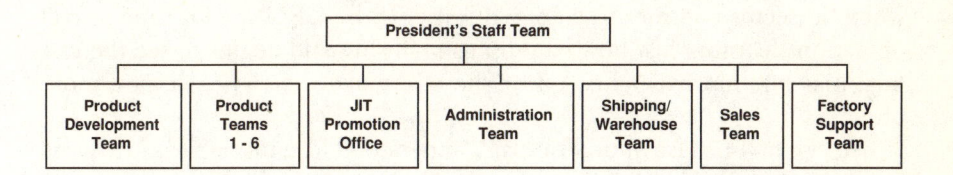

```
                          President's Staff Team
    ┌──────────┬──────────┬──────────┬──────────┬──────────┬──────────┐
  Product    Product     JIT      Administration  Shipping/   Sales    Factory
 Development  Teams    Promotion      Team       Warehouse    Team     Support
    Team      1-6       Office                     Team                 Team
```

particularly given our lack of profits, Art was determined to be generous with people while making it clear that in the future everyone must create value by working together in a different way."

When the headcount reductions were completed, Art Byrne called a meeting of the entire workforce of the parent company and announced that no one would ever lose their job as a result of the improvement activities that would start immediately. "The bad part is over; now we will all learn how to continuously create more value so that we never have bad days again."

Byrne was in effect giving job guarantees to his union workforce without asking anything in return except that they be open-minded to change. "I'm certain that 99 percent of American companies wouldn't do this, but taking away the fear of job loss is at the very core of a lean conversion. Think of it logically from a human perspective rather than as some corporate bureaucrat. If I asked you to help me reduce the number of people needed to make a particular product from five down to two, and after you did, I followed up by laying off three people, one of whom was your cousin and another a good friend, what would you say to me when I asked you to help me do the same thing a month later for another product?"

Teaching People How to See

Based on his experience in "leaning" eight separate businesses in the Danaher group, Byrne had concluded that the single most effective action in converting an organization to lean practices is for the CEO to lead the initial improvement activities himself. "This is where most American companies fail right at the outset. CEOs want to delegate improvement activities, partly because they are timid about going out on the shop floor or to the engineering area or to the order-taking and scheduling departments to work hands-on making improvements. As a result, they never really learn anything about change at the level where value is really created. They continue to manage in their old by-the-numbers manner, which kills the improvement activities they thought they started. The fact is that big changes require leaps of faith in which the CEO must say 'Just do it,' even when 'it' seems contrary to common sense. If the CEO spends time in real operations learning just how bad things really are and begins to see the vast potential for improvements, he or she will make the right decision more often."

Because no one else in the company understood lean principles, Art Byrne led the initial training sessions himself. Using a manual he had written, he conducted two-day sessions on lean principles for 150 employees followed immediately by three-day *kaizen* exercises so employees could use the skills they had just learned. (This was very different from Wiremold's previous improvement activities, conducted as part of TQM, where improvement teams met weekly for an hour or two, mostly to plan improvements to be implemented weeks or months later.)

Byrne then gathered his managers and union head together and took them on "the walk of shame" through every part of the plant and through the engineering and sales departments. "There was *muda* everywhere and my managers were now able to see it. I told them that we were going to convert every process, including product development and order-taking, into continuous flow and that we were going to learn how to pull. I also told them that I was going to get them the best help in the world, from Iwata and Nakao, who were at the end of their exclusive agreement with Danaher and ready to work for Wiremold."

Attacking Every Value Stream Repeatedly

Soon hundreds of weeklong *kaizen* activities were under way (and continue to this day), involving practically every employee, as every value stream in Wiremold was repeatedly evaluated for ways to make it flow better and pull more smoothly. Wiremold's assumption is that every stream can always be improved in pursuit of perfection and that every stream must be improved in pursuit of perfection. Equally important, it is presumed that results can be achieved very quickly, the common expression being that "if you can't get a major improvement in three days you are doing something wrong." Once this mentality is reinforced by results—and employees begin to believe management's guarantee that no job will ever be lost due to improvement activities—improvement can become self-sustaining.

Re-creating the Production Organization to Channel the Value Stream

When Art Byrne de-layered the Wiremold organization (again, see Figure 7.2) he did far more than remove tangential jobs and frills that could no longer be afforded. He smashed the departmental barriers to focus everyone's efforts on the value stream by creating dedicated production teams for each of Wiremold's six product families. The purchasing, manufacturing, and scheduling (MRP) groups within the Operations Department, the Engineering Department, and the "process villages" (stamping, rolling, molding, painting, assembly, etcetera) in the plants were eliminated, with their personnel reassigned to product teams provided with all of the resources needed to produce a specific product family.

Let's take Tele-Power™ Poles as an example. (These are the steel or aluminum columns extending from floor to ceiling in open office settings, with power and communications outlets on every side of the column to permit a host of adjacent workstations to plug in. They are offered in an enormous variety of shapes, lengths, plug configurations, and colors.) Team leader Joe Condeco was given complete responsibility, and profit-and-loss accountability, for Wiremold's "pole" products from initial launch through their production life. More radically, the team leader, the product planners, the buyers, the factory engineers, the production supervisors, and the production associates were all co-located on the factory floor immediately adjacent to the realigned machinery producing the poles in single-piece-flow cells.

The team was given its own punch presses and rolling mills, as well as assembly equipment, so it could be self-sufficient. Before, the assembly activity was dependent on the Rolling Mill Department for their bases and covers. Despite large stocks on hand, they would often lack the right base or enough covers. When they asked the Rolling Mill Department for more of a missing item, the response would often be, "Sorry, but the master schedule generated by the MRP system calls for us to make other items now. You'll have to wait until next week or take your problem to a higher level." Now the Tele-Power™ team has all of the equipment it needs. *There can be no excuses.*

The new setting was initially a great shock to the "white collars" who had always worked in a remote office and seen themselves in a very different light from "factory workers." (Wiremold soon implemented a casual dress code based on Art Byrne's belief that "neckties cut off circulation to the brain and inhibit teamwork." This was another problem for office workers who somehow felt that their appearance rather than their skills and their contributions made them special.) Reassignment to product teams was also a shock to the process specialists working in the process villages like the Rolling Mill Department who had traditionally hoarded their tricks of the trade. However, everyone soon came to like it. For the first time, they could actually see value flowing!

Introducing a Lean Financial System and "Scoreboard"

To get the production teams to work in accordance with lean principles, Wiremold needed to junk its traditional system of standard cost "absorption" accounting, which allocated costs by labor and machine hours in accordance with mass-production thinking. Production managers knew from experience that they had to "absorb" allocated overhead by spreading it over as many machine and labor hours as possible. This system gave an overwhelming incentive to keep every worker and every machine busy—to "make the numbers"—by producing inventory, even if the inventory consisted of items no one would ever want.

As Orrie Fiume remembers, "Standard cost and variance analysis were declared dead as concepts immediately after Art's arrival. We looked at Activity Based Costing but knew it wasn't the answer. Its advocates will tell you it is based on cost drivers, but in reality it's just a different method of allocating overhead. There is still too much allocation of aggregated costs downward. We were determined to work from the bottom up."

The key to the new way of thinking was to organize production by product families, then let each product team do its own purchasing and buy all its own tools. A simple system could then be devised to assign real costs to each product line. Today, more than 90 percent of the costs involved in making a Tele-Power™ pole, for example, come from product-specific cost analysis. Only a small fraction of cost is an allocation outside the control of the team, specifically occupancy costs for whatever space the team is using in a plant. And even in this case, the team is charged only for the space it actually uses, so costs can be reduced by using less.

Some elements of the old standard cost accounting system are retained in the computer because the financial statement needs them—for example, the value of in-process inventories. However, these are deemphasized in evaluating the performance of the product teams, which are told to concentrate on the cost of manufacturing instead. Similarly, the financial implications of running down the inventories during the transition period were not shown to the product team leaders for fear they would do the wrong thing.[3]

In addition to a simple profit-and-loss calculation, Wiremold's production teams were given a new "scoreboard" consisting of some simple, quantitative performance indicators:

- productivity of the product team (expressed as sales per employee),
- customer service (expressed as percent of products delivered on time),
- inventory turns, and
- quality (expressed as the number of mistakes made by the team)

The team leaders and their teams can see these indicators at all times because they are prominently posted. In addition, the two primary ways to improve are obvious. First, smooth the flow of products through the system, with no backflows for reworking quality problems, no scrap, and no in-process inventories. Then, make only those products customers actually want, because productivity is measured as end-market sales (not additions to in-process inventories) per employee.

To keep everyone marching at the same pace, Wiremold equips the scoreboard with a set of expectations as well. Specifically, team leaders and their teams are expected to:

- reduce defects, as shown in the quality indicator, by 50 percent every year;
- improve productivity, expressed as sales per employee in constant dollars, by 20 percent every year;
- deliver 100 percent of products *exactly* on time;
- increase inventory turns to a minimum of twenty per year; and
- increase profit sharing to 20 percent of straight wages (as explained in a moment)

"Variance analysis" is still performed but not based on variances from standard costs. Instead, when the trend line starts to diverge from performance targets, the team collectively searches for the root cause of the variance rather than maneuvering to "make the numbers," as in the old days.

Running Down Inventories

Because Wiremold is privately held and the board of directors understood what was happening, the special financial problem of inventory reduction in a lean transition was not a major concern. For a publicly traded company, however, rapidly running down inventories can be a real problem, one worth a brief digression. As firms move from batch-and-queue to flow systems, enormous amounts of cash are suddenly made available from freed-up inventories. (This offers the firm a special strategic opportunity, as we will see in a moment.) The problem is that the removal of these inventories increases production costs, *as shown on the financial statement*, and can easily wipe out profits.

Let's take a simple example. Firms typically calculate their costs of production and profits in the following manner, as shown in the left-hand column of Table 7.1.

TABLE 7.1: CONSEQUENCES OF INVENTORY REDUCTIONS FOR PROFITABILITY

	MASS PRODUCTION METHODS	LEAN PRODUCTION METHODS
Beginning in-process inventory	$ 576,000	576,000
Direct materials purchased	924,000	637,000
Direct labor	958,000	958,000
Indirect manufacturing costs	465,000	465,000
Subtotal	2,923,000	2,636,000
Minus ending in-process inventory	− 576,000	− 100,000
Total costs of production	2,347,000	2,536,000
Total revenue from sales	2,500,000	2,500,000
Profit (loss)—pretax	153,000	(36,000)
Cash flow—pretax	153,000	440,000

Now, suppose that the new "lean" management takes in-process inventory down dramatically from $576,000 to $100,000 while holding everything else constant (except, of course, material purchasing, because products are being made largely from the inventories already on hand). Running the numbers again, as shown in the right-hand column, it's apparent that the new management, while trying to "do the right thing," has moved the company from a $153,000 profit to a $36,000 loss (even as cash flow has zoomed).

This phenomenon can be very bad for publicly traded companies unless the management actively explains the situation to stockholders in advance. The only alternative to education is a slash-and-burn campaign of headcount and cost reduction (in the direct labor and indirect manufacturing cost accounts) to restore short-term profits. This can, however, easily set back the introduction of lean thinking or even make it impossible if the traumatized workforce refuses to cooperate with lean initiatives.

Creating a "Lean" Function

To help the product teams continuously improve, Art Byrne created a new function, the JIT Promotion Office (JPO). The old Quality Department, some of the training activities formerly conducted by the Personnel Department, and several high-potential associates from different areas of the firm were grouped under the JPO. With the JPO, the task of working through the entirety of Wiremold, value stream by value stream, could be speeded up.

The product team leader and the JIT Promotion Office jointly evaluate the value stream for the product to determine what types of *kaikaku* and *kaizen* activities should be performed and when. A team leader from the product team and a facilitator from the JPO are then assigned to each improvement team (which might be a subset of the product team, the whole team, or some portion of the team plus outside experts with needed skills). Because the team leader will go back to her or his job on the product team once the *kaizen* is finished, the facilitator from the JPO shoulders the critical responsibility for seeing to the completion of the follow-up work invariably resulting from a weeklong improvement effort.

In addition to planning and facilitating improvement exercises, the JPO teaches every employee the principles of lean thinking (identifying the value stream, flow, pull, and the endless pursuit of perfection) plus lean techniques (standard work, *takt* time, visual control, pull scheduling, and single-piece flow in particular) and periodically reteaches them. As Frank Giannattasio notes, "This is an enormous but critical challenge. Your middle management, in particular, feels threatened by the lean transition and the removal of all those safety nets. When in doubt, they will take you right back to making batches and building inventories unless you reinforce the message through continued teaching, coupled with continuous hands-on improvement exercises."

Offering Ironclad Job Guarantees in Return for Flexibility

As we noted earlier, Art Byrne knew that if the value stream for every product was going to be unkinked continuously, people would continually be left by the side of the stream. Resistance to continuous improvement would be chronic unless he guaranteed that workers would not be out on the street, even if their specific job was eliminated. He also knew that the existing work rules in Wiremold's union contract—restricting stampers to stamping, painters to painting, molders to molding, and so on—would make it impossible to introduce flow and to continuously improve every activity. Finally, he knew that his workforce would have a very hard time differentiating layoffs due to weak demand from layoffs due to *kaizen*. Therefore, once the initial retirement offer was accepted, Art went immediately to his union and offered job guarantees for the remaining workers in return for their cooperation in working in a new way.

The union was suspicious at first. Wiremold's former director of labor relations had been an old-fashioned hard-liner and the union presumed that any management offer of job guarantees must contain fine print which somehow reversed its on-the-surface meaning. In the end, however, the union decided that Byrne would deliver on his promises.

Curiously, for reasons Art Byrne finds hard to understand, executives in many companies in the Hartford area were more skeptical about his job guarantee offer than his union. "People tell me all the time that I'm crazy to make an ironclad guarantee of jobs. They say, 'What if something goes wrong and your sales fall off?' But my view is that management has five lines of defense before showing people the door: (1) reduce overtime, (2) put the extra people on *kaizens* (to get a future payback), (3) in-source some components from marginal suppliers we plan to drop anyway (remembering that our equipment is now highly flexible), (4) cut the workweek across the board, and, most powerful, (5) develop new product lines to grow the business. Our employees are now all highly skilled in process improvements and only a concrete head would fire skilled people due to short-term business fluctuations."

Re-creating the Product Development System to Channel the Value Stream

The product development system Art Byrne found in the fall of 1991 was clearly not going to grow the business. Engineering vice president Steve Maynard remembers that thirty products were under development and all were making slow progress. "We had long queues between the stages in development, we had departments within engineering with batch production, and we had expediters. There were absolutely no priorities except that some projects at some times had 'the voice of the president' behind them and received expeditious treatment." The average project actually making it through the system took three years, but many stragglers were lost in action along the way.

Fortunately, Steve Maynard already knew what to do. He had learned, at a University of Hartford seminar in the fall of 1990, that Quality Function Deployment and dedicated development teams are an unbeatable combination. The seminar was affiliated with MIT's Laboratory for Manufacturing and Productivity, and MIT professor Don Clausing, one of the disseminators of the "House of Quality" concept,[4] took Steve through the steps needed to introduce the "voice of the customer" in a highly structured, continuous-flow development process.

However, back at Wiremold, the senior management was so busy with the ongoing TQM effort that there was no time for another program. They told Steve Maynard, "Wait until next year." Fortunately, by "next year" Art Byrne was on the scene. "When I first met Art, I said, 'What do you think about QFD and dedicated development teams?' He said, 'Do both immediately. And by the way, your new target for product development time is now three to six months, not three years.' We were off and running within a week."

Steve Maynard's first step in the fall of 1991 was to start formal in-house training in QFD, using a consultant for technical support.[5] All the senior executives attended this training, just as every manager, no matter how senior, no matter what their job, participated in shop-floor *kaizen* activities. Art Byrne's theory was that every manager in an organization must understand the basic activities of that organization, notably product development, production operations, and sales/scheduling, and that the only way to learn was intense exposure to systematic principles.

Next, Maynard and the senior management team asked an obvious but previously neglected question: What businesses are we really in? They reviewed the thirty ongoing development programs and "deselected" those—most of them, in fact—which did not support a specific business: tele-power, power and data management, plastic products, etcetera.[6] This shrunk the number of projects dramatically, and those which remained were prioritized. These projects were then placed in a product plan, showing their target dates for introduction.

For each program judged worthy of continuing, Maynard designated a three-person team consisting of a marketer, a designer/product engineer, and a production/tool engineer. The team was sent to talk directly with prospective customers in the building design and construction community to come up with a broad definition of the product through an initial QFD process. They asked the "value question" described in Chapter 1 and came back saying, for example, "What we really need is a Tele-Power™ Pole which can accommodate any height of ceiling, which can be ordered in a very wide range of colors, and which is unobtrusive."

Steve Maynard remembers the amazement among many Wiremold old-timers when these teams were formed. "They asked me, 'Why have we got a tool-design guy out in the field talking to customers? Doesn't the need for specialization and the division of labor require that tool designers stick to designing tools?' The security many of them felt in the old departmentalized, everything-in-its-place way of organizing work was truly striking."

Once the broad definition of the surviving products was determined, a truly multifunctional team was formed to develop a detailed product specification in engineering language. The team was co-located in a dedicated space in the Engineering Department and included the team leader from the appropriate product family (Tele-Power™ Poles in our example) plus the production planner, the production/tool engineer (a member of the original three-person, product-definition team), and a buyer. The team was told to achieve a target cost determined by estimating the market price and subtracting an acceptable margin.

When the precise specification of the product was accepted, detailed part and tool design was conducted by the team, again working to target cost. Toward the end of the process, the whole team moved its desks to the factory floor to go through process-at-a-glance and standard work exercises with the production team handling the product. (Remember that thinking about manufacturability has been present from the beginning. The production/tool engineer was on the original definition team.)

By mid-1992, Wiremold was ready with its first product under the new regime. It had taken only six months and tool costs were only 60 percent of what had been originally budgeted, based on past experience. Even as Wiremold's managers in the physical production and order-taking process were learning how to see, Wiremold's marketers, product designers, and engineers were learning how to hear the voice of the customer and how to make designs flow quickly and directly through the development process.[7]

Fixing the Order-Taking Process

The third key activity of any business is order-taking, scheduling, and delivery, and Art Byrne made no distinction between this "business process" and the firm's physical production. It was subjected to the exact same *kaikaku* and *kaizen* process at the same level of frequency as every production activity.

As in most batch production organizations, Wiremold's order entry and shipping was disconnected from physical production. A master schedule in the MRP system, based on market forecasts, was supposed to ensure that adequate stocks of finished goods were always on hand in a massive centralized warehouse, so that when an order was received it could be processed and then shipped from inventory.

The orders themselves were also processed in a batch mode through a central Customer Service Department. This department entered orders throughout the day into a computerized order-processing system. The orders were processed overnight in a batch and, if inventory was on hand, pick lists of what to ship were printed out the next morning in the Shipping Department. Over the next two or three days the Shipping Department at the warehouse would gather the goods and send them to Wiremold's distributors.

However, items on a customer order often were not available, despite large inventories, so very few orders were shipped complete. Instead "backordered" items were shipped over an extended period as they became available. Because of the MRP system and the large batches in each production run, it was not unusual for a single customer order to ship over many weeks or months. Also, because most orders had delayed items, a large Customer Service Department was needed to keep track of orders and to respond to customer questions about delayed items.

The end result of all this handing off of orders and the massive warehouse was that it took almost a week to process and ship an order when everything was in stock. Yet most orders called for items which were delayed for extended periods and the system had many potential sources of errors. The Customer Service Department found it very difficult to keep up with its dual role of making customers happy about delayed or incorrect shipments and spurring the rest of Wiremold to get the job done right.

After a series of *kaizen* teams went through the entire series of activities —from order-taking to shipping—it was possible to shorten the order-receipt-to-ship time from more than a week to less than a day. To achieve this, orders were sent to shipping four times during the day (rather than in one big batch overnight) and the central warehouse was closed, freeing up 70,000 square feet of space. Upon receipt of the orders, shipping circulated carts past the small finished stock racks at the end of each product team's production process.

As the shipper withdrew parts from the rack and pushed empty parts containers down a return chute, this became the signal—the only signal— for the product team to make more of a given part. (The MRP system which formerly kept track of the movements of individual parts within the Wiremold production system was gradually given the much smaller task of long-term capacity planning and ordering parts from suppliers not yet on pull systems.)

This new approach, which required many fewer people and resulted in fewer errors, could only be introduced over a period of about two years as Wiremold began to convert from batches to product teams with single-piece flow. Parts which had been produced in one-month batches were soon being produced every day, a feat which required that many machines be changed over twenty to thirty times per day rather than the former three to four times per week.

Although Wiremold's competitors in the electrical industry are now being forced to match its quick-shipping capability, they seem to be doing it the way so many American firms are achieving "just-in-time," by maintaining even larger inventories of finished units or by switching to a "Max-Flex" system such as we saw at Lantech, in which mountains of component parts are prepared in advance so that final assembly can be conducted in direct response to customer orders. Both approaches are inferior to a truly lean pull system from start to finish.

Linking Compensation to Profits

Wiremold had always paid base wages at slightly above the average level for the Hartford area. It then tried to reward its workers for good results through a profit-sharing plan funded with 15 percent of pretax profits, paid quarterly in the form of a check, and by contributing shares of company stock as the employer contribution to a savings plan. The problem was that, in the years just prior to Art Byrne's arrival, there had hardly been any profits and stock values had slumped. In addition, the old batch production system made it hard for employees to see any connection between their own efforts and the success of the firm.

Art Byrne resolved to keep the existing profit-sharing arrangement but to steadily increase profits ("by working smarter than our competitors") and to show everyone the financials so that the reasons for profitability would be clear. During the first years of "lean management," profits at Wiremold have increased from 1.2 percent of wages in 1990 to 7.8 percent in 1995, and Byrne is still strongly committed to increasing profit sharing to 20 percent of every employee's pay.

Improving Suppliers

After many internal improvements were made, it became increasingly apparent that many of Wiremold's problems were external. Purchased goods and raw materials accounted for a significant percentage of Wiremold's total costs, yet no effort had ever been made to improve supplier performance. Instead, Wiremold's traditional purchasing operation had concentrated on controlling supplier profit margins by ordering every part and type of material competitively from multiple sources.

Kaizen teams moved quickly to dramatically reduce the number of suppliers, from more than 320 in 1991 to 73 by the end of 1995. This was essential if Wiremold was going to be able to take time with each supplier to improve its performance. But then it was necessary to start with the most critical suppliers and teach them to see.

In April 1992, a Wiremold *kaizen* team paid a first visit to Ryerson, a giant steel fabricator much larger than Wiremold, with fabrication facilities spread all across North America. Ryerson supplies Wiremold with large rolls of steel which Wiremold stamps or bends to make the cases for many of its products. Ryerson had adopted state-of-the-art techniques to the extent that it had just begun to deliver to Wiremold every day, "just-in-time." However, at the back of Ryerson's plant, the Wiremold JIT team found just what they had expected: a neat row of steel coils, each a day's supply for Wiremold, fifty days in a row produced by Ryerson in one enormous batch. Just-in-time had been nothing more than an inventory shuffling exercise because Ryerson didn't know how to produce in small lots.

The Wiremold team therefore went to work on Ryerson's massive steel cutting machines, which took two shifts to change over from one cutting pattern to the next. This, of course, was the cause of the massive lot of coils laid out in the shipping area. In a short time it was possible to bring changeover times down from two shifts to about thirty minutes, and Ryerson began to meet Wiremold's needs each day for delivery during the day.

Even better, from both Ryerson and Wiremold's standpoint, Ryerson was soon able to produce for all of its other customers on a true "Just-in-Time" basis, driving down costs across the board. Wiremold, of course, expected something from Ryerson in return for its trouble, and negotiated a range of special services—like absorption of materials cost increases for extended periods and extra-short runs of steel for certain low-volume applications. As a result of Wiremold's proactive stance toward a key supplier, Wiremold, Ryerson, and all of Ryerson's other customers were much better off, a win-win-win achievement for lean thinking.

Devising a Growth Strategy

Art Byrne notes that "our production system and its needs are fundamental to our strategy." Because the application of lean thinking to batch-and-queue organizations liberates tremendous amounts of resources—people (including engineers and managers), space, tools, time (to get to market much faster), and *cash*—it is both possible and necessary to grow rapidly. It is possible to grow rapidly because the means are self-generated; it is necessary to grow rapidly to provide work to support the job guarantees which are the social basis of the system. In consequence, Wiremold has grown rapidly along three tracks.

One important means of growth for a lean organization is to rethink what can be done in continuous flow. We believe that many organizations try to do too much—in particular, to control suppliers of "key" technologies. But many organizations, like Wiremold before Art Byrne arrived, also do too little in the way of physical production because they imagine that scale economies require the purchase of many items from firms using enormous, high-volume machines in centralized plants to supply these items in massive batches to many customers.

Cord sets are a nice example. Wiremold products use enormous numbers of cord sets—the wire and plug ends used to connect surge protectors and other power conditioning devices to a power source. In the past, these were produced in large batches by cord set manufacturers supplying many firms like Wiremold across a range of industries. The problem was that Wiremold's production was constantly being jeopardized by the lack of the proper cord sets as sales trends changed. Wiremold would have brown when only white cords were wanted or have twelve-foot cords when the customer wanted fifteen-foot cords. Resolving these shortages often took two to four weeks due to the batch production methods of cord set suppliers.

When Byrne arrived at Wiremold he asked, "Why can't we produce cord sets, indeed at the same rate and in continuous flow with our end product?" And, as is usually the case, when Wiremold's tool engineers looked at the economics of cord set production, they found that the cost and time savings from using small, simple machines merged into the production sequence for the finished product not only overcame the problem of having the right cord set on hand as demand shifted, but also reduced the cost per cord set. So, Wiremold has begun to supply its cord set needs in-house. After all, Wiremold has plenty of excess space, plenty of extra people, and cash readily available to buy or make the necessary, simple machines.

Any would-be lean producer needs to look at this issue more generally, asking in each case, "What physical activities can we incorporate directly into a single-piece-flow production process?" Doing this also reduces the number of suppliers dramatically, making improvement of the remaining suppliers much easier.

Wiremold's second growth strategy has been to buy up small firms with allied product lines (and who use batch-and-queue methods) in order to increase the scope of Wiremold's product offerings. The first wave of inventory reductions at Wiremold (during the first two years of comprehensive *kaizen* activities) produced $11 million in cash. This money was used to buy five firms with complementary product lines generating $24 million in sales volume.

In essence, Wiremold was able to convert $11 million of *muda* (in the form of inventory), which would have cost about $1.1 million in carrying costs (assuming 10 percent as the cost of money and storage), into $24 million in new sales volume, which at a 10 percent operating margin generates $2.4 million in income. The $3.5 million income swing is highly significant for a company the size of Wiremold (with about $250 million in annual sales). Equally important, because the product lines of the five firms were complements to existing lines, Wiremold's sales force suddenly had a much more complete range to offer customers, which helps increase the overall growth rate.

The fact that Wiremold freed up approximately 50 percent of the space in all of its operations (excepting the central warehouse, which was totally eliminated) greatly helped the acquisition campaign. While Art Byrne's philosophy is to retain and upgrade existing management, several of the companies purchased were available because the family management could no longer run them successfully and wanted out. This provided consolidation opportunities.

For example, two of the firms purchased were consolidated into Wiremold's Brooks Electronics operation in Philadelphia. Prior to the acquisitions, the three companies had operated independently, utilizing 114,000 square feet of space. Now, the combined operation has increased its total sales significantly, yet is located in Brooks's original 42,000 square feet of space. Inventory has been reduced by 67 percent, the number of employees needed to run the combined operation has been reduced by 30 percent, and the surplus buildings have been sold.

In effect, Art Byrne and Wiremold are running a lean vacuum cleaner across the world of batch-and-queue thinking in the wire management industry. Each time Wiremold's vacuum sucks up a batch-and-queue producer it spits out enough cash to buy the next batch-and-queue producer! Because of Wiremold's need to grow to utilize freed-up resources, this process can and must be repeated indefinitely. (As we will show in Chapter 11, the first firm to adopt lean thinking in any industry can and must perform this same feat.)

The third and final element of the Wiremold growth strategy is the rapid introduction of new products, utilizing the new product development system with its dedicated teams and Quality Function Deployment methods described earlier. For example, the new product line described in Chapter 1 has increased sales by 140 percent, both by creating a new niche in the market and by stealing sales from competitors unprepared to match Wiremold's pace of product introduction.

All three strategies are critically dependent on the lean techniques introduced in production, order-taking, and product development. Indeed, the rapid introduction of these techniques *is* Wiremold's fundamental strategy. Art Byrne remembers that in previous jobs he had often wanted to go faster with application of these techniques but his senior bosses were usually more interested in massive long-range "strategic" planning efforts which they believed should take precedence. "To my way of thinking, this is exactly backwards. Introducing lean techniques in every business activity should be the core of any company's strategy. These provide both the opportunity and the resources to generate and sustain profitable growth. Profitable growth is what the strategic planners of the world are always seeking, but find hard to achieve because their company's operations can't deliver on their strategies."

The Box Score After Five Years

As we will see in Chapter 11, three years is about the minimum time required to put the rudiments of a lean system fully in place and two more years may be required to teach enough employees to see so that the system becomes self-sustaining. Wiremold's performance over the five-year period from the end of 1990 to the end of 1995 is therefore a good test of the potential of lean thinking. The results are quite striking.

To begin with product development, time-to-market has been consistently reduced 75 percent, from twenty-four to thirty months down to six to nine months. Sixteen to eighteen new products are being introduced each year (compared with two to three in the period through 1991), but the engineering/design headcount has stayed the same.

Several new computer-aided design technologies might be assigned some of the credit for these gains, except that these techniques were adopted in 1990–91, *before* the time-to-market and productivity gains. As we have emphasized throughout this volume, advances in hard technologies can be useful and in many cases are very important, but they are unlikely to yield more than a fraction of their potential unless they are incorporated in an organization which can make full use of them. By placing product designs in single-piece flow with a dedicated, multiskilled, co-located team and no interruptions, Wiremold has eliminated backflows and rework in the development process while also reducing manufacturing costs and dramatically spurring sales with products which accurately address customer needs.

The rethinking of order-taking, scheduling, and shipping has produced the same results. The old batch system, which needed more than a week to receive, process, and ship a typical order, now needs less than a day. Past-due orders are now less than one tenth of their 1991 level and continue to fall as Wiremold refines its pull system through all six product teams. Order entry errors have been practically eliminated, and misrouted or unanswered queries in the much smaller Customer Service Department have fallen from 10 percent to less than 1 percent.

In physical production, the results are exactly as we would expect. The amount of plant space needed to produce a given volume of product has been cut by 50 percent and productivity has been increasing at a rate of 20 percent per year. The time for raw materials and components to travel from the receiving dock to the shipping dock in Wiremold's plants shrank from four to six weeks to one to two days. Inventory turns have increased from 3.4 in 1990 to 15.0 in 1995.

To make this possible, Wiremold has continued to reduce setup times on all of its machines and to convert all production activities for its product families to single-piece flow. For example, punch presses with large progressive dies that used to take two to three hours to change are now changed in one to five minutes; rolling mills which took eight to sixteen hours to change over in 1991 can now be changed in seven to thirty-five minutes; plastic injection molding machines that took two to four hours to change over in 1991 can now be done manually by one Wiremold employee in two to four minutes. As a result, machines that previously shifted from one product to the next two to four times per week, now change products twenty to thirty times a day.

By aggressively implementing single-piece flow, operations requiring five to eight operators in 1991 are conducted with one to three employees today. By utilizing single-piece flow, JIT, and Total Productive Maintenance in the largest and most complicated assembly operations, productivity has been increased by 160 percent over three years. Equally important, single-piece flow has been instrumental in reducing defects by 42 percent in 1993, another 48 percent in 1994, and another 43 percent in 1995, almost at Wiremold's target rate of 50 percent per year indefinitely. At the same time, standard work, *takt* time, and visual control have been slashing accidents and injuries, which are down by more than half compared with 1991.

Putting the improvements in product development, order-taking, and physical production together, we find that sales per employee more than doubled, from $90,000 in 1990 to $190,000 in 1995. However, this and the figures just cited are all relative to Wiremold's previous performance. The indicators which truly count in the marketplace are sales, profits, and market share. Happily, between 1990 and 1995, Wiremold's sales in its core wire management businesses—owned before the lean vacuum cleaner was turned on—more than doubled in an otherwise stagnant electrical equipment market and profits of the whole firm—including the new businesses—increased by a factor of six. What's more, the growth rate, including acquisitions of related businesses, is picking up, in line with Wiremold's strategy of doubling its sales every three to five years for the foreseeable future.

All of these indicators are summarized in Figure 7.2, a "box score" for Wiremold under lean management.

Table 7.2: Wiremold Under Lean Management

	1990	1995
Sales per employee ($000s)*	90	190
Throughput time to produce average product	4–6 weeks	1–2 days
Product development time	3 years	3–6 months
Suppliers	320	73
Inventory turns	3.4	15.0
Space required (index)	100	50
Sales (index)	100	250
Operating profit (index)	100	600
Profit sharing (% of straight wage)	1.2	7.8

*Note that Wiremold's degree of vertical integration in manufacturing has increased substantially as items such as cord sets and plug outlets have been brought in from suppliers. Thus, value created per employee has increased even more if adjusted for the portion of the value stream under Wiremold's direct management.

But What About Firms with More Severe Problems?

The Wiremold story is extraordinary. The firm has been transformed in a remarkably short time and now gives every prospect of growing rapidly into an industrial giant. What's more, we could repeat this story in dozens of medium-sized firms we have discovered across the United States during research for this book.

Wiremold was a greater challenge than Lantech, given the age and narrow skills of its workforce, the stagnation of its core market, and the entrenched us-versus-them mentality of the old management and union, but is it still a fair test of lean thinking? After all, Wiremold has only fourteen hundred employees, operates primarily in two neighboring countries (the United States and Canada), and has relatively simple product and process technologies. What about the aging industrial giants who present the most visible managerial challenges? What about the publicly traded, mass-production firm with tens of thousands of employees, global operations, complex technologies housed in deep technical functions, and a complex network of component systems suppliers? Can lean techniques produce the same results, and in the same time frame? We turn now to Pratt & Whitney, which is truly the acid test of lean thinking.

CHAPTER 8
The Acid Test

On June 1, 1991, Mark Coran drove across town, from the Hartford, Connecticut, headquarters of the United Technologies Corporation, to the East Hartford headquarters of Pratt & Whitney, UTC's largest subsidiary and the world's largest builder of aircraft engines. UTC chairman Bob Daniell had just given him a new assignment—one for which his background as UTC's corporate controller and star cost-cutter seemed ideal preparation.

The problem at Pratt appeared to be structural and substantial but not desperate. As the world's largest builder of military jet engines[1] (accounting for a third of its total business in the 1980s), Pratt was faced with the end of the cold war, a reality to be confirmed shortly with the collapse of the Russian countercoup in August 1991. It suddenly seemed likely that much of the military engine business was gone for good.

In the short term, the loss of military business was offset by an extraordinary boom in orders for commercial engines. As the world's market-share leader[2] in commercial aircraft engines, Pratt had ridden the wave and racked up a record operating profit of $1.01 billion in 1990 on a record $7 billion of military and commercial sales. However, anyone familiar with the roller-coaster demand cycle in the commercial engine business knew that sales at this level couldn't be sustained for long, and in fact, orders for spare parts had already started to fall. Therefore, Mark Coran's job, as the new executive vice president for operations at Pratt, was to prepare the manufacturing operations in a massive company with 51,000 employees for a perhaps 10 percent permanent reduction in the size of the business, and to do this before the commercial-order boom collapsed.

As it turned out, Mark Coran had no time to work with. June 1991 would prove to be the peak month of production volume in the history of Pratt & Whitney, with "shop hours" of work—the conventional Pratt measure of production activity—running at an annual rate of 11 million. Soon, commercial jet aircraft orders, which had reached a record high of 1,662 in

1989, started to drop steeply as the world recession set in, falling to a low of only 364 in 1993.

Much worse for Pratt's finances, the airlines were dipping into their inventories of jet engine parts to repair their fleets, rather than ordering new parts from Pratt. Orders for Pratt spares were sliding rapidly by the fall of 1991, and by 1992 were running at only 63 percent of the 1989 peak. This was a crushing blow because spare parts account for the great majority of the profits of every aircraft engine company, due to the industry practice of selling new engines at substantial discounts in order to capture market share and create a large user base for their highly profitable, captive spare-parts businesses.

To make matters worse, Pratt and its two global rivals—General Electric in the United States and Rolls-Royce in the United Kingdom—were locked into spending large sums right away—$3 billion in total among the three firms—on development of the next generation of jet engines. These are the 84,000 to 100,000 pounds of thrust "monster motors" needed for the Boeing 777 and possibly for the proposed 600-seat Airbus A3XX. (The first of these, the Pratt PW4084, entered airline service on the Boeing 777 in June 1995.)

Because of its four-year product development cycle for new engine designs and the eighteen-month production lead time to physically build an engine once ordered, Pratt was helpless to respond to a dramatically changed world. Capital spending on the PW4084 was locked in and many engines were already under construction for customers who suddenly no longer wanted them. What was more, the airlines were sending a clear signal that they now wanted low-cost rather than high-performance engines for the 1990s, designs that could not be ready for years.

The first half of 1991 had continued the record profits of 1990, but the turn in the market was breathtaking and Pratt was suddenly heading for a $1.3 billion swing in its operating results within a year, culminating in a $283 million loss for 1992. As Coran remembers, "Very suddenly, just when I arrived, everything that could go wrong went wrong. Rather than a simple cost-cutting exercise to deal with a 10 percent drop in volume, I realized that we needed to rethink the whole business."

Fortuitously, just at the time of the crisis, several key executives in the UTC group—including Coran, George David, the president of UTC's Commercial and Industrial Group, and Karl Krapek, the president of Carrier—had become familiar with lean principles, mainly from the accident of being located in Hartford where Art Byrne was working steadily to apply them. In addition, Coran had a major advantage. He had never had an operating job prior to arriving at Pratt and therefore had none of the biases of the traditional mass-production operating executive. He therefore resolved to implement lean thinking as the best way to save Pratt & Whitney.

The attempt to do so represents the acid test. If Pratt can apply these principles quickly in a massive, publicly traded, high-tech organization with extraordinarily deep technical functions and life-or-death demands on product quality, *plus* all of Wiremold's problems, then literally any American firm can.

From the American System to Mass Production[3]

Pratt provides a wonderful example of the mass-to-lean conversion because the firm was centrally involved in creating the very mass-production system which eventually threatened its survival. What's more, it twice went through the progression from flexible start-up to stuck-in-the-mud mass producer that we saw at Lantech.

The original Pratt & Whitney Company was created before the American Civil War by Francis Pratt and Amos Whitney. These "Yankee mechanics" learned their trade as inside contractors at Samuel Colt's armory, opened in Hartford, Connecticut, in 1855. They produced the individual parts needed for Colt pistols and rifles, hiring their own workforce but using Colt's plant and tools.

Of central importance to our story, Pratt and Whitney also built many of the four hundred machine tools and the gauges Colt needed to achieve his goal of totally mechanized gun production in which parts were interchangeable and handwork for "fitting" was eliminated.[4] This approach became known as the American System, in comparison with the European System in which parts were individually handcrafted, with each part fitted to those already in place to create a completed product.

When Pratt and Whitney left Colt in 1860 to establish The Pratt & Whitney Company, they took with them a fundamental set of ideas about manufacturing practice which dominated the company until very recently. They believed that best practice called for the creation of special-purpose machines able to perform specific operations on specific parts, if possible at high speeds in high volumes. They further believed that machines performing similar types of tasks should be grouped together in departments and that simple logic called for setting up a machine to make a given part and then making a batch of them before setting up the machine for the next part. In other words, they built the precision machinery needed for the familiar world of batch-and-queue and, over time, organized their own factory in accord with these principles.

Over the next sixty-five years, Pratt & Whitney grew from a small workshop under the direct management of the two founders into a massive and highly successful organization. In its many departments focused on specific processes—casting, drilling, tapping, heat treating—Pratt produced the parts needed for lathes, grinders, millers, cutters, and borers for metalworking industries. The firm also pioneered extremely precise gauges to check the accuracy of parts and sold these along with their tools. Over the years, Pratt's machines became more complex and capable of more delicate and sophisticated tasks. In addition, advances in metallurgy made it possible to work prehardened metals so parts could be made to net shape without fear that subsequent hardening steps would interfere with interchangeability. However, the basic philosophy of production did not change.

The Rise of the Eagle[5]

In the summer of 1924, Frederick Rentschler resigned as president of the Wright Aeronautical Corporation in New Brunswick, New Jersey, because the bankers investing in the firm would not back his idea for a radial, air-cooled engine much larger than the revolutionary Wright Whirlwind just entering production.[6] He believed this large engine would swing the military away from liquid-cooled designs and make commercial aircraft economically viable for the first time.

With the encouragement of the U.S. Navy, Rentschler sought new financial backers and early in 1925 contacted Pratt & Whitney in Hartford, which was experiencing a slump in its business and found itself with excess plant space and tools. In addition, Rentschler noted that the Hartford area was full of Yankee mechanics skilled in operating the types of tools Pratt produced, precisely the tools needed for aircraft engine manufacture.[7]

Rentschler proposed to play a similar role at Pratt & Whitney to that Francis Pratt and Amos Whitney had played seventy years earlier at Colt's armory. He outlined a plan to set up a company within a company, using P&W's long-established name with its worldwide reputation for precision machinery. He proposed borrowing a million dollars from P&W's owners (in return for giving them 50 percent of the stock in the new Pratt & Whitney Aircraft Company)[8] and using Pratt's underutilized plant space and tools to make his new engine. An agreement along these lines was reached in July of 1925, and Rentschler was back in the aircraft engine business.

In 1925, aircraft engine design was still a trial-and-error process of building a prototype and testing it to failure, then strengthening the part that failed and testing the design again. Rentschler knew that the key to success was to attract the most experienced engineers in the industry and to quickly create a scaled-up version of the Wright Whirlwind that would work well on the first try. He soon convinced several senior engineers from Wright to join him at Pratt, and his new design team made spectacular progress.

In only nine months, Pratt's six engineers and twenty craftsmen (out of a total payroll of thirty including Rentschler) were able to design the new Wasp engine (with about two thousand parts), incorporate a key processing innovation to save weight,[9] build three prototypes, and have them ready for testing by potential buyers. When tested, the Wasp produced 50 percent more power (425 horsepower) than the Wright Whirlwind air-cooled engine and weighed only 650 pounds compared with the 1,650-pound Curtiss Liberty liquid-cooled engine producing the same horsepower. (The latter engine was the standard design used by the U.S. military at that time.)

Orders from both military and commercial customers poured in, and by 1929, Pratt & Whitney was the world leader in the tiny but rapidly growing aircraft engine business. The Pratt engine quickly established a reputation for reliability and was chosen for the next generation of commercial transports, beginning with the Ford Tri-motor. (The corporate logo—an American Eagle encircled by the words "Pratt & Whitney—Dependable Engines" —was affixed to every engine from the beginning and became familiar to airline passengers around the world.) In 1929, Rentschler was able to buy out the Pratt & Whitney machine tool company's interest and build a new headquarters and vast production facility in East Hartford.[10]

In the beginning, the three key activities of Pratt & Whitney—design of new products, order-taking, and production—could be accomplished effectively in an utterly simple organization. Indeed, the initial production run of two hundred Wasp engines for the U.S. Navy was designed and then built in one large room by a group of highly skilled machinists directly interacting with the tiny group of product engineers.

By the early 1930s, as production volumes grew from dozens of engines to hundreds, organizational differentiation like that undertaken by Lantech seemed to be required. Departments were created for each major activity— sales, engineering, prototype building and testing, quality control, purchasing, production, and service. Shops were created inside each department for specialized activities; for example, heat treatment, paint, and final assembly shops were established within the Production Department. As long as Pratt had only one product in development (the Hornet, which followed the Wasp and increased horsepower to 500) and only the Wasp in production, this system worked well without the need for cross-functional management.

However, by the mid-1930s, as Pratt expanded its product offerings to include the 300-horsepower Wasp Junior and the 800-horsepower Twin Wasp, and conducted experiments with a range of new engine configurations, something more was needed. A new position was created, the "project engineer" reporting to the heads of engineering and production. The project engineer was given the job of coordinating all of the activities involved in the design, production, and installation in the customer's airplane of a specific product line (such as the Wasp) as it moved through the host of departments and shops.[11] The project engineer was only a coordinator with no dedicated employees or resources—in today's terminology, a "lightweight" program manager[12]—but a startling conceptual leap had been taken, going far beyond a purely functional organization and common management practices at that time. Indeed, the concept of a project engineer to oversee the entire value stream foreshadows the lean principles described in this book.

As Pratt grew in the 1930s, changes were required in the factory as well. Initially, all of Pratt's metal-cutting tools had been relatively small machines—lathes, drills, millers, borers, etcetera—which could be lined up in the actual sequence of work flow.[13] For example, in 1936, the Cylinder Shop in the East Hartford plant was organized as follows:

> ". . . the first shop . . . immediately following the raw material inspection and the Experimental Department is the Cylinder unit. On one side of the main aisle are produced all of the steel cylinder barrels. On the other side are produced all of the aluminum alloy heads and in addition, the barrels are assembled to the heads, together with valve seats, bushings, valve guides and other minor parts, so that when the cylinder is ready to leave the department, it . . . proceeds directly to the Finished Stores Department. . . . with spare parts requirements, there are approximately 50 separate active cylinder designs. The equipment has been laid out so that the machines are in a sequence and the raw material proceeds in a straight line. Naturally, not all machines are required for any given cylinder."[14]

Similar shops had been created for master links and rods, crankcases, crankshafts, pistons, rocker shafts and valve guides, and cams. These sound remarkably like the work cells for complete components we have encountered throughout this volume and it is clear that Pratt's operations managers at that time had at least a rudimentary notion of flow: ". . .the scheme of production is a relatively simple one. Raw material is received by rail or truck through the front of the shop [factory] and then flows through the various manufacturing departments to the Finished storeroom at the rear."[15]

However, it is also clear that continuous flow was strictly limited to assembly and those activities which could be performed with simple machines. Special shops were created for machining parts made from magnesium and hard steel alloys as well as for heat treating, painting, and polishing. Because most of the parts in each completed component needed at least some of these treatments, much material was moved back and forth from shop to shop.

In addition, an elaborate system of centralized storage areas, tool cribs, and inspection stations was in place. It was taken as a given that quality inspections must be done independently of the primary workers by technicians reporting to the head of that function, not to the head of production, and that production could be more tightly controlled by storing tools, fixtures, and parts-in-process in a central location. These decisions meant that every part and every worker moved to a central storage area between each major production stage and during setups for the next job.

Finally, the philosophy of the company was that many defects could only be detected by test running of completed engines. Therefore, a row of test cells went across the entire rear section of the factory. Each engine was run for eight to thirteen hours, then completely disassembled. The parts were inspected, replaced as necessary, and reassembled. The engine was run for five to twelve more hours and then, in the event no problems were found, it was shipped.[16] As we will see, this final safety net created an "assemble it, then tinker until we get it right" mentality which persisted at Pratt until 1994.

Even with a relatively simple plant layout and product line, it is clear that, by 1936, Pratt was having to work very hard to get products through the system. An organized system of "shortage lists" and "follow-up" (read "hot lists" and "expediting") was in place and the assistant general manager was eager to tell an audience of peers that "high-tech" help with these tasks was already in place:

> It might also be of interest to point out that all the shortage lists and schedule sheets are made on electrically operated Hollorith machines[17] from punch cards made in the store room office so that these lists are printed and supplied to the Schedule Dept. and Follow-up Dept. in a neatly printed segregated form and without any delay. This is a major factor in the efficient control of shop production.[18]

In short, Pratt & Whitney was for the second time moving down the path from a lean workshop to a massive mass producer. The major innovation during the second transition was that the growing emphasis on complex tools housed in specialized departments could be supported by automated information management to shepherd products from raw materials to finished goods.

What should have been the major organizational innovation, the project engineer, never worked as planned. By 1939, Chief Engineer L. S. Hobbs was writing to his superiors, "It has been fairly obvious from the time of our institution of the Project Engineer system that in reality the system has not functioned as such."[19] Instead, the project engineer was a lightweight manager within the product development organization and products moved through sales, scheduling, production, and installation as best they could, with expediting by the centralized information management system but with no individual or team fully responsible for their progress.

World War II as the Engine of Mass Production

When the flow of orders increased from hundreds to hundreds of thousands in World War II,[20] Pratt made the final leap to mass production in the factory. A shortage of skilled workers meant that the new machine tools for the war effort were designed for very specialized tasks with only modest skill requirements by the operator. The number of shops, each assigned a narrow task, grew dramatically as the division of labor continued. What's more, the volume of orders meant it was often feasible to dedicate a given machine to a given part, perhaps for years at a time, so the need to do frequent setups was reduced. Work-in-process, travel within the production system, rework in the test department at the end of production, and managerial complexity all increased but engine output increased even more, and the latter was the only important consideration during the war.

Not surprisingly, by the end of the war, the mentality of the workforce had changed. Rather then being highly skilled, semi-independent craftsmen, the new workforce was much more narrowly trained, assigned to largely interchangeable jobs, and under much tighter management control. A conventional union had little appeal to the initial generation of craftsmen at Pratt, but by 1945, a different mentality and a different shop-floor reality created an environment in which the International Association of Machinists easily won an election to unionize the workforce.[21] A maze of work rules and grievance procedures soon followed as a mirror image of the division of labor instituted by management.

The second important consequence of World War II was in product development, where the growing complexity of designs and the need to extract ever more power from the basic radial engine configuration created the need for very deep technical functions. The key disciplines were materials scientists to develop new materials, structural engineers to address weight and durability problems, aerodynamicists to tackle the problem of airflow and drag through and around the engine, and mechanical engineers able to design and link together the thousands of individual parts required for each engine. Each of these specialties gained its own department within the vast Pratt & Whitney Engineering Division.

By the end of the war, Pratt's Wasp Major engine had thirty-six cylinders in four rows turning a single crankshaft. It was both supercharged and turbocharged to yield 4,600 horsepower (compared with the 425 horsepower of Pratt's original nine-cylinder Wasp). Along with the turbo-compound engine being developed at the same time by the Curtiss-Wright Company (the merged successor firm to Wright Aeronautical and Curtiss), the Wasp Major was one of the most complex pieces of purely mechanical apparatus ever devised.[22]

The Jet-Propelled Eagle

During World War II, the U.S. government directed Pratt and Curtiss-Wright to stick to what they knew: designing and building reciprocating piston engines. Other American firms with no previous experience in aircraft engine building (General Electric, Westinghouse, and Allison) took the lead in jet engines, and by war's end Pratt was the clear world leader in a technology with no future. What was worse, it was nowhere with the technology that did have a future—the jet turbine.

In 1946, P&W took a tremendous but unavoidable gamble by abandoning research on piston engines. It attempted to leapfrog its new jet-age competitors with a two-shaft, axial-flow jet engine considerably larger and more complex than any previously envisioned. Curtiss-Wright, by contrast, continued to elaborate the piston engine with its turbo-compound version for the Douglas DC-7 and the Lockheed Super Constellation in the early 1950s. C-W exited the industry when jet aircraft quickly supplanted these final iterations of the piston-engine airplane.

Jet engines were based on different principles but required many of the same technical skills in Pratt's existing engineering functions. The materials scientists were now concerned with managing the extreme heat in the hot parts of the engine. The structural engineers were concerned with vibration in complex turbo-machinery. The aerodynamicists were concerned with airflow past the compressor and turbine blades. The mechanical engineers were still concerned with detailed design of the thousands of parts, now rotating rather than reciprocating, aggregating to a complete engine. The big difference was that the nature of the knowledge was now highly scientific and the amount of effort required was much greater.[23]

Pratt's technical functions became deeper and more silolike as the nature of the necessary knowledge became more arcane. The project engineer system within product development groaned as the walls between functions thickened, giving rise to the "Pratt Salute" of arms crossed and pointing in opposite directions to assign fault to other departments for all design and manufacturing problems.

The production system, for its part, was remarkably unaffected by the jet age. Highly specialized machine tools—joined in the 1970s by truly massive special-purpose devices such as electron-beam and fusion welders—were located together in shops inside departments to feed batches of parts to a bench-assembly operation creating the finished engine. Every engine was then extensively tested and "tuned" (reworked) before shipment. The common joke was that the average part traveled farther inside Pratt's plants during production than it did in airline service. But there seemed to be no better way.

Pratt's leap to jet propulsion in 1946 produced a technical and commercial triumph by 1952. The P&W J-57 engine powered the American eight-engine B-52 bomber first flown in that year. Slightly modified and renamed the JT3, this engine captured 100 percent of sales for the initial versions of the four-engine Boeing 707 and Douglas DC-8 by the end of the decade. P&W quickly followed up with an entirely new engine, the JT8D, to power the entire world fleet of Boeing three-engine 727s and two-engine Douglas DC-9s and the initial versions of the two-engine Boeing 737. When the American military awarded Pratt a contract in 1970 as the sole source of the F100 engine for the F15 and F16 fighter planes, the company totally dominated the global aircraft engine business. Indeed, at the end of the 1960s, Pratt held a staggering 95 percent share of the world's commercial jet engine market (outside the Russian bloc) and nearly a 50 percent share of American military orders.

In the process of reaching industry dominance, Pratt and its organization fine-tuned and hardened the standard features of a mass producer. Tasks were finely divided in physical production, with specialized machines making batches of parts with long lead times. During product development lightweight team leaders coordinated engineering efforts across thick functional walls.

In fact, this system was adequate if not perfect for its environment. For decades aircraft engines were ordered by regulated airlines—competing on service but not on price—and by the military—interested in wartime performance with purchase price only a secondary consideration. In addition, advances in materials science and aerodynamic analysis meant that each new generation of product could achieve substantial performance improvements. As long as Pratt's technical depth could produce products which performed better than competing products, the fact that they took unnecessary time to design and manufacture, cost more than they needed to, and sometimes failed to perform properly when first launched in service could all be overlooked.

During this golden age the specification of new products at Pratt tended to work backwards. The senior engineers decided what technologies were ready for introduction in the next product generation and specified the engine configuration needed to utilize them. They then calculated the production cost and selling price as a sort of resultant. Once in production, costs were not rigorously tracked, but instead rolled up in the profit-and-loss statement in the president's office, by which point it was too late to do much about them.

By the 1980s, as airframe makers began to offer a choice of two or three engines (from Pratt, GE, and Rolls) for each wide-body aircraft type, the issue of production costs was confused further by the industry practice of progressively discounting prices for new engines, eventually to far below costs.[24] This was done in the hope that profits could be recovered from sales of spare parts, in particular turbine blades, where the engine makers had a monopoly. For example, the spares purchased by an airline during the operating life of a JT8D were likely to equal five times the initial purchase price of the engine. In this environment, the manufacturing side of the jet engine companies could easily get confused about the importance of costs —after all, the engines were being sold for prices far below any imaginable production cost.

The final feature of this mature mass-production system was its peculiar method of order-taking. The twenty-four-month lead times needed to physically produce an engine conspired with the three-year lead time needed to produce the complete airplane to create gigantic waves of orders for jet aircraft in the postwar era,[25] as shown in Figure 8.1.

As the airline industry emerged from recessions, aircraft customers signed up for planes and engines they might not need in order to ensure themselves a place in the production queue, while sales departments often made special

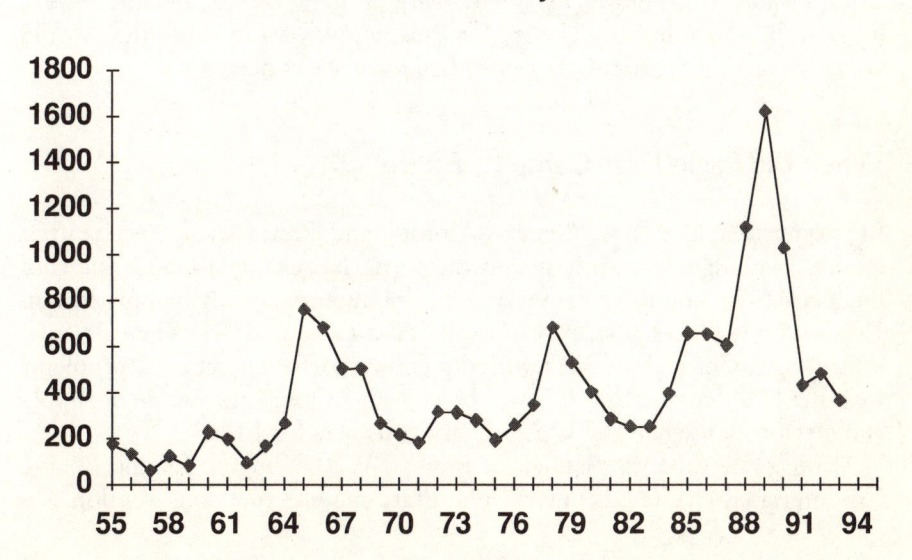

FIGURE 8.1: COMMERCIAL JET ORDERS

deals for large orders even when sales were booming in order to hold market share and protect the spares base. These orders could suddenly evaporate when the economy slumped, but waves of military orders often offset slumps in civilian demand and spare-parts purchases often went up when new engine deliveries slumped after 1980, as shown in Figure 8.2.

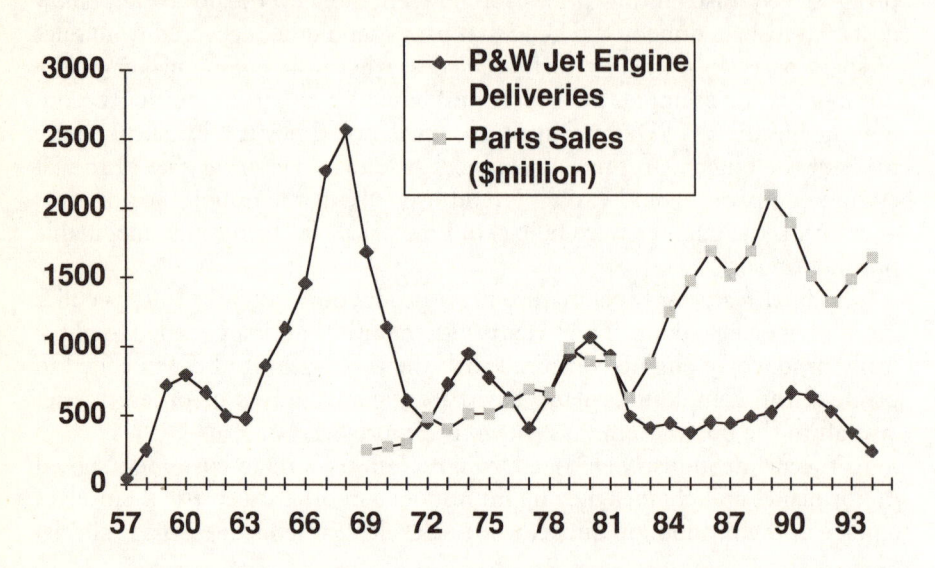

FIGURE 8.2: JET ENGINE DELIVERIES & PARTS SALES

In consequence, employment at Pratt was more stable than orders until 1990, as shown in Figure 8.3. There were periodic layoffs, but these were likely to be short and it was easy for Pratt employees to think they would always have a job, particularly if they had a few years of seniority.

When the Eagle First Came to Earth

Big companies like IBM, General Motors, and Pratt usually receive (but ignore) a number of warnings that the world has changed before the roof finally caves in, and the collapse of both the military and civilian markets in 1991 was not Pratt's first wake-up call. That came in 1984, when Pratt so infuriated military customers with its failure to fix operational problems with the F100 engine that GE was brought in as a second source of supply and given roughly half the U.S. military's business for F16s.[26]

At the same time, the launch of Pratt's PW2037 engine for the Boeing 757 infuriated airline customers. The Pratt engine's fuel consumption was

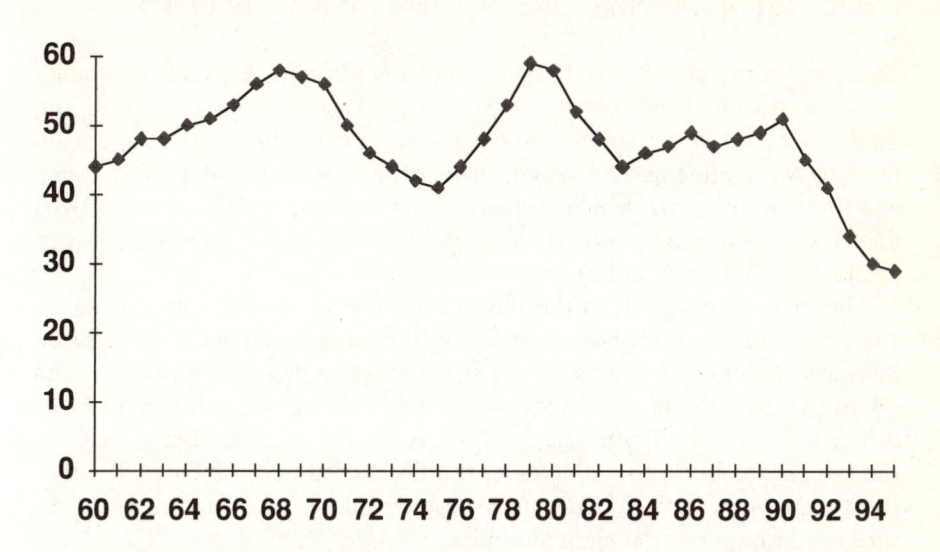

FIGURE 8.3: EMPLOYMENT AT PRATT & WHITNEY (000s)

superior to that of the competing Rolls-Royce RB211-535 and pricing was competitive, but the Pratt engine had a terrible record of mechanical problems, causing flight cancellations when introduced into service. As Fred Hetzer, the project engineer on the PW2037, remembers, "We were like the aging slugger in baseball who can still see the ball clearly but can't swing the bat fast enough to hit it. We knew about the problems in the PW2037 a year before they surfaced with commercial customers, and we worked day and night to fix them, but the organization was so sluggish and cross-functional communication was so difficult that we just couldn't get them fixed in time." As a result, Pratt had a superior engine ready first but wound up with only half the business in the forty-thousand-pound-thrust class.

Finally, Pratt badly misjudged the trend of demand in the jet engine market. Thinking that large, double-aisle aircraft were the primary growth market and reluctant to compete against its currently best-selling JT8D, Pratt failed to develop a replacement engine for the JT8D powering the 727s and 737s. When Boeing decided in the early 1980s to modernize the 737 by lengthening the fuselage to carry more passengers and updating its systems, Pratt did not have an engine with modern, high-bypass technology and lower specific fuel consumption. A consortium formed by GE in the United States and Snecma in France (CFM) did and ran off with most of the business for what became by far the world's best-selling airplane. When Airbus introduced the A320 to compete against the 737, 100-to-160 passenger, single-aisle jets became by far the largest aircraft market segment.[27]

Leaner but Not Lean; Necessary but Not Sufficient

Suddenly, in the mid-1980s, Pratt faced competition in all its major product categories and its market share began to slip across the board. In addition, total engine deliveries in the industry began to fall due to the shift from four- to two-engine designs. Pratt's management was not completely asleep and three innovations, which seemed earthshaking at the time, were introduced in response, one in production and two to bridge the chasm between product development and production.

The major innovation in the physical production system, introduced in 1984, was the "focused" factory with flow lines and business units organized by categories of parts. Pratt's factory structure emerging from three hot wars (World War II, Korea, and Vietnam) and one cold war was a hodgepodge of isolated shops working on parts with no relation to the part being made in the next shop. In one notable case, the distance traveled by a part within Pratt plants (not counting the distance traveled between plants) was measured and found to total eighteen miles.

In 1984, Pratt reorganized its facilities so each would take responsibility for a major category of engine parts. The massive North Haven plant would work primarily on turbine blades while the Southington plant would work primarily on rotors and discs and the Middletown plant would take on all final assembly work. Within each plant, activities were further reorganized so that many of the steps in the physical processing of each category of part[28] were grouped and lined up in a logical progression in a "flow line," insofar as tool designs would permit. Note that this is exactly the concept described in 1936 by Carlton Ward, the assistant general manager of production at Pratt.

Finally, each part category—for example, high-temperature turbine blades for the JT8D engine—was placed in a "business unit" whose leader knew the cost for his operations. The business unit head was fully in charge of getting the parts made at cost and on time, in accordance with the master schedule (now run off a massive computerized Material Requirements Planning system).

By the mid-1980s, Pratt's senior managers were aware that as the jet engine matured it was becoming sensible to apply similar design principles to "standard" design problems confronting each category of part. For example, why not specify the same grade of chromium for each high-temperature turbine blade, rather than fiddling endlessly with minor changes in the alloy mixture, which produced negligible improvements in performance? Yet it was apparent that Pratt's design engineers working on each category of part were doing the exact opposite. They were doing what comes naturally in engineering cultures far removed from the customer by endlessly reengineering designs in search of novelty and a better solution, no matter how slight the performance gain. In consequence, quite different production methods might be specified for practically identical parts, making their manufacture with the same tools in a common flow cell and business unit impossible.

As senior managers became convinced that many novel designs were novel in name only while costing the company millions in spiraling development and production costs, a solution emerged in the form of cross-functional teams[29] to evaluate each part and process widely used in Pratt engines—for example, turbine airfoils—and to agree on "norms" for part design, material selection, and processing techniques. If any engineer wished to adopt a new design approach differing from the norm, it was her or his responsibility to convince the relevant team that it was superior. In practice, this system greatly reduced the number of novel schemes proposed and reduced costs.

It was also apparent by the late 1980s that the project engineer system of weak coordination was producing poor results, so Pratt augmented this approach with a new system of Integrated Product Development (IPD) being promoted among major defense contractors by the U.S. Air Force. The idea was to form cross-functional IPD teams to resolve major cross-functional conflicts in engine development as they arose. This concept fitted nicely with Total Quality Management, a "program" also embraced under the moniker of "Q-Plus" by Pratt in the late 1980s.

The results of these three innovations were significant but not sufficient. Time-to-market for the new PW4084, entering airline service in June 1995, shrank from five years under the old project engineer system without IPD to about four years with IPD, and the number of engineering hours declined by a similar fraction. Meanwhile, the new plant layouts dramatically reduced travel of parts within the production system but each step in the so-called flow lines still had a pile of inventory on either side because each machine was producing large batches between setups. One worker was still assigned to each machine, often simply waiting for something to go wrong, and many machines were so massive and dedicated that they could not be incorporated into flow lines. What was worse, the system went steadily backwards after being set up in 1984 (just as it had in the 1930s) because Pratt management was not prepared to continuously realign its massive machines as processing steps and part designs changed. As a consequence, physical lead times for physical production of engines from initial order and raw materials to shipped unit shrank from the traditional twenty-four months to eighteen by the end of the 1980s, but then stagnated even though the actual time needed to physically make an engine using lean methods was only a few months or even weeks.

In 1991, Pratt was no doubt leaner than in 1983. (When the same part's journey through Pratt plants was plotted in this latter year, it was found to travel only nine miles rather than eighteen.) The shop floor looked much the way it had under Carlton Ward in 1936, when some measure of flow was still in place, and the IPD system had restored some of the engineering coordination possible when Pratt & Whitney conducted its affairs in one large room. These steps were necessary and are important to note here because they provided the critical foundation for what was required next, but Pratt was not yet lean enough to survive once the crisis struck.

The Creative Crisis of 1991

When the world as it was understood at Pratt came to an end in 1991, there was an understandable sense of confusion and a plethora of competing ideas about what to do.

One school of thought—the product engineers' dream—called for pursuing a technology strategy by pushing ahead rapidly with the next generation of technology. This was the Advanced Ducted Propfan (ADP), utilizing a truly massive fan with reversible blades at the front of the engine. This concept could pull the plane forward with increased fuel economy and stop it on landing by reversing the pitch of its blades and pushing air in the opposite direction.[30]

However, the jet engine had matured to such a degree that the most optimistic estimates about the performance of this engine indicated that it could reduce fuel consumption by 6 to 8 percent at the cost of greatly increased mechanical complexity. It would push passengers along no faster and would probably require more effort for airlines to maintain. In addition, the ADP was some years away from production and depended critically on development of new lightweight composite structures capable of containing the massive fan blades in the event one or more separated in flight.[31] Although the ADP was an attractive option to pursue over the longer term (particularly if energy prices increased and the American government helped pay for its development),[32] it could hardly provide a large enough leap in performance in a short enough time to save Pratt & Whitney.

Another school of thought—the financial planner's dream—called for progressively downsizing the company by finding risk-bearing foreign partners for each major component in Pratt engines. These components are the large fan at the front; the compressor behind it, which squeezes air into the combustion chamber; the combustion chamber, where the dense air is mixed with the fuel and ignited; the turbine, which recovers energy from the exhaust stream as it exits the combustion area (sending the energy backwards by means of a shaft through the center of the engine to turn the compressor and fan at the front); the exhaust nozzle; the nacelle, which streamlines the exterior of the engine, contains the thrust reversers, and captures errant blades; and the accessories, such as the fuel and engine control systems.

Under this approach, Pratt would become the "system integrator" bringing the parts together, but would need to design and make very little itself. Because many foreign firms would see participation in one part of the product as a route of entry for making whole engines, it would be easy to find foreign partners willing to cover the great bulk of development and capital costs. What was more, including foreign firms in new engine programs would help deal with the political problem of selling large orders to foreign military forces and state-owned airlines. The problem for Pratt would be the risk of being supplanted as the system integrator for subsequent engines by one or more of its risk-sharing partners, backed by foreign governments anxious to develop an aerospace industry. Indeed, this approach might easily become an involuntary exit strategy.

A third school of thought called for rethinking the three major activities within Pratt & Whitney—the development of new products, the selling and order-taking process, and physical production—in light of lean principles, beginning with physical production. The idea was simply to start with the existing company, rapidly make it much lower-cost and much more reactive to the voice of the customer, and then consider what to do next. This was the strategy pursued by Mark Coran for Pratt's manufacturing operations in the fall of 1991.

From Big to Not So Big and "Flow" to Flow

Coran's first step was to tackle the obvious fact that Pratt had much more space, tools, and people than it would ever need again, even if it did not improve its productivity. He therefore announced in December of 1991 that 2.8 million of Pratt's 11 million square feet of manufacturing space would be closed.

He next announced that every product, insofar as possible, would be made in continuous flow with the aid of lean techniques, in order to reduce costs by 35 percent (in constant dollars) over the next four years and to dramatically reduce the lead time for physical production from eighteen months down to four. He imported Bob D'Amore, a lean thinker from UTC headquarters who had learned lean principles as a participant in the turnaround of Harley-Davidson in the mid-1980s, to head the new Continuous Improvement Office. D'Amore reported directly to Coran and was given the task of going through the whole Pratt production system and devising a plan for getting every production activity into some type of continuous-flow cell. This was to be Pratt's initial *kaikaku*.

Next, Coran started work on drastically reducing Pratt's supplier base so a small number of suppliers in long-term relationships could be helped to improve their performance, and then dispatched process improvement teams to help with this task.

It was very hard work. Pratt's hourly workforce and middle managers had typically worked for the company all their lives and were often the children and even the grandchildren of Pratt employees. They had seen the ups and downs of the engine business for decades and many preferred to see the current situation as simply the latest cycle. It would surely pass and things could continue as before.

In addition, the ideas Bob D'Amore was pushing challenged everything the workforce had always known. For example, D'Amore wanted to regroup machines in tight cells so that one operator could tend two, three, or more machines, while practice at Pratt for generations had been that each operator was assigned his or her own machine. In addition, he criticized Pratt's bigger-and-more-complex-is-better tool philosophy as being directly contrary to lean thinking. What was more, Pratt couldn't guarantee anyone—hourly worker or manager—a job after the new system was in place.

Mark Coran remembers the situation as rather like an invasion in which a small party waded ashore and tried to take control of a vast territory simply on the strength of their new ideas. "It was hard, hard work, and by the spring of 1992, I was doubtful that Bob and I were going to make it. Every manager was *talking* about making a leap but nothing was actually happening."

Fortunately, Coran got critical help from a high place and had some good luck as well. George David had just moved up to become president of United Technologies and had completed his education in lean thinking. This was facilitated in 1991 by Art Byrne, who gave a talk to one of the periodic meetings of the presidents of all the UTC operating companies.[33] As David remembers, "He asked us a very simple question: Why did we need so many people, so much manufacturing space, so many tools, and so much inventory to get so little done? He argued that we miserably failed to manage our assets, compared with a best-in-class lean company like Danaher or Toyota. I was bowled over with the examples of waste he pointed out in our businesses.

"So I went over to see what he was doing at Wiremold in the fall of 1991 and it was a revelation. I've been an operating executive for years with a good feel for engineering but I've never run a plant. After I watched Art Byrne, Yoshiki Iwata, and Chihiro Nakao doing hands-on *kaizens* on the shop floor at Wiremold I saw the light." So when Mark Coran told David a short time later about his frustration in pushing lean thinking through Pratt, David immediately suggested that reinforcements should be sent in the form of Iwata and Nakao.

There was a problem, however. Shingijutsu was on the verge of signing a long-term contract to work for General Electric's Aircraft Engine Group. When David learned of this, he raced in person to meet Iwata and Nakao at a hotel in Simsbury, Connecticut, and emerged with a multiyear agreement for them to help Pratt instead. As David remembers, "I was thrilled. We desperately needed their knowledge and we snatched them away from GE at the last minute."

Lean Knowledge Is Not Enough

Nakao's initial foray into Pratt in May of 1992 was pure theater, like his visit to Jacobs Chuck. In the space of a week, a series of activities at Pratt's massive Middletown, Connecticut, plant were consolidated and the amount of effort, space, and tooling needed was reduced by 75 percent. Jaws dropped and a wide range of continuing improvement activities were started, which pushed D'Amore's original thinking much farther and faster. As Mark Coran noted later, "Our lean *sensei*'s central contribution was to change permanently our sense of what was possible and in what time frame."

However, the new engine market was now starting to "crater" along with spare-parts orders, which had continued to plummet since 1991. Even as D'Amore struggled to unkink the existing value stream, the amount of work to be done was falling by the day, from the peak of 11 million shop hours (on a annualized basis) sustained from June 1991 through July 1992 down to an annualized rate of 8.8 million by December 1992.

In addition, it was suddenly apparent that Pratt could not sustain the isolated operational gains it was making because there was no support structure for the new, compact cells. Bob D'Amore's Continuous Improvement Office had neither the resources nor the authority to follow up on the myriad of loose ends at the conclusion of every improvement exercise. Nor was it able to provide day-to-day coaching to line managers on how to maintain the progress already made and how to improve on it. Even more unsettling, it was becoming apparent that many managers were actively resisting the new system. As a result, the spectacular gains achieved in the one-week improvement blitzes were quickly being lost as managers and workers went back to old ways.

Finally, the accelerating rate of decline in sales suggested that the whole structure of the business, not just the size of the plants and the amount of hourly headcount, was no longer appropriate. Pratt as a whole desperately needed a rethink.

A Second Change Agent

George David was now carefully observing the crisis at Pratt because it was beginning to affect the whole of UTC. Historically, Pratt had been both UTC's largest operating unit and by far its most profitable one. The sudden loss of profits at Pratt was now driving down earnings and share prices at the parent UTC, despite good performance from the other businesses.

As David looked around in the fall of 1992, he decided he needed a second "change agent," someone to replace Pratt's president, who, as a lifetime P & W employee, understandably reflected the traditional Pratt way of doing business. There was one obvious candidate, forty-three-year-old Karl Krapek, then serving as president of Carrier. David knew that Krapek understood lean thinking and he also knew that Krapek would steamroller any obstacle to get the job done. "Mr. Krapek," he observes dryly, "is the most relentless executive at following up in the world today."

We have now heard many accounts of how the "light came on" as managers first grasped lean principles. Krapek's enlightenment started early but it was a full decade before he was in a position to put lean principles to work on a larger scale. After graduating from the General Motors Institute as an industrial engineer (and after a graduate degree at Purdue in the same subject), he was given increasingly important operating management jobs within GM. In 1979, at age thirty-one, he became one of the youngest assembly-plant managers in GM history, running the five-thousand-worker Pontiac assembly plant in Pontiac, Michigan.

One of the most striking features of the plant, as he noted upon first taking over, was the massive inventory of finished engines ready for installation. Indeed, in the deep recession beginning in 1979, the Pontiac plant had a three-month supply of engines. This caused endless difficulties and it occurred to Krapek that the plant's performance could be improved dramatically if engines were only made and shipped to the plant as actually needed.

He devised a plan to clear out the stockpiled engines and then get deliveries from the nearby Flint, Michigan, engine plant every thirty minutes, just as needed. The concept worked brilliantly as it got started and the positive effects on many aspects of plant operations were apparent. Krapek began to think of how to expand on this fundamental lean principle. Then disaster struck. A shipment from the Flint plant failed to arrive and the entire plant had to be shut down, sending the workforce home four hours early. Senior management at GM demanded to know how he had allowed his plant to operate with no buffers! Krapek was severely reprimanded and threatened with being fired.

After an appeal to a higher level, Krapek was allowed to continue in his job, but he suddenly understood what many managers have discovered before and since: It's impossible to introduce lean, flow concepts piecemeal and in an organization where the senior management doesn't understand them and where the very structure of the organization doesn't support them. When George David, then at Otis Elevator, called with a job offer, Krapek was ready to depart for an organization he hoped would be more capable of change.

Perhaps the most fortuitous aspect of moving to Otis was the firm's location in Hartford. When Krapek first heard about the events at Jake Brake and other Danaher companies in 1987, he took a personal interest. However, because nearly 80 percent of the "manufacturing" conducted by Otis was at the construction site where the elevator was being installed, it was not immediately apparent how to apply lean principles.

In 1990, when Krapek moved from Otis Elevator to become president of Carrier, he inherited a true manufacturing challenge where very nearly 100 percent of costs were incurred inside Carrier's plants or inside those of its suppliers. He was prepared by his early experience at Pontiac to accept lean thinking, so he consulted with Art Byrne on what to do and retained Iwata, Nakao, and their associates to help. They quickly began to convert the operation from departmentalized batches to cells for single-piece flow and made dramatic progress.

When the phone rang in the fall of 1992, Krapek was ready and able but unenthusiastic. "George David called and said, 'You have to go to Pratt.' We were doing great things at Carrier but were only part of the way along in the lean conversion. I said I wanted to stay. In addition, I told him, 'I came from General Motors and I don't want to go back to General Motors.' I meant that I did not want to return to a highly departmentalized, rigid bureaucracy trying to operate as it always had in a totally changed world. But David pointed out, 'You're no longer middle management as you were at GM. You will be the president. If you don't want Pratt to be General Motors, change it into Toyota or something even better!' I really had no choice, so I went."

When Krapek got to Pratt at the end of 1992, he knew he had to devise a dramatic plan to reconfigure the whole company and implement it very quickly. A new analysis of market trends showed that new engine sales had practically come to a halt and that shop load was heading for 5.4 million hours by 1994, down 50 percent from the peak in 1991–92, and that it might never rebound much from this point. However, the multilayered, departmentalized structure of the company, with all its associated overheads, had not changed and nothing flowed easily across the functional and departmental walls. What's more, Pratt was still trying to do too many things itself.

Krapek's first action was to speed up an evaluation already launched by Coran to determine which physical activities Pratt should be performing. As a result, sheet-metal forming, the fabrication of steel engine discs, and the manufacture of gears and gearboxes were soon contracted to suppliers.

Next, the two thousand parts in a jet engine were grouped into seven product categories—rotors and shafts, turbine airfoils, combustors and cases, nacelles, forged compressor airfoils, compressor stator assemblies, and general machined parts. The old organization structure, based on plants, was abandoned, to be replaced by a new system of Product Centers, one for each category of parts plus an eighth center for Final Assembly. Each was given a general manager reporting to Coran; at the same time, the centralized purchasing, quality assurance, and detail part design functions in Operations and Engineering were reconfigured, with most employees reassigned to the Product Centers. This meant closing a large fraction of Pratt's plant space and moving a substantial fraction of total manufacturing activities from one plant to another so that, for example, all of the production work involved in making a rotor could be conducted in nearly continuous flow in one large room in the Middletown, Connecticut, plant.

One great problem facing Krapek was that a massive, immediate reduction in Pratt's headcount was required and some facilities in Connecticut had to be abandoned. As Krapek noted, "Our weekly output of three large engines and six small engines plus spare parts can literally be fitted into my office. So why do we need ten million square feet of manufacturing and warehousing space?"

In addition, Pratt's union had to accept the notions of multiskilling, job rotation, multimachine operation, and continuous movement of jobs and work between plants to accommodate a changing value stream. By contrast, as of 1992, almost all hourly workers tended a single machine and simply watched as it conducted its operations, interceding to gauge parts as appropriate. They were constrained in their scope of activities by the division of labor into 1,151 union-sanctioned job classifications—or about one job classification for every ten hourly workers—and jobs were assigned on the basis of seniority through an elaborate "bumping-rights" system which often caused dozens or hundreds of job reassignments when the pattern of working was modified only slightly.

George David and Karl Krapek conducted a series of high-level negotiations in the spring of 1993 with the International Association of Machinists and with the State of Connecticut before finally reaching an agreement that hourly headcount would be reduced permanently (with total Pratt headcount falling from 51,000 in 1991 to 29,000 by the end of 1994), that flexible working and active participation in job design and the development of standard work would be the new norm, and that the state would help with retraining of displaced employees. In return, Pratt agreed that as long as the ambitious productivity improvement targets were met, no more work would be outsourced to suppliers or moved to Pratt operations in other states.

Remove the Anchor-Draggers

A second great problem facing Krapek and Coran, with the downsizing and labor-management issues resolved, was that Pratt's existing managers either couldn't or wouldn't operate the new Product Centers. Although three of the eight general managers of the new centers announced in August 1993 were from outside Pratt (all with cellular manufacturing experience at General Electric) and knew what to do, many of the Pratt old-timers couldn't seem to get it.

The problems were of two sorts. At the North Haven turbine airfoil facility, the longtime Pratt managers really threw their hearts into change and attempted a very ambitious move from batches to single-piece flow, but they simply didn't have the skills to pull it off. The backlog of orders grew alarmingly and customers began to scream.

Traditionally, managers caught in this predicament at Pratt were fired. (The slogan among parts plant managers had always been, "Ship on time and you'll be fine [even if you're shipping junk].") However, Mark Coran was determined to instill a new spirit in which managers who earnestly tried to manage in a new and better way would not be punished for failure. He therefore moved the plant management to other jobs in Pratt and went outside to find Ed Northern, a former GE manager with extensive experience in lean operations, to carry through the lean transformation.

The other problem was that some general managers simply refused to change their methods. In the spring of 1994, Chihiro Nakao had conducted some more theater in the main assembly hall at Middletown when he walked in, quickly looked around, and then told the general manager of assembly that the time needed to assemble an engine would need to be reduced from thirty days to three, the space needed would have to be cut in half, the amount of human effort required would need to be cut by two thirds, and inventories of parts and engines on hand would need to be reduced by more than 90 percent. What was more, assembly of these massive machines would need to be converted from bench assembly to a moving track in continuous flow. And it would be necessary to start immediately.

The general manager and his deputies argued that this was simply impossible to do quickly for such a complex product in such a complex organization as Pratt & Whitney, using highly skilled craftsmen to correct mistakes made farther upstream. They promised to work on a long-term plan, but it was apparent that nothing would happen soon; shortly afterward they were asked to leave Pratt and Bob Weiner, another Pratt outsider, was installed as the new general manager.

Over the three-year period from 1991 to 1994, the number of senior managers in Pratt's Operations Group was reduced from seventy-two to thirty-six, and only seventeen of the remaining thirty-six were with the company as of 1991. To make the lean transformation happen in this extraordinarily in-grown organization it proved necessary to replace a much higher fraction of the management than in the other organizations we have examined.

Fixing the Two Key Activities

Because Pratt conducts two basic activities in physical production—fabrication of individual parts from castings or forgings and assembly of these parts (along with many more from suppliers) into complete engines—the physical transformation of Pratt that followed comes clearly into view if we look for a minute at what Ed Northern did to transform turbine blade fabrication and what Bob Weiner did to transform final assembly.

The Billion-Dollar Room

Ed Northern manages a single, vast room, in North Haven, Connecticut. It measures 1,000 feet by 1,000 feet and can be easily surveyed from the front door. In this room in 1991, 1,350 Pratt employees used 600 sophisticated machines to manufacture $1 billion worth of turbine blades and guide vanes for jet engines.[34] Because jet engines themselves are usually sold below cost —indeed, in some recent cases, practically given away—and because the frequently replaced guide vanes and turbine blades (often called the "razor blades" of the jet engine business) are sold at multiples of their actual production cost, what happens in Ed Northern's room largely determines whether Pratt & Whitney can make a living.

The problem in 1993 was that North Haven's costs were so high that Pratt was not garnering enough profits on its "razor blades" to sustain its "razor" (jet engine) business. Even worse, in the effort to switch over to lean methods, North Haven was failing to meet its shipping schedules. Back orders were soaring and Pratt's cash flow was severely affected. When Ed Northern first walked into the room in August 1993, he faced a life-or-death task.

Ed Northern's light, like many others we have met, came on in the early 1980s, in his case at the GE Aircraft Engine Group where he first tried single-piece flow. He had some early successes but eventually left for Inter Turbine, a small firm making a living by repairing damaged turbine blades for airline maintenance shops. Inter Turbine, however, lacked the technology base or financial resources to move beyond a narrow market niche, so when Mark Coran called in the summer of 1993, promising Ed complete freedom to institute lean methods at North Haven, he readily accepted.

The room Ed Northern first saw was laid out in the "flow" lines introduced in 1984, except that changing part designs and processing needs had run head-on into the massive, immovable processing machines so that whatever flow had been achieved in 1984 had become a series of dams and stagnant pools by 1993. In addition, he found truly appalling quality. In many processes, first-time-through acceptable quality was less than 10 percent. Parts were going through the system over and over and it was impossible to meet the production schedule.

Northern immediately took a series of steps which we hope are becoming familiar. He assessed his headcount and determined that he would never need more than 60 percent of his 1,350 workers. At the same time, he surveyed the line management and found that a substantial fraction would never be able to work in the environment he planned. A onetime headcount reduction and rapid management changes quickly produced a personnel level he knew he could defend and a management team he could lead.

The next step was to construct a value stream map for the entire turbine blade and guide vane business, to reconfigure the business units so they precisely channeled the flow of value for each product family, and to reconfigure every machine so it could be moved easily at any time by the workforce.[35] Then it was time to move the machines into cells laid out in the same sequence as processing steps so that single-piece flow occurred in as many cases as possible.

The results were immediate and startling. Over the next two years, overdue parts fell from $80 million to zero, inventory was cut in half, the manufacturing cost of many parts was cut in half as well, and labor productivity nearly doubled. In short, just what we would expect. But then it was time to confront the monuments problem.

The Monument of Monuments

Lean thinkers call a "monument" any machine which is too big to be moved and whose scale requires operating in a batch mode. (They would apply the same term to a hub airport, a centralized computer system, or a centralized engineering department—to anything that requires batches to operate and can't be moved as the value stream changes.) Because continuous improvement and changing processing requirements require the continuous movement of machines, monuments are evil, another form of *muda*.

The monument in question in North Haven was the massive, $80 million complex of twelve Hauni-Blohm blade grinding centers, custom-made in Germany and installed in 1988 as Pratt attempted a high-tech leap over its competitors. The idea had been very simple: Totally automate the grinding of the blade roots for turbine blades using the world's fastest and most sophisticated equipment.

Prior to the late 1980s, North Haven had placed each blade in a series of nine grinding machines for a total processing time of eighty-four minutes. The objective was to grind smooth the base of each turbine blade so it would snap snugly into the disc holding it in the engine. This approach was labor-intensive, due to direct labor needed to watch machines, conduct frequent gauging, and position parts in machines. In addition, indirect effort was needed to move parts from machines to storage areas and then to the next machine, now located some ways away in the degraded "flow" system.

The new system used twelve massive grinding centers with twelve axes of motion. Each center could perform all of the grinding steps formerly accomplished by nine machines and could grind a blade in only three minutes. What was more, the centers were fed and unloaded robotically and the parts were carried to and from storage by an automated guided vehicle (AGV). No direct or indirect hourly labor was required.

Still, there were problems. The forces applied to the blade by the grinders were so severe that the blade was destroyed if held by standard positioning fixtures which concentrated the tremendous forces at a few points on the blade. Therefore, it was necessary to encapsulate the blade, excepting the area to be ground, in a low-temperature alloy to spread the forces evenly over the whole blade. Encapsulation, conducted by a machine with a large vat of liquid metal, expensive molds, and long changeover times, was a batch process, so it was necessary to take the encapsulated parts to a storage area until they were needed by the Blohm machines. This task was handled by AGVs and an automated storage and retrieval system. (ASRS, as it was called, was identical in concept to the system Toyota tried in its Chicago warehouse, as described in Chapter 4.)

There was another problem, which was that the low-temperature alloy had to be removed from the blade after the grinding operation. Several sophisticated steps were then required to ensure that the alloy was truly removed. (Even microscopic amounts of the alloy would cause hot spots and rapid failure of the blade once in the engine.) These involved X-rays and an atomic absorption process using caustic chemicals to test for trace elements of alloy. This last step created a serious environmental problem of radioactive acids as well. The system as it was installed is shown in Figure 8.4.

FIGURE 8.4: AUTOMATED BLADE GRINDING CENTER

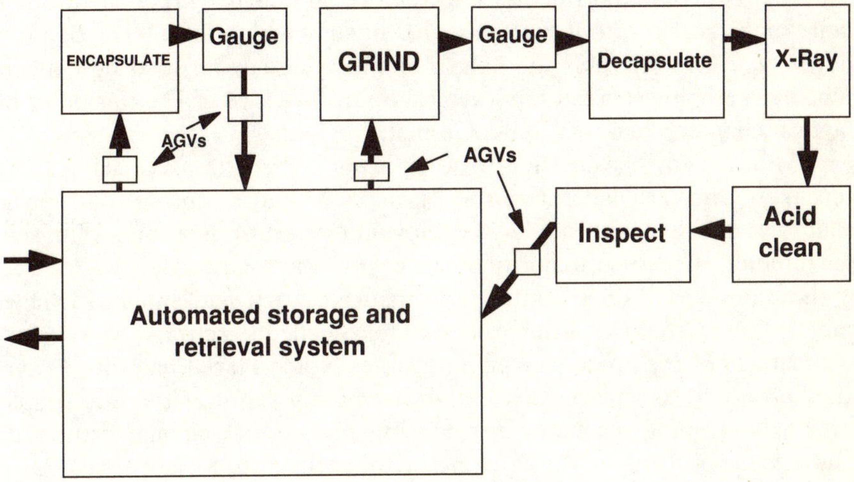

[Figure 8.4: Flow diagram showing ENCAPSULATE → Gauge → GRIND → Gauge → Decapsulate → X-Ray → Acid clean → Inspect, with AGVs feeding to/from an Automated storage and retrieval system]

Yet another problem was the changeover times needed for the Blohm grinders to convert from one family of parts to another. Because of the need to move layer after layer of automation away from the grinding tool in order to change it, eight hours were needed for every changeover. The planners of the system apparently believed that extremely long runs of parts would be possible—permitting completely automated mass production—but in practice Pratt needed to make small numbers of a wide variety of blades. The long changeover times prevented this and required the production of large batches of each part type instead.

Finally, many of the direct and indirect hourly workers had to be replaced by skilled technicians who debugged the elaborate computer system controlling the entire process (with two thousand parameters). In the fall of 1993, when Ed Northern arrived, there were twenty-two technicians tending to the needs of the Blohms, a number not much smaller than the number of direct workers needed for the old manual system.

In the end, eight of the nine processing steps involved in the new system, plus the AGVs and the ASRS, added no value whatsoever. What was more, the three minutes of grinding time were accompanied by ten days of batch-and-queue time to get from the beginning of the encapsulation process to the end of the deencapsulation process. And the complex machinery was temperamental. Even at the end of a lengthy learning curve, it was difficult to get past about an 80 percent yield. A disappointing result from an $80 million investment.

We mention the Blohm grinders because they exemplify a whole way of thinking which is now obsolete. The twin objectives of speeding up the actual grinding—what you might think of as a "point velocity" within a lengthy process[36]—and the desire to remove all hourly workers because of their "high" cost per hour both miss the fundamental point. What counts is the average velocity (plus the length of the value stream) and how much value each employee creates in a typical hour. (We'll return to this point in the next chapter when we discuss German "technik.")

Initially, North Haven tried to work around the Blohms, placing their step in the turbine blade fabrication process behind a "curtain wall" so it would not interfere with single-piece flow in the rest of the process. But this was difficult. The great majority of the cost in the total process was caused by the Blohms, and their erratic performance thwarted attempts to achieve smooth flow in the rest of the process. They needed to retire.

By late 1994 the process mapping team at North Haven had the answer. They proposed to replace each Blohm machining center with eight simple three-axis grinding machines utilizing ingenious quick-change fixtures to hold the blades firmly in the machines without the need for encapsulation.[37] Each cell would have one worker to move parts from one machine to the

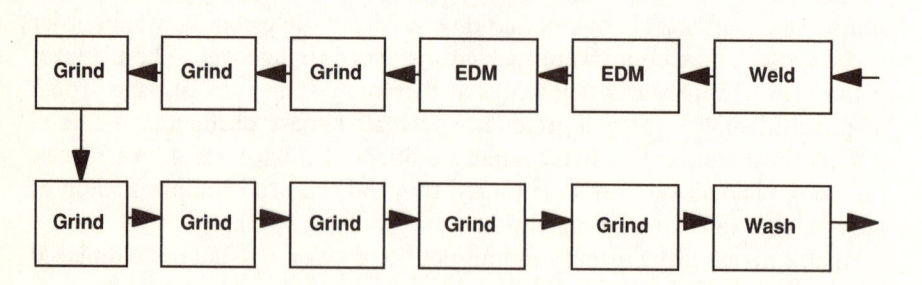

FIGURE 8.5: LEAN BLADE GRINDING SYSTEM

Cell with eight 3-axis grinding machines and two electrostatic discharge (EDM) machines (drawn to larger scale than Figure 8.4)

next by hand, standardize his or her own work, gauge parts to check quality, change over each machine for the next part type in less than two minutes (with the help of a roving changeover assistant), and make only what was needed when it was needed.

By increasing actual processing time from three minutes to seventy-five minutes, the total time through the process could be reduced from ten days to seventy-five minutes. Downtime for changeovers could be reduced by more than 99 percent (as each of the nine machines was changed over just-in-time for the new part coming through). The number of parts in the process would fall from about 1,640 to 15 (one in each machine plus one waiting to start and one blade just completed). The amount of space needed could be reduced by 60 percent. Total manufacturing cost could be cut by more than half for a capital investment of less than $1.7 million for each new cell. No encapsulation; no AGVs; no automated storage warehouse; no deencapsulation with its environmental hazards; no computer control room with its army of technicians. Lean thinking at its best, as summarized in Table 8.1.

TABLE 8.1: LEAN VERSUS MONUMENTAL MACHINING

	AUTOMATED BLOHM GRINDER	CHAKU-CHAKU CELL
Space/product cell (sq. ft.)	6,430	2,480
Part travel (ft.)	2,500	80
Inventory (average per cell)	1,640	15
Batch size (number of blades)	250	1
Throughput time (sum of cycle time)	10 days	75 min.
Environmental	Acid cleaning & X-ray	No acid, no X-ray
Changeover downtime	480 min.	100 sec.
Grinding cost per blade	1.0 X*	0.49 X*
New blade type tooling cost	1.0 X*	0.3 X

*The exact numbers are proprietary. The point is that the cost of blade grinding has been cut in half, and the cost of tooling for a new part has been reduced by 70 percent.

When the first of the new cells—called *chaku-chaku*, meaning "load-load" in Japanese—went into operation at the beginning of 1996, North Haven was on its way to a cost and quality position, using a high-wage, high-seniority workforce with "simple" machines in a World War II vintage (but immaculate) building, that no one in the world could match.

The latter fact led to the final step of Ed Northern's strategy. He knew that lean thinking would continually free up more workers and resources. Unless he proposed to continuously hand out termination notices and explain to his work teams why they should continue to put their hearts into working for a company with no apparent interest in protecting their jobs, he needed to find more and more work and find it quickly. (Ed calls this "keeping hope alive.")

One method was to take work back from suppliers, particularly when incorporating it into North Haven's activities permitted more continuous-flow production. (It's important to understand that this is a one-way process. A firm cannot take work in to suit its needs, then subcontract it again later to suit new needs. The suppliers won't be there.) A second approach was to enter the turbine blade repair business in collaboration with other units of Pratt, taking on engine overhaul work, another world of batch-and-queue thinking awaiting a lean awakening. Both concepts were well along in planning in 1995.

The Continuous-Flow Engine

Meanwhile, in the final assembly hall, Bob Weiner energetically introduced lean principles from the moment of his appointment in July of 1994. As Ed Northern's former deputy at GE Aircraft Engines, it's not surprising that the steps he took were exactly the same: Cut headcount at the outset to a level which can be sustained for the long term, replace managers who couldn't adjust to the new system, standardize work, and deal with quality problems so work could flow continuously. Then introduce continuous flow.

As Weiner and his team studied the situation, they realized that Chihiro Nakao's goal of a three-day engine was achievable, but would require a substantial investment to combine the assembly hall with the test cells[38] in another building. However, simply by introducing modular assembly—what Nakao called a "head of the fish" system, where major components flowed in fully built up and ready to snap together from the Product Centers representing the bones of the fish—they found that by mid-1996 they could cut the time through the process from thirty to ten days and substantially reduce assembly effort. The key was to place the engines on an imperceptibly moving track and to eliminate all backflows and rework caused by upstream quality and delivery problems. The new system brought the component modules and tools to the assemblers in kits so they didn't waste time on "treasure hunts" and provided the assemblers with a simple PC-based system beside the assembly line to display assembly diagrams and instructions relevant to a each step.

A Concurrent Quality Crisis

The final problem to be overcome was a concurrent quality crisis. In 1993, Pratt was besieged with customer complaints about the rate of in-flight shutdowns of its engines, the primary measure of quality in the aircraft engine industry. Indeed, several airlines were threatening to cancel future orders or even to go to court to claim damages, and it appeared that Pratt's in-flight shutdown rate on some engines was running at seven times the level of GE's and Rolls's.

In one way, this seemed impossible. In 1992, Pratt's Quality Assurance Department had 2,300 employees and everything that could be checked was being checked. But on another level, it was clear that the quality movement of the 1980s had gone badly wrong. Quality Assurance had become the classic corporate superego or nagging nanny, checking up on production employees to make sure they hadn't taken shortcuts on quality in order to meet production targets. This, of course, created a very negative, reactive reputation for Quality Assurance.

It also meant that production managers cheerfully referred any alleged quality problem to a series of Material Review Boards (MRBs), which decided long after the problem was first noticed whether parts rejected by Quality Assurance were acceptable to ship. In the early 1990s, Pratt was conducting 66,000 MRBs per year. But 90 percent of the time the part was finally accepted for shipment "as is" because the variation from the formal specification was deemed to be insignificant. This was after lengthy delays and hours of meetings to assess the problem.

One solution to this problem was to completely reorganize the Quality Assurance Department under a new head, Roger Chericoni, a longtime Pratt product engineer with no quality background and no baggage. Only 150 employees were retained in this function, with the rest being assigned to business units on the plant floor to directly resolve quality issues as they arose.

The other solution depended once more on George David, who had in fact been enlightened about lean thinking twice, the first time several years before meeting Art Byrne. In the 1980s, in his position as head of Otis Elevator, he had also been chairman of the Nippon Otis joint venture with Matsushita in Japan. In 1990, David had faced a crisis when Matsushita announced that it felt it could no longer put its National brand name on the joint venture's products.

"The head of Matsushita called me to point out that our product had for years been breaking down four to five times more frequently than competitor products from Hitachi and Mitsubishi. Given our history of product performance in Japan, I knew our relationship was moving toward a breach. I also knew that if Otis couldn't compete with Japanese firms in Japan, we would eventually lose to them elsewhere."

Fortunately, Matsushita offered help in the person of Yuzuru Ito, Matsushita Electric's corporate quality wizard who was dispatched to help fix the quality problems at Nippon-Otis. "We needed his help because we were determined to make our products the best, but we just didn't know how. It was that simple."

With Ito advising an Otis task force on its quality problems, "call back rates" (elevator industry-speak for the number of times per year an emergency call is required to fix a malfunctioning elevator) began to plummet and eventually fell below those of Hitachi and Mitsubishi. David notes, "There's no doubt Ito-san single-handedly saved our relationship with Matsushita and made it possible for an American firm to succeed in Japan against the best Japanese competitors."

When Ito retired from Matshushita shortly after this episode, George David pleaded with him to help Otis full-time, and when David moved up to president of United Technologies in 1992, he expanded his mandate to all UTC companies. Eventually, he even convinced Ito to move his home from Japan to a site near UTC corporate headquarters in Hartford.

When Ito started to help with manufacturing operations at UTC, it turned out that his techniques were based on flow thinking. He used "turn-back rate charts" to see how many times mistakes interrupted the flow of production. He always found that continuous flow and perfect quality were achieved together, after rigorous root-cause analysis and corrective action.

"When the Pratt quality problems at the customer level began to reach a crisis in 1993, I knew there was a perfect interlock between Ito's quality philosophy and Shingijutsu's flow philosophy. I realized that together they were an unbeatable combination, so I told Ito to devote all of his time to helping Roger Chericoni at Pratt."

After targeting the root cause of the in-flight shutdowns, Ito turned his attention to the general problem of backflows in the Pratt production system. For example, at North Haven, the 10 percent of product getting through a typical manufacturing process the first time was soon raised to practically 100 percent.

The Bottom Line in Physical Production

By mid-1995 Pratt had totally revamped its entire physical production system. The mass-production, batch-and-queue, "tinker till we get it right" philosophy built up over nearly 140 years was gone and the company was completely converted to a flow organization stressing first-time quality with no backflows.

The MRP system formerly driving the movement of every part had been reassigned to the task of long-term capacity planning and long-lead-time delivery of parts from suppliers not yet lean, while flow through each module center and into final assembly was regulated by a simple pull system.

The eighty business units, one for each major part family within a component module, were reconfigured both organizationally and physically. Business unit heads were given a much simpler "scoreboard" with a much smaller fraction of allocated costs (in a system similar to the Wiremold approach we saw in Chapter 7), and told to manage costs down through *kaizen* activities. Production engineers and quality experts were physically reassigned—that is, their desks were moved—from "upstairs" in plant offices or at engineering headquarters to space on the shop floor within or immediately adjacent to the work cells.

In the end, all seven thousand of Pratt's machines were moved (some many times), and by the end of 1995, every production process in the entire Pratt & Whitney Company had been *kaikaku*ed and *kaizen*ed at least once, with the objective of creating a continuous-flow cell for each part with substantially zero in-process inventory within the cell. At the same time, a host of improvements in quality thinking spurred by Ito were leading toward "certification" of every process—that is, redesign of activities and adjustment of tools—so that first-time quality with no backflows for rework could be absolutely assured.

As a result, throughput time fell from eighteen to six months (with a near-term target of four); inventories of raw materials, work-in-process, and finished goods on hand fell by 70 percent and are still falling; the massive central warehouse which formerly stored all parts moving between production steps was closed; referral of quality issues to MRBs declined by more than half (with a goal of eliminating MRBs by the end of 1996); and unit costs for a typical part have fallen 20 percent in real dollars even as production volume has fallen by 50 percent. This last measure is perhaps the most important because in the old days of mass production, Pratt's unit costs would have gone up by 30 percent or more in this circumstance and the company would probably have been forced to merge or exit the industry.

The original goal of a 35 percent cost reduction, set at the beginning of the crisis in 1991, remains in place but the collapse in demand, which only began to reverse in mid-1996, means it's going to take a bit longer to get there. In addition, while Pratt's own costs have fallen dramatically, the supply base, which now accounts for more than half of Pratt's total production costs, must now be *kaikaku*ed and *kaizen*ed to the same extent as Pratt. In many cases this will involve rethinking whole industries, in the fashion of the glass example in Chapter 5, in order to introduce time and cost savings and quality improvements back through casting and forging all the way to base metals.

The Point of No Return

The critical moment for the lean transformation at Pratt occurred in the spring of 1994. Although upstream aspects of production were steadily improving, problems in delivering engines to customers meant that nothing was visible to the external world. The unwillingness of the old management to adopt to the new system and errors in implementation at various points upstream caused Pratt to deliver only 10 percent of its engines on time, a historic low.

As Mark Coran remarked later, "I kept wondering that spring why I still had a job in a situation where the results of our efforts weren't yet showing up. But in retrospect, the secret was simple: George David and Karl Krapek, unlike most senior executives in American firms, actually understood what I was doing. They realized we were going to have steps backward along with our steps forward and that the trick was to hold an absolutely steady course."

As soon as the new management was in place in final assembly in the summer of 1994, and once Ito's quality initiatives began to show results and a pull system from final assembly began to replace MRP across the company, everything came around very quickly. What was more, the new general managers began to clamor for more time and help from Bob D'Amore's beefed-up Continuous Improvement Office, and Pratt was able to sustain the gains made in the weekly improvement blitzes. However, it had taken more than three years of hard work to reach a point where turning back became unthinkable.

The Next Leap

In 1995, Karl Krapek began to turn his attention to the rest of Pratt, where the slow-moving, inward-looking product development and engineering system had changed only modestly. The organization chart at this point, with the new Product Centers fully in place, looked unsettlingly like a Rubik's Cube (as shown in Figure 8.6). Any new product program involved an elaborate matrix of divided responsibilities and loyalties between the product development teams (called Propulsion Centers), Pratt's core technologies in seven Component Centers, and the detailed engineering and manufacturing in eight Product Centers.

In simplest terms, developing a new product meant defining the whole (thrust, weight, fuel consumption, product cost) in a Propulsion Center, engineering and producing each major component in Component Centers, and then engineering the individual parts making up each component in the Product Centers. The project was essentially handed off twice between three massive organizations reporting separately to the president. Confusion and high costs were the predictable results.

The solution, which was announced at the beginning of 1996 but which will take all of 1996 to implement, is to create much stronger Propulsion Center product teams, including dedicated component design engineers. The de-

FIGURE 8.6: PRATT & WHITNEY ORGANIZATION, 1994

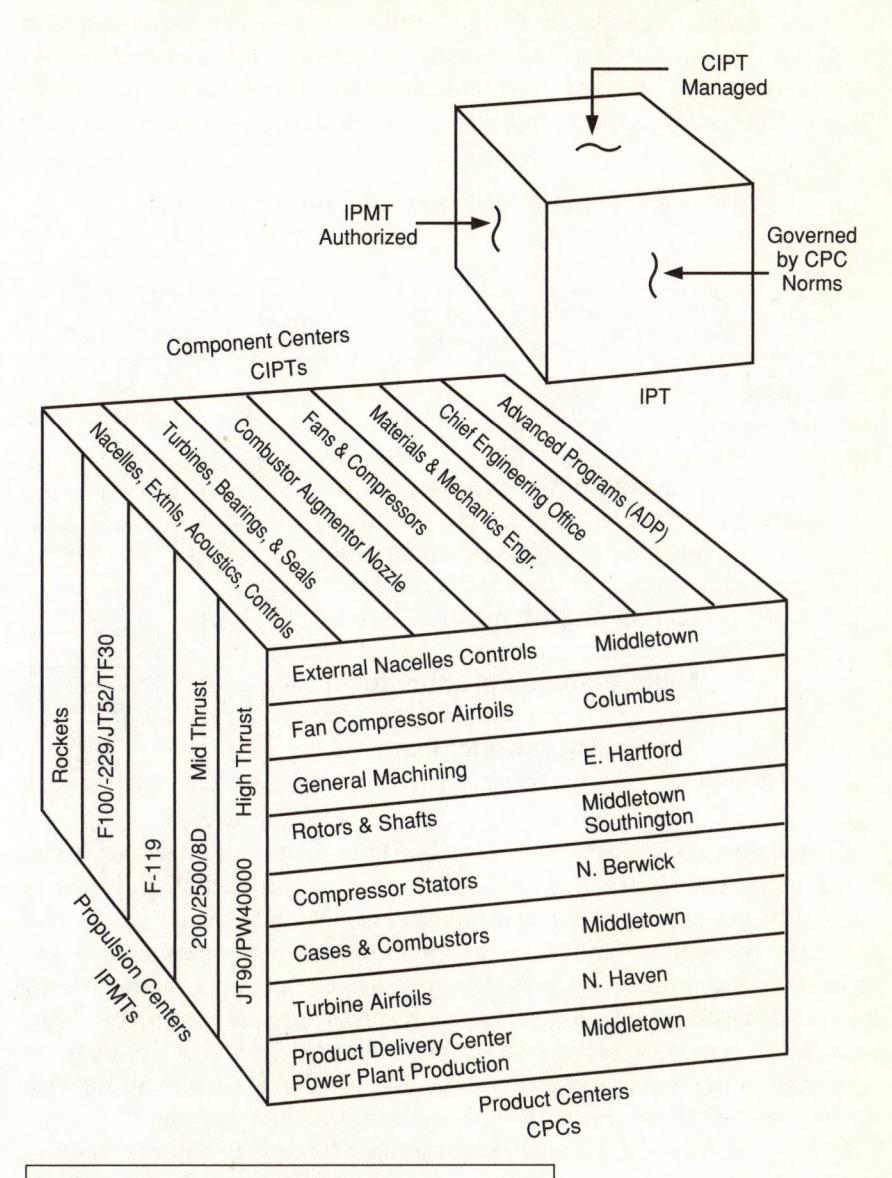

IPT	= Integrated Product Team
CIPT	= Component Integrated Product Team
IPMT	= Integrated Product Management Team
CPC	= Charter Part Council
GESP	= Government Engines & Space Propulsion
LCE	= Large Commercial Engines

sign engineers remaining in the Component Centers will be relocated either to a small engineering function charged with developing new design methods and technologies, as well as maintaining design standards and engineering systems, or to one of the new Module Centers created out of the current Product Centers to give a "lean organization" as shown in Figure 8.7.

FIGURE 8.7: PRATT & WHITNEY ORGANIZATION, 1996

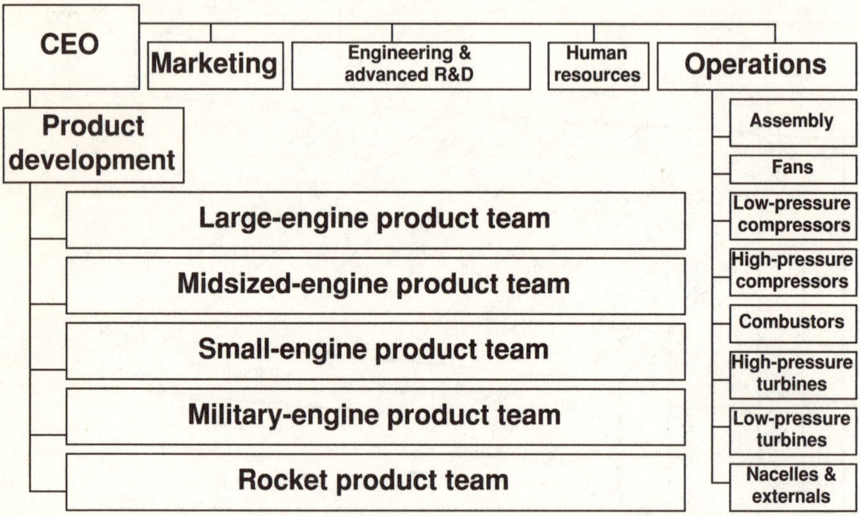

```
CEO ── Marketing ── Engineering & advanced R&D ── Human resources ── Operations
 │                                                                    ├── Assembly
 └── Product development                                               ├── Fans
       ├── Large-engine product team                                   ├── Low-pressure compressors
       ├── Midsized-engine product team                                ├── High-pressure compressors
       ├── Small-engine product team                                   ├── Combustors
       ├── Military-engine product team                                ├── High-pressure turbines
       └── Rocket product team                                         ├── Low-pressure turbines
                                                                       └── Nacelles & externals
```

The Module Centers will essentially be stand-alone businesses with vice president/general managers responsible for current production and for supporting the development of new products. Each Module Center will be able to completely engineer and fabricate one of the seven modules making up a jet engine: fans with their cases, low-pressure compressors, high-pressure compressors, combustors, high-pressure turbines, low-pressure turbines and nozzles, and nacelles and externals. These will be delivered at precisely the right time to the Assembly, Test, and Delivery Module, which will snap the engine together almost instantly and deal with the final customer.

At the same time this change is taking place (and there will no doubt be problems initially, just as there were in physical production), Pratt is rethinking sales and service. As product development lead times fall to perhaps two years and physical development times fall below the current target of four months, it will be necessary to eliminate the waves of sales, followed by droughts, which make it impossible to run Pratt on a level schedule even though end-user demand—that is, airline passenger miles—is very stable.

Lessons and Next Steps

What are the lessons of the Pratt experience for American managers who want to create lean organizations? The most obvious is to begin with what you do right now. Don't think about what your workforce doesn't know, their lack of education, or their age. Don't think about the past obstructions of your union or the need for good quarterly "numbers." These barriers exist mainly in your own head.

Instead, line up your value-creating activities in a continuous flow to improve quality while taking out large blocks of cost. This can be accomplished quickly if you have the knowledge—it has taken three years in the massive Pratt production system, which provides the toughest possible test—and it never requires significant sums for new equipment or plant. As costs fall, freeing up resources for new initiatives, it is much easier to see what to do next, including up-skilling your workforce.[39] Indeed, a fundamentally different cost structure for existing operations will often suggest a very different strategy from what would have been pursued if the old cost structure had been taken as a given. (Pratt, for example, could never have dreamed of competing in the engine overhaul business with its pre-1992 cost structure.)

For Pratt, of course, the effort to convert to lean principles is still only part of the way along. Physical operations have been dramatically transformed but product development is only now being revamped and the marketing and sales system are still to be made lean.

Even when this is done, strategic issues will remain of whether the aircraft engine business itself is viable and how the company will need to deploy its activities around the world to better correspond with its markets of sale.[40] One promising path is to rethink whether Pratt is in a product or service business, and the dramatic reduction in costs plus lean thinking may make it possible for Pratt to take the engine overhaul and maintenance business away from independent repair firms and from the hard-pressed airlines as well. For example, can flow thinking make it possible to perform a complete engine overhaul overnight at a Pratt facility so that planes never need to be out of service and airlines do not need to keep large stocks of spare parts plus a considerable number of spare engines?

In any case, by starting with what it does now, Pratt has dramatically reduced its costs while pleasing its customers. As a result, operating results rebounded from losses of $283 million in 1992 and $262 million in 1993 to profits of $380 million in 1994 and $530 million in 1995, even as sales continued to sag. Pratt has bought the time needed to complete the introduction of lean principles across the business and given itself considerable latitude in deciding what to do next.

What About Lean Thinking in Alternative Industrial Traditions?

We've now looked very carefully at American firms, through a progression of age, size, and complexity, from Lantech, with simple process technologies, a 20-year history, 400 employees, and $70 million in sales, to Pratt, with complex technologies, a 140-year history, 29,000 employees, and $5.8 billion in business. The same principles were applied in each case and they have produced remarkable and sustainable results.

But what of the other great industrial traditions? Our previous book found a large audience in Germany but also met with great skepticism among German managers and workers. Because we had no examples of lean practice to point to in Germany at that time, it was possible to contend, at least in theory, that lean thinking simply could not work, that some other approach was needed for revitalizing German industry. We now turn to an example in Germany which proves this theory dead wrong.

CHAPTER 9

Lean Thinking versus German *Technik*

On July 27, 1994, something remarkable happened in the assembly hall of the Porsche company in Stuttgart, Germany. A Porsche Carrera rolled off the line with nothing wrong with it. The army of blue-coated craftsmen waiting in the vast rectification area could pause for a moment because, for the first time in forty-four years, they had nothing to do. This was the first defect-free car ever to roll off a Porsche assembly line or to emerge from the earlier system of bench assembly.[1]

This first perfect Porsche—and there have been many more since—was a small but highly visible milestone in the efforts of Chairman Wendelin Wiedeking and his associates to introduce lean thinking into a veritable industrial institution—indeed, into one of the great symbols of the German industrial tradition. This struggle has not been easy and some aspects of a totally lean system remain to be implemented, but it is now also apparent that it can be done. What's more, there's already evidence that when lean concepts are married to the strengths of the German tradition, embodied in the concept of superior technology, or *technik*, a remarkably competitive hybrid form can emerge.

Modest Success to Rags to Riches

The Porsche company was founded in 1930 by Ferdinand Porsche, the legendary Austrian engineer who subsequently designed the Volkswagen Beetle.[2] Porsche had been the technical director of Daimler (up until the time of the merger creating Daimler-Benz) but found it better to work on his own, so he established the first independent automotive engineering consultancy in Germany.

Through the 1930s and during the war, Porsche was a small engineering firm but one of a very high order, often called on to tackle the toughest problems and to propose dramatically different solutions. The Beetle design was the most famous, but there were many others.

At the end of the war, young Ferry Porsche took over from his father in extremely difficult economic conditions. The large firms Porsche had consulted to were in ruins and demand for automobiles was severely depressed by postwar economic chaos. Nevertheless, the younger Porsche not only made plans to continue the engineering consultancy but was also determined to begin manufacture of cars carrying the Porsche name. He soon set up a small workshop in the village of Gmünd, Austria, near the family's ancestral estate, and the first copy of the first Porsche, called the Model 356, was produced there by hand in 1948. Forty-six additional cars were built over the next three years by craftsmen, mainly using hand tools.

It was soon clear that if Porsche wished to become a "real" car company it needed to relocate back to Stuttgart to be near suppliers, and for the engineering consultancy to be near its most likely clients. The first Porsche 356 from the company's new location in Zuffenhausen, a Stuttgart suburb, was completed in the spring of 1950 and the current Porsche company was truly launched.

The company was initially very simple, consisting of an Engineering Department and a Production Department. The latter had a small machine shop which fabricated and assembled parts to modify the basic VW engine used in the 356. The bodies for the car were constructed and painted by Reutter, a traditional coach builder located nearby. They were then dropped onto a chassis assembled largely from Volkswagen Beetle parts at stationary assembly stands in Porsche's small assembly hall. Finally, they were inspected, test-driven, adjusted and repaired as appropriate, and shipped.

Soon a racing team was added, which hand-built one-of-a-kind race cars, sometimes in the week between races, and the engineering consultancy expanded dramatically, working mostly for Volkswagen but for other car companies as well. Therefore, the product engineers continued to be the dominant voices in the firm even as the Porsche car manufacturing business became profitable and grew dramatically.

By the early 1960s, Porsche had gradually substituted parts of its own design for the original VW parts and engines. However, the 356 design was getting old and it was hard to explain to the public that the car was no longer merely a VW with a different body and refined suspension. So in 1964, the 356 was replaced by a completely new car, the 911.[3]

The new car was entirely a Porsche in terms of its engine and body components, and the building of the body was taken over from Reutter. Porsche was therefore becoming a much more integrated and complex company. This was even more the case when it was decided in 1969 to launch a lower-priced car line in collaboration with Volkswagen. The 914 model was succeeded in 1976 by the 924, assembled at the Audi plant at Neckarsulm, using many Audi mechanical components including an engine reworked by Porsche.

A second up-range car, the 928, was added in 1977, along with a new moving assembly track in the Zuffenhausen assembly hall. This eventually handled the entire model range when the 968 successor model to the 924 and 944 models was moved there from Neckarsulm in 1991.

The Porsche company therefore grew steadily as a specialist automobile manufacturer. By the mid-1980s, it had become spectacularly profitable as its products became an essential possession of young entrepreneurs and investment bankers making large sums in the worldwide economic boom of the Reagan era and the Japanese Bubble Economy. In 1987, its 8,300 employees produced 22,000 911s and 928s at Zuffenhausen, joined by 26,000 944s from the Audi plant. Sales of cars and engineering services combined totaled $2 billion.

Porsche as a Classic German Firm

A snapshot of the Porsche company in the years up to the late 1980s shows a classic German model of successful industrial capitalism, especially of a successful *Mittelstand*, the mid-sized engineering firms which have been the great strength of the German economy. First, control of the company was continued firmly in family hands into the third generation through the creation of a series of holding companies. As Ferry Porsche remarked in his memoirs, "If it had been my intention to set up a company for the purposes of speculation, I would have given it a fancy name from the beginning, because I refuse to sell my own name."[4]

Management passed into professional hands in 1972 when Ferry Porsche decided that no one in the next generation of Porsches and Piechs (his sister's married name) should succeed him as managing director. However, the Porsche and Piech families continued to look after the firm just like their ancestral estate at Zell am See in Austria, as a sort of perpetual enterprise of which they are the stewards. The accounts of the firm were replete with reserves for the future which subtracted from short-term profits but built a cushion to safeguard the firm's independence in times of trouble.

A second feature marking Porsche as a classic German firm was the intense focus on the product itself, its superior performance being the firm's most important concern. American firms were typically run by executives with a financial background who were comfortable dealing with public equity markets, and Japanese senior executives tended to have had experience in a variety of functional areas within their firms, but the senior managers of Porsche, as is typical in Germany, were brilliant product engineers who believed strongly that the firm with the best product, designed by the best engineers, would win in long-term competition. Indeed, even the legal name of the firm seemed to express this sentiment: Dr. Ing. h.c. F. Porsche AG.

In 1969, the product engineers were moved from Zuffenhausen to a new facility at Weissach, twenty-three kilometers out in the countryside from the Stuttgart-Zuffenhausen factory. Here they conducted all of Porsche's engineering consultancy work, designed new Porsche models, and built prototypes both for new Porsche models and for outside firms. The major investment in Weissach and the distance it created between the product engineers and the production staff in the plant were both symbolic of what was most important at Porsche.

Yet a third feature of Porsche marking its German pedigree was an organization chart which was entirely departmental and steeply hierarchical. Each major activity was conducted inside its own organizational unit and every important decision was referred upward through layers of management. Careers moved up the departmental hierarchies as well.

Activities needing the input of many departments typically proceeded by passing the work—a design, an order, a physical product—from one department or function to the next, usually with delays due to the batch-and-queue nature of the system.

A special feature of Porsche's organizational structure introducing a rigidity beyond the German norm was the consequence of its second business as an engineering consultancy. Auto companies and large-parts makers often wanted help on narrow technical problems. The knowledge base to address these problems—suspension dynamics, engine vibrations, or minimum-weight body structures, for example—required deep depositories of know-how in each department, ready for sale to outside organizations. However, this meant that Weissach experts could often ignore the need for cross-department cooperation on Porsche's own car designs while making handsome profits for Porsche on outside sales of engineering services.

The Porsche supply base was yet another typical feature of German industry. By the late 1980s, the firm had 950 suppliers even though Porsche — like most *Mittelstand* companies—made many of its parts itself. This meant one supplier for every nine employees and a vast Purchasing Department to manage them. Relationships were typically very long term, dating in many cases to the start of production in Stuttgart in 1950. They were also very cooperative, so much so that Porsche would sometimes become involved in bailing out small suppliers on the edge of bankruptcy.

Looked at another way, supplier relations were in-grown and reactive. Porsche was primarily interested in the contribution of purchased parts to the performance of the car, not in their cost, the frequency and reliability of deliveries, or the percentage of defective parts. It was taken as a given that Porsche would perform 100 percent inspection on incoming goods and maintain a vast warehouse to guard against supply disruptions. In any case, Porsche lacked the technical skills to help its suppliers improve their production operations and the firm accounted for only a tiny fraction of the sales of its larger suppliers. In addition, the long-term relations between individual purchasing agents and supplier sales representatives had created a "don't rock the boat" culture in which change was very difficult.

Perhaps the most striking feature of Porsche in the late 1980s was its craft culture, which went far beyond the norms of Mercedes and the other big German engineering-based industrial firms. From the early days Porsche had stressed its craftsmanship, and many workers with craft skills migrated to Porsche from the larger firms in reaction to the introduction of deskilled high-speed, mass-production operations with short work cycles. As a result, the skill level on the floor was truly extraordinary and Porsche, unlike the other big German engineering firms, had almost no recent immigrants on its payroll. In the late 1980s, nearly 80 percent of Porsche's employees in the engine shop and 54 percent of the workers in the assembly hall had completed the rigorous three-year German apprentice program, meaning that the ability of the workforce to rectify technical problems was probably unmatched anywhere in the world. These workers had deep knowledge of materials and individual operations: what methods to use to fabricate aluminum, what type of machine to use to cut steel, at what speeds to run machines, and at what rate to feed parts into machines.[5]

Its craftsmen were organized in hierarchical layers, just like the rest of the organization. Primary workers reported to *gruppen meisters* (work group leaders), who reported to *meisters* (foremen), who reported to *ober meisters* (group foremen) in each work area. As Ferry Porsche noted with approval in his memoirs, by 1960, one employee in five in production activities was involved in supervisory tasks.[6] The hierarchical nature of the craft skills within the workshop also meant that Porsche was very late in adopting the German version of teamwork, often called autonomous group work. These ideas were first tried only in 1991 after Porsche had entered a deep crisis.

Porsche management stressed long work cycles (typically twelve to fifteen minutes) and workers could take pleasure in seeing much of a product come together. In the early years it was even possible for one worker to assemble a whole engine and sign it. This practice, while not the norm, continued to be the ideal for most Porsche workers.

Unfortunately, much of this craft work was *muda*. For a start, the factory was not closely involved in designing the product, so Porsche designs were high on performance but very low on manufacturability. Far from protesting, the skilled workers resolutely shouldered the burden of making unmakable designs, often by means of lengthy adjustments and fitting of parts.

Similarly, it was accepted that many parts from suppliers would be defective, would arrive late, and might even be the wrong part altogether. In the late 1980s, 20 percent of all parts arrived more than three days late, 30 percent of deliveries contained the wrong number of parts, and ten thousand parts in every million were defective and unusable. By contrast, as shown in Table 10.1 in the next chapter, Toyota's first-tier suppliers in Japan deliver about five defective parts per million and make 99.96 percent of deliveries exactly on time with exactly the right number of parts. It was the job of the Porsche purchasing staff to find the defects with the help of one hundred inspectors and to somehow get hold of missing parts with a legion of expediters.

In the paint booth, it was accepted that "first-time-through" quality would not be very high due to contamination which was very difficult to eliminate, but that skilled paint specialists could eventually bring the body paint up to an acceptable level. Finally, once the moving track was installed in 1977, the operating philosophy was to quickly put all of the parts on the car, then test them as a system after the car rolled off the line, and to rectify errors in a highly skilled troubleshooting and rework process which eventually produced a product with a world-class low level of defects as reported by customers. Skilled work was, therefore, defined as the ability to operate specific machines and to diagnose anomalous conditions during long work cycles and to take corrective action on a case-by-case basis.

This approach was also applied in downstream portions of the product development system, where manufacturing engineers took product designs and either figured out how to make them or secretly reengineered them. Even worse, as anyone owning a Porsche has learned, there was practically no attention to serviceability because the voice of the service bay was simply not represented in the system. In consequence, a whole new skilled trade was created around the world, the Porsche mechanic.

The Porsche craft tradition had great appeal to many workers because of the long cycles and the opportunity to put every worker's considerable skills to the test continuously. It also appealed to many managers because there was no need to take up the messy and unpleasant task of confronting the cause of problems at upstream stages and rectifying them at the source.

The Crisis

Porsches offered truly superlative performance based on a deep technology base and filled a special niche in the market for true sports cars just tame enough for everyday use. As a result, it was difficult for either giant car companies or tiny specialists to challenge Porsche. Sales volumes were too low for the high-volume car companies to bother with, reaching only 33,000 units in the peak year for the highest-volume model, the 944, and never exceeding 21,000 for the upmarket 911. Smaller specialist firms who might have copied Porsche's product philosophy and worked cost-effectively at low volumes lacked the necessary product technologies built up over many years by Porsche's consultant engineers.

However, the firm's special situation also created vulnerabilities. For one, any model change was truly a "bet-the-company" proposition, so over time the management erred on the side of caution. The 928 model was planned as a replacement for the 911, but when customers balked at the 928's front-engine, rear-drive design, the 911 was simply continued indefinitely alongside the 928. Another critical vulnerability was that a majority of those with the money and desire to buy a Porsche in the 1980s lived in North America, while practically 100 percent of Porsche's value was created in or near Stuttgart.

As a consequence of these vulnerabilities, the boom year of 1986, when Porsche sold a record 50,000 cars (62 percent of them in North America), gave way to nightmare years from 1987 on as the mark strengthened against the dollar and sales steadily tumbled. By 1992, Porsche was selling only 14,000 cars worldwide and only 4,000 rather than 30,000 in North America. (Table 9.1 provides a production history of the Porsche Company.)

The initial response of the Porsche and Piech families to the sales collapse was hesitation. They hoped it was only a blip in the market. However, by 1989, the downturn was continuing and the family brought in new senior management with a marketing focus to revitalize sales. Arno Bohn, the marketing director of the Nixdorf computer company, was hired as the new chairman to concentrate on rethinking the model range.

Bohn's efforts mainly produced an intense and protracted conflict over just what a Porsche should be. Widely divergent concepts were proposed, ranging from the revival of an "affordable" Porsche like the 914 and the 924 to a four-door model to be sold as an ultra-high-performance luxury sedan, to an even more performance-oriented Ferrari-type two-seater, following on the success of the 959 model in 1987.[7] In any case, new products were five or more years away due to the sequential nature of Porsche's development system.

Because sales of the mid-priced 944 had collapsed after 1987 but demand for the more expensive 911 and 928 continued to be fairly stable until 1992, Bohn concluded that the mid-priced market ought to be left to the Japanese, with new Porsche offerings concentrated on the highest-priced segments of the market. In other words, Porsche was to pursue a classic segment retreat

TABLE 9.1: PRODUCTION HISTORY OF PORSCHE CARS (000s)*

Year	911	928	968	Contract†	Zuf. Tot.	912/914	924/944‡	Porsche Total
1965	3	0	0	0	3	6	0	9
1966	4	0	0	0	4	9	0	13
1967	5	0	0	0	5	6	0	11
1968	8	0	0	0	8	6	0	14
1969	13	0	0	0	13	4	0	17
1970	14	0	0	0	14	23	0	37
1971	14	0	0	0	14	16	0	30
1972	15	0	0	0	15	25	0	40
1973	15	0	0	0	15	28	0	43
1974	10	0	0	0	10	17	0	27
1975	9	0	0	0	9	9	0	18
1976	12	0	0	0	12	1	20	33
1977	13	2	0	0	15	0	22	37
1978	10	5	0	0	15	0	22	37
1979	11	5	0	0	16	0	21	37
1980	10	4	0	0	14	0	15	29
1981	10	4	0	0	14	0	18	32
1982	12	5	0	0	17	0	20	37
1983	13	4	0	0	17	0	31	48
1984	12	5	0	0	17	0	28	45
1985	16	5	0	0	21	0	33	54
1986	18	5	0	0	23	0	31	54
1987	17	5	0	0	22	0	26	48
1988	13	4	0	0	17	0	9	26
1989	14	3	0	0	17	0	10	27
1990	21	2	1	0	24	0	4	28
1991	17	1	3	5	26	0	0	26
1992	10	1	5	4	20	0	0	20
1993	8	1	3	2	14	0	0	14
1994	16	0	2	2	20	0	0	20
1995	18	0	0	1	19	0	0	19

Source: Dr. Ing. h.c. F. Porsche AG.

* The production figures in this table do not exactly match the sales figures given in the text because of substantial lags in adjusting output to changes in sales.

† Porsche assembled the 500E luxury sedan for Mercedes and the Audi 80 Estate with four-wheel drive.

‡ The 924 model was replaced by the updated 944 model in 1983.

strategy, and the decision was finally made in 1990 to develop totally new two-door and four-door models with the engine in the front and rear-wheel drive to replace, by 1996, the 911, 928, and 944 and move Porsche further upmarket in price.

In the meantime, it seemed essential to cut the costs of production by about 30 percent to address the currency realignment between the dollar and the mark, yet no one inside the company seemed up to the task. The solution was soon found in thirty-eight-year-old Wendelin Wiedeking, the chairman of Glyco, a German auto parts maker. Wiedeking already knew the company and its problems because he had been manager of the paint and body shop at Porsche ten years earlier, before leaving for Glyco, where he had had great success, rising quickly to chairman, and had demonstrated both extraordinary energy and the courage to undertake dramatic change.

The Change Agent

Wiedeking arrived at Porsche in October 1991 as the sales slide was steepening and earnings were slipping from a meager $10 million profit in 1990–91 toward a loss of $40 million in 1991–92 on $1.5 billion in sales. It was also just at the time that the Japanese car companies were launching their attack on German luxury cars and our MIT study, *The Machine That Changed the World*, was revealing to the Germans how far behind they had fallen in fundamental productivity.

However, Porsche's problem was not primarily Japanese clones because even the "sportiest" Japanese cars, like the Toyota Supra and the Nissan 300ZX, were still several notches away in the direction of touring cars from Porsche's pure "drivers' cars." Porsche's fundamental problem was cost—its cars were simply too expensive for 1990s buyers to afford. And it was suddenly obvious that the amounts of time, effort, inventories, tools, and space needed by the best Japanese firms like Toyota to make "almost a Porsche" were a tiny fraction of those used at Zuffenhausen to make a real Porsche. It followed that costs and throughput times could be cut dramatically at Porsche if the right means were applied.

Wiedeking therefore called his direct reports together, had everyone read *Machine* very carefully, and arranged for an initial study tour in Japan. He remembers that the first shock was that the Japanese car companies they visited were willing to show them everything. "No one in the Japanese auto industry considered us serious competition and so they were very open. This was a major affront to our self-image."

Upon their return, the team was terribly discouraged. "We could see that we were far, far behind and we had some general sense about why, but we lacked the techniques to tackle our productivity and first-time quality problems and we had no priorities. When you are way behind on every competitive dimension, how do you begin and where?"

Just then, at the beginning of 1992, the world recession caught up with sales of Porsche's upmarket cars. Production at Zuffenhausen, which had rebounded in 1990 and 1991, suddenly fell by 23 percent from 26,000 to 20,000 and losses for the company as a whole were suddenly soaring past $150 million on only $1.3 billion in total sales.

Despite the growing sense of crisis, Wiedeking continued a series of trips to Japan, totaling four by mid-1992. These included managers but also shop-floor workers and members of the Works Council (the Metalworkers Union). He was intensely aware of the insularity of thinking at Porsche (which we believe is no worse than in the typical German engineering firm) and the need to open the windows.

Previously, Porsche operations managers had rarely traveled abroad, and then it was typically to look at high-tech machinery but not at management practices. This was on the premise that advances in management methods in foreign companies could not be relevant in Germany. The rank-and-file workforce and the union leaders had never been abroad on study tours and clung to a belief that all that was wrong at Porsche was a downturn in the market and some bad product decisions.

The Plan of Attack

As these visits continued, Wiedeking decided that he must take bold steps to dramatically reorganize the company, and that he must get help directly from Japanese experts, a decision he knew would be highly unpopular within Porsche. He already had a consultant working on a reorganization plan and he had met Maasaki Imai[8] of the Kaizen Institute when visiting Japan. In May 1992, Wiedeking invited the Kaizen Institute to work for Porsche as part of a four-pronged offensive to overcome the crisis.

The first step in the campaign was to restructure operations from six layers of managers to four (as shown in Figure 9.1) and to create four cost centers and three support functions to make responsibilities much clearer (as shown in Figure 9.2). The number of managers was reduced by 38 percent—from 362 in July 1991 to 328 in July 1992 to 226 by August 1993. In the new system, the support functions concentrated on developing the supply base, devising quality systems, and planning improvements while day-to-day operating tasks were assigned to the cost centers.

FIGURE 9.1: DELAYERING OPERATIONS AT PORSCHE

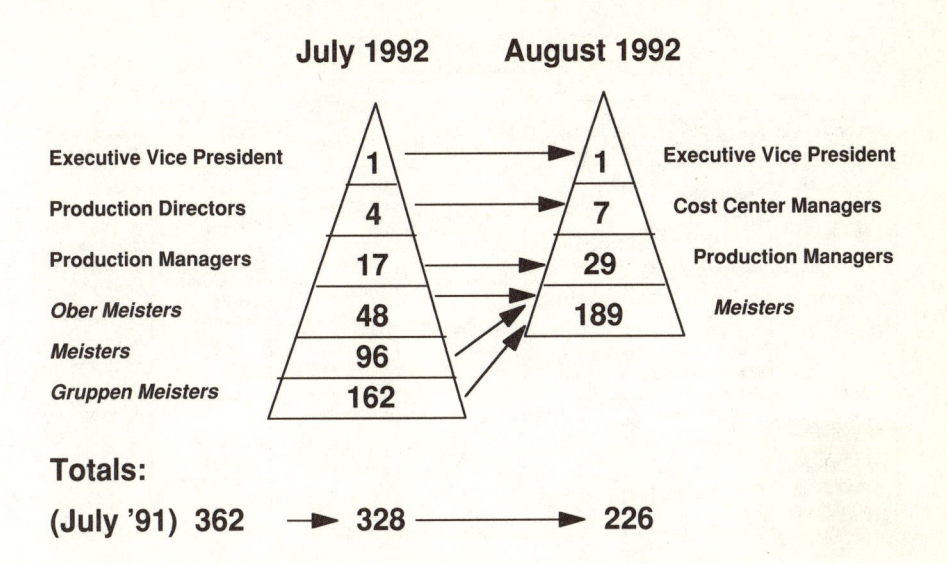

July 1992   August 1992

July 1992			August 1992
Executive Vice President	1	1	Executive Vice President
Production Directors	4	7	Cost Center Managers
Production Managers	17	29	Production Managers
Ober Meisters	48	189	Meisters
Meisters	96		
Gruppen Meisters	162		

Totals:

(July '91) 362 → 328 → 226

At the same time, Wiedeking negotiated with the Porsche Works Council for a new team structure on the plant floor. Production departments of twenty-five to fifty employees reporting through several layers of *meister* were broken down into two to three teams of eight to ten workers with each group of teams reporting directly to a single *meister*. (The *ober meister* and *gruppen meister* jobs were eliminated, as shown in Figure 9.1.)

Wiedeking's second step was a "quality offensive" to show the workforce the true costs of Porsche's quality practices and to devise alternative methods. The most effective tool was to estimate the cost of catching a defect at the moment it occurred, compared with the cost at the end of the line, in the vehicle rectification area at the end of the plant, and in the hands of the customer. A problem costing 1 mark to fix at the spot it happened on the assembly line was estimated to cost 10 marks to fix at the end of the line, 100 marks in the vehicle rectification area at the end of the plant, and 1,000 marks at the dealer under warranty! This came as a revelation to the Porsche workforce, which had simply never looked downstream from their own work area to see the consequences of their mistakes.

A defect detection and reporting system was instituted so that everyone in every area of production could see immediately where mistakes were occurring and what was being done about them.

Wiedeking's third step was in the form of a new suggestion system in which work team members were rewarded for submitting suggestions for improving both quality and productivity. The *meister* evaluated the sugges-

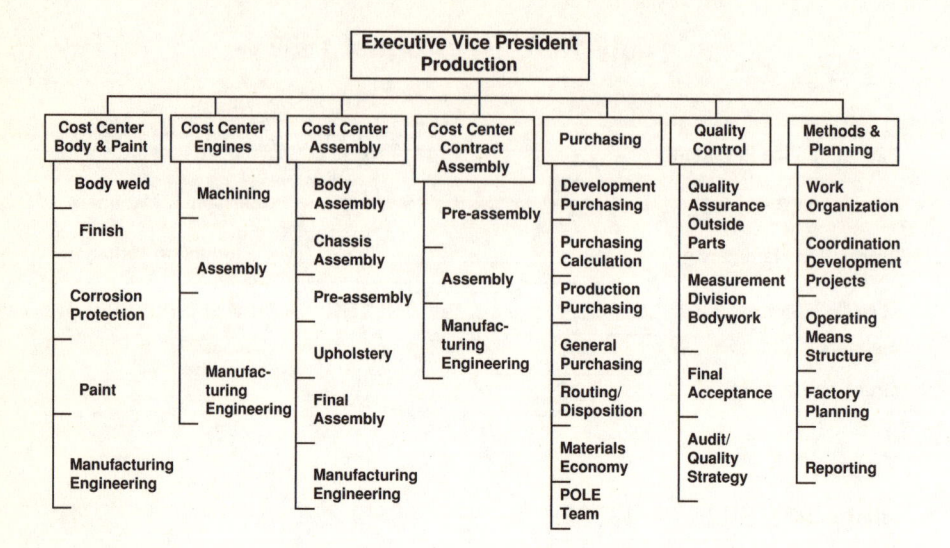

Figure 9.2: New Production Organization

```
                        Executive Vice President
                               Production
┌──────────┬──────────┬──────────┬──────────┬──────────┬──────────┬──────────┐
Cost Center  Cost Center  Cost Center  Cost Center   Purchasing   Quality      Methods &
Body & Paint  Engines    Assembly    Contract                    Control      Planning
                                     Assembly
Body weld               Body         Pre-assembly  Development   Quality      Work
            Machining   Assembly                   Purchasing    Assurance    Organization
Finish                  Chassis      Assembly                    Outside
                        Assembly                   Purchasing    Parts        Coordination
            Assembly                 Manufac-      Calculation                Development
Corrosion               Pre-assembly turing                      Measurement  Projects
Protection                           Engineering   Production    Division
                                                   Purchasing    Bodywork     Operating
                        Upholstery                                            Means
            Manufac-                               General                    Structure
Paint       turing      Final                      Purchasing    Final
            Engineering Assembly                                 Acceptance   Factory
                                                   Routing/                   Planning
                                                   Disposition
                        Manufacturing                            Audit/
Manufacturing           Engineering                Materials     Quality      Reporting
Engineering                                        Economy       Strategy

                                                   POLE
                                                   Team
```

tions immediately and took responsibility for implementing them quickly. Previously, suggestions had been sent to a special staff department from which they either never emerged or were seen only at a point so much later that the worker making the suggestion had moved on to a new job. As a result, the average employee made 0.06 suggestions a year.

Under the new system, the number of suggestions per employee per year has risen to twelve, which is among the highest in Europe for European-owned firms. By contrast, the Lean Enterprise Research Centre survey of European auto suppliers in 1993 found that the average number of suggestions per employee per year at German-owned auto parts firms was less than one and that British-owned auto parts firms reported only two suggestions per employee. At the same time, Japanese auto parts firms in Japan reported twenty-nine.[9]

The final step in the Wiedeking offensive was a policy deployment and visual management system called the Porsche Improvement (*Verbesserungs*) Process, or PVP for short. This set measurable targets, monthly and annual, for each cost center and for each work team along four dimensions:

- cost, measured by reductions in hours of fabrication and assembly effort, and reductions in the amount of rework, scrap, and breakdown time for machinery.
- quality, measured as the number of first-time-through defects per component or per vehicle and defects discovered in the final road test of each vehicle.

- logistics, measured by on-time delivery to dealers, on-time delivery of parts to the next manufacturing operation, and reductions in inventory levels.
- motivation, measured by suggestions per employee, housekeeping, absenteeism, accidents, and PVP workshops and training hours per team.

When this system was launched—with great fanfare to coincide with the production launch of the 911 Carrera model in mid-1993 [10]—each work *meister*'s group agreed to the monthly and yearly targets for these measures and took responsibility for meeting them by posting their results prominently in their work area so that anyone walking by could see whether the team was succeeding. This was in complete contrast to the previous system, in which performance measures were secrets to be tightly guarded by top management and all proposals for improvement came from staff departments.

As the training progressed and it came time for the cost centers and work groups to take decisive steps to achieve their goals, Wiedeking was once more discouraged. He needed to introduce a total change in the thought process and practices of his craft-oriented workforce, yet he and his direct reports had only a theoretical knowledge of what to do. They had never actually implemented a lean system and the situation in the company was so desperate that they could not afford any initial failures. Wiedeking decided that Porsche needed shock treatment in the form of hands-on improvement activities from the Shingijutsu group he had met during his study tour of Japan. After several personal visits by Wiedeking and lengthy negotiations to prove Porsche was serious, Yoshiki Iwata and Chihiro Nakao agreed to take on the task.

The Arrival of the *Sensei*

As always, Chihiro Nakao's initial foray into Porsche was a theatrical tour de force. When he arrived for his first visit in the fall of 1992, he insisted that Wiedeking immediately accompany him to the assembly plant. After walking through the door and looking at the stacks of inventory, he asked in a loud voice: "Where's the factory? This is the warehouse." Upon being assured that he was indeed looking at the engine assembly shop, he declared that if this was a factory Porsche obviously could not be making any money. And upon being told that Porsche was, in fact, losing more money every day, Nakao announced that a drastic improvement activity must be conducted in engine assembly along with many other places and that these must start immediately, indeed that day.

This, of course, was not the normal practice at Porsche, where all changes were carefully planned months in advance and negotiated with the Works Council. Any change in job content and the movement of any machine needed to be negotiated in advance, making *kaikaku* and *kaizen* in the normal "just do it" manner illegal in Germany.

Nor was it the normal practice for a stranger—a Japanese, no less, who spoke no German and communicated through an interpreter—to speak this way to a Dr. Ing. head of production (Ph.D. engineer) in a loud voice in front of the workforce. Finally, it was not normal practice to announce that the participants in the initial improvement projects must include all of the senior managers as well as the primary workforce.

The initial reaction on the shop floor was shock followed by considerable resentment, and the Works Council only very reluctantly consented to the initial improvement exercise. Most Porsche workers still found it difficult or impossible to believe that the problem was inside Porsche rather than outside in the marketplace. In addition, it was hard to believe that Japanese production engineers who knew nothing about the sports car industry could actually be helpful.

When the Works Council agreed to the experiment with the Japanese consultants, it stipulated that Porsche workers would conduct their own parallel workshop to show that if change was really needed it could perfectly well be achieved by long-term employees rather than outsiders.

The objective of the first *kaikaku* in the engine assembly area was very simple: Get rid of the mountains of inventory and the treasure hunting for parts which occupied a substantial fraction of each assembler's daily effort. Then make the parts flow from receiving to engine assembly to the final assembly plant very rapidly with no stopping, no scrap, and no backflows to fix defects.

A start must be made somewhere, so the objective of the first weeklong improvement activity was to cut shelf height in half from 2.5 to 1.3 meters in order to cut the inventory of parts on hand in engine assembly from an average of twenty-eight days to seven and to make it possible for everyone to see everyone else in the shop. (The underlying idea, of course, was to "lower the water level" so the snags in the prompt resupply of parts would be brought to the surface and the next step could be taken toward eliminating inventory and speeding flow.)

As the team formed its plan, a crucial moment arrived. Nakao handed a circular saw to Wiedeking, now dressed in the blue Porsche jumper worn by all production workers, and told him to go down the aisle sawing off every rack of shelving at the 1.3-meter level. As Manfred Kessler, then the head of the Methods and Planning Department and now the head of the Supplier Development Group, remembers, "It was the defining moment.

Historically, senior management never touched anything in the plant and no one ever took such drastic actions so directly and quickly."

At the end of the week, the initial rundown in inventory was complete (there was no longer anyplace to store twenty-eight days' worth of parts) and the effects were both dramatic and completely visible. The Porsche internal teams, meanwhile, had made hardly any progress on their parallel tasks and concluded that they should simply join the next consultant-led *kaizen*.

Many improvement activities lay ahead in engine assembly, as shown in Figures 9.3, 9.4, and 9.5, tracing the transformation of engine assembly between the fall of 1992 before the transformation started to the end of 1993 when a fully lean system was in place. Over this period, the amount of space for inventories was reduced from 40 percent of the assembly area to zero, the amount of parts on hand was reduced from twenty-eight days to essentially zero, and parts were in the assembly area for only about twenty minutes before the completed engine was sent to the final assembly area.

Instead, parts kits for each engine were built up in a kitting area on the floor below and sent up to the assembly floor in little carts at exactly the rate engines were being assembled. (The kits were themselves a *poka-yoke* device because the parts were placed on the cart in their exact assembly sequence. Any part skipped over would be spotted immediately.)[11] Meanwhile, a *kanban* system was being installed with major suppliers so that the

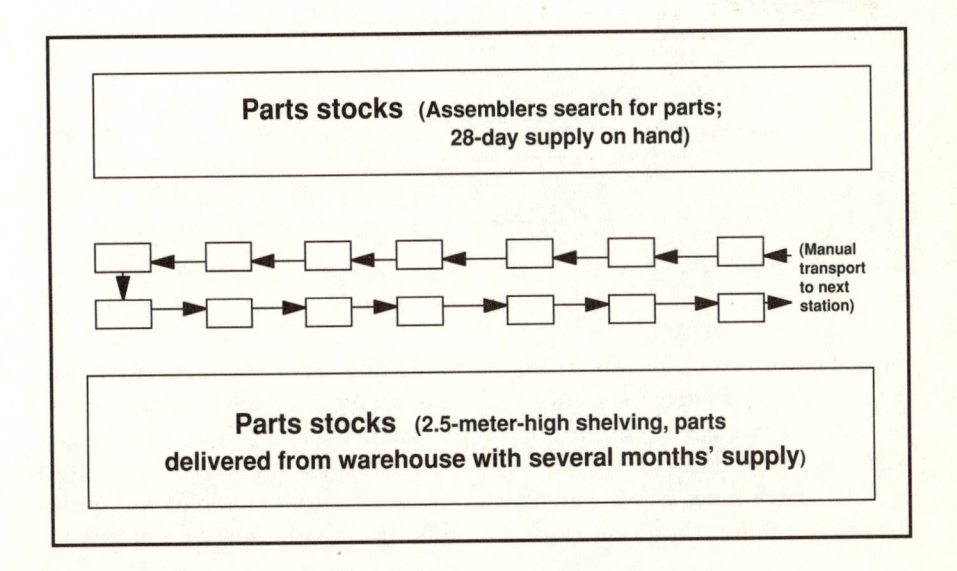

FIGURE 9.3: PORSCHE ENGINE ASSEMBLY, OCTOBER 1992

204 LEAN THINKING

FIGURE 9.4: PORSCHE ENGINE ASSEMBLY, DECEMBER 1992

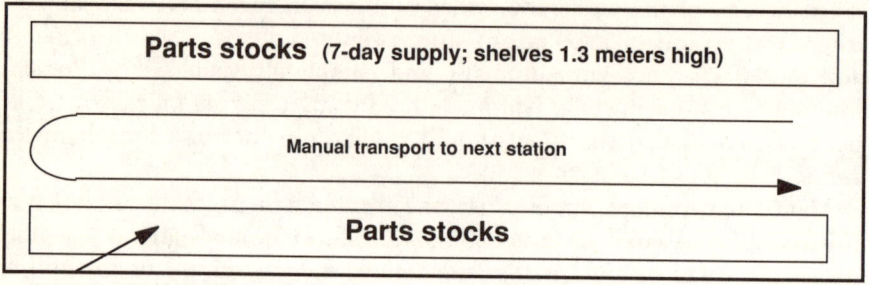

Parts stocks (7-day supply; shelves 1.3 meters high)

Manual transport to next station

Parts stocks

(Parts ordered by kanban from central warehouse with several months still on hand)

FIGURE 9.5: PORSCHE ENGINE ASSEMBLY, DECEMBER 1993

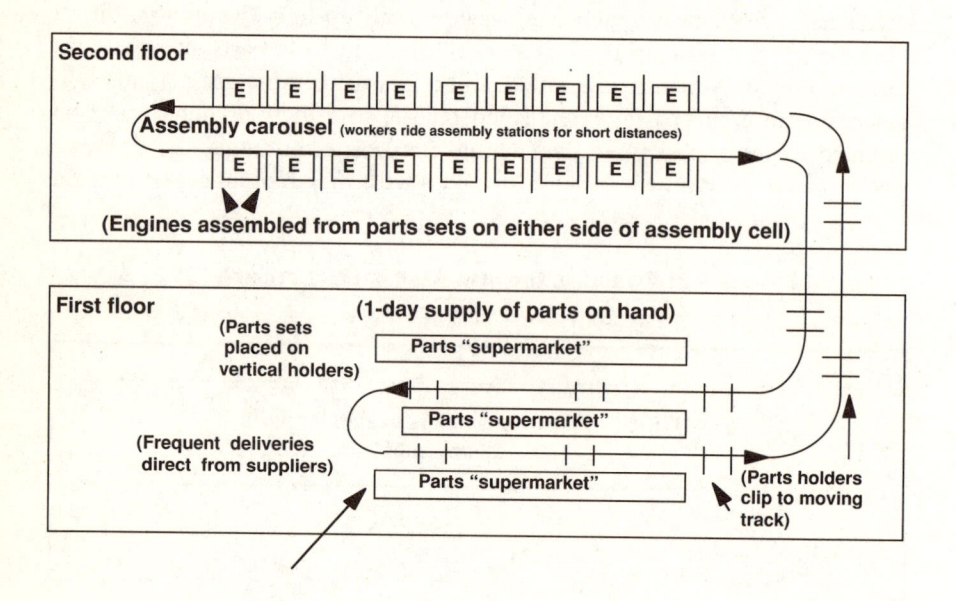

Second floor

E E E E E E E E E
Assembly carousel (workers ride assembly stations for short distances)
E E E E E E E E E

(Engines assembled from parts sets on either side of assembly cell)

First floor   (1-day supply of parts on hand)

(Parts sets placed on vertical holders)
Parts "supermarket"

Parts "supermarket"

(Frequent deliveries direct from suppliers)
Parts "supermarket"

(Parts holders clip to moving track)

needed parts were delivered directly to the kitting area at frequent intervals. The massive automated central warehouse Porsche previously used for received parts was partly emptied and the space made available to the service parts organization.

At the same time, improvement activities were started in the paint booth, the body welding shop, the engine machining shop, chassis assembly, and final assembly. On their monthly one-week visits, the Japanese consultants would oversee the efforts of all six improvement teams beginning with an analysis session on Monday morning and a report to all six teams in the afternoon on the proposed plan of attack.

Because they had invariably seen the same situation before—remember that they and other Japanese *sensei* have been conducting similar exercises every week for nearly thirty years—they could instantly point out opportunities for additional improvements going beyond what the team had initially proposed. As Wiedeking commented, "You have to actually apply lean thinking in real situations to learn to see. Nakao and our other advisers have developed 20/10 eyesight, so we could all learn at a multiple of our normal speed. It was astonishing."

With the six plans agreed upon, the teams went to work—senior managers, production workers, support staff—to build any necessary equipment, move machines, run the new layout, standardize the work, and stabilize the whole activity. It was generally possible to continue production while conducting the improvements because machines could be moved in the evening or over the lunch hour. By Friday, it was time to summarize the improvements, hear the reports of all six teams, make a list of follow-up activities required to sustain the improvements (often very long), and celebrate.

Gradually, over a two-year period, the PVP teams that planned and followed up on the consultant-led workshops gained the experience to join with work teams and conduct activities without outside help. A policy was then adopted that every work team would conduct a major weeklong improvement project on its activities every three months, in addition to taking immediate action on improvement suggestions from work team members at any time. These activities in turn became the key to meeting the measurable improvement targets for every work team set as part of the Porsche Improvement Process.

Dealing with the Jobs Problem

Wiedeking would not have gotten very far if he had not faced up to the jobs problem. Part of the problem was addressed by the prior decision to bring assembly work back in from Audi for the 968 model. Another part could be handled by contracting with Audi and Mercedes to assemble a few of their ultra-low-volume models. And part of it could be handled by assigning excess workers with special skills to *kaizen* activities for extended periods. For example, in the paint booth, some of the skilled paint finishers were assigned to improvement teams trying to eliminate contamination from the system by finding the root causes so less end-of-the-line touch-up would be needed. When volume picked up again (as it had to if Porsche was going to survive at all) these workers would be needed once more for painting.

However, production at Zuffenhausen was falling from 26,000 in 1991 to 14,000 in 1993 and it seemed unlikely that it would return to the 1980s levels for years, until the introduction of new models. In addition, it was apparent that Porsche was engineering and making a wide range of parts and components in-house at absurdly low volumes and high costs. These needed to be bought instead from the firms supplying similar parts to the big car companies. Therefore, it was apparent that Porsche simply had too many people to survive.

A onetime adjustment in the workforce of twenty-five hundred employees was carried out over a three-year period beginning in mid-1992 to bring the headcount to a level consistent with long-term needs. Some workers took a special retirement offer and others were given a large severance. Because natural attrition is about 3 percent a year, given the age distribution of Porsche's workforce, an additional 30 percent reduction in the workforce can be achieved in the next decade without resort to layoffs if no additional sources of production volume can be found.

While this reduction in headcount was taking place, the management offered the standard guarantee we've seen in all of the examples cited in this book. It made a commitment to the works council that no one would ever lose their job due to the introduction of lean thinking by means of periodic PVP activities, although the nature of everyone's job would constantly change and a collapse in sales might necessitate another round of departures to save the company. This guarantee was originally given for the three-year period 1991–1993, and later extended for another three years through 1996.

The Reaction of the Workforce and the Union

Both the workforce and the union were initially quite upset at the affront to, respectively, their competence and their role. The lean message was that the traditional craftsmanship was mostly *muda*: correction of mistakes which should never have been made, movement to find parts and tools which should be immediately at hand, wasteful motions through a lack of careful analysis of how to do the job, wasted time while watching machines which could be taught to monitor themselves, waiting for missing parts, and inventories everywhere due to batch-and-queue methods.

Another aspect of the message was that the Works Council should participate directly with the management in problem solving by participating in improvement activities. A hands-off, reactive attitude which implicitly assumed that jobs and living standards could be preserved simply by bargaining to extract them from management was simply irrelevant to the new situation of the German economy.

Fortunately, lean thinking carries a positive message which can redefine craft for a postcraft age. As Porsche employees participated in one improvement activity after another, many began to see that there is a higher form of craft, which is to proactively anticipate problems in a team context and to prevent them while constantly rethinking the organization of work and flow of value to remove *muda*. (Another way to think of it is that Chihiro Nakao is the ideal-type craftsman for the twenty-first century.) Thus the direct worker and the work team subsume many of the traditional activities of "management" while improving activities at a far more rapid rate than management alone ever could.

The special strength of a firm like Porsche in this respect is that the workforce is highly skilled in the fundamental disciplines of manufacturing operations. Multiskilling, job rotation, analysis of root causes, preventive maintenance, and *kaizen* are all more productive activities for a workforce with these skill sets, and Nakao was soon complimenting the improvement teams on coming up with ingenious stratagems which even he had not thought of. (We'll have more to say about this in a moment.) In short, Porsche was and is still a craft company, but the craft is becoming the new lean craft of rapid and radical continuous improvements.

Fixing the Supply Base

Because Porsche buys nearly 80 percent of its manufacturing value from suppliers and is increasing this fraction, it was immediately apparent that teaching the suppliers to see was as critical as teaching Porsche employees. A number of suppliers had recently agreed to just-in-time deliveries, but when Porsche personnel investigated, the suppliers were invariably supplying just-in-time from massive warehouses. The demand for frequent deliveries in small batches had had no effect on production methods for the simple reason that most suppliers had no idea how to perform small-lot production.

Teaching 950 suppliers to see was clearly hopeless given Porsche's resources and the small fraction of most suppliers' output bought by Porsche. So the first step was to start reducing the supply base to 300 firms, partly by standardizing many parts and dropping low-volume options. Within this group of 300, about 60 suppliers were designated as critical systems suppliers and it was often possible for the former direct suppliers to become second tiers to these firms.

Porsche then formed a supplier improvement team, called the POLE team (from the racing term for the lead position at the start of a race), with the objective of obtaining the "pole position" in the race for survival. The team proceeded to conduct the exact same improvement exercises at the most important suppliers as were occurring inside Porsche. They began with those suppliers most receptive to lean thinking, like seat-maker Keiper Recaro, and used the initial successes with these firms to encourage the more reluctant suppliers to join in. The objective was to get material to flow continuously through the suppliers as Porsche pulled it while at the same time dramatically reducing both the number of defective parts (running at 10,000 per million in 1991) and the need for Porsche to assign a hundred workers to incoming inspection.

The experience was always the same. As Manfred Kessler, the director of the POLE team, remembers: "When we arrived at supplier plants, the management would always insist that there was nothing to improve. They'd wearily say, 'We've rationalized everything already in response to visits from the supplier development teams from other manufacturers. There was really no need for you to come.'" The POLE team would then ask the senior management to play the Porsche version of the JIT game,[12] a simple exercise in which five senior managers take roles in a four-stage production process folding and packing three colors of paper boxes. (The game is described in Figure 9.6.)

The first person is asked to bundle up and deliver quantities of unfolded boxes in three colors to the two pre-assembly stations. The quantities are in response to a customer order. One pre-assembly station folds the large boxes while the other pre-assembly station folds the small boxes and both stations secure their boxes with a rubber band. The boxes are then passed ahead to the assembly station where the fourth player opens the large box and places the small box inside. The player writes out a ticket, folds it, places it on top of the small box, and then closes the large box and secures it with a rubber band. The box is then passed to quality control/dispatch where the fifth player opens the large box and checks to see that the ticket is present and properly written. This player signs and stamps the ticket before placing it back on top of the small box. The large box is then closed, secured with a rubber band, and delivered to the customer.

The players are told to work at their own pace to produce the three colors of box in response to the customer order. Soon every player is trying furiously to complete his tasks, first for one color of box, then for the next. However, a huge mountain of boxes quickly builds up in front of the fourth player, who has a bigger job than the others. In addition, the customer announces that he wants to change his order, to receive first whichever color of box the team has left till last. This quickly produces even more of a pile-up as the wrong color boxes are pushed to the side so the right color can get through.

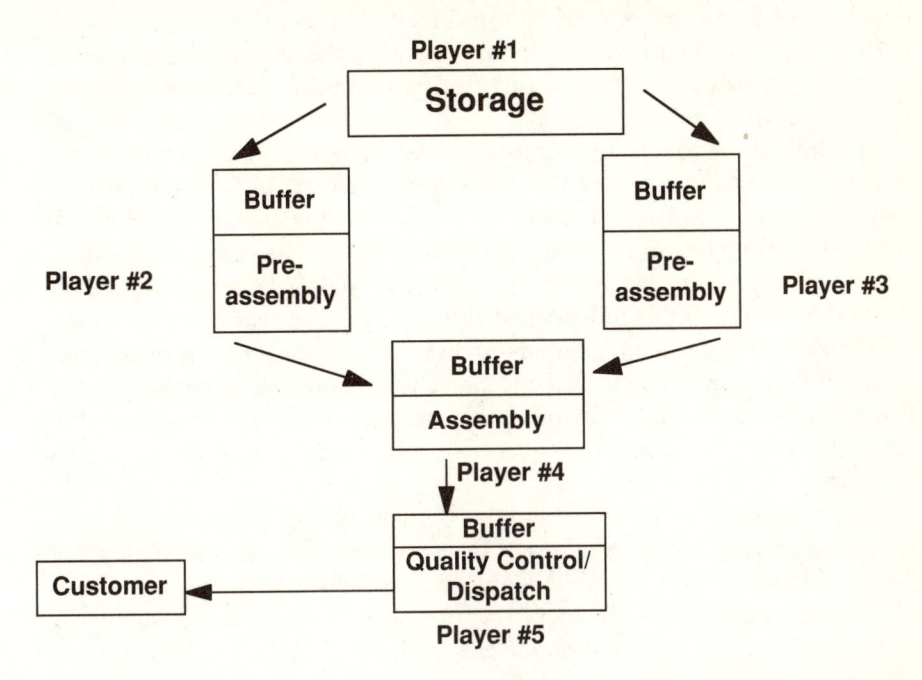

FIGURE 9.6: THE PORSCHE JIT GAME

```
                    Player #1
                  ┌──────────┐
                  │ Storage  │
                  └──────────┘
              ↙                 ↘
        ┌────────┐          ┌────────┐
        │ Buffer │          │ Buffer │
        ├────────┤          ├────────┤
Player #2│  Pre-  │          │  Pre-  │ Player #3
        │assembly│          │assembly│
        └────────┘          └────────┘
              ↘                 ↙
                ┌──────────┐
                │  Buffer  │
                ├──────────┤
                │ Assembly │
                └──────────┘
                  │ Player #4
                  ↓
            ┌──────────────┐
            │    Buffer    │
   ┌──────┐ ├──────────────┤
   │Cust- │←│Quality Control/│
   │omer  │ │   Dispatch    │
   └──────┘ └──────────────┘
                 Player #5
```

The team of five is then asked what's wrong and what could be done about it. The answer is always the same: "The fourth player is the bottleneck so we need to add another worker to the assembly step and build a storage area between steps two and three."

The POLE team then suggests that instead the five players should try a pull system by making only five boxes at a time and only when asked (pulled) by the next player downstream. To the players' amazement, the whole activity proceeds smoothly, with only a tiny buildup of boxes between steps two and three. They then play two more rounds, reducing the lot size to three and then to one, eventually achieving perfectly smooth flow and no buildup of boxes at all.

Next, the POLE team says the customer is going to vary his order at random between the three colors of boxes and asks what will happen. The supplier executives recognize this situation as the key headache in their lives and predict chaos. But, of course, with no boxes piled up in inventory, it's a simple matter to switch from one color to the next.

As the supplier's managers are scratching their heads, the POLE team moves from games to reality by suggesting that the exact same techniques should be introduced in the activities required to make Porsche parts. "Why don't we take a set of activities for one part and try it today?" The POLE team would then stay for a week or two to remove all the waste the team could find and to standardize the process and develop follow-up steps so the new level of performance could be sustained. The understanding with the supplier's management from the outset was that the cost savings would be precisely calculated and divided three ways, one third to the supplier, one third to Porsche, and one third as a pass-through to the Porsche customer.

On some of the toughest cases Nakao was brought along for shock value, but in general the Porsche team was able to do the work itself, and invariably with the same results: a halving of effort, a 90 percent reduction in throughput time from raw material to finished part, the complete elimination of in-process inventories, and a dramatic improvement in quality. At the end of two weeks of full-time work by the six-member team, when the full effect had been demonstrated—generally to widespread astonishment—the POLE team specified that any Porsche systems supplier must develop its own POLE team and go through the *muda* elimination exercise for every part supplied to Porsche. Then, of course, it ought to go to work on its own suppliers.

After two years of full-time effort at the end of 1995, Porsche had conducted *muda* elimination exercises of several weeks' duration at the plants of thirty of its sixty largest suppliers and had worked with a few second-tier suppliers as well. Because of inquiries from many companies not supplying Porsche but who had heard about this activity, Porsche has now started Porsche Consulting, an external consulting practice similar in concept to that started by Freudenberg-NOK in North America. Thus, Porsche is not only a world-class product-technology consultant but hopes to become a world-class consultant on lean thinking.

Fixing the Overall Management

As the results of the conversion to lean thinking began to appear in physical production, something began to happen which we've seen in other companies (for example, Lantech and Pratt & Whitney). Power began to shift from the product engineers who had dominated the firm for its entire history to the operations managers. The supervisory board suddenly noted that what was dramatically improving was physical production, an activity not previously thought to be central to the firm's success. The results were especially spectacular in terms of inventory reductions, which were freeing up the cash Porsche badly needed to fund its new product program.

The supervisory board therefore took a step which previously would have been unthinkable at Porsche. Wendelin Wiedeking, the operations director, was promoted to chairman of the management board and exhorted to apply the same medicine to the entire company.

On taking office in August 1992, Wiedeking shifted all of the senior managers to new positions and persuaded many to retire. He was certain that they were anchor-draggers whose long experience and intense loyalty to Porsche as it had been would prevent them from ever embracing a new way of thinking.

Fixing the Product Plan

The most critical first step was to straighten out the model strategy. The plan had been to withdraw from the mid-price range and to field only ultra-high-performance cars, larger and fancier than the 928 model, on the presumption that Porsche could not offer a mid-priced driver's car with reasonable performance and make a profit. However, it now appeared that costs could be dramatically slashed and that the segment retreat strategy being pursued would pit Porsche against BMW, Mercedes, Audi, and eventually the Japanese.

Wiedeking decided that Porsche must concentrate entirely on the niche it had itself created ("Let's make originals, not copies!" he pronounced) and produce two new two-seat sports cars for this niche at different price and performance levels but sharing about 40 percent of their parts, including the engine block, to make the plan feasible. These are the mid-priced Boxster, introduced in the autumn of 1996 to replace the 968, and an upscale successor to the 911, introduced in 1997.

Because this is clearly a niche with limited volume, the second part of the product strategy was to take on the task of developing and building low-volume coupes, cabrios, and even luxury vans for the big German car companies. (Several projects are under discussion.)

It's impossible to know whether this bet-the-company decision is the right strategy, although this will become clear just as this book appears. It *is* a very clear strategy which vaporized the paralyzing confusion in the company about what a Porsche "is."

Fixing the Product Development System

The success of the new strategy is unavoidably a roll of the dice beyond Wiedeking's control. What Wiedeking *could* control was the method of developing the new cars so they really are superlative additions to the long Porsche tradition of slightly tame drivers' cars, but created in the least time with the lowest feasible engineering, tooling, and production costs.

The classic Porsche development system would never be able to do this, so it was time to look around for ideas. Wiedeking quickly concluded that the new development system adopted by BMW in the late 1980s was the most feasible. This called for designating a strong product team leader for the new products (which are essentially being developed as one car with two body style options) who would report directly to Wiedeking.

The existing functional engineering structure was retained, partly because this is very useful in selling different categories of engineering consulting services. Thus, most members of the development team are still formally members of the various engineering departments. But the new project director, Rainer Srock, was given broad powers to develop contracts with the heads of each of these departments specifying which engineers would be assigned to the project for how long and preventing the destructive practice of constantly transferring engineers between projects to meet the changing needs of consulting jobs. The team was then co-located and given the mandate of developing the first variant of the new Porsche car in three years from the start of work in the summer of 1993. (The previous development cycle was officially five years but always took longer.)

An important addition to the development teams are the production leaders from operations, who actually make cars; the purchasing staff, who select the suppliers and contract for the parts; the tool engineers, who design the process machinery; and the Service Department, which helps dealers with after-sales service. By working together the team is striving to engineer a product design, a set of production tools, and a set of manufacturing methods for the first easy-to-make, easy-to-repair Porsche. The Porsche product engineer is still important—above all, the cars must have brilliant performance—but the team is now looking at the whole, even including servicing, a traditional Porsche blind spot.

A Box Score

In the summer of 1991, any reasonable observer would have pronounced the Dr. Ing. h.c. F. Porsche AG company of Stuttgart dead. The firm could either exit the sports car business and carry on as an engineering consultancy or it could go the route of Jaguar, Ferrari, Aston-Martin, Lamborghini, Saab, and Lotus by surrendering its independence to one of the giant mass-market car companies. Instead, it embraced lean thinking and stands on the verge of rising from the dead.

The indicators of new life are striking when presented as a box score (see Table 9.2).

In simplest terms, over a five-year period, Porsche will have doubled its

TABLE 9.2: Box Score on Porsche's Lean Transition

	1991	1993	1995	1997[1]
Time[2]				
Concept to launch	7 years	—	—	3 years
Welding to finished car	6 weeks	—	5 days	3 days
Inventories[3]	17.0	4.2	4.2	3.2
Effort[4]	120	95	76	45
Errors[5]				
A. Supplied parts	10,000	4,000	1,000	100
B. Off the assembly line (index)	100	60	45	25
Sales[6]	3,102	1,913	2,607	—
Profits[6]	+17	−239	+2	

[1] Projected by the authors on basis of Porsche design, production, and improvement plans.

[2] Time from stamping of first body panel until finished car is shipped and from the time a commitment is made to develop a new model until the first product for sale is produced.

[3] Days' supply on hand of the average part.

[4] Hours of effort, direct and indirect, to assemble a Porsche 911 and its successor model. Note that the design of the 911 was not changed between 1991 and 1995, thus all of the improvements in productivity are due to rethinking the work flow and eliminating errors. The new cars have been designed with the objective of reducing assembly effort. Therefore, much of the improvement between 1995 and 1997 is due to redesign of the cars.

[5] (A) Defective parts per million; (B) Defects per vehicle at the end of the assembly track.

[6] In millions of Deutschemarks, as reported in the Porsche annual report.

fundamental productivity in operations while cutting defects in supplier parts by 90 percent and first-time-through errors in-house by more than 55 percent. By 1997, it will have launched two highly manufacturable products after only three years of development work, cut the needed manufacturing space in half, shortened lead times from raw materials to finished vehicle from six weeks to three days, and cut parts inventories by 90 percent.

The Next Challenge

The results are remarkable and Porsche is the furthest along in the lean transition of any German firm we have studied. However, as with every example cited, it's important to note that many challenges still lie ahead. The product development system is jerry-built over the preexisting structure and we would predict that the company will need to go much farther in the direction of dedicated product teams once the crisis has past. (Like the Ford Motor Company after the success of the Taurus, Porsche runs a strong risk of sliding backwards after 1997 as the engineering functions reassert their power.)

Similarly, the operating cost centers are a good start, but Porsche is only now realizing that it needs a more formalized "improvement office" (which we also call a "lean function") to absorb the excess people who will be freed up continuously as *kaizen* activities continue.

Perhaps most important, Porsche's whole method of selling cars, handling service parts, and preparing the master production schedule is just beginning to be rethought. Symbolically, the sales and marketing departments are located in Ludwigsburg on the opposite side of Stuttgart from the production organization. The inherent problems with the current system, where marketing adjusts the production schedule only five times a year and releases orders to production four to five weeks prior to actual manufacture, will reemerge when the first new product is ready in 1996 and Porsche, in all likelihood, has more demand than it has supply.

Finally, Porsche's work with first-tier suppliers is commendable, one of the best and most systematic we have seen in any Western-owned firm. Most Porsche suppliers, however, are just getting started with their lean transition, and the bottom of the Porsche supply base in raw materials has not even been scratched.

Thus, Porsche faces a continuing challenge to complete the lean revolution started when Wendelin Wiedeking arrived as the change agent in August 1991. In our experience, it takes a minimum of five years (which would be the fall of 1996) before the transition can be so thoroughly institutionalized within a firm that there is no possibility of turning back. And five more years may be needed to push the new way of thinking through every part of the firm, into the dealer system downstream, and all the way back up the value stream to raw materials.

Implications for the German Tradition

German industry possesses many unique strengths, as we noted earlier when fitting Porsche into the industrial landscape:

• German firms still benefit from a stable system of industrial finance emphasizing the long term, even if it has unraveled a bit recently due to the strain of world competition and due to the problem of succession for the family owner–managers who built the *Mittelstand* after the war.

• Senior management believes in the product itself as the most important factor in competition and German firms are now working hard to rectify the tendency of times past to substitute the engineer's definition of value for the customer's.

- Relations with suppliers are both longterm and supportive, again with a few recent exceptions driven by crises in large firms like Volkswagen.
- Both the factory workforce and technical specialists in manufacturing firms have the highest skill levels in the world. As a senior executive at Toyota told us some years ago, "Who I really fear as competitors are the Germans, if they ever learn how to talk to each other."

But talking to each other has been a key German weakness. As one looks at the educational system, at every level the emphasis is on deep but narrow skills for technical operations rather than horizontal systems thinking to pull all operations together. And this is reflected in career paths which have been up narrow chimneys. It is equally reflected in organization charts full of tiny departments (a term which in German literally means "separate") reporting upward through many layers to the point where cross-department conflicts can be resolved.

Meanwhile, on the factory floor, the *meister* system of a large group of twenty-five workers reporting directly to the shop head, who refers problems up the hierarchy for solution, runs directly contrary to small-scale work teams. These workers should be focused horizontally on a linked set of activities along the value stream and perform many of the indirect tasks associated with managing their work, including quality assurance, machine maintenance, tool changes, development of standard work, and continuous improvement.

A second German weakness has been a fondness for monster machines which produce large batches. For example, we've often looked at gigantic paint booths—classic monuments—painting massive racks of tiny parts and justified on grounds of flexibility. "We never know when we might need to paint something much larger, so we've built in the flexibility to do so." The costs of the initial machine and the continuing costs of keeping it continuously fed (which always requires inventories before the machine and after it) are lost in a narrow calculation of the cost to paint each part and the comfort German managers seem to derive from the belief that their equipment can respond to shifts in the market.

A third German weakness has been the tendency to substitute the voice of the product engineer for the voice of the customer in making trade-offs between product refinement and variety on the one hand and cost as reflected in product price on the other. While quality may be free, variety and refinement almost always entail costs, particularly when products are designed without much attention to manufacturability. Good hearing is therefore needed to ensure that product designs contain what customers want rather than what designers enjoy making.

For example, one of us recently observed a "tear down" of automotive exterior rearview mirrors and discovered that the Nissan mirror design for the Micra model assembled at Sunderland in the U.K. has four parts and is offered in four colors. The Volkswagen Golf, by contrast, offers four completely different exterior mirror designs each containing eighteen or nineteen parts specified by product engineers seeking a high degree of refinement. Each mirror is available in seventeen colors. As a result, Nissan's production system deals with four mirror specifications while VW struggles with sixty-eight, each with more than four times as many parts.[13]

German thinking about the cost/variety cost/refinement trade-offs has long foreshadowed the recent popularization of "mass customization"[14] in North America. The problem as we see it is that minor options like color and trim, and even major options like tiny increments in auto wheelbase, often exceed the ability of the customer to notice them. Additional refinement is always potentially a good thing, but only if the customer notices it and thinks the cost is worth it. The desire to listen to the voice of the customer can create a one-way conversation if the real cost of variety and refinement are hidden, even from the product engineer.

Nevertheless, the German system was highly competitive until recently because each weakness was offset by a strength:

• Because skill levels were so high on the plant floor it was possible to fix each problem as it arose rather than fix the system which created the problems in the first place. The finished product handed to the customer was usually of superlative quality, even if also of high cost.

• Because the skill level of product development engineers was so high, they could reengineer designs coming from upstream rather than talk to upstream specialists about the problems their designs were creating. Again, the end product reaching the customer was superlative in achieving the promised performance, but at high cost.

• Because of the technical depth of a firm's functions, it was often possible to add performance features to products which offset their inherently high development and production costs. In some cases this led to rapid segment retreat (for example, in machine tools), but growth in the remaining high-end segments (for tools like the blade grinders described in the Pratt example) was sufficient to keep German firms busy and profitable.

• Because the German machine tool industry was so advanced, there seemed for many years to be a real prospect that high German wages could be offset by Computer Integrated Manufacturing breakthroughs which would couple highly flexible production operations with automated materials handling to practically eliminate direct labor. The objective of eliminating jobs created friction with the labor unions who responded by bargaining to continually reduce the workweek to offset potential job losses. However, this seemed to be a transitional problem because the eventual outcome was to be a German workforce consisting only of highly skilled technicians making products with performance features foreign competitors could not match.

In the 1990s, these offsetting strengths have been overwhelmed by world conditions. Wages have risen behind a soaring mark, East Asian firms have attacked traditional German market niches, and the limits of the current generation of factory automation have become painfully apparent.[15] Across the board, German products have become too expensive for either foreigners or Germans to afford.

In consequence, a sense of panic and then fatalism has set in. For example, Juergen Schrempp, the new chairman of Daimler-Benz, has recently lamented that "Germany can no longer hope to build airplanes," and some of the biggest firms have been rapidly moving components production and final assembly out of Germany in search of lower labor costs. Meanwhile, the unions have begun to offer to reduce or eliminate wage increases in return for stability in the number of production jobs.

This reaction is understandable but misguided. What the Germans can no longer do in Germany is make airplanes or cars or any other product in the traditional German way. What German firms can do is teach their employees how to talk to each other about the proper specification of value, identification of the value stream, and the elimination of *muda* through flow and pull. Then, when workers and engineers learn to see and to hear, German firms can undertake continuous and radical improvement activities in pursuit of perfection and do this better than anyone else in the world, just as our Toyota executive feared. The result will be sales growth in Germany because real costs to the customer will decline (at constant wages) and revitalize export opportunities.[16]

The Opel Eisenach plant, opened in 1993, was perhaps the first German attempt to introduce lean thinking. Yet, it was only an isolated plant and, in addition, it was a "greenfield" facility with a new, handpicked workforce built in eastern Germany by an American-owned firm. Like the new Japanese car plants built in North America and the U.K. in the 1980s, it doesn't prove that traditional firms can adopt the new practices. Lantech, Wiremold, and Pratt prove this for the United States and Unipart is beginning to prove it in Britain. Similarly, Porsche is the real test, the first proof that a classic German firm can change its fundamental behavior and combine the best of Japanese thinking with the best of German thinking to create something better than either.

As other firms follow Porsche, another benefit will begin to appear: The current debate about whether German wages are too high and who is at fault for falling living standards will give way to the ability to clearly analyze value and the value stream for specific products. Then, as waste is removed and operations are made transparent, everyone will be able to see whether there is still a gap between the value of products as defined by ultimate customers and the cost of creating and producing them.

If most *muda* has been eliminated and costs still exceed value then the issue must be faced of whether Germans are paying themselves too much to make given classes of products in Germany. The issue will be much easier to address at that point because the debate will not be along the negative-sum lines of whether management is extracting money from workers or workers are making excessive claims on their employers. Instead, it will be about the transparent relation between cost and value. Our strong suspicion, just like our instinct about the U.S. auto industry in the 1980s, is that the real problem will prove to be too much *muda* rather than too high a wage. In a lean Germany, high wages should be sustainable even as prices to customers fall substantially, turning the current spiral of ever-higher costs, lower production, and growing unemployment in the opposite direction.

Germany versus Japan

Applying lean thinking to all of German industry can be done and we predict it will be done. But it will require hard work and time plus a couple of additional innovations of an organizational nature to be discussed in the last chapter. By contrast, many observers have assumed that Japanese industry, having perfected lean thinking thirty years ago, has fully embraced it and has little more to do. In fact, this is dead wrong. We now turn to the third of the world's great industrial traditions to consider the dilemmas of the current era.

CHAPTER 10

Mighty Toyota; Tiny Showa

When Taiichi Ohno first visited the Koga foundry of the Showa Manufacturing Company early in 1984, he was his usual diplomatic self. After quickly walking around the facility he told President Tetsuo Yamamoto to bring him the plant manager. When Takeshi Kawabe appeared, Ohno asked, "Are you responsible for this plant?" Kawabe acknowledged that he was. Ohno then roared, "This operation is a disgrace. You are completely incompetent. Yamamoto-san, fire this man immediately!"

Yamamoto noted that Kawabe was no more and no less responsible for the condition of Koga than everyone else at Showa. It was being run the way Showa had always run its plants, no better and no worse. He suggested that rather than firing anyone, Ohno should act as their *sensei* and tell them what to do to make things better.

As a result of this interchange the seventy-two-year-old Ohno, retired from Toyota but still chairman of two Toyota-group firms, Toyoda Spinning and Weaving and Toyoda Gosei, formed a relationship with Yamamoto and Kawabe that lasted until his death in 1990 and eventually led to the total transformation of this typical Japanese manufacturing firm. The events at Showa Manufacturing since 1984 are fascinating because they illustrate so clearly how lean thinking has spread in Japan and why the complete embrace of lean principles is as hard (but as rewarding) for Japanese firms as for American and European ones. They also highlight the tasks which remain to be completed in Japanese firms, even Toyota.

The Crisis at Showa

In 1983, Showa Manufacturing, a maker of radiators and boilers, celebrated its one hundredth anniversary. The firm had been steadily successful in the Japanese market and in the 1960s had even been chosen to build a new heating system for the Imperial Palace in Tokyo. However, the world changed after the second oil shock in 1979, and Showa started to struggle. Demand for its industrial products slumped as Japanese firms cut back expansion plans and considered more modern concepts in heating. Equally ominous, the cost structure at Showa, with its traditional Japanese commitment to its 750 core employees, seemed to be stuck.

Showa's initial response was typical of Japanese firms in these circumstances. To raise the cash to avoid layoffs it sold the valuable real estate under its center-city offices and main plant and began relocating its production facilities to cheaper but more modern sites nearby in hopes of gaining efficiencies. It also diversified into ornamental castings for bridge railings and began to implement a plan for exporting its cast-iron boilers to America to take advantage of the weak yen.

When Showa's original office and manufacturing complex in crowded Fukuoka City (on the northern tip of Kyushu, Japan's southernmost island) was fully relocated in 1983 to new plants in suburban Umi and Koga, the management expected its fortunes to change. Instead, the decline continued. The production system in the new plants was in fact the same as that in the old. Process villages for casting, cleaning, stamping, welding, painting, and assembly were run in batch mode with long intervals between tool changes. This practice created mountains of parts which were then taken to central stores before reshipment to the next processing step. Orders took months to work their way through the system, as chased by expediters with hot lists. (It was the familiar world of every firm we've looked at before the advent of lean thinking.) In addition, the cost of starting exports was high and the diversification into ornamental castings pitted Showa against larger firms with established reputations in the building trades.

It was at this point that Tetsuo Yamamato decided he needed to take dramatic action. He would contact Taiichi Ohno and ask for help.

This was not a trivial decision, because Ohno's reputation was one of unrelieved ferocity. He was barely able to suffer geniuses, and the fools he seemed to find all around him could expect routine tongue lashings for failures they scarcely understood. (Chihiro Nakao, one of Ohno's favorite pupils, worked with the master for more than twenty years but cannot remember ever receiving a compliment of any sort from Ohno for his efforts. He can, however, remember receiving tongue lashings, almost by the day.) What was more, Ohno might not even be available. To date, he had not formally agreed to help any firm outside the Toyota group.

On the other hand, Ohno was clearly a genius—one of the preeminent industrial thinkers of the twentieth century—who had transformed the Toyota group into the most competent manufacturing organization in the world. If it was only a matter of putting up with insults, Yamamoto felt the price would be worth the reward. In addition, as a man of Ohno's generation who was president of a golf club in the Fukuoka area and a mah-jongg master, Yamamoto thought he could entice Ohno beyond the Toyota group with an ample supply of his two favorite entertainments. Perhaps in the process he could divert Ohno's scorn from Showa employees.

When Ohno accepted an offer to address the Fukuoka Chamber of Commerce late in 1983, Yamamoto acted as his host and seized the opportunity to invite Ohno to return early in the new year for a round of golf and a quick look at his foundry. Fortuitously, Ohno at just this time was pondering what to do about some of his lieutenants, including Yoshiki Iwata at Toyoda Gosei and Chihiro Nakao at Taiho Kogyo. He was getting old and they feared that once he was gone they would be penalized for his famous clashes with his peers at Toyota.

These had occurred repeatedly during Ohno's take-no-prisoners campaigns to push the Toyota Production System through Toyota itself in the 1950s and 1960s and then, after 1965, through the supply base. After the conversion of the first- and second-tier suppliers was largely completed in 1978, Ohno was no longer so critical to Toyota, and he had been eased out as executive vice president. His new jobs as chairman of Spinning and Weaving and of Toyoda Gosei sounded impressive but were, in fact, largely ceremonial, designed to give him recognition for his past achievements but to keep him at a comfortable distance from Toyota Motor Corporation at the heart of the Toyota group.

The Showa invitation suddenly raised the possibility of solving several problems. It would give Ohno a continuing testing ground for his ideas in a firm completely outside the Toyota orbit, one mired in the classic world of mass production, and it would provide a chance for some of his loyal deputies to leave the Toyota group to form a consulting firm, to be called Shingijutsu, for "new technology." (As we will see in a moment, he had already had a parallel idea for another organization, called NPS, or New Production System, which he started a few years earlier with other loyal disciples.) So, Ohno took a look at the Koga foundry, roared his famous roar, and then quietly said "yes," he and his associates would take on the leaning of Showa Manufacturing.

The Initial Struggle

We have encountered many Americans and Europeans who seem convinced that lean thinking somehow comes naturally to the Japanese. (These same individuals routinely assume that all Japanese firms are lean and have been for decades, another notion which is completely wrong, as we'll show in a moment.) The reality is better represented by the initial reaction of the workforce when Ohno and his colleagues started their first improvement activities at Showa's foundry.

Ohno immediately asserted that by moving to small-lot production and producing only what was requested by the next production step, it would be possible to reduce the three months of inventory of the typical part to a few days. Time-to-market could therefore be reduced to a fraction of current levels. He stated that it would also be possible to double labor productivity, halve the amount of plant space needed for current output, and to do this very quickly with practically zero capital investment. (These are numbers the reader will no doubt recognize as "normal" in a lean transformation.)

The Showa workforce, however, was completely skeptical and resistant. They were mostly longtime foundry workers, and they simply "knew" that none of these objectives was achievable except, possibly, by means of their working much harder. And the line management felt little different. Plant manager Kawabe, for example, was still smarting from his initial encounter with Ohno and believed that techniques right for the high-volume auto industry were out of place in the low-volume casting and boiler-building business.

Nevertheless, because Ohno and his disciples had President Yamamoto's full backing, it was at least necessary to go through the motions. The first project, as shown in Figures 10.1 and 10.2, was to convert coil making and assembly from a batch process to single-piece flow by creating a cell for the pipe-cutting, fin-press, expansion, cleaning, brazing, leak testing, and final assembly steps. High-speed machines that were hard to change over were replaced by designs created in Showa's tool shop (eventually totaling three hundred throughout the company), so that the cell could convert from one coil design to another in only a few minutes before resuming operations. The output of the cell was then fed directly into a simplified and shortened final assembly track.

Despite the skepticism of the workforce, and pointed disagreements with them at almost every step, in less than a week it was possible to eliminate half the plant space, 95 percent of the in-process inventory, half of the human effort, and 95 percent of the throughput time needed to make a coil. (In addition, quality improved dramatically.) The capital investment and time needed for the transition were trivial in comparison with the benefits.

These were electrifying numbers in an old-line organization like Showa, which had had hardly any productivity growth in decades. Yet they were exactly what Ohno had promised. As the *kaikaku* campaign progressed from activity to activity, substituting single-piece flow for batch-and-queue, the results could not fail to gain the attention of even the most negative among the Showa workforce. As attitudes began to shift, Takeshi Kawabe—the most skeptical of the original management—was even willing to take on a

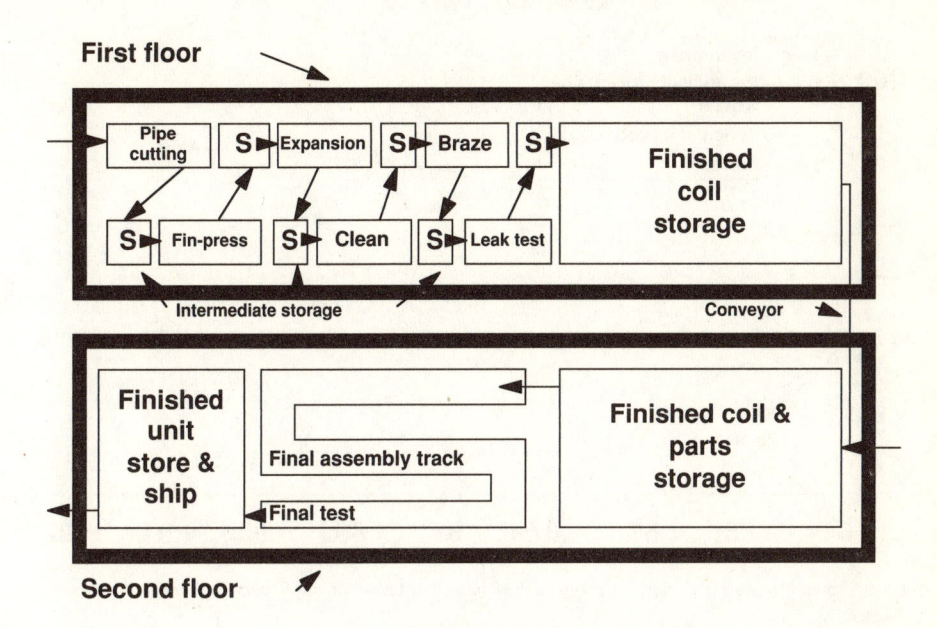

FIGURE 10.1: COIL MAKING AT SHOWA, SPRING 1984

new job as head of the newly created Production Research Department. (Elsewhere, we've seen this new function called the Process Improvement Department [Lantech], the JIT Promotion Office [Wiremold], the Continuous Improvement Office [Pratt & Whitney], and the GROWTH Division [Freudenberg-NOK].) He took charge of improving every activity across the firm and gradually became the in-house Ohno.

Over the next three years, as Kawabe[1] exhibited the enthusiasm of the new convert, every activity was rethought and improved at least once. And

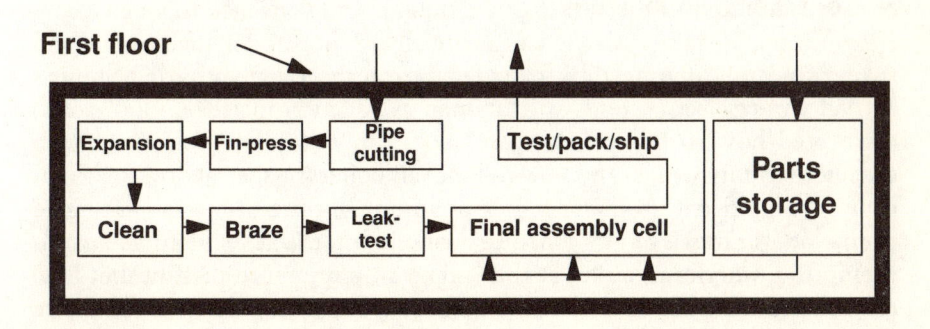

FIGURE 10.2: COIL MAKING AT SHOWA, SUMMER 1984

FIGURE 10.3: SALES, PRODUCTIVITY, SPACE USE, AND INVENTORIES AT SHOWA, 1984-92

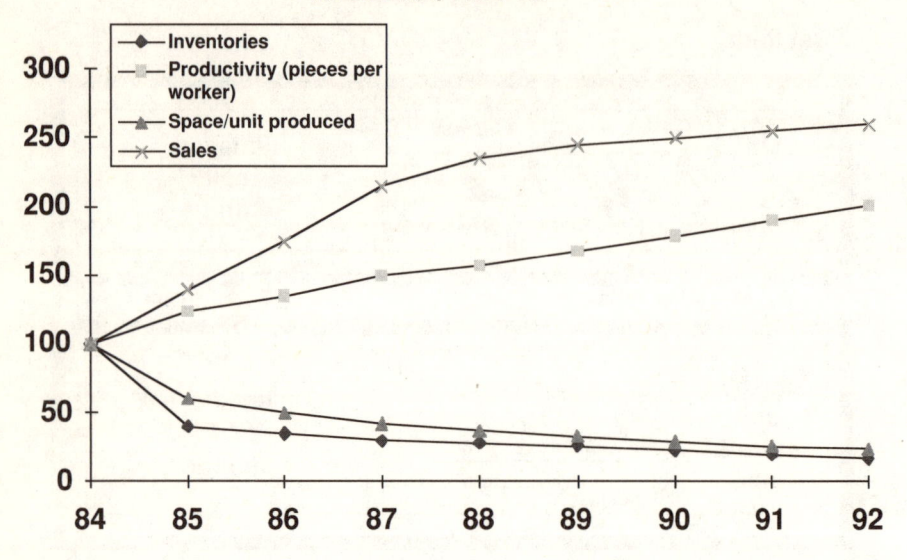

Source: Showa Manufacturing Co., "Background of Implementation of the Showa Production System," 1993, p. 5.

eventually, in pursuit of perfection, every activity was *kaizen*ed at least *ten* times. Productivity soared, inventories were slashed to a quarter of their former value, and the amount of space needed to make a given amount of output was cut by 75 percent, as shown in Figure 10.3.

As a result, Showa clawed its way up from deep losses to modest profits. Still, selling prices for Showa's products continued to decline in a stagnant market. Showa had bought time to think, but it was clear that cost cutting alone would not be sufficient to generate adequate profits.

A Contradiction in Thinking

A key problem—one faced by many Japanese firms today—was that Showa's market strategy was at odds with its new production methods. Showa had discovered how to build a complete boiler in four days (compared with sixteen to twenty weeks) and how to build all boilers to special order without paying a significant production cost premium, yet the firm was looking to overcome weaknesses in its Japanese markets by selling standardized products in the American market at the end of a three-month distribution line. At such great time and distance, no customization or rapid market response was possible. What was more, the export drive had hardly gotten into full swing before the yen began to strengthen steadily, soon doubling in value from 260 yen to the dollar in February 1985 to 129 in February 1988.

Clearly something was wrong when a highly flexible firm was looking desperately on the other side of the world for standardized business, so President Yamamoto launched a rethink of Showa's whole strategy and product line. He concluded that there was simply no future beyond replacement demand in Showa's traditional product line of cast-iron boilers, even if some competitors could be forced out of the business. (Remember that to keep his core workforce busy and reap the full financial benefits of the lean transition, he needed to *double* sales very quickly at constant prices.) He also concluded that profitable exports through long supply lines were a mirage.

Yamamoto therefore decided that Showa should reverse course and work backwards, asking what its key technologies and capabilities really were and how these could be matched up with new needs among domestic consumers. As he looked at the booming Japanese economy it seemed obvious that the Japanese were underspending on themselves—both in their public goods and in their private lives. Therefore, the most promising growth opportunity would be to build lower-volume, customized goods supporting a new and higher-quality lifestyle for domestic customers. However, Showa's functional organization was ill-suited for this new task.

A New Organization to Support Leanness

In 1987, Yamamoto broke up 104 years of centralized corporate structure by creating new, horizontal product teams, one each for a range of new product lines. These product families eventually ranged from custom-designed and strikingly original cast parts for "showcase" bridges (for example, in public parks) to low-volume air-conditioning units for specialized applications. Other business units were created for custom-designed truck bodies for the construction industry, special aluminum castings—practically sculptures—for public buildings, and custom castings in exotic alloys for the aircraft engine and nuclear power industries. A particularly important initiative was an "environmental products" unit making home air filtration systems and home bath heating and filtration systems to keep the water in the tub hot and clean twenty-four hours a day. (One business unit established to manufacture the automated parking carousels tucked away in the back of most Japanese apartment buildings failed and was eliminated.)

Each product team had its own marketing, product design/engineering, and production system, renting space in Showa offices and plants as appropriate. Within a brief period the centralized, "batch" operations of the old

Showa—marketing, design, and production—were eliminated and replaced with dedicated, continuous-flow teams for each product family. These employed a very high fraction of Showa's total headcount. Only a few workers were left in the tiny, centralized functions consisting of production scheduling, finance, supplier development and logistics, human resources, quality assurance (to deal with complaints from customers), and, of course, "production research" to continually improve every activity.

In the new system, a high fraction of costs were directly assigned to individual products and only a small fraction were allocated from general overhead, so it was possible to know whether product families were producing an adequate profit. As a result, the leaders of each product team could easily be judged on their bottom-line success. The team leaders were told to continuously renew their product ranges and to be prepared to exit product lines where they could not make money.

Between 1984 and 1995, Showa replaced 100 percent of its product range. In the process, it eliminated two thirds of the products and production tasks which had been so carefully and repeatedly *kaizen*ed. Showa's current president, Keiji Mizuguchi, notes that rapid entry and exit from product lines is "normal" in a world of custom products but would never have been possible in the centralized organization of the pre-1987 Showa. Nor would anyone have known which products were making money and which were dragging down the firm.

From Hard to Soft *Kaizen*

The objective of each product team was to introduce single-piece flow in product design, order-taking, and production—the same approach taken by Freudenberg-NOK, Lantech, Wiremold, Pratt & Whitney, and Porsche. Because the production steps were soon all *kaikaku*ed (then *kaizen*ed and re-*kaizen*ed), it was gradually both possible and appropriate for the Production Research Department to move beyond the plant to help rethink product development and order-taking.

The first step, beginning in 1991, was to rethink the already streamlined design process to take full advantage of Showa's commitment to customization. Clearly, if boilers, bridge railings, and ceilings for shopping malls were going to be customized, the customer needed to be directly involved in the design from the outset, but Showa, in far-off Fukuoka, had no easy technical means for doing this. Therefore, Takeshi Kawabe (who only seven years earlier had been the manager of a classic batch-and-queue foundry) undertook a three-year project to develop an interactive design software which the customer and Showa designers could look at together in real time to make decisions about product specifications and the state of orders. This was introduced in 1994.

At the same time, Showa rethought its boiler technology and materials, switching to stainless steel and to new production tools designed in-house which eliminate the need for workers to weld inside the boiler vessel. Using the new design method and the new production system, boiler costs were reduced by an additional 30 percent in Showa's most mature and problematic product family.

The Final Element: Rethinking Order-Taking and Scheduling

By the time Tetsuo Yamamoto retired as president to become chairman in 1993, Showa had nearly completed its transformation from mass to lean producer. The major organizational step left for new president Keiji Mizuguchi (who came from the giant Sumitomo Trading Company, which handles the distribution of many of Showa's products) was to rethink order-taking and scheduling. In doing this he was inspired by the American reengineering movement, but in the end he went further.

As Mizuguchi looked at the situation in 1993, Showa was able to physically build almost all of its products in less than a week. Yet it was accepting orders months in advance, particularly in the building industry, where many of the items needed to complete a project really did require months to fabricate in other, mass-production firms. Part of the problem was that customers were constantly changing their orders right up to the last minute. What was more, Showa was running all of its orders through a centralized Production Scheduling Department which processed orders (and changes) in batches before sending them along to the design and production groups in each business unit. Due to time pressures (because orders required several weeks to process) and the many hand-offs from one department to the next, orders were sometimes started into production that were clearly nonsense —impossible specifications, for example—creating the need for expensive rework.

A simple approach would have been to create a streamlined order scheduling department with multiskilled workers to handle orders one at a time and see them through the system. However, this method retained the centralized Scheduling Department and Mizuguchi concluded that this was not lean enough. Instead, the reengineering team eliminated the Scheduling Department and gave the task of scheduling orders to the marketing group in each product team.

The product teams were told to schedule backwards (working to *takt* time) to precisely synchronize orders with available production slots at a point exactly four days before shipment when the firm order needed to be inserted in the production schedule. This is exactly the system used at Lantech, as described in Chapter 6.

In this new system, orders with incorrect information must never be passed forward by the designers and engineers. (Scheduling equivalents of *poka-yoke* devices have been developed to make sure all mistakes are caught.) Meanwhile, the customer must be educated to understand that Showa needs only four days of lead time before the product is ready to ship so that there is little point in specifying exactly what is wanted (and then changing the order repeatedly) until it is time to build it. The customer must also be educated, as at Lantech, about the curious fact that Showa now ships exactly on schedule.

The final element of the Showa ordering and scheduling system is that it is completely open for everyone along the value stream to see—the customer, the distributor, the Showa product team, and the component and materials suppliers. Only the product team can change the information on the electronic schedule board, but everyone with an interest in the outcome can electronically check on the status of orders at any time. Another example of the power of visual control.

As a longtime executive of a major trading company, Keiji Mizuguchi was fully aware as he took on the presidency of Showa that the world consists of many markets, some offering interesting opportunities, and that Showa should develop a new strategy for serving markets beyond Japan. But he was determined that Showa's new global strategy would not repeat the mistakes of the past. The first step (in 1995) was to establish a subsidiary in China, but one with a very different purpose from those of many other Japanese, European, and American firms.

The new Showa subsidiary customizes designs and then manufactures Showa products for the Chinese domestic market. Most of the manufacturing is done at one site in China—using lean techniques with no compromises—for rapid delivery to Chinese customers. The objective is to take full advantage of the strengths of a lean firm by customizing and manufacturing in the market of sale and developing strong relations with local customers. There is no intention to export Showa products from Japan to China or from China back to Japan or to other markets. In the future, any major market with promise for Showa will get its own design and production system to serve that market. What will be shared globally is a set of technological capabilities and the vital lean know-how for managing production, product development, and order-taking.

The Bottom Line: A Lean Success

By 1995, after a decade's march, Showa was finally reaping the full rewards of its conversion to lean principles driven by a lean strategy. As shown in Figure 10.4, Showa quickly improved its productivity and reduced its space needs and inventories after 1984. These steps stemmed the company-threatening losses and bought vital time to consider what to do next (just like similar steps at Pratt & Whitney and Porsche), yet as of 1991 the firm was still not making an adequate return because it was selling products into declining markets.

As the new business units gradually found their markets and product development and order-taking were improved after 1991, Showa began to take off, just as the rest of the export-dependent Japanese economy fell into a prolonged slump. As typical Japanese manufacturing profits (for the 1,033 largest firms) fell by 70 percent after 1989 (as shown in Figure 10.4), Showa, now selling 100 percent of its output into a stagnant domestic economy, lifted its profits by nearly 100 percent compared with 1989.

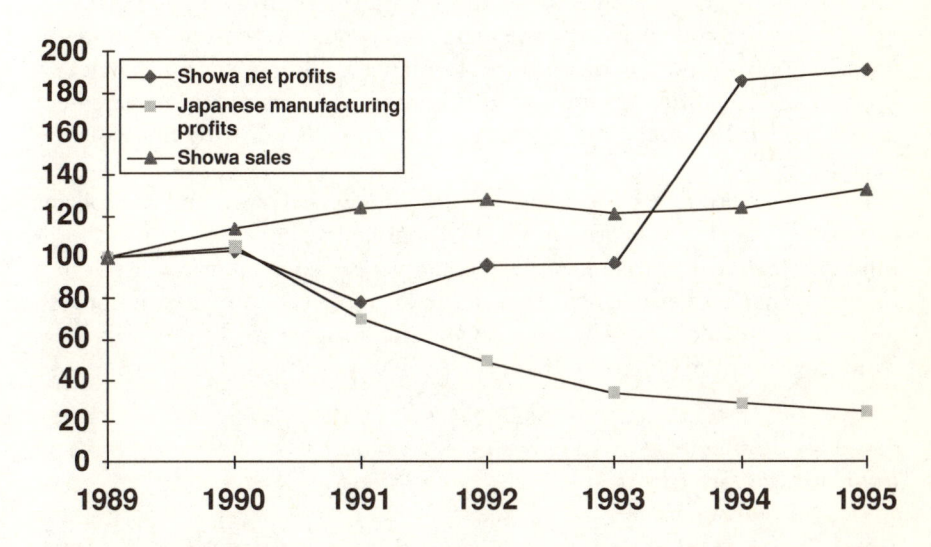

FIGURE 10.4: SHOWA SALES AND PROFITS, 1989–95

Sales themselves rose nearly 33 percent in the first half of the decade, against a slumping economy, but President Mizuguchi has set a target of a 50 percent increase in sales in Japan by the year 2000 as the Japanese economy recovers and additional products are launched. This will be achieved using only existing office and plant space and with existing headcount, as Showa once more launches into a wall-to-wall *kaizen* exercise to look again at every element of its value streams. Meanwhile, Showa will be testing its "lean globalization" strategy in China and will pursue it elsewhere as appropriate.

What About the Rest of Japan?

Showa's transition to leanness may seem to have occurred at a snail's pace, especially for readers accustomed to the magic world of business books, where any firm can be fixed almost overnight by following the author's simple advice. Surely, you say, there are shortcuts, and surely Showa was a late and slow adopter of lean ideas in Japan, an outlier in the hinterlands.

In fact, Showa could have gone faster. None of the methods ultimately used, including the reorganization into tightly focused, integrated product teams, the product customization system, and the new order-taking and scheduling techniques, was unknown in 1984. In a society demanding more rapid returns from capital than Japan and one willing to bear the human consequences, perhaps Showa would have gone faster. (Remember that the first rule of business at Showa—as in most Japanese firms—was not to lay off employees unless it faced immediate bankruptcy, so there were inherent limits on how quickly its financial performance could improve in a stagnant product market if headcount was held constant.) Certainly, a management determined to go faster can go faster, and we will return to this point in Chapter 11.

However, Showa was not a late adopter among mid-sized and small firms in Japan. Indeed, it was among the first manufacturing firms in Kyushu to fully embrace lean ideas, and there is ample evidence (as we will see in a moment) that a substantial fraction of the Japanese economy is still not lean today. We can see why when we review the struggle to diffuse lean ideas from their point of origin in Toyota.

Leanness at Toyota

When Taiichi Ohno first came to tiny Showa Manufacturing in 1984, mighty Toyota was just at the end of a thirty-five-year process of diffusing lean thinking across the Toyota Group within Japan and was just beginning to spread it across the world, beginning at the NUMMI plant in California.

Two of the basic lean concepts in physical production—automatic machine and line stopping whenever a mistake is made so no bad parts will be passed forward to interrupt the downstream flow (which Toyota calls *jidoka*) and a pull system so that only parts actually needed are made (which Toyota calls Just-in-Time)—had been formulated by Sakichi Toyoda (the founder of the Toyota group) and his son Kiichiro Toyoda (first president of its offshoot, the Toyota Motor Company) in the 1920s and 1930s. However, these concepts of physical production were only linked and operationalized by Taiichi Ohno and his disciples beginning in the late 1940s. At the same time, Toyota was pioneering ideas on the organization of product development, supply chain management, and order-taking from customers, which ultimately constituted the complete Toyota system. Soberingly, Toyota was only able to make the historic leap to fully implement these ideas when it faced a deep crisis in 1950.

". . . The Advantage of a Defiant Attitude"

Looking back in the 1980s, Taiichi Ohno noted that "Companies making even a modest profit never use the Toyota Production System. They can't. On the other hand, there are nearly bankrupt companies that implement the Toyota Production System to the fullest, knowing they won't lose much even if it fails. . . . This is the advantage of a defiant attitude."[2]

Certainly, loss-making Toyota did not have much to lose in the immediate postwar period and Ohno was master of the defiant attitude. When he was promoted to manager of the Engine Manufacturing Department at Toyota in 1948, and suddenly had the authority to make changes, he found a classic batch-and-queue operation with all machines of a type in one location. The shop's performance was even worse than one might expect because other Toyota departments supplying the engine shop rarely delivered on time and then delivered only in huge batches. Therefore, the engine shop spent the first half of the month waiting for all of the necessary parts to arrive and the latter half working furiously to meet the monthly production quota.

It was soon after arriving that Ohno had his most fundamental insights. First, he noted that workers spent most of their time simply watching machines do their work and that many bad parts could be produced before they were discovered by inspectors from the Quality Control Department. He remembered Sakichi Toyoda's self-monitoring looms (which he called "a laboratory in front of your eyes") that used devices measuring thread tension to shut themselves down immediately if a thread broke and the loom began to make defective cloth. Using this idea as his inspiration, he quickly devised a set of simple limit switches and go/no-go gauges so that machines, once loaded, could do their work to completion without human intervention and stop working immediately if they detected an error in their efforts. With these simple devices added to conventional machine tools, it was quickly possible for one worker to superintend many machines and perform quality checking as well, intervening only to load machines (as in the *chaku-chaku* line just installed at Pratt & Whitney) and to deal with malfunctions.

Ohno's second insight was that "when you have lots of inventory you are always one part short." He decided that the problem could only be solved if each processing step went frequently to the previous processing step and picked up exactly the number of parts needed for the next increment of production. By adding the ironclad rule that the previous step would never produce more parts than the next step had just withdrawn, a rudimentary JIT system was put in place. The famous *kanban* cards were introduced in 1953 to formalize the system and make information flow smoothly backwards at the same rate products flowed forward. The quick changeovers of tools needed to permit the previous process to rapidly respond to the needs of the next process were first attempted in the late 1940s, but the dramatic ability to change even the most massive tools was not fully perfected until the late 1960s.

Ohno's third insight was that machines should be moved from process villages into "cells." There, in a horseshoe pattern, they would be placed in the exact sequence required by the part being made. By focusing on the needs of the object undergoing manufacture, rather than the maintenance needs of the machines, the traditional skill sets and work methods of the workforce, or conventional thinking about scale economies, he focused the value stream and eventually perfected the concept of "single-piece flow." Note also that the introduction of single-piece flow eliminates much of the need for in-plant JIT linking departments and process villages. In addition, by adding or subtracting workers from a cell, Toyota could increase or reduce the rate of production to keep it exactly synchronized with the "pull" of the market.

Ohno's insights and actions marked a fundamental departure from other Japanese firms in the post–World War II era (including arch-rival Nissan). Many companies focused on larger and larger high-speed machines grouped in process villages, eventually linked by MRP, or on elaborate, automated transfer and assembly lines linking dozens of manufacturing steps and increasingly employing robotics to eliminate human effort. The latter might be thought of as "high-tech" mass production and these methods were perfect for the high-volume production of standardized products, largely for export. However, such goods are today a vanishing species, and high-tech mass production is often a loser when confronted by a flexible lean producer that has introduced continuous flow through its entire value stream.

The Creative Crisis

One of Ohno's favorite sayings was that "Common sense is always wrong." He viewed his life as an effort to reverse common sense—for example, the belief that batch production is more efficient—and find a better way. However, his temperament and the very notion that the "common" was wrong destined him for collisions with most of his colleagues and workers. From the moment he discovered that one worker could load and monitor as many as fifteen machines, and further concluded that machines needed to be arranged and rearranged in the sequence of production steps without regard for traditional skills, there was potential for conflict with the workforce. And from the moment he concluded that upstream departments should do precisely what the next department downstream requested precisely when it requested it, the life and work of managers all along the value stream was permanently changed.

As it happened, Ohno's productivity campaign collided with a collapse in sales in 1949. Even as the number of workers needed to produce a given volume of vehicles was falling rapidly, sales plummeted in the depression brought on by the "Dodge Line" introduced by the American Occupation to break the back of inflation. Toyota, unlike Showa years later, had insufficient financial reserves to survive while keeping all its workers on the payroll, and faced a desperate crisis. What was more, many first-line workers and their direct managers (who were in the same union) found Ohno's new approach to manufacturing highly upsetting. The traditional skill trades—welders and machinists—and many support skills—like quality checking and machine maintenance—were threatened with elimination by the new methods and managers found the extreme synchronization of the production process, with ever-declining buffers, to be very demanding.

Early in 1950, the crisis came to a head when Toyota announced it would terminate 2,146 employees, a third of its workforce. The remainder of the workforce went on strike for two months until President Kiichiro Toyoda agreed to take responsibility for management's failure to protect the workforce and leave the company. But Toyoda's ouster had no effect on the adoption of lean techniques. Ohno stayed and the new agreement between Toyota and its union made clear that Ohno's working methods would become the norm. In return for flexibility in working practices, this agreement guaranteed the jobs of the remaining workers for life and promised that no one would be laid off in the future due to process improvements.

The Slow March Through Toyota

Fortuitously for Toyota, the end of the strike in June 1950 was exactly coincident with the outbreak of the Korean War. Suddenly, Toyota had a full order book making trucks for the American army in Korea and the financial crisis was past. Still, no Toyota executive wanted ever again to face the trauma of layoffs, so the problem immediately became how to increase production without significantly increasing headcount. This was exactly what Ohno knew how to do.

However, Ohno taught through hands-on demonstrations to his direct reports, and his ideas were often counterintuitive and difficult to accept unless you tried them yourself. (This is still true today, as we have seen repeatedly.) As a result, most managers and line workers not under Ohno's direct supervision remained skeptical about his "reverse common sense," which no one else in the world was pursuing, and the diffusion of the Toyota Production System was surprisingly slow within Toyota.

It was only when Ohno was promoted to general manager of engines, transmissions, and assembly in 1953 that these steps were fully synchronized and such techniques as the *andon* line-stop system were transferred from their first implementation in the engine shop (in 1950) to the final assembly line. And it was only when he took over the new Motomachi plant in 1960 that Toyota attempted to get its outside suppliers to deliver Just-in-Time. Indeed, right up until his retirement in 1978, the progression of the Toyota Production System within Toyota was linked directly to Ohno's career. He not only invented much of the "knowledge" but was also the relentless "change agent," two of the three roles which we have found essential in every successful firm we have studied. (The third role, the force of continuity, was played by President Eiji Toyoda—Kiichiro's cousin—who steadily backed Ohno, surely one of the world's most demanding and difficult personalities, in his run-ins with other Toyota executives.)

The Parallel Revolutions

The invention and perfection of the Toyota Production System was a staggering achievement, but at the same time Ohno was rethinking the factory in the late 1940s, President Kiichiro Toyoda was putting in place the *shusa* product development system, the Toyota supplier group, and the Toyota distribution and sales system, each of which complemented the new logic of physical production.

Because Toyota was determined not to build foreign manufacturers' cars on license (as all other Japanese car companies did until well into the 1950s), it needed a superior product development system with strong leadership. Kenya Nakamura was therefore chosen as the first truly strong chief engineer (or *shusa*) for Toyota's first postwar, "clean sheet" car, the critical Crown model set for launch in 1955. Nakamura and the three other chief engineers selected when the Chief Engineer's Office was established in 1953 were forceful personalities who built strong teams of helpers and guided their designs rapidly through a firm with relatively weak technical functions.[3] The overwhelming success of the Crown in the Japanese market and Toyota's decision to adopt a short, four-year model replacement cycle created a special role for Toyota's *shusa* which served the company well for a generation.

The crisis of 1950 had another effect on Toyota because its banks partly blamed the crisis on overproduction due to optimistic forecasts by the Sales Department. They demanded the creation of an independent company (called Toyota Motor Sales) starting in July of 1950 that would buy all of the Toyota Motor Company's output and distribute it to customers. In theory, Toyota Motor Sales would resist overproduction because the inventory would be carried on its books. The bankers' theory was dubious (because Toyota Motor Company controlled Toyota Motor Sales), but the arrangement did give the brilliant Shotaro Kamiya (TMS's president for twenty-five years) more room to maneuver in perfecting his "customers for life" selling system and to think very hard about how to shorten the order cycle to a point very near the day of manufacture so unwanted cars would not be built.

At the same time the *shusa* product development system and level selling were being introduced, Toyota made a dramatic departure from conventional industrial practice on vertical integration. Beginning with the creation of Nippondenso, Aisin Seiki, and Toyoda Gosei as independent companies in 1949, Toyota rapidly deintegrated itself. By taking former internal departments and turning them into independent but affiliated businesses, Toyota reduced the value it added to the average vehicle within its narrow corporate boundaries from about 75 percent in 1937 to 25 percent by the late 1950s. Even 50 percent of final assembly was contracted out.

The reasons this radical policy was pursued are difficult to establish with precision. The initial spin-off of Nippondenso, Aisin Seiki, and Toyoda Gosei may have been encouraged by the American Occupation, which objected to concentrated industrial holdings. (Toyota's industrial group was designated in September of 1947 as an unacceptable industrial concentration to be disbanded within a few years, but this mandate was never enforced.) However, the continuing process of de-integration of Toyota, even after the Occupation abandoned its deconstruction campaign, and the later de-integration of Nippondenso and the other "first-tier" suppliers, was apparently caused by the desire of Toyota managers to spread risks and to gain the advantages of a lower wage base for subcontracted parts.

Whatever the reason, it seems unlikely that Kiichiro Toyoda fully anticipated the brilliant effect of the group structure, which was to create permanent relationships between firms whose wages and executive compensation depended on their individual performance rather than on the performance of the whole group. The methods of interaction devised for dealing with the closely affiliated companies were later applied to all 190 members of the Toyota supplier association, creating a totally different style of supplier relations from any seen before.

The group structure also turned out to be uniquely supportive of Ohno's concept of target costing, where Toyota Motors at the top of the pyramid determined the value of a given component to the customer and then worked backwards with the supplier to figure out how to remove enough cost to produce the part at the target cost with an acceptable profit. As we will see in a moment, the best way to remove cost was almost always to embrace the Toyota Production System (TPS).

As Toyota group supplier costs fell, the 190 firms soon discovered that they could make much more money selling to customers other than Toyota who did not understand the logic of lean production. Toyota soon began to receive a cross-subsidy from all of its competitors except Nissan, which Toyota's core suppliers were barred from selling to until 1994.

Completing the Revolution in Production

By the mid-1960s, Ohno had finally pushed his ideas all the way through Toyota's own production facilities. The logical next step was for all Toyota suppliers to begin delivering parts Just-in-Time. However, as delivery frequency was increased in response to *kanban* signals, Toyota discovered that its suppliers were relying on finished goods warehouses filled with small piles of parts assembled far in advance for their hourly or several-times-a-day shipments. The piles were created from large production batches because the suppliers had no idea how to produce in small lots to replenish the amounts withdrawn from stocks several times a day by Toyota.

In 1969, Ohno therefore directed a new group of direct reports he had trained personally, the Production Research Office (now called the Operations Management Consulting Division [OMCD]), to set up mutual-help groups among Toyota's forty-two largest and most important suppliers. The companies were divided into six groups of seven, each with a team leader from one of the companies. The groups were asked to conduct one major improvement activity each month between them, with the technical assistance of OMCD. The results of the activities were then to be examined by senior executives of the other six firms whose task was to offer suggestions on how the activity might be improved even further. Next, the suppliers were asked to establish their own OMCDs and get on with the task of making every activity lean. Toyota pulled the transformation along by demanding continuing reductions in part costs on every part every year from every supplier.

After 1973, when growth briefly stopped but Toyota kept demanding continuous price reductions based on continuous cost reductions, Toyota's first-tier suppliers realized that they would need to reduce costs at their second-tier suppliers by teaching them the Toyota system. In this way, TPS trickled most of the way down the supply chain by the end of the 1970s.

Completing the Parallel Revolutions

As hard as it was to fully diffuse lean principles across Toyota's physical production system, it proved even harder to complete the revolution in other aspects of the business. For example, Toyota Motor Sales gradually reduced its lead time to ten days for car orders from Toyota but it still retained a large bank of finished cars. It was not until Shotaro Kamiya finally retired from the chairmanship in 1981 (at age eighty-one) that Toyota could do the logical thing and merge TMS and TMC to form the Toyota Motor Corporation. After 1982, the inventory of finished vehicles in the Japanese domestic market withered to practically zero (before the collapse in demand after 1991 temporarily reversed the trend).[4] Most cars are now built and delivered within about a week of customer order.[5]

Parts distribution long proved resistant to lean thinking, and Toyota did not apply lean techniques in its domestic service network (as described in Chapter 4) until the early 1980s. Up to that time, it was operating classic batch-and-queue warehouses even though the warehouses were supplied by the world's leanest producers.

Finally, the initial *shusa* system Toyota put in place with the Crown in the early 1950s worked less and less well as the number of products began to proliferate. (Even as late as 1966, when the Corolla was launched, Toyota had only three automotive products, the Crown, the Corona, and its ill-starred "people's car," the Publica.) By 1991, Toyota was offering thirty-nine models of cars and trucks, based on nineteen separate "platforms" (autospeak for the underlying body structure beneath the exterior sheet metal and interior trim).

The problem was that the initial, strong-willed *shusa* gave way to more bureaucratic personalities and Toyota's functions became much deeper and stronger as the firm accumulated knowledge. The *shusa*, from their position deep inside the firm, had more and more trouble hearing the voice of the customer and often stumbled while pulling products through the development process. What was more, there was no adequate mechanism to inform *shusa* of each other's work. As a result, many parts for new cars were being designed from scratch although almost identical components were either already available or were being developed simultaneously for other new vehicles. The results were excessive costs, a failure for more than a decade to reduce time-to-market (which became stuck at about forty-two months), and spectacular misreading of consumer desires as the Bubble Economy came to an end in 1991.

In 1992, therefore, Toyota reorganized its products into three platform groups (front-drive cars, rear-drive cars, and light trucks) overseen by truly heavyweight program managers with a much higher level of dedicated engineering resources. (The organization, in fact, now looks startlingly similar to Chrysler's in North America, although Toyota would be reluctant to admit this.) The objective is to focus on product families which share components rather than on stand-alone products (each of which still has its own chief engineer), to dedicate engineering resources to the platform groups, and to streamline the flow of designs all the way into production so new vehicles can be carried from concept to launch in twenty-seven months. These are precisely the features of the product development systems we've seen repeatedly in our successful lean firms, except Toyota was late to adopt them.

Toyota Today

By the time we completed our previous book, *The Machine That Changed the World*, in 1990, Toyota had become the preeminent production organization in the world, and we believe this is still the case. Although the rules on data gathering for *Machine* prevented us at that time from identifying specific companies and facilities, Toyota finished first—and generally by a substantial margin even in comparison with other Japanese firms—on practically every benchmarking exercise we conducted—factory performance, product development time and effort (even before the 1992 reorganization), supply chain performance, and distribution. Surveys conducted since that time, as summarized in Table 10.1, indicate that there has been considerable convergence in productivity and quality across the world but that Toyota and its parts group in Japan have retained their superiority.

Clearly, "the machine that changed the world" was Toyota's intercon-

TABLE 10.1: RELATIVE PERFORMANCE IN AUTO ASSEMBLY AND PARTS MANUFACTURE, 1993–94

	TOYOTA* (in Japan)	JAPAN (Average)	USA (Average)	EUROPE (Average)
Productivity (Toyota = 100)				
Assembly	100	83	65	54
1st-tier suppliers	100	85	71	62
Quality (delivered defects)				
Assembly (per 100 cars)	30	55	61	61
1st-tier suppliers (ppm)	5†	193	263	1,373
2nd-tier suppliers (ppm)	400†	900	6,100	4,723
Deliveries (percent late)				
1st-tier suppliers	.04†	.2	.6	1.9
2nd-tier suppliers	.5†	2.6	13.4	5.4
Stocks (1st-tier suppliers)				
Hours	na	37	135	138
Stock turns (per year)	248†	81	69	45

* The figures in the TOYOTA column for assembly productivity and quality and for first-tier supplier productivity have been estimated from industry sources by the authors. The IMVP and Anderson data sets used to compile the other columns do not provide data on the performance of specific companies but instead show best, worst, and average performances within each geographic region.

† These figures have been calculated by Peter Hines of the Cardiff Business School for a different mix of products compared with the other groupings. There may be some minor differences in performance due to this difference in the "market basket" of parts in the sample, but we believe it is negligible.

Sources: For assembly: John Paul MacDuffie and Frits Pil, "Regional Convergence in Manufacturing Performance: Round Two Findings from the International Assembly Plant Study," MIT International Motor Vehicle Program Research Report, Cambridge, Mass., 1996.

For suppliers: Nick Oliver, Daniel T. Jones, Rick Delbridge, Jim Lowe, Peter Roberts, and Betty Thayer, *Worldwide Manufacturing Competitiveness Study: The Second Lean Enterprise Report* (London: Andersen Consulting, 1994).

For Toyota suppliers: Peter Hines, "Toyota Supplier System in Japan and the UK," Lean Enterprise Research Centre Research Paper, Cardiff, U.K., 1994.

nected ideas about product development, production, supply chain management, and customer relations systems. But pushing these concepts all the way through only one company, its suppliers, and its distributors, took thirty-five years. What's more, even Toyota still occasionally wobbles in its course and the process of introducing lean ideas from one end to the other of Toyota's value streams for its products is not complete even today.

In the late 1980s, after Ohno and his generation left the company, Toyota began to consider the possibility that perhaps it should adopt more automation, indeed some of the aspects of high-tech mass production. The Tahara plant near Toyota City was the test case, where a much higher level of assembly automation was introduced with the launch of a new model in 1989. However, Toyota soon learned the same lesson as Roger Smith at General Motors: High-tech automation only works if the plant can run at 100 percent output and if the cost of indirect technical support and high-tech tools is less than the value of the direct labor saved. Tahara flunked both tests.

In its next plant, the Miyata facility on Kyushu, which opened in 1991, this lesson was taken to heart with a return to a much lower level of automation in final assembly and a reorganization of the assembly line so that related activities—for example, the electrical system—are installed and then tested in one focused area. This gives the workforce immediate feedback on whether everything has been done correctly, a key factor in creating a psychological sense of "flow."

Most recently, in the revamped Motomachi plant relaunched in 1994, Toyota has dealt with a key weakness of its system, the failure to evaluate the actual level of human effort involved in each production job and not just its feasibility within a given cycle time. By asking work teams to precisely determine the amount of fatigue and stress caused by each motion and then summarizing these for each job, Toyota for the first time can talk objectively about the level of effort required. This in turn permits the company to make jobs comparable (or to adjust the effort level for older workers or those with physical problems) and to answer critics who have frequently claimed that Toyota (and the Toyota Production System more generally) demand an impossible pace from workers.[6] If unacceptable levels of stress and fatigue are discovered, the work team then *kaizen*s the activities to redesign jobs and develop simple operator assist mechanisms.

Taking this step, involving a very considerable research effort, is a tacit acknowledgment by Toyota that for the indefinite future it will need about the same degree of direct human involvement in production tasks. The lights will still be on in the oft-predicted "lights out" factory well into the twenty-first century.

The new RAV4 vehicle for Motomachi also takes account of the fact that reducing the number of parts and simplifying their fabrication can be much more effective than either automation or a fast work pace in reducing product costs. For example, the body panels for the RAV4 take a maximum of three strikes to complete in the stamping shop, while panels in other Toyota models generally require five strikes. Going from five strikes to three automatically reduces tooling bills by 40 percent and increases the throughput of the stamping shop dramatically. Many other components in the RAV4 have been simplified as well. As a result, Toyota estimates that it has reduced the human effort needed to assemble a RAV4 by 20 percent, compared with the most comparable previous product, even while reducing the amount of assembly automation, the cost of production tools, and slightly reducing the work pace.

With regard to its total value streams, Toyota's first- and second-tier suppliers all operate their production facilities in accord with the Toyota Production System, and have since the late 1970s. But the performance of the third-tier makers of small parts is still inconsistent. Some are good, some aren't, and it remains to be seen if the latest yen shock is the crisis needed to push TPS all the way to headwaters of the parts fabrication value stream.

More striking, most raw materials suppliers (steel, aluminum, glass, and resins for molding plastics) are still stuck in the world of batch production. These firms, accounting for more than two-fifths of the total manufacturing cost of a vehicle, are outside the Toyota Group's reach and most have been resistant to Toyota's requests to streamline their thinking. For example, Japan has only three domestic glass producers, and until 1994 they were permitted by the Japanese government to operate a tight "capacity" cartel to control pricing and new entrants. Not surprisingly, one-month batches of pressed glass for automotive use have been the norm in the glass industry, and this seems to be typical for steel, aluminum, and plastic resins as well.

The magnitude of this problem for Toyota is shown by a simple calculation by Peter Hines of the Lean Enterprise Research Centre.[7] In the fall of 1994 he estimated manufacturing costs incurred along Toyota's value streams as follows: Toyota itself, 22 percent; first-tier suppliers, 22 percent; second-tier suppliers, 10 percent; third- and fourth-tier suppliers, 3 percent; and raw materials suppliers (directly to Toyota and to each of these tiers combined), 43 percent. In the West, raw materials probably account for no more than 25 percent of manufacturing costs, but because Toyota has been so effective in cutting costs in its supply base through four tiers of suppliers while raw materials costs have not been managed in the same way, the real cost saving for Toyota today lies in changing the thinking and behavior of materials suppliers.

Finally, Toyota's approach to aggressive selling was a great breakthrough in the 1950s but has hardly evolved since. The number of steps and the amount of effort involved in meeting customer needs through door-to-door selling creates a high-satisfaction/high-cost selling system when Toyota needs a high-satisfaction/low-cost system. Another leap will be needed (to be described in Chapter 13) if truly lean selling is to emerge at Toyota.

So even Toyota, the leanest organization in the world, has not yet succeeded in creating *lean enterprises* by removing all of the unnecessary time, effort, and error sources from raw materials to finished vehicle, order to delivery, and concept to launch, for each family of products. Part III of this book will propose ways to make this final leap.

The Spread of Lean Thinking Outside of Toyota[8]

Because Toyota pioneered the full complement of lean techniques, it would seem that other Japanese firms should have been able to apply them much more quickly than Toyota. Yet, this was not the actual pattern. In the 1950s, Japanese electronics firms independently invented strong program management and a short product cycle, essential to their strategy of making a living by combining commodity electronic bits into clever packages and flooding markets with a variety of rapidly renewed products. However, only Mitsubishi, headquartered in nearby Kyoto and a member of the Chubu Industrial Engineering Association (of which Ohno was intermittently president), seems to have pursued Toyota's experiments in production.[9]

Other Japanese firms *were* making dramatic progress during this period, but along a complementary path and from a different starting point. They were steadily extending the original statistical quality control concepts introduced by the Americans immediately after the war[10] to involve the shop floor in Quality Circles using the seven quality tools and Deming's Plan-Do-Check-Act problem-solving cycle. Soon they were experimenting with early forms of policy deployment and the management of quality improvement across each functional process. Within a few years, Total Quality Control (followed by Total Quality Management) was widely applied across the industrial landscape in Japan.[11]

Stung by Nissan's winning the Deming Prize in 1960, Toyota also began to adopt TQC in parallel with Ohno's ideas and won the Deming Prize itself in 1965. By then, both quality and continuous flow were being managed as cross-functional activities reporting to the highest levels in Toyota. Toyota's real advantage, as it turned out, was that it alone was able to combine TQC with TPS to stand out from others.[12]

No one in Japan—even in the auto industry—seems to have paid much attention to Toyota's unique approach until the first energy crisis in 1973. When most firms began losing money after years of steady growth, yet Toyota continued to earn healthy profits in a slumping market—by avoiding production of unwanted products and continuously pushing down costs—the virtues of Toyota's lean system were suddenly apparent.

Mitsubishi Motors, which had already embraced many elements of the system, moved ahead rapidly on full implementation, and Mazda made TPS a central pillar of its comeback after 1974 (just in time for Ford to learn the system secondhand, beginning in 1979, when it took a 24 percent equity stake in Mazda). Nissan, Honda, and the other Japanese car companies began to do their homework as well, with mixed results. Nissan, to take the most striking example, found it very hard to give up on its own strategy of progressively automating activities to eliminate both human effort and the need for tight coordination by means of TPS. As a result, it fell steadily behind Toyota, after enjoying a comparable market share in the early 1960s.

Ohno realized that a major reason the Toyota system did not spread rapidly was that it required hands-on teaching. Yet no one with deep experience ever left Toyota except to go to a Toyota supplier. (Consultant Shigeo Shingo, who advised Toyota but who worked for many other firms as well, was the one major exception.) Therefore, as Ohno contemplated retirement in 1978, he decided that a highly useful activity would be to take some of his most loyal and gifted disciples and form external propagation mechanisms.

The first of these, headed by his closest disciple, Kikuo Suzumura, was called New Production System, or NPS.[13] Ohno's idea was to form a group of the chief executives from a range of Japanese firms outside the auto industry, including retailing. These were all firms selling directly to the public and none were competitors. They agreed to conduct hands-on improvement activities on the same model used by Toyota to spread TPS through its first-tier suppliers after 1969. Ohno was the "supreme adviser," with Mr. Suzumura the day-to-day leader. As we have seen, Ohno also played a role in the formation of Shingijutsu as a more conventional consulting organization in the mid-1980s.

It seems fair to say that by the mid-1990s most major Japanese manufacturing firms and many of their first-tier suppliers were fully aware of lean concepts and most had at least some examples of implementation. However, we have been struck in our travels through Japan by the unevenness of implementation and the striking fact that many big companies placed their bets on the very different concept of high-tech mass production.

For example, we recently visited a large facility of a technically advanced firm where a race was being conducted between the rising yen and the elimination of expensive human effort. The process villages molding, cutting, and painting parts for the plant's complex product were entirely automated, with robots neatly stacking the parts emerging from various fabrication steps on pallets to be taken by automated guided vehicles to an automated storage and retrieval center. From there, in-house parts and those received from vendors were taken automatically to a completely automated final assembly line which could instantly adjust its fixtures to hold any of the one hundred models of the basic product and assemble it solely through the efforts of pick-and-place robots. (The plant still employed 3,600, but *none* was involved in direct labor.) The facility exported 50 percent of its 7.5 million units of output and supplied one sixth of world demand for its product from one final assembly line in one room. For the future, this company is looking to China as a source of cheap subcomponents, currently supplied by local first-tier suppliers.

It is obviously possible to combine lean techniques with high-tech mass production. For example, the firm we have just cited applies the concepts of Total Productive Maintenance (another idea originating in the Toyota Group, at Nippondenso) and self-managed work teams (consisting only of technical support staff because there are no direct workers) to its fully automated production system. However, there is a fundamental problem with the strategy in most applications, notably that it is a classic case of optimizing one tiny portion of the value stream while ignoring the costs and inconvenience to customers created elsewhere.

To achieve the scale needed to justify this degree of automation it will often be necessary to serve the entire world from a single facility, yet customers want to get exactly the product they want exactly when they want it. This is generally immediately. It follows that oceans and lean production are not compatible. We believe that, in almost every case, locating smaller and less-automated production systems within the market of sale will yield lower total costs (counting logistics and the cost of scrapped goods no one wants by the time they arrive) and higher customer satisfaction.

When one looks at smaller Japanese companies, like Showa, the record is more mixed with many still essentially batch producers. (Showa formed a self-help group with ten other firms in the Fukuoka area in the late 1980s and many of these firms have made dramatic progress in applying lean techniques, but many other nearby firms have continued along their traditional path.)

And the farther one travels from the manufacture of discrete products the more Japanese practice looks similar to (or even inferior to) practices elsewhere in the world. To take an important example: Distribution is still largely conducted in the multitiered, batch-and-queue manner described in Chapter 4 before Toyota began applying lean thinking. (It's curious that the international debate about the Japanese distribution network has focused on its impenetrability to foreign producers. We have never seen any mention of the efficiency of the actual activities being performed at each level, which seem to be a major drag on the Japanese economy as a whole.)

Finally, regarding services, it's clear that many Japanese firms—for example, domestic airlines—offer a high level of quality and customer satisfaction but by means of batch-and-queue methods which doom them to high costs.

So, after forty years, the Japanese economy is leaner than most by virtue of some superlative manufacturing activities, but it is still not lean enough and much of even its strongest activity, manufacturing, is not lean at all. The implications become clear when we look at the world situation and Japan's future.

Tiny Showa; Mighty Toyota: The Japanese Challenge Today

We believe that the world has now changed in a fundamental way: Lean techniques are spreading rapidly to all regions, and currencies have fundamentally realigned as American domination of the world economy has come to an end.

As a result, tiny Showa now has interesting lessons to teach other Japanese firms, even mighty Toyota. Showa has refocused its efforts on the Japanese domestic market and diversified into products which meet emerging Japanese needs, public and private. Its lean production system reinforces its lean ordering and product customization capabilities to deliver exactly what customers want exactly when they want it. The direct manufacturing costs may be higher than making the product in Sri Lanka or Burkina Faso (if this is technically possible), but total costs (including logistics) are lower and the combination of low cost, superlative quality, customization, and immediate delivery is unbeatable. At the same time, Showa is establishing a top-to-bottom production system in its other major market of sale.

This is not the only imaginable path of adjustment, of course. An alternative way to surmount the changes in the world economy is for Japanese firms to become technological innovators and pioneer new classes of products which no one can duplicate. (The world will then either buy them at whatever cost and with whatever wait, or do without.) This may preserve the ability of Japanese firms to serve the entire world market from one location even if logistics costs are high and customers cannot custom-order. However, as we will explain in some detail in Chapter 12, the underlying reasons why Japanese manufacturing firms have been better than foreign competitors at embracing lean techniques—company- rather than function-based focus of careers and the relative weakness of technical functions—make it very difficult for Japanese firms to be technological leaders. A few may succeed, but most will fail.

A second solution is for firms to "hollow" themselves out by importing a high fraction of the actual manufacturing content in their products, conduct assembly in Japan using high-tech mass production, and continue to export the finished products to world markets. The problem here, as we've seen in every chapter, is simply that firms in Europe and North America are rapidly figuring out how to conduct lean manufacture within the region of sale. (Indeed, Toyota, through its direct investments in North America and Europe, has been the most effective teacher.) To repeat, oceans and leanness are usually incompatible. This strategy will often be a loser.

The third way out is to find new things for Japanese manufacturing firms to do at home while aggressively replicating lean systems for product development, order-taking, and physical production in every major region. This is clearly the winning combination. Tiny Showa is in fact a model for Toyota.

An additional, and very important, step is to begin applying lean thinking to Japanese distribution systems and services. Otherwise a reorientation of the economy from selling manufactured goods to foreigners at high margins to serving new domestic needs may cause a steep drop in the standard of living. Indeed, the fear of this drop has apparently deterred government policymakers from pushing Japanese firms in the direction we believe is essential.

The Steps Are Always the Same

We're now at the end of our march around the world, from North America, to Europe, to Japan. At every stop we've found that all firms—including Toyota—face the same challenges in embracing lean thinking, and that managers must take the same steps. We're therefore ready, in the next chapter, to summarize just what these steps are and how you can take them as quickly as possible.

CHAPTER 11

An Action Plan*

We hope you've learned to distinguish value from *muda* and that you want to apply lean thinking to transform your business. But how do you "just do it"? We've learned from examining successful transformations across the world that a specific sequence of steps and initiatives produces the best results. The trick is to find the right leaders with the right knowledge and to begin with the value stream itself, quickly creating dramatic changes in the ways routine things are done every day. The sphere of change then must be steadily widened to include the entire organization and all of its business procedures. Once this is in hand and the process is irreversible inside your own firm, it's time to start looking up- and downstream far beyond the boundaries of individual firms to optimize the whole.

GETTING STARTED

The most difficult step is simply to get started by overcoming the inertia present in any brownfield organization. You'll need a change agent plus the core of lean knowledge (not necessarily from the same person), some type of crisis to serve as a lever for change, a map of your value streams, and a determination to *kaikaku* quickly to your value-creating activities in order to produce rapid results which your organization can't ignore.

Find a Change Agent

Maybe the change agent is you, and if you run a mid-sized or small business like Pat Lancaster we hope it is. However, if you are the senior leader of a

---

* In preparing this chapter we are deeply indebted to George Koenigsaecker, president of the Hon Company, for sharing his experiences and his unpublished essay, "Lean Production—The Challenge of Multi-Dimensional Change" (1995). Because Koenigsaecker has now implemented lean techniques in a number of organizations in different industries, his perspective has been invaluable.

large organization, you may not have the time or opportunity to lead the campaign yourself. You'll need your chief operating officer, or your executive vice president of operations, or the presidents of your subsidiary businesses to introduce the necessary changes, and these individuals may need some direct-report helpers as well. Sometimes there are inside candidates for these jobs, but often it's necessary to go outside for a Wendelin Wiedeking or a Karl Krapek or a Mark Coran.

Individuals with a make-something-happen mind-set are not a commodity available freely, but in the fifty firms we've looked at it was possible to find the right change agent, and generally after only a short search. While chief executives in organizations failing to get started on a lean transformation often tell us that the problem is a lack of good candidates to take on the challenge, we generally find instead that it's reluctance to bring in executives who will introduce truly fundamental change.

GET THE KNOWLEDGE

The change agent doesn't need detailed lean knowledge at the outset but instead a willingness to apply it. Where can the knowledge be obtained?

There are lots of resources for learning in North America, Europe, and Japan. Lean firms are themselves continually improving and most are happy to include visitors—in particular their customers and their suppliers—in their improvement activities. Freudenberg-NOK, for example, has involved more than five hundred executives from outside firms in its three-day *kaizen* activities over the past four years. And there is a vast literature available, some of it very good, on various lean techniques and when to apply them.[1]

Because most change agents new to lean ideas need considerable time to master them, additional help is usually needed right away. In particular, firms will need someone in-house, like Ron Hicks at Lantech or Bob D'Amore at Pratt, who can act as the expert in quickly evaluating the value stream for different products and initiating *kaikaku* and *kaizen* exercises. In our research, we've been struck by just how many managers there are in Japan and North America, and increasingly in Europe, who are masters of lean techniques but who are frustrated with their ability to implement them in their current organization. This may make these experts available to you.[2]

Even if you find one or more executives with the necessary knowledge, they may well need outside help to move your organization ahead rapidly. There are many consultants claiming lean credentials and some of them are very good. But several cautions are in order. Any consultant who has no links back to the roots of lean thinking and who relies mainly on seminars and off-site classroom instruction, or who wants to do the improvement for you with a large team of junior consultants without fully explaining the logic of what is happening, should be avoided. Similarly, a consultant offering massive offensives to quickly fix specific activities—the pulling-rabbits-out-of-hats phase—but with no interest in working with you to create an organization which can sustain lean concepts for the long term is unlikely to be of real help in the end. This is the type of activity—usually aimed simply at quick headcount reduction—which has given the reengineering movement such a cynical cast and has caused so many reengineering projects to fail the moment the consultant leaves.

In addition, it's unlikely you'll find one adviser who can impart all the knowledge. Applying QFD to product development, introducing lean techniques on the shop floor, and creating a self-help supplier association require different skills and firms may discover they need a portfolio of advisers for specific types of knowledge.

One underused resource for firms all over the world is the generation of Japanese now in their sixties who helped pioneer lean thinking and create order out of chaos in the 1950s and 1960s. (For example, Yuzuru Ito, who took retirement from Matsushita and is now working to introduce lean quality tools across the entire United Technologies group.) The nature of these individuals seems to be that they can't stop trying to eliminate waste, no matter how many years past "retirement" they may be. Like Ohno and Shingo in the generation before them, who continued to conduct improvement exercises right up to their deaths, they have no desire to slow down.

We've heard many Western firms give excuses for not availing themselves of this resource—the two most common being that Japanese of the immediate postwar generation typically speak only Japanese, and that these pioneers in lean implementation are too demanding (having learned this from Ohno and other leaders of the Japanese miracle after the war) and short on diplomacy when their clients fail to follow through.

But these are only excuses. Many of the change agents we've studied developed a successful relationship with a Japanese *sensei* after a careful search and a period of learning how to work with each other. Typically, the executive made several requests for help before an arrangement was finally worked out. For example, George David at United Technologies asked Ito to come to UTC on a half dozen occasions before he finally agreed and George Koenigsaecker asked his Japanese advisers to visit his plant many times before they agreed. For the true *sensei*, the change agent's level of commitment is the single most important issue.

Finding a *sensei* who does not speak your language (and therefore needs an interpreter) can even be a help because it highlights the unusual nature of the interaction: This is not just another consultant peddling another quick fix; it's someone changing your whole way of thinking about your business. Similarly, any teacher who doesn't vigorously protest when a pupil fails to live up to his promises and potential is probably more interested in a secure fee than in lasting change.

A final point about lean knowledge is very important. The change agent and all of the senior managers in your firm must master it themselves to a point where lean thinking becomes second nature. What's more, they should do this as soon as possible. If the change agent doesn't fully understand lean thinking, the campaign will bog down at the first setback (and there *will* be a first setback). So he or she (or you) must truly understand the techniques of flow, pull, and perfection, and the only way to gain this understanding is by participating in improvement activities, hands-on, to a point where lean techniques can be taught confidently to others. While doing this, the change agent needs to involve the other senior executives of the firm as well, so everyone's knowledge is brought up to a minimum level to grasp the power of lean thinking.

Find a Lever by Seizing the Crisis, or by Creating One

We have not found an organization free of crisis that was willing to take the necessary steps to adopt lean thinking across the board in a short period of time. So if your firm is in crisis already, seize your invaluable opportunity. Just remember that you can achieve spectacular results on cost reduction and inventories in six months to a year, but it will take five years to build an organization which can sustain leanness if your change agent is hit by a bus.

In the 1990s, most executives in North America, Europe, and Japan have come to realize that even large firms are more fragile and more prone to crises than they had imagined.[3] At any given moment, however, most organizations aren't in crisis, and a substantial fraction is doing very well. How can you, as the change agent, take a seemingly secure organization (for example, like IBM in the 1980s) and introduce lean thinking, which you know will be needed to head off a crisis in the future?

One approach is to take some subunit of the organization which *is* in crisis and focus all your energies on applying lean remedies to it.[4] Ideally, this would be a business unit with a set of product families, but it could be a single plant, one product development group, or even one product line in a plant or one development team for a specific product. This is also the way leaders who are not near the top of their organization can take the lead on a lean breakthrough: Apply lean thinking to your own troubled business unit or facility, or get transferred to a unit which is in a crisis. Then, once dramatic change has been introduced in the unit, the leaders of other units can be invited over for hands-on learning and can take ideas back.

Even if no sub-unit of your business is in crisis, there may be an opportunity for dramatic change if you can find a lean competitor. (In our role as advisers to firms we've often wished that Toyota would diversify to compete against our clients!) For example, we recently encountered a case where a classic mass-production firm's competition was mediocre and generally not a threat. However, one small business unit of a key competitor had recently made a lean transition with striking results. By focusing on this one instance of superior practice it was possible to introduce significant change in the corresponding business unit of the client, which then started a change process across the firm.

Yet another approach is to find a lean customer or a lean supplier. When John Neill at the Unipart Group in the U.K. set out to transform his company at the end of the 1980s, a key element of his strategy was to begin supplying Toyota and Honda in the United Kingdom because he knew they would make demands on Unipart's performance far beyond those of any European-owned customer. He realized that the customer would not only create the crisis but could also offer hands-on assistance in introducing lean methods to resolve it.

For the truly bold executive there is one more lever of change available, and that is to consciously create conditions in which there will be a firm-threatening crisis unless lean actions are taken. For example, we've studied a manufacturer of long-lead-time, complex machinery which has recently begun to sell a critical new range of products, set for initial deliveries in a couple of years, at prices that can only be profitable *if* the firm quickly adopts lean methods to bring down costs dramatically across the board. This is clearly a high-risk path, but if the change agent truly wants to create a crisis, there are many ways to orchestrate one.

Forget Grand Strategy for the Moment

We've encountered many firms that truly are in a crisis but respond mainly with strategic analysis: "Are we in the *best* businesses for us to be in? Should we sell some of our troubled businesses [presumably to buyers who don't know their problems] and buy some new businesses [presumably from sellers who don't know their businesses' worth]? Should we increase R&D spending and try to create a product no one else can duplicate? Should we form a strategic alliance with other firms to achieve synergies? Should we merge with competitors or wage a takeover campaign to gain scale economies and reduce competition?"

Some of these firms really are in industries with no opportunities, but it's all too easy to start blaming your industry rather than yourself. If you quickly eliminate *muda* in product development, sales and scheduling, and operations, you'll soon discover that as you fundamentally change your cost base, shorten production lead times and time-to-market for new products, and increase your flexibility, the prospects for your business(es) will look very different. Even if it turns out that some businesses have severe structural problems, you won't be worse off for making them lean because very little capital investment will be needed. (Remember: If a major investment is required, you're not getting lean.) Your cost base will fall, meaning your operating results will improve even if sales volume and prices don't. You will also have bought time to think (for a very modest price), even if it turns out that a very lean business (like Showa's parking carousels) is not sufficiently profitable to continue.

Map Your Value Streams

Once you've got the leadership, the knowledge, and the sense of urgency, it's time to identify your current value streams and map them—activity by activity and step by step—by product family.

Many firms embracing business process reengineering may think they have already done this, but in fact they've only gone a small part of the way. Typically, a reengineering approach concentrates on information flow rather than production operations or product development (because functional resistance is much lower for these office activities formerly organized by department). Reengineering rarely looks beyond the firm to delve into the operations of suppliers and distributors, even when these account for the great majority of costs and lead times. And even within narrow business processes, the focus is usually on streamlining aggregated activities rather than on addressing the needs of individual product families.

Other firms we've recently visited have told us at the front door that they are "lean" because they have introduced cellular assembly or dedicated product development teams. In the words of the typical Porsche supplier, "There is really nothing more for us to do." Yet we almost always discover that their accomplishments to date are tiny islands in a sea of *muda*. For example, we recently examined a computer firm which conducts final assembly of computer workstations in continuous-flow cells, one for each product family, rather than on the long assembly line used previously for all products combined. Time and effort for assembly itself have been reduced substantially and the new approach is more flexible. However, problems with in-house and upstream supplies necessitate an eight-week supply of the average part, so the plant still builds to forecast rather than to precise customer order, and the forecast is often wrong. The problem, of course, is that lean techniques have been applied only to the tiny course of the value stream which was easy to fix, specifically flow in one part of one plant, and which did not require any change in the behavior of internal or external suppliers.

So, to repeat, look at the entire value stream for individual products. Your customers are only interested in their product and they generally define value in terms of the whole product (often a good plus a service). They are not interested in your organization or your supplier and distributor relations, and they are certainly not interested in the security of your job. Market-based societies permit to exist and thrive those organizations which do a good job of identifying and serving customer needs rather than the organization's own interests.

Begin as Soon as Possible with an Important and Visible Activity

It would be wonderful if you as the change agent could simply decree a new way: "We will take all of our value-creating activities and make them flow, starting this morning. Then we'll introduce pull beginning tomorrow." Unfortunately, that's not how things work. Instead, you need to start as quickly as you can with a specific activity—perhaps it's the fabrication and assembly of Product G. You need to involve the direct work group, the managers of all the levels between you and them, other senior executives you hope to convert to lean thinking, your *sensei* (internal or external), and yourself. Often, although not in every case, it's best to start with a physical production activity because the change will be much easier for everyone to see.

We advise people to start with an activity that is performing very poorly but which is very important to the firm. That way, you can't afford to fail, the potential for improvement is very large, and you will find yourself drawing on resources and strengths you didn't know you had in order to ensure success.

Demand Immediate Results

One of the critical features of lean techniques is immediate feedback. The improvement team and the whole workforce should be able to see things changing before their eyes. This is essential to creating the psychological sense of flow in the workforce and the momentum for change within your organization.

So, don't conduct a lengthy planning exercise. Your value-stream maps can be completed in only a week or two. And don't bother with simulations to see about the "what ifs." We have studied one firm which had even developed a complex computer simulation package to predict what would happen if a single machine was moved anywhere in its production system. Because the predictions were always unsettling, the company never moved anything!

Finally, don't waste time on benchmarking if there is any way to get your firm moving without it. We gave the benchmarking industry a big boost with our previous book, which described the most ambitious benchmarking ever attempted in a single industry, and for companies that are completely asleep, benchmarking may be an essential first step. However, if you already understand lean thinking and lean techniques, you should simply identify the *muda* around you through value stream mapping and get started immediately on removing it. Benchmarking as a way to avoid the need for immediate action is itself *muda*.

Once you dive in, if nothing dramatic is accomplished in the first week of working on a problem activity—typically a halving of required effort, a 90 percent reduction of work-in-process, a halving of space requirements, and a 90 percent drop in production lead time—you've either got the wrong *sensei* or you are not really a change agent. Figure out which it is and take appropriate action immediately!

When you get your first results invite a cross-section of your firm to the report-out. The best way to communicate the changes under way is simply to take everyone to the scene of the action and show precisely what is happening.

As Soon as You've Got Momentum, Expand Your Scope

We've found that it's critical to quickly produce some dramatic results everyone can see by focusing on a particularly troubled activity, usually in physical production. However, as soon as the first round of improvements are in hand, it's time to start linking the different parts of the value stream for a product family.

To take a simple example, once you've learned how to convert fabrication and assembly of Product G from large batches to flow, it's time to learn to pull, both by converting the next upstream processes to flow and also by establishing a level schedule and a formal pull system. As you do this, "backward steps" are bound to occur because the precise purpose of these techniques is to expose and eliminate all types of waste. It's only when the flow stops that you know you've found the next problem to work on.

Once you have flow and pull started on the shop floor, it is time to go to work on your ordering system. *Kaikaku* in the office is not as easy to see as moving machines on the shop floor, but it's equally vital. Start with office activities that are directly linked to the activities you just changed on the floor. Prepare the way by involving office staff in the early shop-floor *kaikaku* weeks—where they can play a useful role just by asking dumb questions: Why do you do it this way? After they grasp the fundamentals and see the potential, they are ready to ask the same questions about office work. Then, once a bridgehead is established, go to work on all of your activities related to selling, formal order-taking, and scheduling.

At the same time you start to introduce pull in production and order-taking, you need to start thinking about flow and pull in product development for each product family. This is particularly the case because for most firms the quickest way to grow sales in order to absorb freed-up production resources is to speed up products already in the pipeline. We routinely found cases in our research of firms which were able to eliminate three quarters of their previous development time for routine or follow-on products while reducing manufacturing cost and improving quality and user satisfaction. In every case they boosted their sales substantially (at no cost) and found uses for their excess people.

As you progressively move your lean transformation beyond a physical manufacturing environment, you will find more of a need to transpose the logic of lean thinking to suit different mind-sets and circumstances. Even with the most positive attitude, staff in a warehouse or a retail activity will find it very hard initially to see how flow and pull apply to their activities. After all, they don't "make" anything in a physical sense and they've spent years blaming manufacturing for not getting its job done on time.

For example, Unipart's Industries Division had been receiving help for several years from Toyota's supplier development group at their U.K. plant, but Unipart found it difficult to know where to start in applying lean thinking to its warehousing and distribution businesses. It was only after a recent visit to Toyota's Parts Distribution Centers described in Chapter 4 that "the light went on" and Unipart's managers could see how to apply lean concepts to their spare parts distribution operations for Rover and Jaguar.

For instance, once they understood that the *muda* of overproduction translates in the warehouse world as a "faster than necessary pace" and that leveling incoming orders is a necessary precondition for creating flow, they were able to make rapid progress. In their first weeklong *kaikaku* they freed up enough space and people to take on a large new account distributing service parts for a major manufacturer of laser printers.

Creating an Organization to Channel Your Streams

Many leaders who don't fully understand lean thinking jump to the wrong conclusion after the exhilarating success of the initial "breakthrough" exercise. "We've done it for one activity," they'll say. "Now all we need to do is replicate what we've done in every other activity and we will be lean within a few months." The reality is that you are only at the beginning. The next leap is to create an organization which can channel the flow of value and keep the stream from silting up again. You'll also need to devise a practical strategy to fully utilize all of the resources being freed up.

Doing this requires reorganizing your business by product families with someone clearly in charge of each product and creating a truly strong lean promotion function which becomes the repository of your hard-earned skills. It also requires a consistent approach to employment in your firm and a willingness to remove those few managers who will never accept the new way. Finally, it means creating a mind-set in which temporary failure in pursuit of the right goal is acceptable but no amount of improvement in performance is ever enough.

Reorganize Your Firm by Product Family and Value Stream

As we noted in the Introduction, the proper purpose of a business organization is to identify and channel the value stream for a family of products so that value flows smoothly to the customer. As you get the kinks out of your physical production, order-taking, and product development, it will become obvious that reorganizing by product family and value stream is the best way to sustain your achievement. And as you right-size your tools, it will become apparent that a large fraction of your people and tools can be dedicated to specific product families.

This means identifying your product families and rethinking your functions to realign marketing/sales, product development, scheduling, production, and purchasing activities in coherent units. The exact way to do this will vary with the nature of the business, the sales volume for products, and the type and number of customers. But the basic idea can be applied in most businesses. The organization chart for your lean business will begin to look like the one in Figure 11.1.

The boxes are drawn in proportion to the number of employees in each, making clear that the product family teams account for the great bulk of human effort in the business. The functions with their allocated overheads have shrunk dramatically by contrast.

Create a Lean Promotion Function

Your *sensei* will need a place to sit down (although a good *sensei* doesn't sit very often). Your process mappers will need somewhere in the organization to call home. The extra people you will soon be freeing up will need a place to go (which explains the size of the "lean" function in Figure 11.1). Your improvement teams will need logistics support. And your operating managers will need continual education in lean methods and periodic evaluation of their efforts to make sure there is no backsliding. In short, you need a permanent lean promotion group and it should report directly to the change agent.

FIGURE 11.1: PROTOTYPE LEAN ORGANIZATION

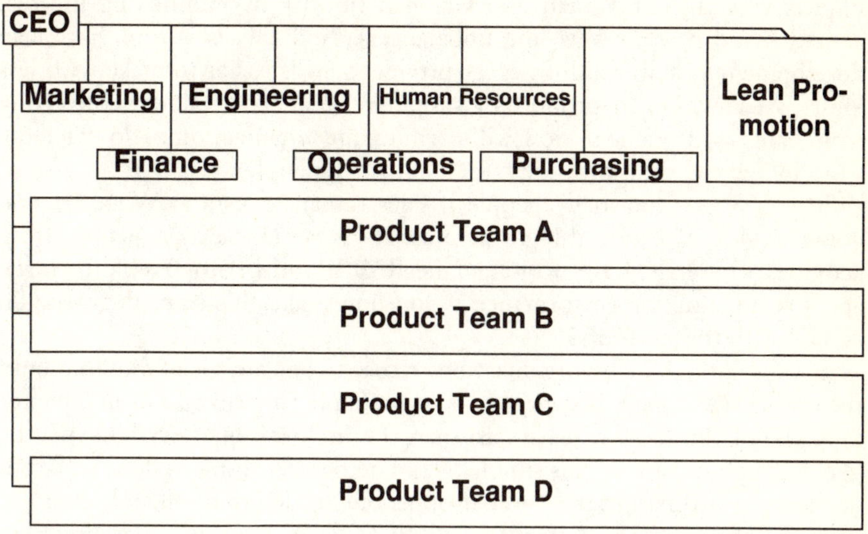

```
CEO
 ├── Marketing   Engineering   Human Resources   Lean Promotion
 │      Finance     Operations     Purchasing
 ├── Product Team A
 ├── Product Team B
 ├── Product Team C
 └── Product Team D
```

An even better idea is to combine your quality assurance function with your lean promotion function so that quality enhancement, productivity improvement, lead-time reduction, space savings, and every other performance dimension of your business are considered equally and simultaneously.

One of the standard problems in getting started on lean implementation is that your operating managers may think that your quality assurance experts and your lean experts are telling them to do different things. In fact, they are telling them to do the same thing—eliminate the *muda* of errors and of waiting at the source so value can flow smoothly—but they use different terminology. (For example, Ed Northern at Pratt remembers that "Mr. Ito was yelling one thing in my right ear while Mr. Iwata seemed to be yelling something different in my left ear. I found this frustrating and confusing until I realized their messages were consistent once you got the terms straightened out.") Some initial attention to "standard language," so everyone is using the same terminology, and a consolidation of the quality and lean functions is an excellent investment.

Deal with Excess People at the Outset

Our rule of thumb is that when you convert a pure batch-and-queue activity to lean techniques you can eventually reduce human effort by three quarters with little or no capital investment. When you convert a "flow" production setup—like the Henry Ford–style production line at Porsche—to lean techniques, you can cut human effort in half (mostly by eliminating indirect activities and rework plus line imbalances). And this is before your lean development system rethinks every product so it is easier to make with less effort. Meanwhile, in product development and order-taking, converting from batch-and-queue to flow will permit your organization to do twice the work in half the time with the same number of people.

So you've got too many people if sales remain constant. What are you going to do? The one thing you must do is remove excess people from activities where they are no longer needed. It will be impossible to make and sustain superior performance if you don't take this step. But what do you do with these people?

As we've noted, many organizations refuse to consider lean thinking until the crisis is very deep. If your ship is truly foundering (like Pratt in Chapter 8), some of the crew will have to man the lifeboats or everything will be lost, and you must face this simple fact. The correct thing to do is to face it up front, by estimating the number of people needed to do the job the right way, and moving immediately to this level. Then you must guarantee that no one will lose their job in the future due to the introduction of lean techniques. And you must keep your promise.

What you can't do is conduct drip torture in which you move through your organization activity by activity, asking your employees to help you eliminate their jobs with no end in sight. As we've tried to explain, in a lean world there is no end to improvement: Jobs are always being eliminated in specific activities. Your employees will react as they should to the introduction of what they will call "mean" production with subtle but effective sabotage. Improvements will be impossible to sustain.

If you are not foundering, you have a luxury and you have a problem. You can protect jobs, but it's harder to get people to change. The correct approach is to concentrate on particularly troubled activities and build momentum for change while sending people no longer needed for these activities to the lean promotion function or elsewhere in the organization. As you demonstrate over time that no one loses because lean techniques are introduced, and that in fact everyone's job security is increased, employees gradually become more cooperative and proactive. On the other hand, just one slip—one failure to honor your commitment to protect jobs—will take years to overcome.

Devise a Growth Strategy

We are sometimes contacted by managements who are making adequate profits but see lean techniques as a clever way to quickly raise margins by eliminating as many people as possible under the guise of "embracing the new paradigm" and "world-class competitiveness." We always tell executives with this mentality the same thing: Don't bother. You can save some money at the outset but you will never sustain leanness.

A far more promising approach is to devise a growth strategy which absorbs resources at the rate they are being freed up. Precisely what to do will depend on a firm's situation, but the arrows in the lean firm's quiver are easy to list. Some may wish to pass cost savings directly through to gain volume. (This has been Freudenberg-NOK's prime strategy to get started. Total sales have tripled in only five years while headcount has been held constant.) And some may wish to speed up development of projects in the pipeline to spur sales and increase market share. (Wiremold did this.) Others may focus on shortening production lead times, delivering exactly on schedule, and making exactly the configuration of product the customer wants, again to boost sales of conventional products. (Lantech.) Still others may try to convert their product from a good to a service and add downstream distribution and service activities to their traditional production tasks. (A path Pratt has just entered into.) And some firms may integrate backwards upstream to consolidate previously scattered production activities into single-piece flow. (The example we cited in Chapter 3 on the glass industry.) Ultimately, most lean firms may want to do all of these things for their existing product lines.

However, this may still not be enough. You may need an additional strategy, but it's best to devise it after you've changed the way you think and run your business rather than making a desperation lunge at your problems beforehand. Once you've seen what lean techniques can do in your firm and reviewed the map of the entire value stream for every product family, you are ready to figure out what to do.

The lean firms we have examined usually find that they can capture adequate growth and profits by sticking to what they know, often by acquiring related lines of business. (Showa was the one exception.) What's more, they find that they can largely finance their acquisitions with the cash they free up in the inventories of the batch-and-queue firms they acquire.

Those firms which need to branch out into unfamiliar activities can do so by establishing product teams for each new product family and continually evaluating their performance against expectations. The virtue of this approach is that product families can be added or dropped without changing the fundamental structure of the firm.

REMOVE THE ANCHOR-DRAGGERS

In every organization we've looked at there was a small group of managers, generally less than 10 percent, who simply could not accept new ideas.

Hierarchical personalities needing a clear chain of command and something to control were particular problems.

And in every successful transition we've examined, change agents, in looking back over their experience, wish they had acted faster to remove managers who would not cooperate. This sounds harsh, of course, but it is the simple lesson of experience. A small percent of managers will move quickly to accept lean ideas—the "early adopters" in marketing parlance—but the great mass will be undecided. The problem is with the few percent who will never go along, because they send an opposite message from the early adopters and take special pleasure in highlighting all the mistakes made along the path to leanness. The result paralyzes the great mass in the middle and jeopardizes success.

To repeat: As you begin the process, most managers and employees will not understand what you are doing but will be neutral to positive if you make employment guarantees. Take action quickly to remove those managers who won't give new ideas a fair trial.

When You've Fixed Something, Fix It Again

At the end of the first improvement initiative on an activity, tell the line management and the work team that in three months it will be time to fix it again. It's critical to get your employees to understand at the outset that no level of performance is ever good enough, and that there is always room for improvement. This will usually mean moving every machine and changing every job.

In the early years of the lean transition, the lean promotion function will have to take the lead in planning successive improvement campaigns. Increasingly over time, however, improvement becomes the most critical job of the product team leader and the primary workforce. You must instill the idea that management is no longer about running activities in a steady state and avoiding variances. Instead, it's about eliminating the root causes of variances (so they permanently disappear and managers can stop fighting fires) while improving performance in periodic leaps that never end. How much did you improve performance? must become the critical question in evaluating managers.

"Two Steps Forward and One Step Backward Is O.K.; No Steps Forward Is Not O.K."

A critical moment in the lean transition at Pratt & Whitney occurred when the energetic general manager of the turbine blade plant took on a task which was correct in principle but too ambitious in practice. When Mark

Coran reassigned this manager and his direct reports to other jobs in Pratt instead of firing them (the usual step taken in this situation in the past), he sent a critically important message that mistakes in pursuit of the right goal are not a failure.

When Coran at the same time terminated the general manager of another Component Center for anchor-dragging on the lean conversion (in an operation that was performing no worse than it had historically), he sent the complementary message that it's not acceptable to do nothing to improve your operation on the grounds that the risk of failure is too high. Getting these twin messages across is a critical task of the change agent.

Install Business Systems to Encourage Lean Thinking

Once you've got momentum (in the first six months of the transition) and have rethought your organization (over perhaps the next year), you're a long ways toward your goal of a lean transformation. However, additional steps are important to make the new approach self-sustaining. Once you've overcome the initial inertia, the number of proposals for improvement will snowball and you'll need a mechanism for deciding what's most important to do now and what can wait until resources are available. You will also need to create a new way to keep score and to reward your people so they will continue to do the right things, and you'll need to make everything in your organization transparent so everyone can see what to do and how to improve. In addition, you will need a systematic method for teaching lean thinking to every employee (including your customers' and suppliers' employees along your value streams). Finally, you'll need to systematically rethink your tools, ranging from monster machines in the factory to computer systems for scheduling, with the objective of devising right-sized technologies which can be inserted directly into the value stream for individual product families.

Utilize Policy Deployment

We've tried to emphasize that to get started in a brownfield you need to "just do it." Get started and show some striking results. However, Lantech's experience of taking on too many lean initiatives once the ball was rolling is the norm rather than the exception. Therefore, it's vital to use the tools of policy deployment to reach agreement across your whole organization on the three or four lean tasks your firm can hope to complete each year. An example for year three might be: Reorganize by product families, introduce a Lean Accounting System, *kaizen* every major production activity four times, and *kaikaku* order-taking and scheduling.

An even more important task for your annual policy deployment exercise will be to identify the tasks you can't hope to succeed at just yet but which some parts of the organization will badly want to tackle right now. You'll need to publicly acknowledge that these are important but they will need to be "deselected" until the next year or the year after, when resources are available.

Create a Lean Accounting System

Many firms today still run standard cost accounting systems, although many more have made some move toward Activity Based Costing. The latter is a great advance, but you can go even further. What you really need is value-stream/product-based costing including product development and selling as well as production and supplier costs so that all participants in a value stream can see clearly whether their collective efforts are adding more cost than value or the reverse.

Once you reorganize by product family and shrink your traditional functions with their allocated overheads, it becomes a lot easier to assign rather than allocate costs to products so that product team leaders and their team members can see where they stand. Your own accounting group should be able to figure out how to do this—you don't need a consultant—but we strongly recommend that you start with the chief financial officer and involve him or her in several weeks of hands-on improvement activities to get started. Then ask the simple question: What kind of management accounting system would cause our product team leaders to always do the right (lean) thing?

You will still need a financial accounting system for your profit-and-loss statement, which does strange things like value potentially obsolete inventories as assets, but you won't need or want to show it to your product team leaders. What's more, you will need to make a gradual transition from your current system to the new lean approach over a year or so to avoid chaos.

Pay Your People in Relation to the Performance of Your Firm

The ideal compensation scheme would pay each employee in exact proportion to the value they add, as value is determined by the customer. However, actually doing this would present insurmountable technical problems and could in any case only be achieved with enormous, non-value-adding effort.

We have found that in a lean firm the simplest and cheapest method of calculating compensation is generally the best. This means paying a market wage to employees based on their general qualifications—for example, whatever assembly workers or entry-level product engineers receive on average in the area of a facility—along with a bonus tied directly to the profitability of the firm. Because a lean firm should be substantially more profitable than average, the bonus should be a significant fraction of total compensation. (For example, Wiremold has set a target for its bonus of about 20 percent of base pay, on the presumption that Wiremold should be at least this much more profitable than the "average" manufacturing firm in the Hartford area and in its industry.)

As you consider bonus schemes, it will quickly become apparent that the total amounts on offer, while substantial, will not be enormous. This underlines the reality that the primary incentive for working in a lean system is that the work itself provides positive feedback and a psychological sense of flow.

We are often asked about incentive pay for employees in the manufacturing area and about adjusting compensation by product family. There is something to be said for both of these ideas, but on balance, we don't support them. Incentive pay is really a carry-over from the old days of piecework and is sometimes used today to deal with the perception that work pace is harder in lean systems. In fact, the pace of minute-to-minute exertion is the same. The difference is that lean systems identify and eliminate practically all of the nonproductive slack time for employees at every level. Therefore, it initially feels as if the work is harder, but after a period of acclimation, when a lack of *muda* begins to seem normal, people often report that the pace is actually much easier than before. In any case, trying to buy the allegiance of your workforce to a lean system with cash is approaching the problem from the wrong direction. Instead, stress the positive aspects of the new work environment.

With regard to separate bonuses for members of each product family, lean accounting makes them technically feasible, but we think they're also a bad idea. In a lean system, work tasks are evaluated very carefully by the work team itself to achieve an even pace with no wasted time. Looking across a firm, the pace of work inside each product family should be very similar. What's more, it will frequently be necessary to reassign employees from one product family to another, sometimes after an interlude in the lean promotion function, as the needs of the business change. Reassignments will generate continuous conflict if bonuses vary from product family to product family because of varying competitive conditions in the marketplace.

Make Everything Transparent

Benchmarking others usually wastes time you could better spend doing the right thing. However, benchmarking your internal performance, especially your rate of improvement, is critical. In addition, it's vital to create a "scoreboard" which shows everyone involved in a value stream exactly what's happening in real time. These don't need to be complicated or require significant investment. We're always amazed in touring lean firms (like Porsche) at how much about the status and improvement trajectory of an operation can be shown with simple diagrams and process status boards. Many of these require little in the way of language or math skills to understand yet give a clear sense of what's happening.

Teach Lean Thinking and Skills to Everyone

It has become conventional wisdom that higher levels of management should learn to listen to the primary work team since they know the most about how to get the job done. Unfortunately, this bit of common sense is only half right. Your primary workforce probably does know the most about the hard technical aspects of getting isolated jobs done (including all the deviations from poorly maintained official procedures which are necessary in order to get products made at all). But what primary workers and front-line managers typically don't understand is how to think horizontally about the total flow of value and how to pull it. Nor do they typically understand the methods of root cause analysis to eliminate the need for fire fighting. Therefore, if you ask your primary workforce to implement lean techniques or permanently solve problems today, you are likely to get a rush of suggestions followed by general disillusionment when they fail to work properly.

To gain the critical lean skills, your workforce needs training, but of a special type. One of us (Jones) has recently worked with the Unipart Group in the U.K. to totally rethink skills acquisition and to create a "Unipart University" immediately adjacent to the value stream. While many firms have created corporate "universities" in campus settings in recent years (of which Motorola University is probably the best known), these mostly utilize dedicated faculty and off-line learning activities. At Unipart, the faculty are entirely line managers (which means they must learn operational skills themselves, skills rarely mastered by senior managers in Western firms) and the skills being taught are precisely those needed immediately for the next phase in the lean transition.

Thus lean learning and policy deployment can be carefully synchronized so that knowledge is supplied just-in-time and in a way that reinforces the commitment of managers and all employees to doing the right thing. Everyone learns the same approach to problem solving and everyone experiences the direct benefits of continuous learning, even though they may have left formal education many years ago. Over time, the investment in training can also be directly connected to the resulting improvements in the business.

Right-Size Your Tools

By tools we don't mean just production equipment but also information management systems, test equipment, prototyping systems, and even organizational groupings. For example, think of a department devoted to a specific activity—let's say accounts receivable—as a type of tool.

You can begin to rethink your tools from your very first *kaikaku*. However, your major monuments will present a major challenge and one which can't be solved immediately. First, you will need to counter the ancient bias of your managers that large, fast, elaborate, dedicated, and centralized tools are more efficient. This, of course, is the cornerstone of batch-and-queue thinking. Instead, for every activity you should ask them to work backwards by asking, What kind of tools would permit products in a given family to flow smoothly through the system with no delays and no back loops? And, What types of tools would permit us to switch over instantly between products so there would be no need to make batches?

As you think about this, you will be surprised to learn that many of your existing "monuments" can be made much more flexible with a bit of creative thinking. You will be further surprised to discover that two small machines with only the features needed generally cost much less in total than one big one with all the bells and whistles. Finally, you will be surprised to discover how much of your new tooling can be built inside your firm using excess materials at very low cost by excess people freed up by lean techniques. (Consider throwing away your industrial equipment catalogues and getting directions to your local junkyard!)

The more you think, the more you will realize that you can provide most value streams with their own dedicated equipment to completely cut out bottlenecks at monuments and stoppages due to changeovers. Then, when the value stream shifts its course, you can quickly redeploy your right-sized tools to serve new needs. However, tackling your major monuments and completely replacing them with right-sized apparatus will probably only get into full swing after several years of making the best of what you have already.

Completing the Transformation

When you're moving ahead at full speed, have your organization reconfigured, and have the appropriate business systems in place (probably after three to four years of strenuous effort), you're well on your way to a complete transformation. The final steps needed are to make sure that your suppliers and distributors are following your lead, that you are creating value as close to your customer as possible, and that you are making lean thinking automatic and bottom-up, rather than merely top-down.

Convince Your Suppliers and Customers to Take the Steps Just Described

It's a rare firm today whose internal activities account for more than a third of the total cost and lead time needed to get its product to market. The de-integration Toyota started in 1949, which eventually decreased its in-house "cost added" from 75 percent to less than 25 percent of total costs, has become the norm for firms across the world. Therefore, you will get only so far along the path to leanness—one quarter to one third of the way in most cases—unless you get your suppliers and customer firms to take the steps just described.

It won't help much to hurl insults or play suppliers or customers against each other. You can make them mad and squeeze their margins, but these tactics generally do nothing for their costs and lead times because they simply don't know what to do. And as time goes on, they either find someone else to do business with or underinvest in product development or their distribution channels.

The only alternative is to actually fix their production, product development, and order-taking systems by sending them your lean promotion team. (This is also an excellent way to be alert to broader trends in industry and to keep your lean thinkers sharp by continually exposing them to new situations.) Don't do this until you've fixed your own activities which the supplier or downstream firm links into, but then go as fast as possible and accept no excuses. "We've done it quickly. We know you can, too. Here's how. Let's get going."

To make this approach feasible, it's obvious that you will need to winnow down your upstream and downstream partner list and prepare to work with them for the long term. When you go to help them, don't charge for your help. Instead, agree up front on how you are going to share the savings. (Porsche and its suppliers decided on a three-way split in which the suppliers kept a third of the cost savings and Porsche got two thirds with Porsche agreeing to pass half of its savings on to the customer in lower prices.) It should be easy to get paid back as well in better quality and shorter lead times for your products.

Point out that there is an extra "win" for your suppliers in this "win-win-win" situation because they will learn how to cut costs and lead times on all of their activities but will probably not need to pass these savings along to their other customers who are still bogged down in short-term, market-based thinking. This is how Toyota and its Japanese suppliers both became fabulously wealthy in the 1970s and 1980s. The suppliers, after learning from Toyota, sold to all of Toyota's direct competitors except Nissan at higher prices than they sold to Toyota while steadily gaining business from these firms by underpricing batch-and-queue competitors in the supplier community.

Finally, as soon as your suppliers and downstream customers start to improve their in-house performance, insist that they send their newly created process improvement teams to fix their own suppliers or downstream customers. (Remember that your suppliers and downstream partners are typically no more integrated than you are.) Set continually declining target prices and continually increasing quality and reliability goals, which make it impossible for them to relax.

It will help this process to bring your first-tier suppliers together in a supplier association for mutual learning of the type long utilized by Toyota.[5] Your first tiers may then wish to draw up a short list of second-tier suppliers they wish to work with. Then the resources of the first tiers can be concentrated on a much smaller number of second-tier firms. (Chrysler has recently launched an initiative in North America to do just this.) Similarly, the assembler firm near the customer at the end of the physical production stream may need to join forces with other lean-minded assemblers to take on the most intractable "batch-head" raw materials suppliers and show them a better way. (Buying raw materials in large lots at lower prices on behalf of your suppliers will seem like a much easier path, but this approach can only squeeze the margins of the raw materials firms unless someone shows them how to run their businesses in a different way.)

Develop a Lean Global Strategy

Some firms can exist happily by doing everything in only one place. For example, Porsche can sell a modest volume of exotic cars to the entire world from one design/scheduling/production location in southwest Germany. Ferrari can do the same thing from northern Italy. The mystique in their products protects firms of this type from knockoffs. In addition, volatility in some export markets, due to currency shifts or changes in tastes, can be tolerated if no one market accounts for a large fraction of total sales. The world as a whole will provide a stable enough market.

Other firms may be happy to remain small. Wiremold, for example, sees no prospect or need for significant markets for its products in Europe or Asia while Lantech is happy to take advantage of export opportunities as they arise but to treat them as a windfall rather than a core aspect of the business. There is plenty of growth potential for these firms in their home markets to utilize the resources freed up during the transition. What's more, expansion into related product lines will be sufficient to absorb resources in the future.

Many other firms, however, like the major automotive, electronics, and aerospace firms and their first-tier suppliers, need a global market and production presence. The adoption of lean thinking will call for a very different strategy from many of those being pursued today.

Many people initially believe that lean techniques are mostly about cost reductions. In fact, they provide the one feasible way to cut costs while also shortening production lead times and time-to-market, improving quality, and providing customers with exactly what they want precisely when they want it. They also make it possible to design, order, produce, and deliver goods at smaller production scales by means of dedicated product teams, without paying a scale or investment-cost penalty.

It follows that for most products with global market potential, the correct global strategy is to develop a complete design, order-taking, and production system within each major market of sale. This makes it much easier to communicate with the customer and also makes it possible to design, produce, and deliver the product very quickly with just the right specifications. "High-tech" mass production at a centralized global location—an example of which we examined in Chapter 10—and a far-flung design and production system seeking to find the lowest wage cost for every activity along a complex value stream can never achieve these combined objectives. These alternative strategies optimize one course of the value stream at the expense of the whole.

Convert from Top-Down Leadership to Bottom-Up Initiatives

Initially, the process improvement group will work top-down because the pressing need is to change the way your employees think by directly demonstrating a better way. Over time, however, the process improvement group will focus more on making every line manager a *sensei* and every employee a proactive process engineer. The function can then tackle only the very toughest problems where line managers still need outside help. This is the present-day assignment of the Operations Management Consulting Division within the Toyota group.

One of the paradoxes of lean thinking is that the ideas themselves are extraordinarily antihierarchical and pro-democractic. Every worker inspects his or her own work, becomes multiskilled, and participates in periodic job redesign through *kaizen* activities. Layers of management are permanently stripped away. Transparency makes every aspect of the business open for everyone to see. Yet getting the critical mass of employees to change their traditional way of thinking requires stern direction as employees are commanded to try things which seem completely crazy.

So, there is a critical transition as you move your organization through the lean transformation, a point when managers must become coaches rather than tyrants and employees become proactive. This transition is the key to a self-sustaining organization. And please note: If you are the change agent, you may become the biggest problem. We've encountered more than one change agent who wanted to continue commanding change from the top when those on the bottom were quite capable of sustaining it on their own. This can easily become a negative sum situation.

One solution is to change your behavior. Another is simply to move on. Many of the best change agents we've encountered seem to work best by converting an organization over a period of several years, then turning senior management over to a more collegial personality, and moving on to another firm still full of "concrete heads."

The Inevitable Results of a Five-Year Commitment

Whenever we encounter a would-be change agent who wants to transform his or her firm, we ask a simple question: Are you willing to work very hard, accept the one step backward which comes with the two steps forward, and stick to your task for five full years? Taking all the steps forward typically takes about this long, as summarized in Table 11.1

While a few firms (for example, Wiremold) can go much faster if the change agent is firmly in command and has done it all before, this extended period is usually needed because a large number of people, including the senior leadership, must be taught to see the difference between value and *muda*. And a significant period of experimentation by ordinary managers—complete with backward steps—is necessary before everyone begins automatically to apply lean thinking and move the organization ahead from the bottom and the middle ranks. It's only at this point that the change agent can step in front of the bus without being missed and it's at this point also that the full financial benefits of lean thinking are apparent. From this point we believe there will be no turning back and the change agent may even want to move on to a new challenge.

There is today an enormous amount of cynicism in the industrial world —cynicism fueled by the latest quick-fix "program," business process reengineering. However, a growing fraction of managers seem to understand that real change and building a solid foundation simply take time. We believe, based on conversations with many of you, that you're willing to rise to the challenge if you are sure that something is really there at the end of the rainbow. One of our major objectives in this book has been to show that there is.

If you are really determined to be the change agent and you get a good

TABLE 11.1: TIME FRAME FOR THE LEAN LEAP

Phase	Specific Steps	Time Frame
Get started	Find a change agent Get lean knowledge Find a lever Map value streams Begin *kaikaku* Expand your scope	First six months
Create a new organization	Reorganize by product family Create a lean function Devise a policy for excess people Devise a growth strategy Remove anchor-draggers Instill a "perfection" mind-set	Six months through year two
Install business systems	Introduce lean accounting Relate pay to firm performance Implement transparency Initiate policy deployment Introduce lean learning Find right-sized tools	Years three and four
Complete the transformation	Apply these steps to your suppliers/customers Develop global strategy Transition from top-down to bottom-up improvement	By end of year five

sensei (or become one yourself), we *guarantee* you will achieve extraordinary things. The techniques we have described in the earlier chapters have been tested around the world in a wide variety of industries, and they always work.

Of course, even a brilliantly performing firm can fail for reasons beyond anyone's control—an unsuspected environmental problem with the product, a drastic shift in consumer tastes, the sudden appearance of a new technology which totally eliminates the need for the old product (for example, the clothespin after the home dryer, the vacuum tube after the transistor). Nevertheless, with a lean tool kit, the chances of succeeding in your chosen activities will soar.

The Next Leap

Just as the introduction of lean thinking forces problems and waste to the surface in all operational areas, new organizational problems will inevitably arise as you apply these ideas. As you shrink your traditional functions, which were formerly the key to career paths in your organization, many employees will start to express anxieties about where they are going and whether they have a "home." And as you place more employees in development and production activities relentlessly focused on the here-and-now, you may begin to wonder about their hard technical skills. Are your engineers retaining leading-edge capabilities or are they simply applying over and over what they already know?

Perhaps most striking, as you take all of the inventories and waste out of your internal value stream, you will become much more aware of the costs and performance problems of firms above and below you along the stream, including your suppliers' suppliers and your distributors' retailers. Offering them technical assistance will be necessary, but it won't be sufficient. To move farther down the path to leanness it will soon be apparent that you will need to work with all the participants in a value stream in a new way.

We believe that adequately addressing these problems will require a final organizational leap, one not even Toyota has taken. We call it the *lean enterprise* and we will explain it in Part III.

PART III
LEAN ENTERPRISE

CHAPTER 12:

A Channel for the Stream; a Valley for the Channel*

We're sometimes asked, What's new here? What are you saying that we haven't heard before? This is an excellent question with a simple answer: We are putting the entire value stream for specific products relentlessly in the foreground and rethinking every aspect of jobs, careers, functions, and firms in order to correctly specify value and make it flow continuously along the whole length of the stream as pulled by the customer in pursuit of perfection.

This is an extremely creative and productive thing to do, but it is not natural. Most of the time, the majority of us think first about our jobs and then about our careers. Because our careers often progress through departments and functions, we also look out for the interests of these organization building blocks. Most senior managers are rewarded on the basis of how well their firm does, and specifically by how much money it makes. Note that no one is looking out, first and foremost, for the performance of the whole value stream, the only issue of relevance to the customer.

In previous chapters, a solution to the jobs problem has been proposed: Eliminate at the outset those jobs which can't be sustained *if a firm is to survive* and then guarantee those which remain. This is not a perfect solution, because some managements only face reality when it is extremely near at hand, making large job losses unavoidable. But at least the correct approach is simple and understandable. What's more, as more managers start to embrace lean thinking, corrective actions can be taken before the crisis emerges and most jobs can be safeguarded. Indeed, we are certain that the total number of jobs will grow as lean thinking becomes normal thinking. By contrast, the careers, functions, and firm "problems" are more complex.

---

* This chapter elaborates on ideas first presented in James P. Womack and Daniel T. Jones, "From Lean Production to the Lean Enterprise," *Havard Business Review*, March–April 1994, pp. 93–103.

The Lean Enterprise

As we thought about these problems it occurred to us that the first step was to create a new mechanism for looking at the whole, a channel for the value stream. We called this the *lean enterprise* and have briefly alluded to it at several points in the text. Now we need to describe it in detail.

The objectives of the lean enterprise are very simple: Correctly specify value for the customer, avoiding the normal tendency for each firm along the stream to define value differently to favor its own role in providing it (for example: the manufacturer who thinks the physical product itself is the customer's primary interest, the independent sales and service company that believes responsive customer relations account for most of the value perceived by the customer, etcetera). Then identify all the actions required to bring a product from concept to launch, from order to delivery, and from raw material into the hands of the customer and on through its useful life. Next, remove any actions which do not create value and make those actions which do create value proceed in continuous flow as pulled by the customer. Finally, analyze the results and start the evaluation process over again.[1] Continue this cycle for the life of the product or product family as a normal part, indeed the core activity, of "management."

The mechanism of the lean enterprise is also very simple: a conference of all the firms along the stream, assisted by technical staff from "lean functions" in the participating firms, to periodically conduct rapid analyses and then to take fast-strike improvement actions. Clearly someone must be the leader, and this is logically the firm bringing all of the designs and components together into a complete product (for example, Doyle Wilson Homebuilder, Pratt & Whitney, Porsche, and Showa). However, the participants must treat each other as equals, with *muda* as the joint enemy.

Ending the Industrial Cold War

As described, the lean enterprise seems so simple and obvious that many readers will think this type of analysis must surely occur routinely in practice, even if not in name. But this is not so. This is partly because most managers lack an understanding for the potential of flow and pull to remove waste when applied to the entire value stream, but there is a more fundamental reason. Jointly analyzing every action needed to develop, order, and produce a good or service makes every firm's costs transparent. *There is no privacy.* Thus the question of how much money (profit) each firm along the value stream is going to make on a specific product is unavoidable.

Historically, relations between the firms arrayed along a value stream have been rather like the behavior of the United States and the Soviet Union during the cold war. Some minimum level of cooperation was necessary in order to keep from blowing up the world (thus the innovation of the "hot line" and tacit agreements on intelligence gathering on third parties with uncertain intentions such as countries in the nonaligned bloc), but the operative assumption was that both sides would take advantage of each other in any way they could short of mutual annihilation. Value stream participants often behave in a very similar way, cooperating at the minimum level necessary to get a product made at all, but hoping that the other parties' ignorance of just what they are up to (and what it cost) will permit them to grab a financial jackpot. For example, firms hope for a financial windfall when costs are dramatically reduced inside their own operations through some innovation which the other firms along the stream don't learn about and therefore never ask to share in.

No one would have suggested that the geopolitical cold war could have been halted if only the two sides had suddenly decided to "trust" each other. Yet one routinely hears that suppliers and their customers along a value stream can somehow end the industrial cold war through generous application of mutual "trust," a term which seems to have no operational meaning. (Just ask yourself how long "trust" lasts when market conditions change and a formerly profitable product line suddenly falls into loss. The party closest to the customer will immediately start demanding cost reductions from those upstream without much reference to who has eliminated waste and who hasn't. Thus, the behavior of General Motors and Volkswagen toward their suppliers during their recent crises are bound to be the norm in a situation where there is no mutually agreed upon operational definition of fair behavior.)

We would propose instead that states of war can only be ended when all of the parties willingly negotiate a set of principles to guide their joint behavior in the future and then devise a mechanism for mutual verification that everyone is abiding by the principles. In the context of a lean enterprise, these principles might be something as follows:

- Value must be defined jointly for each product family along with a target cost based on the customer's perception of value.
- All firms along the value stream must make an adequate return on their investments related to the value stream.
- The firms must work together to identify and eliminate *muda* to the point where the overall target cost and return-on-investment targets of each firm are met.
- When cost targets are met the firms along the stream will immediately conduct new analyses to identify remaining *muda* and set new targets.
- Every participating firm has the right to examine every activity in every firm relevant to the value stream as part of the joint search for waste.

The lean enterprise is itself the verification mechanism and would continue for the life of the product. This could be a very short period—for example, a two-year movie production exercise in the rapidly changing entertainment industry—or it could continue for decades—a Chrysler-led automotive "platform" team periodically offering a new minivan of very similar description to the old product with parts from most of the same suppliers.

We've only recently tried to create lean enterprises ourselves, working with several of the firms mentioned in this book to identify every action along lengthy value streams, and we know it will not be easy even when every firm is strongly committed. (A simple example of a problem to be overcome is the need for a firm far up the stream to invest in new technology to produce in small lots rather than large batches. Because most of the benefit is gained by downstream firms but all of the costs are borne by the upstream firm, some means must be developed for the former to compensate the latter.) But we also know the rewards can be very large for the enterprise collectively as well as the customer at the end of the stream, and we're confident that this mechanism can be perfected.

Alternating Careers

A brief look at the lean organization chart in Chapter 11 (Figure 11.1) indicates that as lean enterprises are created to channel the flow of value, a larger and larger fraction of employees in firms along the stream are directly involved in value-creating tasks at stream side. Much of the indirect effort formerly required simply disappears, along with most of the headcount of the departments organizing this effort.

This is a disconcerting development for many people because the typical method of constructing a career—that is, the sequence of jobs requiring higher levels of skill and broader discretion, which lead to higher compensation—has been upward through these "functional" activities such as engineering, sales, purchasing, scheduling, quality auditing, centralized information systems, and accounting.

If, for the most part, employees are assigned to a particular product team to apply their skills to the value stream, they may begin to wonder if they are "going anywhere" and get confused about "who I am." ("I trained as an electrical engineer but I seem to spend most of my time on integrative tasks which don't utilize all of my training.") While the actual work is likely to be much more rewarding than in the previously disconnected world of departmentalized batches and queues, the lack of perceived progression and the loss of a commanding skill may be dispiriting.

What's more, it may be bad for the enterprise if employees gradually lose their edge and simply spend all their time applying what they already know to standard problems. The Japanese call this the "generalist engineer" problem and see it quite correctly as a potential weakness in competing over the long term with a German firm like Porsche, which has extremely strong technical functions.

This suggests that a new form of career must be devised, an "alternating career" in which employees go back and forth between applying what they know in a team context and taking time out to learn new skills in a functional setting. The basic idea would be to assign employees to product teams for the life of a development exercise or during a product's production life, but to send them back to their "home functions" when a project is completed or they are no longer needed. In the home function, they could receive training on new skills, or work on advanced projects which apply existing skills to the limit, or analyze the flow of engineering, order-taking, and production activities as a technical adviser to a lean enterprise seeking to identify and eliminate *muda*.

The conventional idea of a career progressing up a ladder toward general management, with more and more direct reports, now needs replacement because the value stream doesn't benefit. However, a new concept of a career in which more and more skills are gained and applied to more and more difficult problems is both good for the employee and good for value flow. What's more, gaining the agreement of employees that this is the path to the future is the key to self-perpetuating lean enterprises. The experience of the reengineering movement, which has also sought to remove many indirect workers and to attack the very legitimacy of many functions and departments, argues strongly that when employees are rudely shoved out of the way with no new self-image provided, their natural response is to restore the old system as soon as the reengineers are gone. With some resort to sabotage, this is generally possible, and we find it hard to blame employees trying to set the clock back. The real problem is the lack of creative thought in redefining conventional careers.

Functions for the Future

Just as we need to rethink careers, we need to rethink departments and functions. As lean enterprises are created to channel the value stream, it becomes apparent that the traditional functions should not perform most of their traditional tasks. Engineering should not engineer, in the sense of performing routine engineering on a product. Purchasing should not purchase, in the sense of making individual purchase decisions and holding the hand of the supplier in getting products to launch. Operations should not direct employees in day-to-day production activities. Quality should not conduct detailed audits of products or conduct fire-fighting exercises to eliminate problems with a specific product. These are all tasks for the dedicated product teams, dealing with the issues of the present.

What functions should do is think about the future. Product engineering should work on new technologies that will permit products to do new things for the user and develop new materials and methods which make it possible to eliminate fabrications steps and reduce costs. Tool engineering should work on "right-sized" devices—from computers to production hardware—which make it possible for product teams to create value in continuous flow and rapidly shift over between product variants. Purchasing should identify the set of suppliers a firm will work with in the long term and develop a plan for each supplier to ensure they will have the technologies plus the design and production capabilities to assure the highest-quality performance. Quality should develop a standard set of methods which the product teams can apply to ensure that every product is right every time with no backflows and no "escapes" of bad products to the customer. Indeed, as we noted in Chapter 11, the traditional quality function should be combined with a productivity (or "lean") function to create an "improvement function" able to eliminate *muda* of all sorts.

Every function would provide a "home" to employees with given technical specializations (including production workers who must become operations specialists able to detect and eliminate *muda*). A primary job would be to systematize current knowledge and procedures and teach these to function members as needed (ideally "Just-in-Time" for application because most knowledge is quickly lost if not immediately applied). The function's other job would be to search for new knowledge and summarize it in a form which can be taught when needed.

The Role of the Firm

We can now think of functions as the hills and mountains forming the valley for the value stream. Their knowledge washes down toward those working alongside the stream to create value and speed its flow. However, this thought leads to one last bit of mental rearrangement: If functions create a valley for the stream flowing past and through many firms, what purpose does the firm itself serve? The fundamental building block of traditional thinking about economic organization suddenly seems to lack a purpose except to "make money." And when there are cold war relationships between firms along a value stream, this can often be done by off-loading costs and diverting profits but without making much contribution to actually creating value.[2]

Our answer is that firms provide the link between streams. They are the means of crossing from one valley to the next in order to make maximum use of the technologies and capabilities accumulated by each firm's technical functions. They also provide the means of shifting resources—people, space, and tools—from value streams which no longer need them to other streams which do. From this it follows that most firms will want to participate in multiple value streams, often with different upstream and downstream partners, as shown in Figure 12.1.

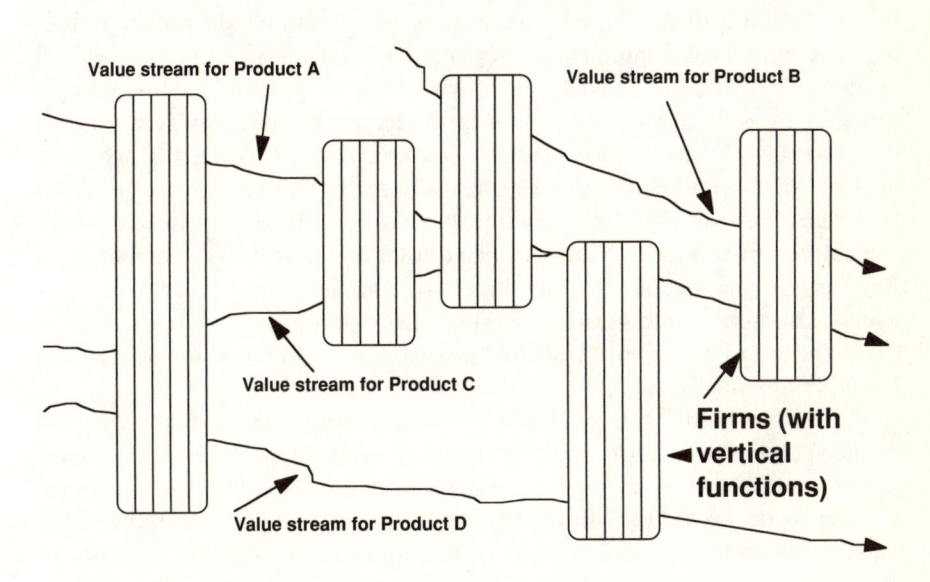

FIGURE 12.1: FIRMS VERSUS VALUE STREAMS

Lean Enterprise in Three Industrial Traditions

Is it actually possible to apply these ideas everywhere? After all, the American, German, and Japanese industrial traditions described in the preceding chapters are very different. Taiichi Ohno could develop the "general case" for flow and pull thinking by applying Ford's "special case" ideas to all types of economic activity, and we can now see that the ideas themselves work everywhere, but is it really reasonable to propose "universal" organizational rules for creating value by means of lean thinking?

We think it is and that it's essential to try. The desire by the customer for the best product of exactly the right specification supplied in the least time at the lowest cost *is* universal, and much easier to satisfy now that most trade and investment barriers have fallen. So it is hard to understand how national approaches to value creation which are suboptimal can endure in the long term. However, as we've seen in the examples of lean transition, the transitional problems will be different in different places.

The American Challenge

The great challenge for Americans is to overcome their "every firm for itself" individualism in which each organization along the value stream optimizes its own stretch while suboptimizing the whole. Perhaps the most striking recent example is Wal-Mart, which became every financial analyst's favorite firm by streamlining its own internal operations, drastically reducing its number of suppliers, asking them to deliver the precise amount needed daily (in some cases, such as with Procter & Gamble, by allowing suppliers to look directly into Wal-Mart's electronic inventory system), and then bargaining hard to drive supplier *margins* down (by offering access to massive sales volumes to only one firm in each supplier category). What Wal-Mart has not done (but which it will need to think about soon) is how to analyze entire value streams to drive total *costs* down. This tendency of American management is exacerbated by the industrial finance system, which asks each firm to optimize its short-term performance but ignores the performance of the whole because no shares of a whole value stream are traded in any market.

The solution, we believe, lies with management rather than with the financial system. If senior managers begin to realize that it's extremely hard to truly optimize their stretch of the stream for any extended period without seeking to optimize the whole, ways can be found to work together with other firms on the basis of clear principles and to deal with the demands of the investment community.

What's more, we believe this is happening as leaders of industry after industry—aerospace, computers, motor vehicles, construction, health care, air travel, retailing—realize that cost is the great challenge for the next decade, pending breakthroughs in new technologies (which may or may not materialize), and that costs can only be attacked through collective analysis and action. Once this reality is acknowledged, the natural capacity of Americans for pragmatism and teamwork will provide a real advantage in pursuing perfection.

The German Challenge

The German challenge is in many ways the reverse of the American. The idea of cooperation between assembler and supplier firms along value streams is well established and the industrial finance system understands and encourages this need as well. (This financial system has been under stress in recent years, but primarily because German firms have had such poor fundamental productivity.) However, workers in German firms show a clear discomfort with horizontal teamwork of the sort needed to operate lean enterprises.

In the 1980s, in response to the perception that Computer Aided Manufacturing (or what we have called "high tech mass production") would soon eliminate millions of jobs and de-skill those workers who survived, the German union movement promoted the concept of shorter working hours and "autonomous work groups" to hive off portions of the production system under the management of "self-directed" work teams.

As we have seen, the threat of CIM was largely a mirage and the real risk to German jobs has come from the inefficiency of German organizations. However, autonomous group working is still an approach which appeals to many German workers. The problem as we see it is that self-directed group work can at best create islands of superior practice in a disconnected process. By design, no one can see and optimize the whole. Even worse, autonomous group working, as commonly pursued, is hostile to standard work, visual control, and continuous improvement for fear these lean techniques will dilute "craft" skills and lead to further job losses. So the prospect for superior performance even within each work group is not high.

Given this background, it's not surprising that in our visits to German firms trying to make a lean leap we are often struck by the disorientation of workers on the shop floor caused by the introduction of lean working methods and organization. These supplant the traditional *meister* hierarchy of command and transfer highly skilled workers (including product and tool engineers) into product teams where they need to take on broader responsibilities and assume a broader outlook.

German firms therefore face a particular adjustment challenge in addressing the jobs problem at the outset and in creating a system of alternating careers for all workers. Doing this is critical in retaining each employee's loyalty and sense of possessing special skills (which are themselves extremely valuable) while reducing the reluctance of the shop floor worker, *meister*, and engineer to participate in cross-skill problem solving. If this can be done, the greatest strength of most German firms, the superlative operations skills of most employees and their strong identification with the product, can be fully utilized for the first time.

THE JAPANESE CHALLENGE

The Japanese challenge is quite different. Collective analysis of costs along the value stream, although never extended all the way upstream to raw materials and all the way downstream into retailing, is clearly accepted and practiced, as is the notion that employees should go wherever they are needed without much regard to functional career paths. (Ask an NEC employee who he or she "is" and the answer will always be "an NEC employee"; ask an AEG or a Microsoft employee who he or she is and the first answer will usually be "a mechanical engineer" or "a software engineer" or some other functional skill.)

What's more problematic is the role of vertical functions—which accumulate knowledge, teach it, and push it ahead—in a society based on horizontal leveling. What's also problematic is the appropriate relocation of production near to the customer in a society which very much wants to stay at home.

While the German firm needs to accustom employees to working in horizontal teams, the typical Japanese firm needs to accustom employees to the idea that skills must be continually upgraded and carried to the cutting edge through periodic in-function assignments which overcome the generalist employee problem. At the same time, many Japanese firms need to acknowledge that the fundamental logic of lean thinking requires production to be conducted near the customer and that many tasks long conducted in Japan simply do not make sense there. The horizontal *keiretsu*, rather than individual firms or the vertical [supply group] *keiretsu*, are the essential mechanism for redeploying people from one valley to another in this situation because most individual firms have stuck to a very narrow range of products and cannot easily shift people within their own operations, all of which face the same problems.

Curiously, the Japanese challenge is perhaps the greatest among the three great industrial traditions because of a widespread conviction that lean thinking has already been universally applied in Japan (when, in fact, it has never been applied to a substantial fraction of production operations and hardly at all in distribution and services) and that there is nothing Japanese firms can profitably do at home except conduct high-volume, export-oriented manufacturing. The idea that low-volume, build-to-order, domestically oriented Showa rather than high-volume, export-oriented Toyota is the future will require some getting used to.

Nevertheless, Japan pioneered the general case for lean thinking and Japanese society has repeatedly shown resilience in adapting to new conditions. Thus the prospects are bright for recasting the Japanese economy once more, this time in full accord with lean principles.

The Distance Still to Go

As we've seen from the examples in Part II, lean thinking works and can be applied to both simple and complex firms in the three major industrial traditions. But what we could not show was the application of lean thinking to entire value streams, in real lean enterprises which have properly specified value from the perspective of the customer, identified the value stream, and squeezed out most *muda* by applying flow and pull. The reason is simply that no one has yet done this. We'll therefore conclude this study in the final chapter with a bit of practical dreaming, by asking what some major economic activities will look like once value stream thinking is universally applied.

CHAPTER 13

Dreaming About Perfection

To make progress toward perfection—perfectly specified value flowing along a perfect value stream channeled by a perfect enterprise—it's useful to dream a bit in order to form a vision of what might be possible. We'll therefore conclude this investigation of lean thinking by taking a moment to dream about a range of activities already encountered in this book and how they might be conducted in a far better way. By rethinking long-distance travel, the "routine cures" aspect of medical care, food production and distribution, construction, and short-range personal mobility in light of lean principles, we can begin to discover better ways to perform these humdrum but essential daily activities which account for the great bulk of all consumer spending and economic activity in advanced economies.

Long-Distance Travel

What does the long-distance traveler really want? How should *value* be defined? While some people seek the travel experience as an end in itself (including those who take a scenic train, a bus tour, or a cruise), most of us simply want to get from A to B with the minimum of time, cost, and hassle, almost always by air. In trying to do this, most travelers deal with the long list of independent firms listed in Chapter 1, and their travel nightmares generally sound like our own. Each organization has its own departmentalized structure and its own optimized tools. Each typically ignores the role of the other parties and is oblivious to the total "service" the traveler receives. And the specific activities involved are conducted with inefficient batch-and-queue methods. So how can lean thinking be employed to do better?

First, the traveler must be placed in the foreground. The time, comfort, safety, and cost of the total trip must become the key performance measure of the "system" rather than optimization of specific assets like airports and airplanes. Then the organizations carrying the traveler along need to jointly think through the total trip to identify the value stream and eliminate all of the unnecessary waiting, confusion, and wasted steps in order to create continuous flow upon request. At every step they need to ask, Why is this necessary? and to think of a better way to get the job done.

Who can do this? Who can lead the lean enterprise? One candidate is the travel agent who could put all of the pieces together, giving the traveler an optimized itinerary, a unified travel document (which might not exist physically at all), and single-point billing. Alternatively, the airline could integrate the system in cooperation with all of the other parties. However, the chronic stagnation and losses currently found in the industry are currently pushing travel agents and airlines in North America in the opposite direction. They are engaged in a zero-sum fight over how to cut costs by pushing them off onto each other, with the opening shot in the campaign being the decision of most airlines to substantially reduce the commissions they pay travel agents for handling ticketing. From the traveler's standpoint the winner is irrelevant because the total costs don't change, only who garners the revenues.

And one can imagine other integrators such as the rental car firms, hotel chains, and credit card companies who currently cooperate with the airlines by offering frequent flyer mileage in proportion to car and room billings and with travel agents through their computerized reservations systems. More realistically, the integrator will be some new entrant—let's call this organization a service provider—willing to introduce a new lean logic to the whole system.

A new entrant might start with small to mid-sized cities currently only feeding hubs and think of ways for travelers to fly direct in small jet aircraft to other small to mid-sized cities, largely bypassing the current system. To do this, both the terminal and the airplane would need to be rethought to create a situation where one could drive (or take a taxi or limo) very near to the gate and then walk quickly to the plane (rolling one's luggage). Reservations could be made by phone or computer (including the taxi, rental car, and hotel reservation) without the need for a traditional ticket. Instead, a credit card could be passed through a reader in the taxi, at the entrance to the plane, and at the hotel to take care of billing and as the room key. En route, this would also signal the rental car company and the hotel that the traveler is on the way.

Baggage handling could be eliminated as well if the passengers simply rolled their bags (perhaps of special design) the few feet to the plane and the role of the gate agent could be eliminated with electronic ticketing and an "*andon* board" to inform passengers of the status of their flight. Because the taxiing time to takeoff and after landing could be very brief in small and medium-sized airports (compared with about twenty minutes taxiing out and ten minutes taxiing in at large hub airports today), and because the jet plane could proceed direct to the desired destination, the current meal and entertainment services could be largely eliminated. These are designed to keep captive passengers occupied and sometimes to garner a bit of extra revenue for the airline.

Most of the ground staff could be eliminated (no gate agents, no baggage handlers, no tow truck drivers) along with the Taj Mahal terminal complex and the check-in/check-out crew at the hotel. (Since your credit card is your room key, you could go straight to your room.) And aircraft could be designed to "turn around" for the next destination within perhaps five minutes. Revenues per employee and per aircraft per day could therefore be very high, reducing costs despite a reduction in the "scale" of aircraft and terminals.

Thinking this way, one begins to wonder why door-to-door travel times can't be cut in half by eliminating all queues and intermediate stops while the cost of travel is substantially reduced and most of the hassle is eliminated. But . . . is any of this practical? Smaller aircraft, even smaller than the new generation of fifty-passenger mini-jets, would be needed and their design would need to be rethought to permit low maintenance, quick turnarounds with no ground crew, and quicker access for both passengers and luggage. Airport terminals would need to be redesigned and security arrangements reevaluated. And everyone jointly involved in providing the service would need to work together to look at the whole.

But what's the alternative? The prospects for faster flying speeds ("point velocities" in our terminology) are nonexistent over land and doubtful over the oceans. And in any case, queue and wait time accounts for more than half of total time on shorter trips, so speeding up the plane wouldn't help very much. The present hub-and-spoke systems might be refined slightly, but they have reached their economic limits. Indeed, most of the reductions in the cost of air travel in recent years been due to cutting the wages of airline personnel and using older airplanes. This is another instance of simply shifting cost burdens rather than reducing the amount of effort needed to get the job done.

One American airline, Southwest, has taken the first few steps along the lean path by flying direct, simplifying the boarding process, and turning its airplanes in fifteen minutes rather than the industry standard of thirty. As a result, it has been by far the most profitable airline in North America. Why not carry lean thinking much further, all the way to its logical conclusion?

A final benefit of rethinking long-range passenger travel bears note. The same hub-and-spoke concept used for passengers in the daytime delivers freight at night, except with dedicated aircraft feeding dedicated freight sortation centers in different cities from the passenger hubs. Why can't a new entrant fly packages direct at night with the same smaller planes and use redesigned passenger terminals for package distribution centers? As one starts to think about the possibilities of using lean principles, opportunities start to appear in many places.

Medical Care

When you visit your doctor you enter a world of queues and disjointed processes. Why? Because your doctor and health care planner think about health care from the standpoint of organization charts, functional expertise, and "efficiency." Each of the centers of expertise in the health care system —the specialist physician, the single-purpose diagnostic tool, the centralized laboratory—is extremely expensive. Therefore, efficiency demands that it be completely utilized. Obvious, isn't it?

To get full utilization, it's necessary to route you around from specialist to machine to laboratory and to overschedule the specialists, machines, and labs to make sure they are always fully occupied. (And, as medical costs spiral, the pressure for full utilization steadily increases. Lines lengthen, often as rationing in disguise.) Elaborate computerized information systems are needed to make sure you find your place in the right line and to get your records from central storage to the point of diagnosis or treatment.

How would things work if the medical system embraced lean thinking? First, the patient would be placed in the foreground, with time and comfort included as key performance measures of the system. These can only be addressed by flowing the patient through the system. (By contrast, conventional thinking places the organization in the foreground, to be efficiently "managed," while the patient is left in the background to wander through an organizational forest too full of trees.)

Next, the medical system would rethink its departmental structure and reorganize much of its expertise into multiskilled teams. The idea would be very simple: When the patient enters the system, via a multiskilled, co-located team (or "cell" in the language of physical production), she or he receives steady attention and treatment until the problem is solved.

To do this, the skills of nurses and doctors would need to be broadened (in contrast to the narrow deepening of skills encouraged by the current system) so that a smaller team of more broadly skilled people can solve most patient problems. At the same time, the tools of medicine—machines, labs, and record-keeping units—would need to be rethought and "right-sized" so that they are smaller, more flexible, and faster, with a full complement of tools dedicated to every treatment team. (As their size and cost shrink, the problem of full utilization shrinks as well.)

Finally, the "patient" would need to be actively involved in the process and up-skilled—made a member of the team—so that many problems can be solved through prevention or addressed from home without need to physically visit the medical team, and so that visits can be better predicted. (We are always amazed that as members of "health maintenance organizations" in the U.S. and the U.K., we have received zero training in simple diagnosis, prevention, and scheduling of visits. The system has been set up so that we overuse it, through ignorance, but wait in long lines whenever we do use it.) Over time, it will surely be possible to transfer some of the equipment to the home as well, through teleconferencing, remote sensing, and even a home laboratory, the same way most of us now have a complete complement of office equipment in our home offices.

What would happen if lean thinking was introduced as a fundamental principle of health care? The time and steps needed to solve a problem should fall dramatically. The quality of care should improve because less information would be lost in handoffs to the next specialist, fewer mistakes would be made, less elaborate information tracking and scheduling systems (the MRPs of medicine) would be needed, and less backtracking and rework would be required. The cost of each "cure" and of the total system could fall substantially.

The problem of cures beyond our current knowledge would remain and the proposed lean transformation in health care is not directly helpful here. However, the lean transition could free up substantial resources which could be used for fundamental research to find new cures. Instead, what's happening today is that the inefficiencies of the existing system are eating up all available resources, so spending on finding new cures is being curtailed to pay for present services. And most of today's health care debate in the political arena is simply a cost shifting or service elimination contest as the various parties along the value stream try to defend their own interests at the expense of others.

Food Production and Distribution

What does the food shopper want? What's the *value* derived from the food production and distribution system? As with travel, some people actually enjoy shopping. They want a fancy store with a nice ambience, and someone should provide this service. However, most of us find that time is our scarcest resource, so we want to obtain precisely the items we need at the lowest possible cost with the least possible hassle. The present system clearly doesn't offer this. How could lean thinking change things?

We've already seen in Chapter 2 how the grocer—the obvious leader of lean enterprises for food—can examine the multitude of value streams emptying into the supermarket aisle. It should be possible, for most food items, to reduce the amount of time needed to get raw materials into the arms of the consumer by more than 90 percent, to substantially reduce the cost and effort involved, and to largely eliminate "stock-outs" where the desired product is not available. This can be done using the flow and pull techniques we've described in detail.

A dramatic improvement in the responsiveness of the production and distribution system would mean that the grocer could convert to a simple replenishment system, in which today's purchases trigger tonight's restocking deliveries and tomorrow's production of replacement items. It could also reduce costs dramatically and eliminate the need for grocers to periodically reduce overstocks with low-price special offers.

But this is not the end. If the grocer can get deliveries in small lots daily from his suppliers and eliminate warehousing and lines all the way back up the value stream, why not take the last step and get rid of the final warehouse, the grocery store itself? Why not use information technologies to take customer orders, based on weekly adjustments to a standing order, and ship direct to the customer from the distribution centers, using milk-run vehicles with a separate container for each customer.

Total costs could fall while the most precious resource of many shoppers —their time—would be saved. What's more, additional services could easily be added; for example, menu planning, shipment of the exact items needed for that week's home-cooking menus, and even completely precooked meals. Finally, the grocer could gather data on the shopping habits of his stable customer base that would be useful in introducing new products with a higher success rate and in eliminating the traditional promotion mentality in the grocery business in which large sums are spent on promotional selling just to wrest a point or two of market share from competitors for brief periods.

This would be a tremendous leap if taken to its logical conclusion. But it will require readjustment in everyone's thinking along the value stream. For example, ask yourself how comfortable you and your grocer will feel in moving to a completely lean and transparent system in which you can see the status of your order but never see a store and the grocer knows everything about your eating habits. Nevertheless, lean food production and supply is completely feasible with the technologies and management techniques available today, and the current system is ripe for change. The important question is who will make the leap.

Construction

What do you want when you construct an office or factory or buy a new home? How is *value* defined? While a few buyers probably enjoy the complexities of today's construction industry, including the opportunity to change their minds about the details of their building during the six months to a year of typical contract-to-close cycles, most buyers would like to get exactly the building they need as quickly as possible at the lowest price. And if the issue is remodeling, where your home or office must be used while it is being renovated, the current system is truly a nightmare. Substantially all customers want to get the job done as quickly as possible.

Not only does the current system require an extended interval from start to finish, but when the work is officially finished there is typically a considerable to-do list which strains relations between the user and the builder. What's more, more than 80 percent of this time and up to half the total cost goes to carrying charges, contractors hurrying up to wait for previous contractors, and ripping out and redoing work that does not meet the formal specification or suit the customer.

We saw the beginnings of lean thinking in the homebuilding portion of the construction industry in Chapter 1 when we met Doyle Wilson, but he has just begun to scratch the surface. The actual amount of time needed to progress from contract to completion for the typical home, if all of the relevant skills and materials were marshaled in the proper sequence, could be reduced from six months to fifteen days using current construction techniques. And the great bulk of errors and rework incurred in home building are completely avoidable if the customer, the contractor, and the subcontractors learn to talk to each other. Finally, the cost of the whole process could be dramatically slashed if rework is eliminated, even before taking the next logical step of transferring the construction of the major components to a factory setting where conditions can be controlled and where lean techniques can be fully implemented.[1]

Imagine the next leap in a lean system in which the buyer can visit the homebuilder, modify the structure on the screen, pick the desired options, perform a credit check, arrange insurance, and sign the contract in one sitting. Then imagine assembling the finished house in less than a week from the moment of the order until time to move in, by use of factory-made components. Imagine further that none of the components needed for this home—windows, doors, hardware, appliances—are made until a day or two before they are needed in lean component factories. This would slash costs further and in the process create a revolution in a massive business with stagnant productivity.

The same concepts could be applied to construction in general. That it's possible is not in question. The real question is who will rationalize the value stream and when.

Short-Range Personal Mobility[2]

We've spent many years associated with the auto industry, so it's satisfying to finish this dream exercise in the place where we started. The first question to ask, as always, is how is *value* defined? For some people it's a vehicle with special performance features or simply the car you want to be seen in—perhaps the new Porsche!—at an appropriate price. However, many current buyers of what is now a very mature product probably don't want to buy a product at all. What they want is personal mobility, obtained at the lowest cost with the least hassle. A physical product, such as a car, truck, van, or sport-utility vehicle, is simply part of the means to this end.

Looked at this way, the current "product" is certainly suboptimal. Buying and selling cars, registering, insuring and repairing them, and taking care of operational details from fueling to cleaning are mostly a time-consuming hassle conducted with a welter of different firms pursuing their own interests. Special needs calling for a taxi, a limo, or a rental vehicle with special capabilities (for example, for hauling personal goods) are another hassle requiring another set of relationships.

Meanwhile, the conventional auto industry has been focusing (and with considerable success) on applying lean thinking, but only to the design and manufacture of the vehicle itself. It has done little or nothing to rethink the total product—personal mobility—which many of us want. This is why many people find today's "post-Japanese" auto industry a very dull place and why customers frequently ask how the industry can be getting more efficient while the cost and ease of buying and operating vehicles has hardly budged.[3] A major reason is that the manufacturing activities are only a fraction of the value stream for the total product, and the cost and inconvenience of the other aspects of the value stream have been rising. How might lean thinking help?

Just as long-distance travel needs a team leader to help the participating firms look at the whole, short-range personal mobility needs some type of mobility provider to see the complete product. This might be a rental car company, a public utility, one of the new "mega-dealer" car retailing organizations, or even a reconstituted automobile company. The idea would be to work with the customer to supply precisely the vehicles and services needed with zero hassle and a lower cost. How could this work?

The mobility provider and the customer would work out the type of vehicles and services needed both now and in the future (including taxi, limo, transit, and specialty vehicles for spot use) and the mobility provider would "put them in the driveway." Insurance, registration, routine service, and repairs would become the responsibility of the provider. (The phone in the vehicle could routinely call the provider and report the status of the vehicle.) The provider would also take care of replacing the vehicle as appropriate to maintain a constant level of service for the user and would bill the user periodically for the services rendered. The relationship would be long term, indeed open ended, so the search costs of finding the right company to provide each part of this total product would be avoided. Going even further, if the mobility provider provided "open-book" cost information (a real leap in the motor industry to be sure), the user would not feel the need to shop constantly for a better "deal" and could comfortably stick with a provider for years or decades. The hassle of personal mobility would largely go away.

This is certain to cost a fortune, right? Wrong. It should cost less for a multitude of reasons. First, the provider can work with the supplier of vehicles to get a steady flow of vehicles manufactured to the precise specification needed because long-term user needs have been assessed. The current sea of new cars no one has ordered which choke car dealer parking lots goes away. So does the car dealership itself with many of its costs. Then the manufacturer can size its production capacity for a steady stream of vehicles because the mobility provider can counteract the business cycle by replacing aging vehicles at a steady rate. (Remember that the demand for travel changes by only a small percent during the business cycle while the sale of new cars in North America, Europe, and now Japan rises and falls by 20 to 40 percent. This requires the industry to maintain large amounts of excess capacity on average.) As demand stabilizes, the supply base can be tightened up and the total lead time for building vehicles can be compressed with dramatic savings in inventories, space, and effort.[4]

As a final benefit, the system could be a closed loop. If the mobility provider retains control over the vehicles and recycles them at the most economic time, and if the new vehicle maker can share the mobility provider's data base on user needs in order to develop vehicles which meet these needs, vehicles should cost less to operate over their lifetimes and last longer. (Just ask yourself how long maintenance intervals for cars will be if the mobility provider does all the maintenance and has a direct say in product designs.) The mobility provider is in a position to obtain the lowest lifetime costs possible because it is in control of the whole cycle.

Would this approach be easy to introduce? Obviously not, and it seems unlikely that the conventional car companies will lead the way. But what is the alternative? Once the introduction of lean techniques in the design and manufacturing portions of the motor vehicle value stream is completed over the next decade, customers will gain a major price benefit, but then the auto industry will be stuck. Lean thinking provides a way to revitalize a highly mature "product" by converting it from a hassle-laden good to a hassle-free service.

The Power of Dreams

These are all dreams. No one has performed any of these industrial transformations. Indeed, there are hardly any *lean enterprises*, even in the most advanced industries, in our sense of the term where value creation is smoothly linked all the way from concept to launch, order to delivery, and raw material into the arms of the customer and on through the life cycle of the good or service. But these transformations can be achieved and with current know-how. All that's needed is for someone to turn dreams into actions in pursuit of perfection.

The Prize We Can Grasp Right Now

We're now at the end of our inquiry into lean thinking. A series of simple but counterintuitive ideas with humble origins in the factory turn out to apply to a whole range of economic activities. They require few new technologies—although the "right-sizing" of many existing technologies is needed to insert them directly into the value stream—and they can be implemented very quickly. It requires only a few years to totally transform even a gigantic firm and somewhat longer to apply them to an entire value stream.

Lean thinking can dramatically boost productivity—doubling to quadrupling it, depending on the activity—while dramatically reducing errors, inventories, on-the-job accidents, space requirements, time-to-market for new products, production lead times, the cost of extra product variety, and costs in general. At the same time, these simple ideas can make work more satisfying by introducing immediate feedback and facilitating total concentration, and they can damp the business cycle, itself the cause of an enormous waste of resources. They require little capital and they will create rather than destroy jobs as managers learn to use them properly. Finally, they provide a bridge to the next great technological leaps by pulling the economies of the developed countries out of their current stagnation and providing resources for research.

All that remains is for enough investors, managers, and employees, like the change agent heroes of these pages and—we hope—you the reader, to create a vast movement, in North America, Europe, Japan, and every other region, which relentlessly applies lean thinking to create value and banish *muda*.

PART IV
EPILOGUE (2003)

CHAPTER 14
The Steady Advance of Lean Thinking

In July of 2000, Art Byrne and his management team at the Wiremold Company reached a somber conclusion. They decided they should accept the $770 million buyout offer from Legrand S.A. of France and bring three generations of Murphy family ownership to an end.

Viewed in one way, this was a sad event driven by the need of the five members of the Murphy family, all in their 80s or 90s, to pay inheritance taxes on the extraordinary appreciation in the value of their company since Art's team took over in 1991. But viewed another way, the sale marked a triumph of lean thinking. A firm near bankruptcy in 1991, with an assessed value of only $30 million, was turned into an engine of wealth creation over the course of a decade. Even better, the newly created wealth—a 2500 percent increase on the level of 1991—was shared widely with Wiremold's employees who collectively owned the largest block of Wiremold stock. In our view, Wiremold's steady advance through an entire decade could have been duplicated by most companies in the 1990s. All they needed to do was follow Wiremold in steadily eliminating waste and pay ever more attention to the voice of the customer in order to create a win-win-win-win for customers, owners, employees, and suppliers.[1] And, as we will see in the pages ahead, Wiremold's continuing success up to the present *was* duplicated in varying degrees by many firms, including those whose lean transformations we chronicled in the first edition of *Lean Thinking*. By contrast, many other firms in the 1990s flew a ballistic trajectory. They zoomed upward in sales and stock valuations on the basis of new business models and optimistic earnings projections before going over the inflection point and heading back to their starting point, if not into bankruptcy.

As managers and investors survey the wreckage of the bubble economy and search for sustainable approaches to wealth creation in the future, a fresh look

The Steady Advance of Toyota

In the summer of 2002 Toyota allowed itself to do something it almost never does. It talked out loud about its plans for becoming the market share leader in the global motor vehicle industry. A remarkable company document titled "2010 Global Vision"[2] projected a future in which Toyota's global market share would continue its steady growth from 11 percent in 2002 to reach 15 percent by about 2010. By contrast, General Motors, the current market share leader, had about 14 percent of the global market in 2002, and its share has been trending downward for decades, as shown in Figure 14.1. Toyota doesn't say so explicitly—this is definitely not the company's style—but everyone in the industry understands that the "2010 Global Vision" is a statement by Toyota that it plans to be number one within a few years.

(Toyota's vision is given credibility by the success of its Global 10 initiative launched in the mid-1990s to gain 10 percent of the global motor vehicle market by 2000. In 2000, Toyota's global share was 10.01 percent.)

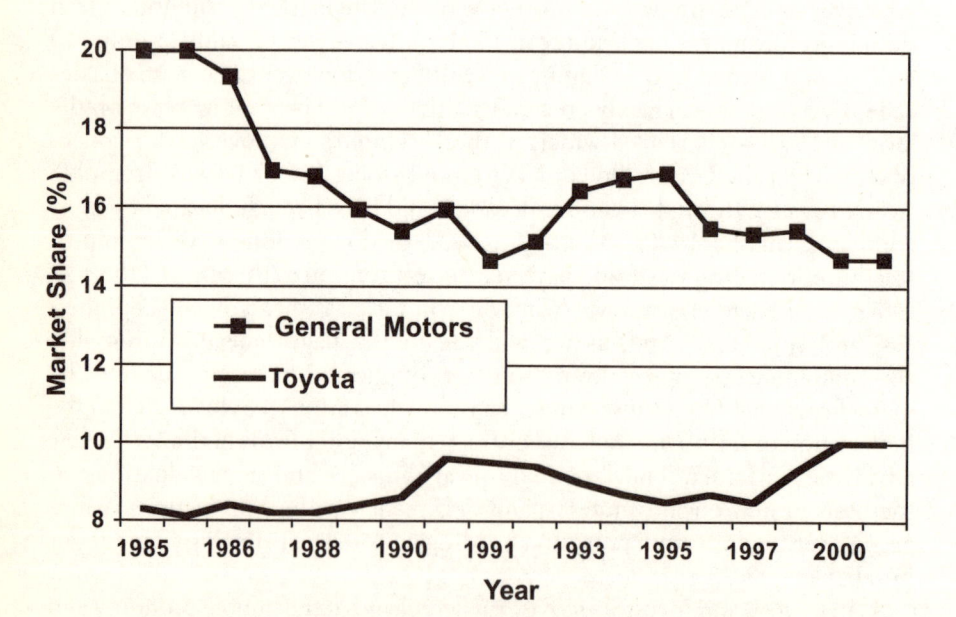

FIGURE 14.1: GLOBAL MARKET SHARE: TOYOTA VERSUS GM

Data includes cars and commercial vehicles. GM includes Saab, Opel, and Holden. Toyota includes Daihatsu and Hino. © Copyright 2003, Ward's Communications.

FIGURE 14.2: U.S. MOTOR VEHICLE MARKET SHARES BY COMPANY

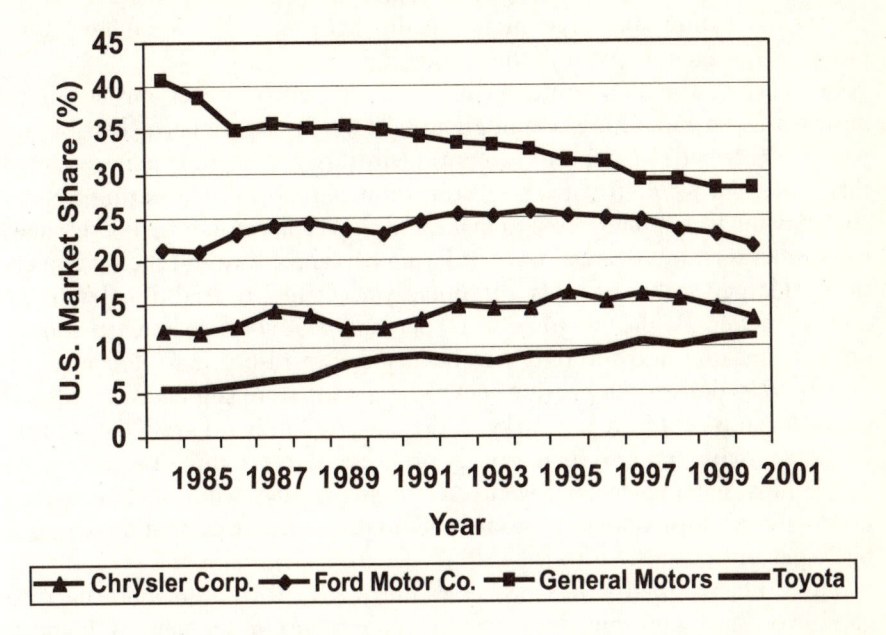

Note: Chrysler Corp. does not include Mercedes; Ford does not include Jaguar, Land Rover, or Volvo; and GM does not include Saab. Source: Ward's AutoInfoBank

Looking at the U.S. market, we note the same trend of steady share gains by Toyota, compared with the declining shares of the traditional Big Three. On current trend, Toyota will pass both Chrysler and Ford in the U.S. market by the time it achieves its global share target (see Figure 14.2).

It's important to note that Toyota's steady share gains are not being bought at the cost of low margins. Toyota reported growing profits through the 1990s and record profits in 2002. Indeed, its return on sales in fiscal 2002 was the highest in the global auto industry, excepting one company we will discuss in a moment.

It's also important to understand that the company marches steadily ahead without needing to be a dramatic innovator in the vehicle market. With the exception of the Prius hybrid, the RX300 "crossover" SUV, and the recently announced Scion line to attract young buyers, Toyota has been a plodding follower in the new market segments with highest growth: pickups, minivans, SUVs.[3]

This strategy has worked and continues to work because Toyota is the most brilliant manager of core processes in the history of industry. Its product development process delivers new products on time with very few defects, products that are more refined and cheaper to make than similar offerings from competitors. And its production and supplier management processes, as described in Chapter 10, deliver higher quality at lower cost with higher selling prices within each segment of the market.

In addition, Toyota relentlessly manages and improves every process in its business. Even something seemingly minor, like the spare parts distribution process described in Chapter 4, is continually pushed ahead. When we visited this process in 1996, Toyota was just introducing its Daily Ordering System and showing its suppliers how to make and ship replacement parts every day. Its competitors, by contrast, were ordering parts monthly and their suppliers shipped large batches of parts infrequently according to traditional auto industry practice. By the end of 2002, 60 percent of Toyota's spare parts suppliers were making and shipping parts every day in response to deliveries by Toyota to its dealers the previous day. These parts were shipped via a central cross-docking center in Kentucky to the eleven Regional Parts Distribution Centers. Toyota has also made steady progress in improving processes in its dealerships, halving dealer inventories of spare parts while increasing the productive area for vehicle service (freed up from former parts storage space) by 20 percent.

The brilliance of Toyota's processes mean that Toyota does not need to gamble on daring product designs within an established segment of the market or to pioneer new segments. Its situation is remarkably similar to that of General Motors in its golden period from the early 1920s into the 1960s, when Alfred Sloan decreed that gambles on product technology were unnecessary as long as the company could quickly match any successful innovation by more daring competitors.[4] Toyota can quickly copy the products others pioneer and win decisively because it continues to pioneer brilliant processes its competitors have taken halting steps to copy.

We emphasize this observation because it is truly good news for companies embracing lean thinking: you usually don't need to play brilliant hunches or score dramatic product breakthroughs to be successful. You can get there with brilliant process management instead, which is within the grasp of any firm with an enduring commitment.

Lean Processes Plus Brilliant Products at Porsche

We told in Chapter 9 of the revitalization of Porsche in the mid-1990s, but noted that its new products set for launch just as the book was published—the Boxster and the new 911—really did need to be brilliant and required perfect placement in a crowded market. Porsche could not afford a major product error and needed both brilliant processes and brilliant products to garner the high prices necessary to survive as the lone midget in an industry of giants.[5]

Fortunately, the new Porsches *were* brilliant, and not by accident—Porsche completely overhauled its traditional functional development process, as we explained in Chapter 9. In addition, Porsche continued to make steady progress in its manufacturing operations[6] in two directions.

First, it was able to offer customers a huge and growing range of options for their vehicles, while steadily reducing the number of hours it took to assemble each car.

Second, by improving quality, both in assembly and in purchased parts (by sending its lean promotion team to work closely with suppliers), Porsche was able to close the Pre-Delivery Inspection Centers in its main markets like the USA, where engineers used to go through each car with a fine-tooth comb to maintain Porsche's leading position in consumer quality rankings. These were simply not needed anymore because the quality at the end of the assembly lines was now truly excellent.

As a result, Porsche is not only the world's smallest independent car company by a large margin, it is also by far the most profitable. Even using the conservative accounting of a family-controlled German firm (where large amounts of revenues are routinely held back as reserves), Porsche reported a 17 percent return on sales in 2002, twice the rate of Toyota, the next most profitable car company.

In Chapter 9 we conjectured that combining German engineering brilliance with Toyota-style process management might produce an industrial hybrid better than either alone, one suited to a low-volume, high-variety

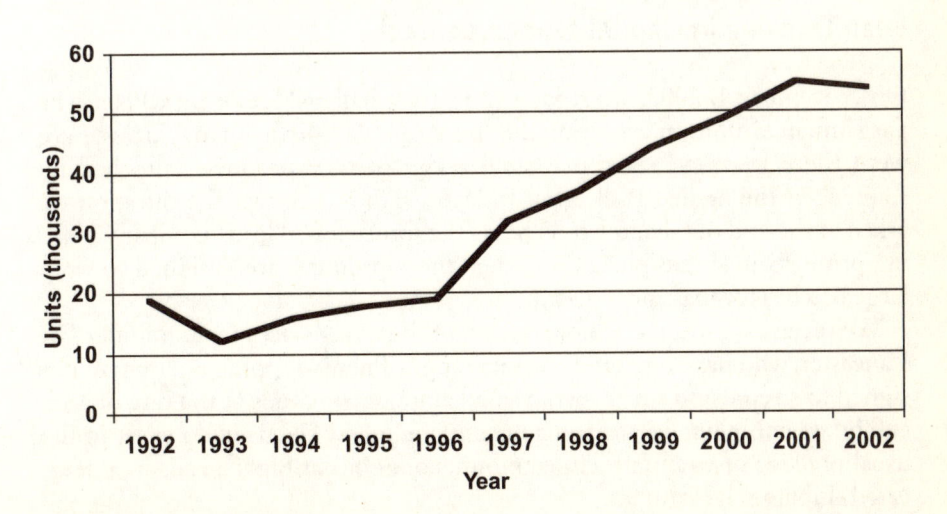

FIGURE 14.3: PORSCHE GLOBAL VEHICLE SALES

Source: Porsche AG Annual Reports

FIGURE 14.4: PORSCHE RETURN ON SALES

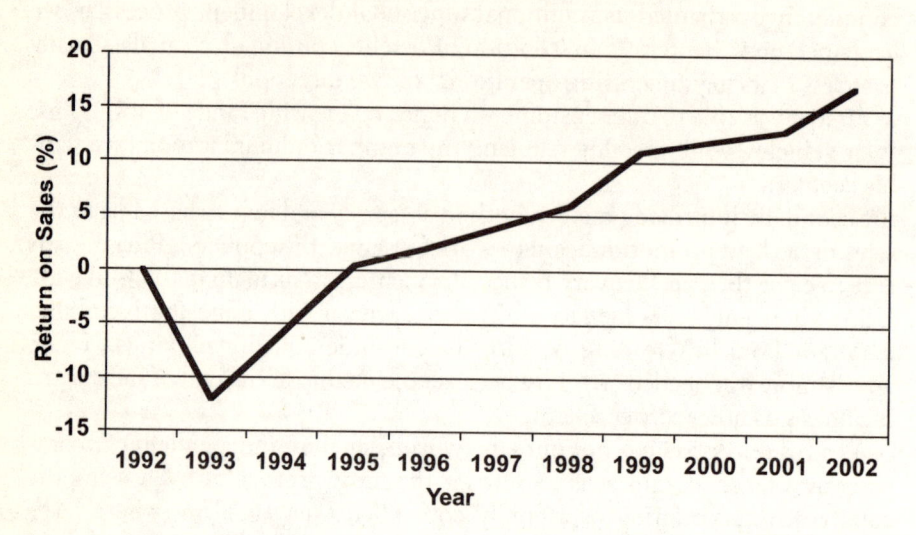

Source: Porsche AG Annual Reports
Note: "Return on Sales" is net profits before taxes divided by sales

business. Our surmise seems to be borne out at Porsche in the years since *Lean Thinking* was launched.

It's great to be brilliant like Porsche, and you may be even more successful than a Toyota, *if* you tend first to your core processes.

Lean Thinking in Capital Goods: Lantech

On November 4, 2002, we stood in the great hall at McCormick Place, the gargantuan exhibition center on the shore of Lake Michigan in Chicago. We were there to inspect a remarkable range of new products launched by Lantech at the annual Packaging Industry Expo to answer the question we asked at the end of Chapter 6. What is the future for a "lean" company making products in single-piece flow when these products are designed to wrap large batches for mass producers?

We received a special demonstration of the new devices from founder Pat Lancaster, who has pioneered a whole range of new wrapping equipment designed to stretch and shrink-wrap small amounts of goods at the rate of each cell or assembly line in a manufacturing company. This is in contrast to the usual practice of wrapping large amounts of goods at high speeds in a dedicated shipping department.

For example, Lantech launched a new integrated palletizer/stretch wrapper at the Chicago show that runs at one-third the rate of previous palletizers, requires one-fourth the footprint on the factory floor, and employs practically no complex electronics to sense where the pallet is, when to start, and when to stop. What makes it a breakthrough into truly continuous-flow manufacturing, with wrapping at the end of the process rather than in a separate department, is that Pat's new invention costs less than one-fifth the amount of any previous palletizer. Thus the cost per pallet wrapped is lower than for large machines even before the economies in handling are added.

In the period since the end of the show, Lantech has used its "right-sized" product to grow sales almost back to their 1999 peak. The truly remarkable aspect of this accomplishment is that the packaging industry as a whole continues to slog through a deep recession, with sales across the industry down by more than 35 percent from the peak in 1999.

Lantech has therefore taken the path of Porsche in combining a brilliant set of internal processes with a brilliant set of new—and very lean—product technologies, to create a bright future for an already outstandingly profitable business.

Pratt & Whitney: Lean Thinking in a Terrible Industry in a Terrible Time

We noted in Chapter 8 that the jet engine industry has long been difficult for producers because the amount of physical goods needed to provide a given amount of value to the consumer continually falls. The number of engines per aircraft has fallen from four for the first generation of jet aircraft—the Comet and the Boeing 707—to two on the highest selling current generation products and the amounts of service parts needed per engine hour of operation has fallen steadily from the beginning of the jet age. Through the 1990s, these two trends largely offset the increase in the number of aircraft in operations so that the total sales volume in the industry was stagnant.

However, the industry has now entered a much more difficult era, one with no visible endpoint. By the beginning of 1991—well before the shock of September 11—the hub-and-spoke business model of the major airlines was under severe assault from low cost point-to-point carriers. In addition, disgruntled "road warriors" (high volume business travelers) were rethinking whether the hassle plus the cost of current air travel was worth the benefit. These customers were critical to the hub-and-spoke carriers; in the 1990s high-volume travelers unable to take advantage of special fares requiring advance purchase or Saturday stays accounted for 8 percent of passenger miles but 50 percent of airline revenues. By the first quarter of 2001 they had seemingly gone on strike and have not returned.

The meltdown of the business model plus the new security environment have resulted in the world's airlines collectively losing $12 billion in 2002, with a number filing for bankruptcy. As a consequence, new orders for large jet aircraft (netting out cancellations) fell from about 1,100 in 2000 to fewer than 600 in 2002, and engine hours of operation (the key long-term driver of demand for spare parts) fell by 5 percent over this same period, the first sustained decline since the beginning of the jet age.

The other half of industry revenues comes from military customers. Given the war on terrorism we might expect the situation here to be different. However, the end of the Cold War and confusion about the military's needs in the new security regime have actually worked against Pratt & Whitney's interests.

To take the most striking example, Pratt provides the sole engine option for the F-22 and F-35,[7] the new front-line American fighter and attack aircraft for at least the next twenty-five years. Pratt's position sounds like an excellent recipe for sustainable long-term sales and profits. Yet these aircraft have come under continual challenge by new views on defense priorities. As a result, the original projection of 750 twin-engine F-22s for the U.S. Air Force (to replace roughly the same number of F-15s) has been steadily scaled back to 276 aircraft as of mid-2003. Meanwhile, orders for the single-engine F-35, to replace the F-16, originally targeted at 3,000 units, are already down to 2,500, with production still four years away.

Thus, the core of the military market for new Pratt engines has been shrinking, with capital investments spread over smaller and smaller production runs. Continuing orders for spare parts for the large number of military engines currently in use is keeping revenues healthy for now but not to the extent of offsetting the distress in the commercial engine business.

So far we have only described the challenges from the market. We need to complete the picture by pointing out that the industry has three competitors for a shrinking volume of large jet engines—Pratt, GE, and Rolls—and none shows inclination to exit. Even worse, from Pratt's standpoint (but not in the view of lean thinkers), the two lean laggards as of 1996, GE and Rolls, have been energetically copying the operational leadership of Pratt, intensifying competition even further.

Putting this all together, it's easy to see why Pratt has not been able to grow its top line (its revenues) since the mid-1990s, as shown in Figure 14.5.

What is remarkable is what Pratt has been able to do with its bottom line by continued application of lean thinking.

For starters, Pratt has continually shrunk its physical footprint, as shown in Figure 14.6. The billion-dollar room in North Haven, Connecticut (de-

FIGURE 14.5: PRATT & WHITNEY REVENUES, 1992–2002

($ millions)

1992	1993	1994	1995	1996	1997	1998	1999	2000	2001	2002
$6,972	$5,956	$5,545	$5,767	$6,201	$7,402	$7,876	$7,674	$7,366	$7,679	$7,645

Source: Pratt & Whitney

scribed on page 174) has been closed, with production moved into a much smaller existing space in East Hartford. The military engine business in Florida has been relocated to existing space in East Hartford as well. And

FIGURE 14.6: PRATT & WHITNEY MANUFACTURING NORTH AMERICA MANUFACTURING FOOTPRINT

(million square feet)

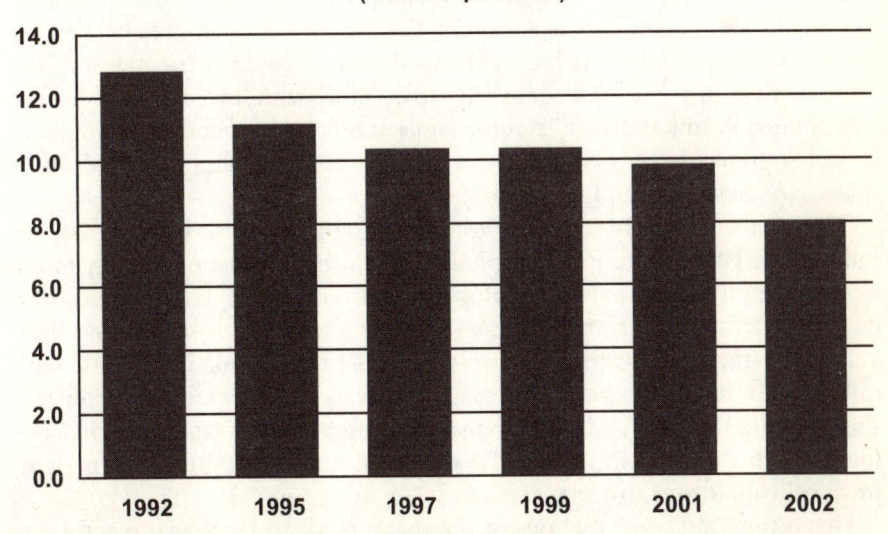

1992	1995	1997	1999	2001	2002
~12.9	~11.2	~10.4	~10.5	~10.0	~8.2

Source: Pratt & Whitney

FIGURE 14.7: PRATT & WHITNEY RETURN ON SALES AND RETURN ON ASSETS

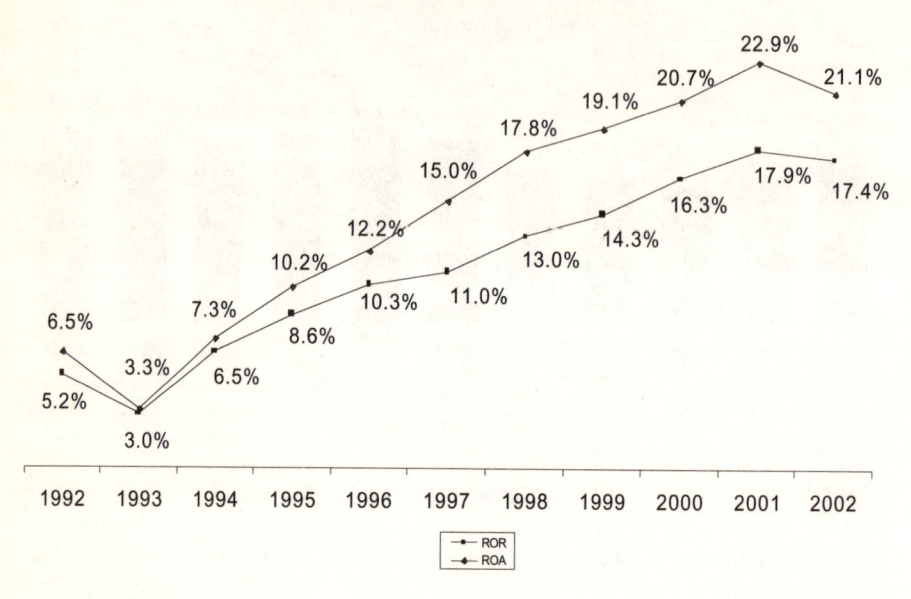

Year	ROR	ROA
1992	6.5%	5.2%
1993	3.3%	3.0%
1994	7.3%	6.5%
1995	10.2%	8.6%
1996	12.2%	10.3%
1997	15.0%	11.0%
1998	17.8%	13.0%
1999	19.1%	14.3%
2000	20.7%	16.3%
2001	22.9%	17.9%
2002	21.1%	17.4%

Source: Pratt & Whitney

even with these relocations, the footprint of the main Pratt complex in East Hartford has been continually reduced.

In addition, capital spending for new equipment has been reduced by buying small, "right-sized" tools with only the capacity and features needed for the job at hand, and Pratt has challenged every new investment using the same thought process. By finding ways to do more with less in every aspect of its business, Pratt has driven its return on assets employed and return on sales steadily upward despite stagnant revenues and severe pricing pressures in its spare parts business (see Figure 14.7).

This performance is a remarkable contrast to the last crisis in the aerospace industry, in 1991, when Pratt's capital heavy business fell immediately into a deep loss[8] and threatened to drag down the parent United Technologies with it. After a decade of lean thinking, spurred by the 1991 crisis, Pratt has been able to weather the loss of volume and prices pressures of 2001–2002 with only a minor drop in its return on sales and assets and its operating profits, as shown in Figures 14.7 and 14.8. To use an aerospace metaphor, this is like flying through a severe wind shear (like the downdrafts in a thunderstorm) with practically no loss of altitude.

Given the long-term realities of the market—distressed customers, large minimum scale requirements for new commercial product programs, and a

FIGURE 14.8: PRATT & WHITNEY EARNINGS BEFORE INTEREST AND TAXES, 1992–2002

($ millions)

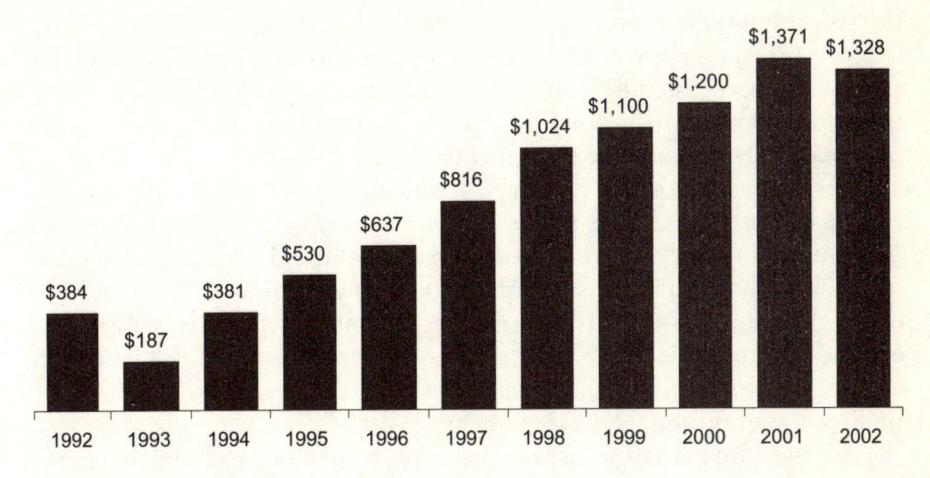

1992	$384
1993	$187
1994	$381
1995	$530
1996	$637
1997	$816
1998	$1,024
1999	$1,100
2000	$1,200
2001	$1,371
2002	$1,328

Source: Pratt & Whitney

large number of competitors in relation to the stagnant manufacturing volume—the 150-year-old Pratt may well face the need for another dramatic transformation into a different type of business. This was achieved twice before: in 1925, when it jumped from machine tools to aircraft engines, and in the late 1940s, when it abandoned piston engines for jets.

The most promising strategy would seem to be diversification into the $10 billion overhaul and repair business, where lean thinking can be applied with the same results as in manufacturing. Pratt is already well along the path and recently has been acquiring overhaul businesses around the globe as well as growing its small in-house overhaul business. These initiatives have increased its global market share in overhaul and repair from 1 percent in 1992 to 10 percent in 2002.

Whatever the path to growing the top line of the business, Pratt's lean practices are providing the operating margin and cash needed to steer a new course.

Beyond Isolated Advances

These are stories of sober success, of companies doing well despite difficult market conditions.[9] They are not the giddy tales often heard during the recent boom, but rather successful keep-on-keeping-on efforts by early adopters (excepting Toyota of course) of the lean thought process we have described. However, they are only meaningful for society at large if many other firms are following them along the path. What evidence can we provide that our ideas are being embraced by firms across the economy?

The best measure is also the simplest: the inventories needed in the economy to support a given level of sales to end customers. It is simply impossible to create a lean business or a lean enterprise encompassing an extended value stream without greatly increasing the velocity of value flowing from raw materials to customers and greatly reducing inventories. This is because the essence of leanness is to eliminate time-consuming but wasteful steps and to create a condition in which the remaining value-creating steps occur in continuous flow at the pull of the customer.

When we sum the experience of our sample firms along with the thousands of other firms comprising the American economy, using data collected by the American government in a consistent format since 1958, we discover that for a very long time, nothing changed. The level of inventory turns (that is, sales to end customers divided by the total inventories in the manufacturing

FIGURE 14.9: U.S. INVENTORY TURNS: AUTOMOTIVE AND MANUFACTURING

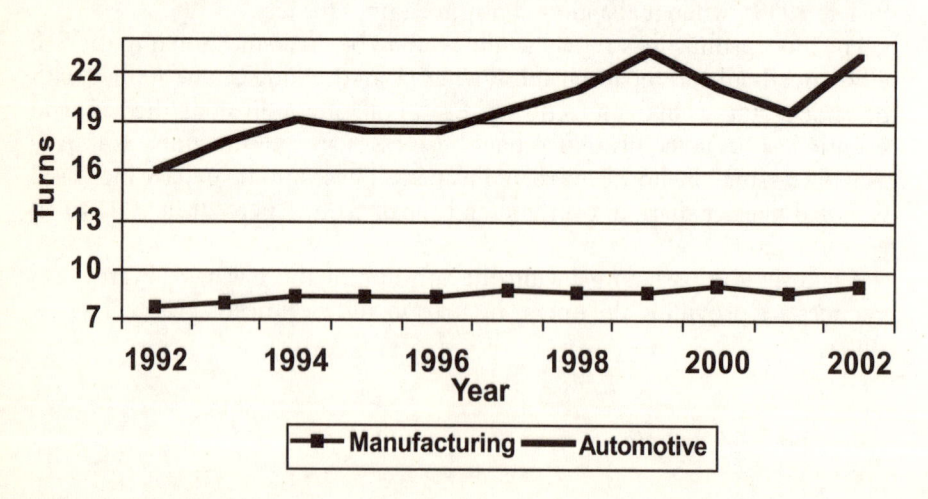

Source: U.S. Census Bureau

FIGURE 14.10: U.S. INVENTORY TURNS: MANUFACTURING, WHOLESALE, AND RETAIL

Source: U.S. Census Bureau

process including raw materials, work in process, and finished goods) was level for nearly forty years from 1958 into the mid-1990s. Turns moved up and down slightly with the business cycle, but showed no trend toward improvement.

During this same interval, the trend in inventory turns in wholesale and retail was much worse. It moved steadily downward from 1958 through 1995 in lockstep with the ever-growing variety of products on offer and the need to support each product with inventory. This trend was despite many innovations in information technology, logistics, and retail formats.

And then the needle began to move. The trend is clearest in motor vehicle manufacturing, as shown in Figure 14.9. This is not surprising given Toyota's powerful presence in this industry. But a steady improvement trend is apparent in many other manufacturing activities and the rate of improvement appears to be picking up again after the recession of 2001, which, like all recessions, caused a temporary fall in inventory turns.[10]

Perhaps more interesting is the upward in trend in inventory turns in wholesale and retail where the simple principle of replenishing small amounts frequently from manufacturers (as explained in Chapter 4), instead of prepositioning large amounts of goods ahead of demand on the basis of forecasts, seems to be taking hold (see Figure 14.10).

FIGURE 14.11: U.S. INVENTORY TURNS: TOTAL ECONOMY

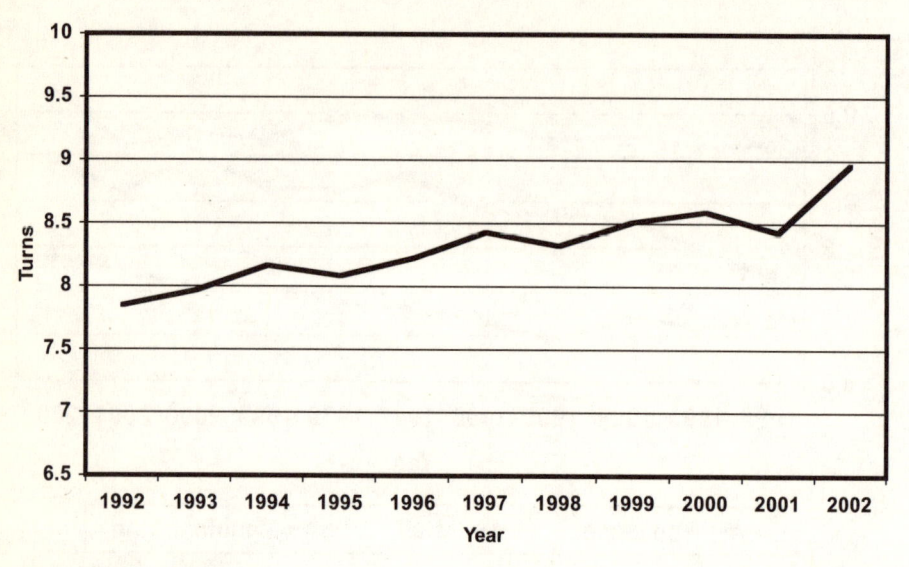

Source: U.S. Census Bureau

When the manufacturing, wholesale, and retail turns are combined, we see a steady increase across the entire economy, as shown in Figure 14.11.

It is certainly too early to claim victory, but the trend since the initial publication of this volume in 1996 is very promising and we look forward to a leaner future than we could have imagined only a decade ago.

This said, the pace is still too slow! What can we do to make greater progress toward the perfect land of zero waste and pure value we envisioned in Chapter 13? What can we do to institutionalize and spur the slow revolution in value creation that we believe is under way?

In fact, we have learned a lot about this question in observing the progress of many companies during the years since the launch of this book and we will devote the remainder of this Epilogue to sharing our new wisdom about the lean leap.

CHAPTER 15

Institutionalizing the Revolution

Revolutions in business practice don't just happen. There must be an action plan that real managers in real companies can deploy. We therefore presented a step-by-step action plan in Chapter 11 that summarized and condensed the plans of attack of our sample firms. Now we'll enhance this plan based on direct observation of the change process in a much wider range of organizations over the past six years.

An Enhanced Action Plan

We believe that our original plan is still remarkably sound and we retain all of the steps in the same sequence. However, for many of the steps we have gained additional insights. We will therefore go through our checklist in the same sequence shown in Chapter 11, adding to each step where appropriate.

FIND A CHANGE AGENT

This first step is as important as ever, but we have discovered in recent years that the typical change agent is evolving as lean thinking spreads. When we began our research a decade ago, a truly inspired and forceful leader at the very top—an Art Byrne, Pat Lancaster, Karl Krapek, or Wendelin Weideking in the position of CEO—seemed to be required to overcome corporate inertia. More recently we have observed a number of lean transformations in companies of different sizes in which the point of origin was mid-level managers and where quiet leadership was effective without need for shouting or theatrics.

But still, a leader—someone who will take personal responsibility for change—is essential. No organization has ever undergone dramatic and comprehensive change without someone somewhere, softly or in a loud voice, taking the lead.

We've learned something else about transformational leadership involving a phenomenon often remarked in human political history: Revolutionaries are often poor managers of the new order once it is put in place. Many of the most effective change agents succeed in the long term because there is someone behind them putting a rigorous system of lean processes in place, someone who can take over and push improvement continuously ahead when the change agent leaves or moves on to other issues. This may be the COO behind the CEO or the head of the Lean Promotion Office under the COO or the product line manager reporting to the head of product development or the value stream manager under the plant manager. The key is that someone somewhere needs to turn a revolution into a rigorous system and make sure that everyone understands and follows the new system.

When there is no one there to put the system in place, the higher level of performance usually lasts only as long as the change agent is directly in charge. (We've learned this several times from hard experience when a dynamic leader left and the organization quickly regressed to the mean.) So our advice, based on years of experience, is that every organization should carefully team a system builder with each of its revolutionary change agents in order to sustain results.

GET THE KNOWLEDGE

Our view of the second step has evolved as well. When we started our research in 1992, the highest levels of lean knowledge were usually resident in Japanese *sensei*,[1] often graduates of Toyota or its supplier group, who taught by starting with a simple problem. For example, they identified a multistep process within a single facility, with materials transfers and inventory between each step, and quickly converted the isolated steps to single-piece-flow within a cell. They then went to the next isolated problem—perhaps in the area of 5S or simple pull systems—and solved it. This created a dramatic sense that rapid change was possible while the *sensei* taught lean thinking and lean methods along the way.

For the *sensei*, the most valuable aspect of these exercises was not the improvement in performance in a specific process. Rather, it was the raised consciousness of the managers involved in the change process and their enthusiasm for tackling other problems using the knowledge they were slowly acquiring from the *sensei*.

Behind the stern mask of the *sensei*, there was a detailed master plan of how all the parts would eventually fit together to create a complete lean production system. But this was not revealed at the outset and became apparent to managers only over time as they learned to see.

The problem with this teaching system, once consultants with no direct link to Toyota and many self-taught managers began to practice it, was that there tended to be no big picture waiting to be revealed. Instead of flow *kaizen* directed at the total flow of value for a product family, there was only process *kaizen*, and usually lots of process *kaizen*, focused on isolated individual steps in many value streams. We coined the term "kamikaze *kaizen*" (and the accompanying term "kamikaze Six-Sigma") to describe the likely result: lots of commotion, many isolated victories in the great war against *muda*, widespread initial enthusiasm on the basis of early results, impressive amounts of consciousness raising, and . . . loss of the war when no sustainable benefits reached the customer or the bottom line.

The solution, which we believe is increasingly accepted, is for firms without access to a master *sensei* to start consciously at the system level for each product family. This means looking at the big picture, including the most important business needs, and determining the overall plan of march before conducting process *kaizen* on the individual steps. As we will see in a moment, this is a job for line managers, not for technical advisers who often have reservoirs of specific lean knowledge but who lack expertise in flow *kaizen* and insight into the most important needs of the business. The value-stream map is an invaluable tool to help line managers along the value stream see the whole, as we will explain shortly.

For firms with access to a master *sensei*, we have some similar advice. Invest early in systematically writing down the knowledge of the *sensei* and inquire about the big picture before too many process *kaizen* events are lined up. This may not be an easy conversation, but we believe a higher-level, system focus by senior managers, as the *sensei* proceeds with process *kaizen*, will produce a better result than either approach alone.

Find a Lever by Seizing the Crisis, or by Creating One

Our third step is still critical and the reason that recessions are so valuable to firms and society. They create the necessity to seize the opportunity that was always there, by embracing lean thinking. And we know that recessions do at least raise consciousness because sales of our books—including this book—always rise in bad times. But just because there is a crisis does not mean the opportunity will be grasped. The hapless manager we describe on page 251 created a profound crisis for his firm by dramatically reducing selling prices for his durable good. But he soon lost his job for failure to take out the necessary costs through dramatic restructuring of his entire design and production process. For a crisis to be useful, leadership and knowledge must lead to decisive action on the tough issues of excess assets, wrong locations, and excess people.

We are also seeing many managers who use the current era of stagnation as an excuse to abandon any efforts to improve their current operations. Instead they relocate design and production, almost always using mass production methods, to remote locations, often thousands of miles from their customers. The new locations have one key attribute—low factor costs, particularly in the form of cheap labor—and they seem irresistible.

The problem is that every competitor can immediately pursue the same strategy, so the advantage is short-lived. In addition, because firms following this strategy add nothing to their knowledge of lean practice, they are vulnerable to shifts in currency rates and geopolitics that may require them to move again soon. We'll return to this point in a moment in discussing the need to optimize entire value streams on a global basis.

Map Your Value Streams

This has been the greatest area of learning for us because we had not grasped just how much help the average manager needs to see the value stream. The maps we drew on pages 39 and 42, although accurate and provocative, turned out to be too simple. And we made a critical error by failing to connect on one map the flow of *information* going back from the customer to the producer with the *transforming actions* on the product, in response to this information, as the good or service moves toward the customer. Making this connection is the critical leap in being able to see the closed circuit of demand and response that is the essence of value creation, an insight that traditional process maps, showing physical transformations alone, fail to provide.

Thus we are deeply grateful to Mike Rother and John Shook for adapting Toyota's standard method for portraying material and information flows into the value stream maps we now use.[2] These maps can be drawn at any scale, from a simple administrative process within an office to the global flow of an extended value stream running from raw materials in the ground to the end consumer.

The objective in each case is to write down all of the steps in the process as it currently operates to define what we call the Current State. For each step we urge managers to ask a set of very simple questions. Does the step create value for the customer? Is the step capable? (That is, does it produce a good result every time?) Is it available? (That is, can it produce the desired output, not just the desired quality, every time?) Is it flexible? (Can it be changed over quickly from one product to the next so that items can be produced in small lots or even lots of one?) Is capacity for the step adequate so the product doesn't need to wait on the process? Or is there too much capacity (due to designing equipment in large increments of capacity based on demand forecasts that are often wrong)?[3]

Steps that do not create value should, of course, be eliminated, while steps that are incapable, unavailable, inflexible, inadequate, and under- or overcapacitized should be perfected. But this step-by-step analysis provides only part of the picture because the relation between the steps is equally important. Does the information coming back from the customer flow smoothly without delays? Does the product moving toward the customer flow smoothly from step to step so that total throughput time is only slightly more than the sum of the times needed for individual processing steps? Does the product flow at the desire of the customer rather than at the push of the producer? Finally, is demand "leveled" at each stage so that small perturbations are smoothed rather than amplified?

By writing down all the steps as a team, as shown in Figure 15.1 for the flow of value within the walls of a factory, it's possible for everyone to see the whole value stream under discussion and to agree on its current level of performance.

The map below shows the flow of information from the customer to the various points in the production process, moving from right to left in the upper half. Orders go from the customer to a Material Requirements Planning computer, where they are held in inventory awaiting the weekly run of the system to devise the production schedule for the following week. A considerable amount of information expediting occurs as floor managers discover shortages or customer demand suddenly changes.

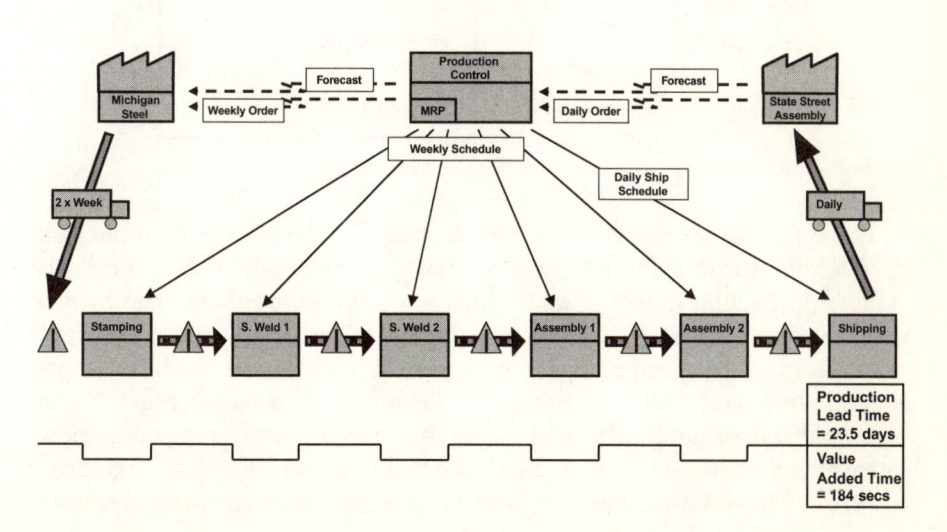

FIGURE 15.1: CURRENT STATE VALUE STREAM MAP

The map also shows the flow of products from raw materials to customer, moving from left to right in the lower half. It summarizes the performance of the five necessary steps, shows the inventory currently accumulating between them, compares value-creating time (very small) with total throughput time (very large), and helps managers envision the initial flow *kaizen* needed to drastically compress the throughput time for the product, eliminate wasted steps, and rectify quality, flexibility, availability, and adequacy problems.

All of this information can be summarized in a box score of Current State performance as shown in Figure 15.2.

FIGURE 15.2: CURRENT STATE BOX SCORE

	Current State
Total Lead Time	23.5 days
Value Creating Time	184 seconds
Changeover Time	10 minutes in assembly 1 hour in stamping
Uptime	80% in weld/assembly 85% in stamping
Scrap/Rework	5%
Inventory	17,130 pieces
Every Part Made Every	2 weeks

The visioning process facilitated by the map and the box score should lead to a vastly improved Future State, as shown in Figure 15.3. Reaching this state requires achieving the "*kaizen* bursts" on the Future State map, which show the necessary points for flow and process *kaizen*.

In this case, the specific steps required are to improve the capability (first-time quality), availability (uptime), and flexibility (changeover time) of the four weld and assembly steps and to eliminate the inventories impeding flow by turning the four steps into a cell. (Note that one fewer operator is required as a result.) In addition, setup times of the stamping press are greatly reduced

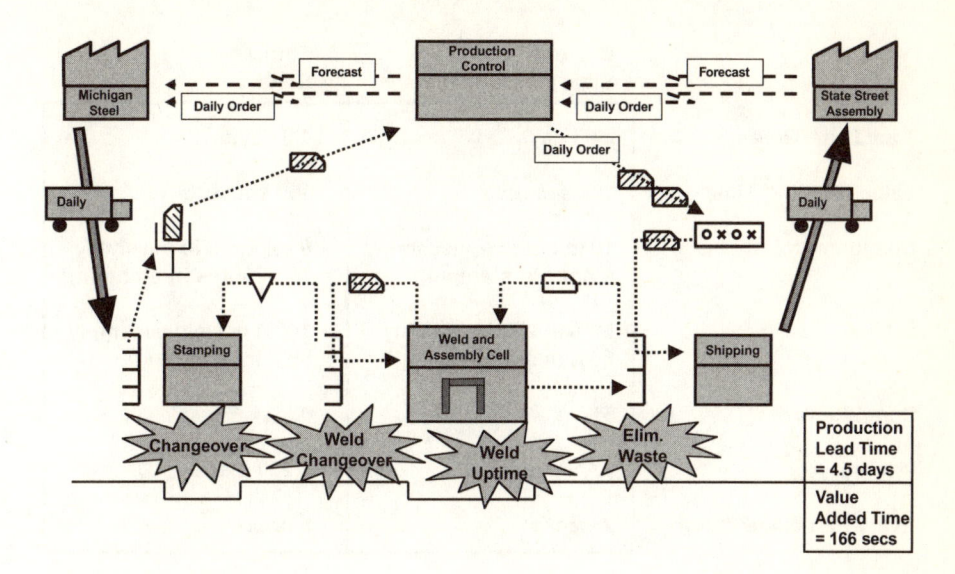

FIGURE 15.3: FUTURE STATE VALUE STREAM MAP

to permit the production of much smaller batches, further reducing inventories.

The final step is to disconnect the Material Requirements Planning system previously giving production orders to every step in the process. A simple pull system is put in its place that sends *kanban* signals from a *heijunka* box (a demand leveling device) at precisely paced intervals to the weld/assembly cell, which is the "pacemaker process" for this value stream. Additional pull loops are installed from the weld/assembly cell to the stamping machine and from the stamping machine to the supplier of steel coils. As a result, the entire process of information management is vastly simplified and transitioned from push to pull.

The implications for performance of this Future State are shown in the expanded box score contrasting the Current State and the Future State in Figure 15.4.

The mapping process clearly reveals the potential for a major leap in performance if a relatively small number of flow and process *kaizens* can be conducted and then sustained. And this is not the end of the potential for improvement. As we will show below, in the section on perfecting the value stream, it is always possible to make further progress by designating the Future State, once achieved, as the new Current State and beginning the improvement cycle again.

This brings us to our major concern about value stream mapping. We've

FIGURE 15.4: CURRENT TO FUTURE STATE BOX SCORE

	Current State	Future State
Total Lead Time	23.5 days	4.5 days
Value Creating Time	184 seconds	169 seconds
Changeover Time	10 minutes in assembly 1 hour in stamping	0 minutes in assembly 10 minutes in stamping
Uptime	80% in weld/assembly 85% in stamping	100% in weld/assembly 99% in stamping
Scrap/Rework	5%	0.5%
Inventory	17,130 pieces	3,250 pieces
Every Part Made Every	2 weeks	8 hours

found overwhelming acceptance of this tool across the world[4] and we now find many managers with beautiful Current State maps and with equally beautiful Future State maps indicating the potential for major leaps in performance. But, when we take a walk along the value stream, there is no actual Future State. The promised leap in performance has never occurred or has been achieved to only a fraction of the extent possible.[5]

When we see this situation we always ask to see the plan for achieving the Future State, which should look something like Figure 15.5, and we ask to meet the individual responsible for managing and improving the value stream. And this is the great problem: usually there is no real plan, or at least no implementable plan, because no one has the responsibility. There is no value stream manager to perfect the process.

REORGANIZE YOUR FIRM BY PRODUCT FAMILY AND VALUE STREAM

Just as we underestimated the importance of the value stream map, we also failed to grasp the significance of the value stream manager. This is the person who leads the mapping process and takes responsibility for removing the *muda* from the value stream for a product, while introducing flow and pull. Instead of describing the role of this critical individual in detail (whom we did mention briefly as the Directly Responsible Individual at Lantech, the Product Team Leaders at Wiremold and Pratt & Whitney, and the Chief Engineer

Figure 15.5: Implementation Plan

V S Manager Date												Product Family	
Product Family Business Objective	Value Stream Objective	Measurable Goal	\multicolumn{9}{c	}{Monthly Schedule}	Person in Charge
			1	2	3	4	5	6	7	8	9	
Improve Profitability in Steering Brackets	Pacemaker *Continuous flow from weld to assembly *Kaizen to 168 secs *Eliminate weld changeover *Uptime weld #2 *Finished goods pull *Materials handler routes	Zero WIP < 168 s/t < 30 sec c/o 100% 2 days FG Pull Schedule	→	→	→	→						John Dave Sam Mike Sue James
	Stamping *Stamping Pull *Stamping changeover	1 day inventory + pull schedule batch size 300/160 pieces c/o < 10 min					→	→				Fred Tim
	Supplier *Pull coils with daily delivery	daily delivery < 1.5 days of coils at press								→		Graham

at Toyota), we concentrated on changing the organization of the firm so that all of the needed skills within functional areas would be directly under this person's authority.

We've subsequently found in a number of organizations that to get the attention of self-absorbed functions, it can be helpful to change reporting arrangements and move personnel under a product line manager or team leader, at least for one product generation. We've also realized that Toyota and more mature lean firms (now including Lantech) get brilliant results from giving the value stream manager complete responsibility for the value stream and the success of the product but hardly any direct reports or traditional authority.

Instead, the value stream manager develops the vision for the product, determines the Current State of the value stream, and then envisions the Future State. She or he then treats the functions as the suppliers of the essential inputs (for example, engineering, operations, purchasing, sales, lean knowledge) needed to reach this state. If the functions fail to perform, the value stream manager typically goes directly to the CEO, the COO, or the director of the office of value stream managers, to describe the problem, get to the root cause, and install a fix.

Finally, we've discovered that these value stream and product line managers, like so much in the lean world, are "fractal." That is, a product line manager overseeing an entire product may work with a number of value stream managers at lower levels taking responsibility for different courses of the value stream. For example, a chief engineer (to use Toyota's term for a product line manager overseeing an entire automotive platform) works with a development leader in design, a value stream manager in the assembly plant, and value stream managers in each of the component plants working on major items assembled into the finished product. Each manager is essentially doing the same job but with varying scope—wide at the top and narrow at the bottom.

That this approach works for maturing lean firms besides Toyota became apparent to us in talking with Pat Lancaster at the trade show where he launched his new right-sized wrappers (described in Chapter 14). We asked how Lantech's dedicated product teams were functioning and got a quizzical look.

"Actually, we've found that the Directly Responsible Individual [the value stream manager] is the critical player in our organization. Once the functional departments got enlightened, we found we no longer needed to change the organization chart and move people onto product teams for each new product family. Instead, the DRI explains to the functions what they need to do as his suppliers to ensure the success of the product. And they do it."

CREATE A LEAN PROMOTION FUNCTION

In the first edition of *Lean Thinking*, we proposed that a lean promotion function be created to house the functional expertise from old-fashioned industrial engineering, quality, and maintenance departments along with the newfound knowledge about flow and pull. Many readers found this suggestion problematic because they could not imagine that experts from a quality background, a total productive maintenance (TPM) background, and a lean (TPS) background could work in harmony.

As time has passed and we have listened to many pointless arguments between *sensei* from TPS, TPM, TQC, and TQM backgrounds, we've become even more certain that all of the expert animals in the lean zoo should live in the same cage. That's because all of these experts—once differing vocabularies[6] and professional rivalries are stripped away—are in pursuit of the same goal: the perfect process.

Each expert would like to create value streams where every step is valuable, every step is capable (the starting point of quality experts), every step is available (the point of origin of maintenance experts), every step is adequate (with neither too much nor too little capacity), and all steps are highly flexible and linked by pull and flow with leveled demand (the starting point of TPS experts). And every value stream manager would like to be able to tap a single supplier of the knowledge needed to achieve perfection.

The challenge is to create a dialogue between all the experts so the value stream manager gets consistent, quality advice in a single voice. Only in this way can the rate of improvement can be maximized.

The Lean Promotion Office should be small, except for periods when excess employees from line jobs are being redeployed and put to work on short-term *kaizen* projects. It needs only a few experts who are willing to master all of the knowledge and methods needed to create perfect value streams and to teach this knowledge, as necessary, to value stream managers and line employees. And it may get smaller over time.

After all, lean knowledge is most needed early in the transformation when most value stream managers lack critical knowhow and the value streams themselves are choked with *muda*. As time goes on, the value stream manager can devote more time to individual product considerations—many of them due to changing markets and customer needs. Less time is needed for identifying Current States and achieving Future States once Current States are already performing at a very high level. (At Toyota the core lean knowledge is located in the Operations Management Consulting Division, but the professional staff totals only about sixty for a global organization with $127 billion in revenues.)

When You've Fixed Something, Fix It Again

Most managers accept the intellectual proposition that improvement is never finished. Yet we repeatedly visit organizations that make an initial leap to lean and then stop, while talking endlessly about the endless journey. We were therefore delighted recently to revisit Freudenberg-NOK, a firm that had already shown an aptitude for pursuing perfection over an extended period. For example, in Figure 5.1 (page 91), we presented their progress over a three-year period in a vibration damper product line.

This time we looked at an oil seal product and found a path of steady improvement for a full decade, with no plans to quit. As the diagrams and charts in Figure 15.6 show, FNGP made the initial leap with this product—from process villages to cells—in 1992. (This is the point at which many firms seem to stop.) They followed up this first step with careful attention to the operation of the cells to create "best practice" and then "model" cells in 1993 and 1994.[7] In 1995 they introduced pull systems throughout the facility to send production instructions to the cells and remove products frequently at a fixed pace. In 1998 they undertook a Production Preparation Process (3-P) for a new product generation. And in 2000 they applied all the tools of Six Sigma to improve the capability of their process to a point where scrap is less than one-

324 LEAN THINKING

FIGURE 15.6A: FREUDENBERG-NOK

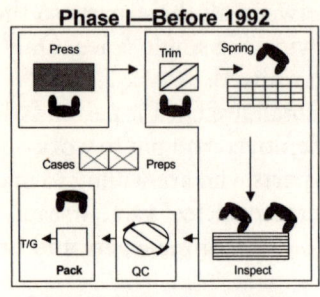

Phase I—Before 1992
Original State, with activities scattered throughout plant

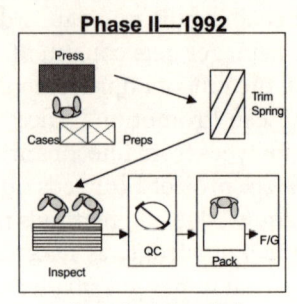

Phase II—1992
Best Practice Cell

FIGURE 15.6B: FREUDENBERG-NOK

Phase III—1994
Model Cell

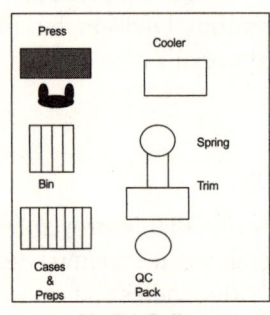

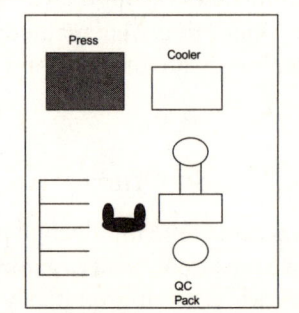

Phase IV—1995
Set-Up Reduction—Pull System

FIGURE 15.6C: FREUDENBERG-NOK

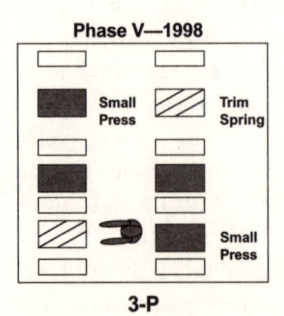

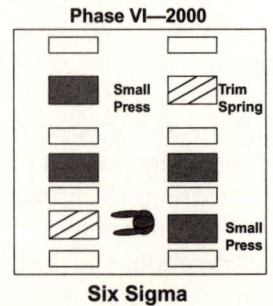

Phase V—1998
3-P

Phase VI—2000
Six Sigma

FIGURE 15.6D: FREUDENBERG-NOK

	Phase I <1992	Phase II 1992	Phase III 1994	Phase IV 1995	Phase V 1998	Phase VI 2000
Performance Impact						
Pieces per Shift	5,800	6,060	6,840	7,000	9,570	9,630
Labor Hours per Day	46	34	24	24	24	24
Inventory (WIP)	36,000	18,000	240	240	70	70
Distance Traveled (feet)	2,214	670	20	20	20	20
Scrap	6.8%	4.1%	1.3%	1.3%	0.8%	0.1%
Lead Time (Door to Door)	30 days	20 days	5 days	24 hours	16 hours	16 hours
Pieces per Labor Hour	383	534	855	875	1,196	1,203
Financial Impact						
Revenue	+	+	+		+++	
Labor	–	–	---	-	–	-
Overheads	-	–	–	---	–	-
Capital	---	---	---	–	–	-

FIGURE 15.6E: FREUDENBERG-NOK SUMMARY

Oil Seal Study

Improvement Summary

6- Phases, 8 Years

Productivity	+214%
Inventory (WIP)	–99.8%
Scrap	–98.5%
Distance Traveled	–99.1%
Lead Time (dock to dock)	–97.7%

FNGP Company-Wide

1992 to Present

- Over 8000 *kaizen* projects conducted in North America
- Saved over $100 million
- Reduced PPM from 2000 to <50
- Cost of quality cut by 60%
- Work in progress inventory slashed by 80%
- Labor productivity increased by 25% per year
- Revenue per 1000 sq. ft. floor space increased by 350%
- Dock-to-dock lead time of 16 hours or less

tenth of a percent in an industry where no one else is below 1 percent. Perhaps a TPM program to obtain 100 percent equipment availability is next?

In any case, the point is clear. It really is possible to continue improvements indefinitely for the same value stream. The question is whether value stream managers (and their top-level superiors) will emphatically demand truly continuous improvements and whether the Lean Promotion Office can continually supply the necessary knowledge.

Utilize Policy Deployment

In the past few years we've had extensive experience with policy deployment in our own research institutes. And it's the hardest thing we've tried to do. Policy deployment forces senior managers to make painful choices about what is really most important for the organization and what is truly achievable. At the same time, policy deployment exposes the contradictions between the plans of every unit of the organization as these affect the other units.

We wish we could say it gets easier. But it doesn't. Old conflicts will always give way to new in any organization as long as it is growing or faces resource constraints. So the intensity of the policy deployment process seems to be a constant. What's more, we have found that the process can be led only by the senior executive.

Paradoxically, we have discovered that the actual plans emerging from our policy deployment exercises are only good for about three months, despite our hopes (and our initial expectations) that they would guide our organizations for at least a year. As we reflected on this, we remembered a principle central to lean thinking: A value creation system must be flexible and responsive because *forecasts are always wrong*. And we realized that a policy deployment plan is nothing more than an organizational forecast, which future events quickly conspire to prove wrong.

At first we were bewildered but then found that Toyota long ago discovered the same thing. Today Toyota senior managers commonly note that "planning is invaluable but plans are worthless."[8] Their conclusion is that going through the process forces everyone in the organization to understand the needs and constraints of everyone else and greatly heightens consciousness about the most promising future path even if the specific course of action chosen during the process needs frequent modification.

Convince Your Suppliers and Customers to Take the Steps Just Described

In 1996, we hoped that the participants in the extended value stream—the firms stretching all the way from raw materials to the end consumer—were ready to go down a new path beyond meaningless "partnerships" (always fashionable in good times) and margin squeezing (the hallmark of every recession). However, in the giddy period of the New Economy in the late 1990s most firms seemed to focus instead on new information technologies, notably web-based reverse auctions, which were bound to show very limited results.

Reverse auctions always seemed a dubious prospect to us. Unless the customer and the supplier can learn to remove costly waste from their joint value-creating process, there is an inherent limit on the long-term price savings available to the customer. The maximum saving is the amount of margin the supplier can afford to give away over an extended period while still remaining in business. And this is typically a very small number—only a few percent—because the great bulk of the supplier's price is determined by real costs resulting from the waste in the value stream.

Recently, as customers and suppliers have found the limits of new IT tools and gone through one more recession-driven round of traditional price squeezing, we have introduced a simple mapping tool that can teach the customer and the supplier to see the whole flow of value. This is the extended value stream map that is the logical complement to the facility-level value stream maps popularized by Mike Rother and John Shook in *Learning to See*, which we described above in our discussion of mapping value streams.

The objective of this tool is not to perform costing studies (although it could be adapted to this task), but instead to raise the shared consciousness of every participant along a given value stream about the performance of the whole stream, the causes of waste, and the best approaches to improvements that can make all participants better off.

By taking a brief walk together, the participants in a shared value stream can quickly determine the Current State and identify the magnitude and sources of the waste, which then can be turned into benefits. For example, on a value stream walk we recently conducted while preparing our workbook *Seeing the Whole*[9] (similar to dozens of others we have conducted over many years), we found that only 8 of the 73 steps performed to physically transform a product (a windshield wiper and arm for an auto manufacturer) created any value for the end customer (the car buyer). And none of the 25 information processing steps actually created any value.[10] Of the total time involved, only 54 minutes out of the 44 days required to produce the finished product actually created value and none of the 58 days elapsing between placement of an order by a customer and its transmission to the most upstream producer were of any value from the standpoint of the customer (see Figures 15.7 and 15.8).

328 LEAN THINKING

FIGURE 15.7: CURRENT STATE EXTENDED VALUE STREAM MAP

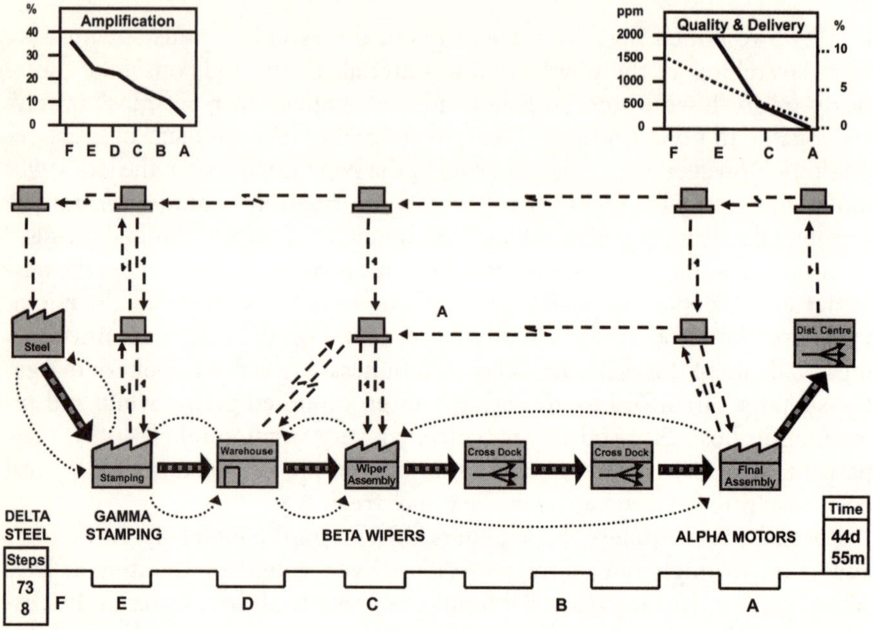

We also found that demand varied only about 3 percent at the customer end of the value stream but gyrated by 40 percent at the most upstream producer (the raw materials supplier). And as we continued our investigation, we found that defects became 7 times more likely and defective shipments to customers 8 times more likely as we walked back up the stream. In consequence, large inventories were present at many points to buffer the system and protect downstream customers from shortages, and large amounts of rework and expediting occurred at every transition from one firm to the next.

We could also see, however, that all of the wasteful steps and time were absolutely necessary because of the configuration of the value stream and the logic of the shared production process. Perhaps most important, no one looking at their stretch of the value stream alone had much hope of seeing the totality of the waste or of reducing it.

On the basis of our walk it was easy to envision a series of future states the participating firms might create that could make every firm better off. For example, simply agreeing to implement the type of Future State shown in Figure 15.3 *within* every plant, to introduce flow and pull, should cut throughput time in half and eliminate 25 percent of the wasted steps.

A second Future State (see Figures 15.10 and 15.11) could introduce lev-

FIGURE 15.8: CURRENT STATE BOX SCORE

	Current State
Total Lead Time	44.3 days
Value Creating to Total Time	0.08%
Value Creating to Total Steps	11%
Inventory Turns	5
Quality Screen*	400
Delivery Screen*	8
Demand Amplification*	7
Travel Distance	5,300 miles

*Ratios of upstream over downstream scores

FIGURE 15.9: CURRENT TO FUTURE STATE 1 BOX SCORE

	Current State	Future State 1
Total Lead Time	44.3 days	23.9 days
Value Creating to Total Time	0.08%	0.16%
Value Creating to Total Steps	11%	15%
Inventory Turns	5	9
Quality Screen*	400	200
Delivery Screen*	8	8
Demand Amplification*	7	7
Travel Distance	5,300 miles	5,300 miles

*Ratios of upstream over downstream scores

330   LEAN THINKING

FIGURE 15.10: FUTURE STATE 2 EXTENDED VALUE STREAM MAP

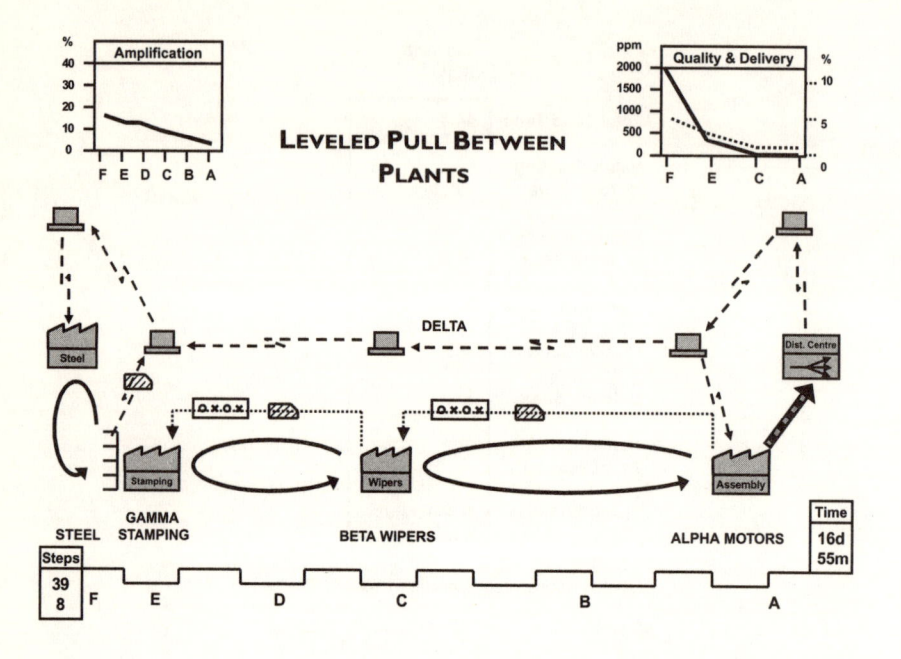

FIGURE 15.11: CURRENT AND FUTURE STATE 2 BOX SCORE

	Current State	Future State 1	Future State 2
Total Lead Time	44.3 days	23.9 days	15.8 days
Value Creating to Total Time	0.08%	0.16%	0.6%
Value Creating to Total Steps	11%	15%	21%
Inventory Turns	5	9	14
Quality Screen*	400	200	50
Delivery Screen*	8	8	3
Demand Amplification*	7	7	5
Travel Distance	5,300 miles	5,300 miles	4,300 miles

*Ratios of upstream over downstream scores

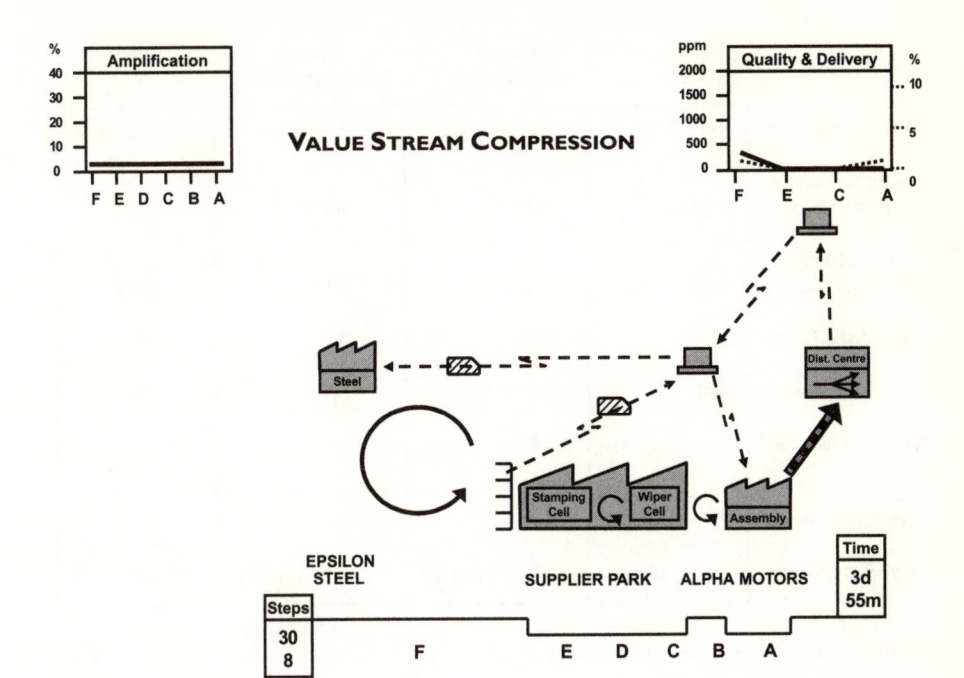

FIGURE 15.12: IDEAL STATE EXTENDED VALUE STREAM MAP

eled pull with frequent replenishment *between* every firm and facility touching the product. This step could reduce throughput time by another third, eliminate more wasteful steps, and reduce the number of warehouse and cross-dock facilities as well.

Finally, if every feasible step was taken to eliminate handoffs and transport links between the firms and physical operations on the current generation of product, it might be possible to shrink the total lead time from 44 to 2.8 days, which is to say to within the time the customer is willing to wait for the product. If this could be accomplished, the whole value stream could be converted from make-to-forecast to make-to-order, with large cost savings for every firm (see Figures 15.12 and 15.13).

And we can even imagine a succeeding Ideal State employing a new generation of product designs and process technologies, so that the manufacturer could produce completed wipers in a single molding step. This would eliminate practically all of the remaining steps and effort and permit production to proceed in line sequence to exactly match the production rate and mix of wipers needed by the final assembler across the road.

Few value streams will ever get this far, but the mapping process itself can

FIGURE 15.13: CURRENT STATE TO IDEAL STATE BOX SCORE

	Current State	Future State 1	Future State 2	Ideal State
Total Lead Time	44.3 days	23.9 days	15.8 days	2.8 days
Value Creating to Total Time	0.08%	0.16%	0.6%	1.5%
Value Creating to Total Steps	11%	15%	21%	27%
Inventory Turns	5	9	14	79
Quality Screen*	400	200	50	2.5
Delivery Screen*	8	8	3	1
Demand Amplification*	7	7	5	1
Travel Distance	5,300 miles	5,300 miles	4,300 miles	525 miles

*Ratios of upstream over downstream scores

at least produce agreement among the value stream partners on the current reality and facilitate achieving one or more future states. If rules can be agreed to on splitting the benefits—and there will probably be no benefits to split if they can't—this simple mapping process can produce truly meaningful "partnerships" for every value stream, moving a long way toward the Lean Enterprises we described in Chapter 12.

DEVELOP A LEAN GLOBAL STRATEGY

We've been amazed in the years since the launch of *Lean Thinking* that many firms in the manufacturing world have continued to pursue mass production logic with respect to production location. They have disaggregated their value streams, seeking to place each processing step with significant labor content in that global location with the lowest wage costs and seemingly locating the processing steps as far apart as possible. The consequence is that many points are optimized but the whole surely is not.

We recently talked with a household name shoe manufacturer that has moved all of its shoe assembly for products sold in North America to South-east Asia. This has lowered the labor cost per shoe from the level previously achieved in Mexico, but has also greatly increased the time needed to get products to the customer. The twenty weeks of lead time in the new system effectively make it impossible to reorder during the short selling season of its models. Instead, this firm places all orders with its contract manufacturers on the basis of forecasts and ends up remaindering 40 percent of its shoes in secondary sales channels at very low prices. And this does not count the lost revenues from customers who visited retail stores or the manufacturer's website and failed to find the models they wanted because they were out of stock.

Similarly, we recently encountered a large components manufacturer that some years ago decided to retain its capital-intensive part fabrication operations in the United States and Canada but moved its labor-intensive assembly operations to northern Mexico. As competitors have duplicated this strategy (moving assembly out of the U.S.) and as Mexican wages have started to rise, the firm is now looking to transfer its assembly operations to China or Vietnam, still shipping parts from the United States. We asked a very simple question: Instead of shipping parts from the U.S. to China and finished products from China to the U.S., with many weeks of cumulative lead time, why not move all of the parts fabrication next to the assembly operation in Mexico so the product can be ordered and shipped within three days to North American customers?

This mass production logic is also applied to the location of engineering. We recently visited the Mexican engineering center of a well known electronics multinational and found a large team of engineers hard at work on a product to be manufactured in Poland for sale in Europe. We immediately had some simple questions: "Don't any Polish engineers know anything about electricity? We can understand why you [the multinational] have sought out cheaper engineering resources for your relatively mature product, but why not locate the engineers next to the point of production to gain the many benefits of co-location?"

After reflecting on these experiences—which seem to be typical—we've developed a very simple way to think about location for producers currently in high-cost areas. Let's call it lean math.

- Start with the piece part cost of making your product near your current customers in high-wage countries (the U.S., Western Europe, Japan).
- Compare this number with the piece part cost of making the same item at the global point of lowest factor costs, probably dominated by wage costs. (The low-factor cost location will almost always offer a much lower piece part cost.)
- Add the cost of slow freight to get the product to your customer.

You've now done all the math that many purchasing departments seem to perform. Let's call this mass production math. To get to lean math you need to add some additional costs to piece-part-plus-slow-freight costs to make the calculations more realistic.

- The overhead costs allocated to production in the high-wage location, which usually don't disappear when production is transferred. Instead, they are reallocated to remaining products, raising their apparent cost.
- The cost of the additional inventory of goods in transit over long distances from the low-wage location to the customer.
- The cost of additional safety stocks to ensure uninterrupted supply.
- The cost of expensive expedited shipments. (You'll need to be careful here because the plan for the item in question will typically assume that there aren't any expediting costs, when a bit of casual empiricism will show that there almost always are.)
- The cost of warranty claims if the new facility or supplier has a long learning curve.
- The cost of engineer visits, or resident engineers at the supplier, to get the process right so the product is made to the correct specification with acceptable quality.
- The cost of senior executive visits to set up the operation or to straighten out relationships with managers and suppliers operating in a different business environment. (Note that this may include all manner of payments and considerations, depending on local business practices.)
- The cost of out-of-stocks and lost sales caused by long lead times to obtain the correct specification of the part if demand changes.
- The cost of remaindered goods or of scrapped stocks, ordered to a long-range forecast and never actually needed.
- The potential cost, if you are using a contract manufacturer in the low-cost location, of your supplier soon becoming your competitor.

This is becoming quite a list—and these additional costs are hardly ever visible to the senior executives and purchasing managers who relocate production of an item to a low-wage location based simply on piece-part price plus slow freight. Lean math requires adding three more costs to be complete:

- Currency risks, which can strike quite suddenly when the currency of either the supplying or receiving country shifts.
- Country risks, which can also emerge very suddenly when the shipping country encounters political instabilities or when there is a political reaction in the receiving country as trade deficits and unemployment emerge as political issues.

- Connectivity costs of many sorts in managing product handoffs and information flows in highly complex supply chains across long distances in countries with different business practices.

These latter costs are harder to estimate but are sometimes very large. The only thing a manager can know for sure is that they are very low or zero if products are sourced close to the customer rather than across the globe.

What does lean math usually say about location? We've found that most products fit into one of three categories:

- For products where rapid customer response can substantially raise sales and selling prices (probably including the higher-end shoes produced by the firm just mentioned), work hard to conduct every step of the production process as near the customer as possible. In many cases, the full application of lean techniques to production steps that are located immediately adjacent—a process we call value stream compression—can produce an acceptable combination of higher revenues and lower costs in a high labor-cost location.
- For products that are more price-sensitive but where rapid customer response is still important, co-locate all steps in the design and production process—that is, compress the value stream including engineering—at a low labor-cost site within the region of sale. For the U.S. and Canada, this will usually be Mexico; for Western Europe it will be Eastern Europe. By using trucks, which are fast and cheap, rather than boats, which are cheap but slow and often require fast but expensive airfreight backup to deal with inaccurate forecasts, it is still possible to replenish products in two or three days as they are sold or consumed rather than waiting weeks or maintaining large just-in-case stocks near the customer. Remember: lean thinkers love trucks (when transport is needed at all), but they try to eliminate boats and planes!
- Finally, for commoditized products that have a fairly high value to weight ratio and where demand can actually be forecast due to stable sales over the long term, co-locate all production steps at the lowest labor-cost point, even outside the region of sale. (The best approach is to compress the value stream to conduct as many steps as possible, including engineering, at the low cost point, requiring only a single transport link to move the finished item from the point of design and manufacture to the market of sale.)

Even when these conditions are met, bear in mind currency risks (because shifts are often quite rapid), country risks (of trade protection in the receiving country and political chaos in the shipping country), and the connectivity costs (ranging from air freight expediting to unplanned engineer visits to the other side of the world to deal with quality issues) that are inherent in managing decompressed value streams. It's our belief that when all these factors are weighed, this third category is much smaller than most managers currently think.

CONVERT FROM TOP-DOWN LEADERSHIP TO BOTTOM-UP INITIATIVES

As we've gained experience in recent years, we've become ever more aware that in a truly mature lean business there is a transition from Policy Deployment to Policy Management.[11] This happens when there are value stream managers for every value stream and employees across the enterprise have learned to see. As a result, ideas for further improvements in every value stream continually bubble up to senior management, which needs only reconcile conflicts and make sober judgments on just how many improvement initiatives can be supported at one time.

This happy situation was brought home to us in a conversation with a senior manager at Toyota, in talking about the current state of affairs in the motor industry. He noted that Toyota at this point in its development obtains brilliant results from average managers utilizing brilliant processes, while its competitors often obtain mediocre (or worse) results from brilliant managers utilizing broken processes.

The natural instinct in this situation is to find more brilliant managers; many American firms went down during the bubble economy with only brilliant hands on deck. The correct response is to perfect the process—the value stream—for every value-creating activity and then rejoice in the fact that average people—and this group, if we are honest, includes most of us most of the time—can get brilliant results and get them consistently. A few brilliant process thinkers are still needed, perhaps housed in the Lean Promotion Office, to tackle the most difficult problems in perfecting every process as average managers bring these issues to senior management's attention as part of Policy Management.

The Opportunity Now at Hand

As we've noted at a number of points, recessions are precious things because they shake conventional wisdom, even complacent lean wisdom, and motivate mangers to make hard choices. The current era is no exception. We are currently at the point of greatest opportunity during the boom-bust-boom cycle that still plagues market economies. This is because unnecessary investments (and investments in the wrong place) can still be avoided as the economy begins to expand from the trough while the dispiriting job losses of the down cycle are past. But the window of opportunity stays open for only a limited period before tradition reasserts itself and false confidence in a firm's processes sets in.

The stories in this book are those of firms who were forced to look in the mirror during the recession of 1991 and who found a new and better way of living as lean thinkers during the 1990s. As we've seen in this epilogue, they not only did well during the boom but have also prospered in the ensuing recession. The question now is which firms will seize the opportunities of the recession of 2001–03 to become the next wave of lean thinkers pushing the whole economy ahead.

We have all the necessary knowledge. Indeed, we know much more about the lean transformation than we did in the early 1990s. There is, therefore, no excuse for failing to act in this golden moment for lean thinkers.

AFTERWORD

The Lean Network

Our problem in writing this book was never theory. Authors with academic backgrounds will generally have no trouble spinning theories, and this task happily occupied us during the first year of this project (1992-93). But then we needed proof that our theorizing actually works, examples of real managers in real firms who are succeeding by employing ideas similar to ours. This threatened to become a serious problem because we really knew only one industry—automobiles—yet we were determined to apply our ideas to every type of economic activity, including services. It was essential therefore to find chief executives from a wide range of industries in North America, Europe, and Japan who would let us use their experiences, both good and bad, to prove our theories.

Just as we identified this need in the spring of 1993, Joe Day, the CEO of the Freudenberg-NOK General Partnership, asked one of us to talk at a media presentation of his firm's lean initiative. In doing this we met Anand Sharma, whose consulting firm, TBM, was offering technical advice to Freudenberg-NOK. Anand soon introduced us to a host of other executives he has advised on the lean conversion including Pat Lancaster at Lantech and George Koenigsaecker at the Hon Company.

At almost the same time, through the MIT Japan Program, Jim Womack came into contact with United Technologies (a Program sponsor) and its subsidiary, Pratt & Whitney. An invitation to visit Pratt led to a completely accidental meeting in the final assembly hall with Chihiro Nakao, one of Pratt's key advisers on its lean transformation.

Nakao-san, as it developed, had along with Yoshiki Iwata of Shingijutsu taught lean thinking to Anand Sharma in the late 1980s, and later collaborated with him on some projects. The Shingijutsu network soon carried us all the way across the world to Porsche in Germany; to Hitachi, Yamatake-Honeywell, and Showa Tekko in Japan; and back to other firms in North America.

While visiting one of these (the PCI Group in New Bedford, Massachusetts) with Chihiro Nakao, we encountered another link in our North American chain in the person of Bill Moffitt, a former Jacobs Manufacturing Company vice president and survivor of the Nakao school of "special *sensei* treatment." He and his associates have been a transforming force in ten of the firms mentioned in this book.

Because the concepts presented in *The Machine That Changed the World* were devised originally by Toyota, it was not surprising that the next link we discovered was Toyota's own Supplier Support Center (TSSC) in Lexington, Kentucky, where General Manager Hajime Ohba was cheerfully teaching lean thinking to forty American firms, many of them neither suppliers to Toyota nor in the auto sector. Ohba-san took us under his wing and escorted us through a range of companies trying to transform themselves into exemplars of lean thinking. (One of our major regrets in preparing this book is that TSSC's clients were only at the beginning of the lean transformation when we had to decide in 1994 which firms to profile. If we had started this volume a year or two later, the achievements of TSSC's clients, like Grand Haven Stamped Products, might well have been described.)

Once we started down the path with Toyota, we found two additional networks, those of Toyota Motor Sales in California (whose dramatic success in introducing "pull" all the way from the customer back to raw materials was the subject of Chapter 4) and of the Toyota Motor Corporation in Japan, where Kiyotaka Nakayama of Toyota's Operations Management Consulting Division led us through today's Toyota operations and the supply base.

As Jim Womack searched for firms in North America, Dan Jones was searching for additional firms in Europe and found many of them through the research activities of the Lean Enterprise Research Centre at the Cardiff Business School. Unipart in particular became a test bed for lean thinking in a U.K. context.

Our final learning opportunity was completely inadvertent. Jim Womack invested in a small bicycle firm and took a hand in a lean conversion. An ancient saw in the academic world is: "If you really want to master a subject, try teaching it." This concept turns out to apply with equal force to lean conversions: If you really want to understand the problems to be overcome, try doing it yourself.

As the reader has probably noted, we became very fond of our subjects and began to think of them as a community of like-minded souls. It was logical, therefore, to bring them together in a series of Lean Summits in North American, Europe, and Latin America beginning in 1995. As these events grew ever larger we realized that we needed to create nonprofit organizations to tie the Lean Community together. The mission of these organizations is to move beyond consciousness-raising events to create and teach tools for implementation.

The Lean Enterprise Institute was founded by Jim Womack in the United

States in 1997 to publish the ideas of lean thinking in a workbook format and to teach these tools to professional audiences. Its publications and activities are described at www.lean.org.

Lean Institute Brasil was founded in 1998 by Professor Jose Ferro in Sao Paulo to promote lean thinking in Brazil and throughout Latin America. For more information, see www.lean.br.org.

The Lean Enterprise Academy in the U.K. was founded in 2003 by Dan Jones to promote lean thinking across English-speaking Europe. Learn more at www.leanuk.org.

The only task that remains is to list all of the members of our lean network who have shared their experiences with us—and these are detailed in the Appendix. Our only regret is that we have had space to tell so few of their stories, for many of those we have had to leave out are as informative and inspiring as those we have included. We hope that in the years immediately ahead many of our readers will add their names and stories to this list as they join the network and pursue lean enterprise.

APPENDIX

Individuals and Organizations Who Helped

Organizations (all affiliations listed as they were at the time of interactions during the writing of the first edition)

Alexander Doll: Patty Lewis
Bene Buromobel: Ing. E. Weichselbaum
Boeing Commercial Airplane Group: Dave Fitzpatrick
Britvic Soft Drinks, Ltd.: Richard Archer, Paul Howard, Martin Thomas
Brooks Electronics: Gary Brooks, Marty Carroll, Mary Pat Pietrzak, Hans Cooper
Calsonic International Europe, Ltd.: Mike Reilly, Lyndon Jones
Chrome Craft: Richard Barnett
Chrysler: Bob Eaton, Bob Lutz, Tom Stallkamp, Francois Castaing, Glenn Gardner, Ed Sprock
Coleman Foods Ltd.: Ian Glenday
Doyle Wilson Homebuilder: Doyle Wilson
Federal Express: Fred Smith
Flex-N-Gate: Shahid Khan
Freudenberg-NOK: Joe Day, Gary Johnson, Sharon Wenzl
Grand Haven Stamped Products: Frank Nagy
Grand Rapids Spring and Wire: Jim Zawacki
H&W Screw Product: Gary Soloway
Hitachi Air Conditioning & Refrigeration Systems: Tsuneharu Takagi
Honda UK Manufacturing, Ltd.: Andrew Jones
Honda of America Manufacturing: Hiroyuki Yoshino, Scott Whitlock, Toshi Amino, Dave Nelson, Tom Griffiths, Doug Chamberlin, Rick Mayo
IG Lintels Ltd.: Keith Williams
ITT Alfred Teves, Ltd.: Horst Vogt
Kaizen Institute: Masaaki Imai, Peter Willats

Keiper Recaro GMBH: Rainer Simon
Lantech: Pat Lancaster, Jim Lancaster, Ron Hicks, Jose Zabaneh, Bob Underwood, Jean Cunningham, John Fain
Leyland Trucks Ltd.: John Gilchrist, John Oliver
Linread Northbridge Ltd.: Ed Brooks
Mexican Industries of Michigan: James Merkhofer
Moffitt Associates: Bill Moffitt, Bob Pentland, Jim Cutler
Nippondenso: Masayoshi Taira, Mineo Hanai, Ryozo Mitsui
Nissan Motor Manufacturing, Ltd.: Ian Gibson, John Cushnaghan, Peter Hill, Peter Wickens, Terry Hogg, Bob Hampson, Colin Dodge, Mike Peacock, Arthur David
Northern Engraving: Philip Gelatt
Parker-Hannifan Automotive & Refrigeration Group: Larry Hopcraft
PCI Group: John Cosentino, John Rachwalski
Perkins Group Ltd.: Tony Gilroy, Mike Baunton
Dr. Ing. h.c. F. Porsche AG: Wendelin Wiedeking, Gerhard Hofig, Uwe Huck, Anton Hunger, Manfred Kessler, Raimond Klinkner, Wolfgang Laimgruber, Dieter Lange, Uwe Loos, Michael Macht, Hans Riedel, Eckart Riefenstahl, Dietmar Scherzer, Michael Schimpke, Rainer Srock, Franz Steinbeck, Gunther Wittenmayer
Pratt & Whitney: Karl Krapek, Mark Coran, Curtis Cook, Ed Northern, Bob Weiner, Bob Jackson, Angie Negron, Grace Reed
Robert Bosch Ltd.: Gerhard Turner, Stefan Asenkirschbaumer
Rohr: Greg Peters, Martin Lodge
Rover Group, Ltd.: JIT/DE Team—Alan Naylor, Peter Bailey, Bob Hollier, Mike James Moore
Senco Products: Dennis Pinkelton, John Dean, Bob Clark
Shingijutsu Co., Ltd.: Yoshiki Iwata, Chihiro Nakao, Kumi Iwata
Showa Manufacturing: Keiji Mizuguchi, Takeshi Kawabe, Tsuneo Aiga
Sloane Toyota: Bob Sloane, Fred Slyhoff
Summit Polymers: James Haas, James Askelson
TABC: Tom Tullius
TBM: Anand Sharma, Bill Schwartz, Sam Swayer, Stuart Fisher
Tesco Stores Ltd.: Graham Booth, Barry Knichel, Peter Worsey
Toyoda Iron Works: Shigeru Hayakawa
Toyota Motor Corporate Services, U.S.A.: Tim Andree
Toyota Motor Corporation (Japan): Fujio Cho, Kiyotaka Nakayama
Toyota Motor Manufacturing U.K., Ltd.: Yukihisa Hirano, Osamu Komori
Toyota Motor Manufacturing, U.S.A.: Tom Zawacki
Toyota Motor Sales, U.S.A.: Richard Gallio, Bob Bennett, Bob Arndt
Toyota Supplier Support Center: Hajime Ohba, Mark Reich, Lesa Nichols
TRW Steering Systems Ltd.: Bob Morgan

Unipart Group of Companies, Ltd.: John Neill, Tony Butcher, Mike Carver, Ian Campbell, Frank Burns, Frank Hemsworth, Doug Henderson, Graham Jackson, Keith Jones, Andy Lee, David Nicholas, Mike Pybus, Corinne Richman, Peter Taylor, Sue Topham, David Whale, Val White

United Electric: Bruce Hamilton

United Technologies: George David

Wiremold: Art Byrne, Steve Maynard, Orrie Fiume, Judy Seyler, Frank Giannattasio

Yamatake-Honeywell: Ichiro Ido

And our consulting clients during the writing of this book, who shall remain nameless but who taught us much.

Individuals

Martin L. Anderson (who has shared our lean thinking for more than fifteen years)

Dominick Anfuso, senior editor, Simon & Schuster (who would probably rather be shot than hear one more lecture on how lean thinking applies to publishing)

Graham Baere, president, Managerial Design International (who shared thoughts on creating organizations to support lean thinking)

John Carlisle (who shared his thoughts on managing relationships in a value stream)

Don Clausing, Xerox Research Fellow in Comparative Product Development, Massachusetts Institute of Technology (who taught us much of what we know about product development)

Alain de Dommartin, Renault Institute for Quality Management (who gave us a window on French reactions to lean thinking)

Stephane Doblin (who gave us an important leg up many years ago through introductions to senior executives of European companies and who continues to provide help along the way)

Friedrich Glasl, Trigon Consulting, Salzburg (who shared his insights into organizational development and who led Dan Jones on many missionary excursions in Germany, Switzerland, and Austria)

Jan Helling (who shared his insights from lean missionary work in Sweden)

Bruce Henderson, president, Robertshaw Controls (who carefully reviewed the final drafts and made many suggestions for improvements)

Gwyn Jones, founder, Merlin Metalworks (who cheerfully took on a theoretician [Womack] for an investment partner)

George Koenigsaecker, president, Hon Industries (who freely shared a decade's experience in transforming mass producers)

Joel Kurtzman, former editor, *Harvard Business Review* (who with Steve

Prokesch suggested we write "From Lean Production to the Lean Enterprise" for *HBR*)

Yasuhiro Monden (who shared his insights into lean accounting and the Toyota Production System)

Toshio Niwa, director, International Exchange, Institute for International Economic Studies, Tokyo (who aided our research in Japan)

Professor Eiji Ogawa, Chukyo University (who helped us understand the origins of lean thinking)

Guy Parsons, president, Merlin Metalworks (who has helped Jim Womack turn theory into practice)

Tom Poynter, president, The Transitions Group (who provided Jim Womack an invaluable education in strategic thinking and implementation)

Steve Prokesch, associate editor, *Harvard Business Review* (who solicited our 1994 article and provided perspective on lean thinking)

Rafe Sagalyn, Sagalyn Literary Agency (our agent, who tried to make us perfect)

John Shook (formerly deputy general manager of the Toyota Supplier Support Center; now director of the Japan Technology Management Program and lecturer in the Department of Industrial Engineering, University of Michigan, who introduced us to many aspects of lean practice and who saved us from a number of errors in the final draft)

Eberhard Stotko (whose tireless enthusiasm for lean thinking encouraged us)

Brian Swain, Rubicon Associates (who shared his experiences in trying to use our ideas in the U.K.)

Michael Tansey, professor of economics, Rockhurst College (who pointed out a major flaw in the structure we first considered for this book)

Betty Thayer, Andersen Consulting (who supported Dan Jones's work on benchmarking)

Professor Kazuo Wada, University of Tokyo (who revealed unknown origins of lean thinking and "group" structures in Japan)

John Womack (who has been a vital sounding board for his brother's ideas)

Special Acknowledgments

Dan Jones would like to thank research colleagues at the Lean Enterprise Research Centre, Cardiff Business School, especially Peter Hines, Nick Rich, and John Kiff, and Professor Roger Mansfield, director of the Cardiff Business School for their support and encouragement. He would also like to thank sponsors and participants in a series of activities coordinated by the Centre: The Lean Enterprise Benchmarking Project (auto parts manufacturing performance benchmarking), the Supply Chain Development Pro-

gramme (value stream mapping and supply chain responsiveness), the BRITE EURAM Future Working Structures Project (engine manufacturing benchmarking and team working), and the International Car Distribution Programme (analysis and simulation of the car distribution system).
In addition, he would like to thank Professor Denis Towill of the Logistics Systems Dynamics Group, School of Engineering at Cardiff, research collaborators at the University of Bath, especially Professors Richard Lamming and Andrew Graves, and Malcolm Harbour, Philip Wade, Derek Whittaker, and Professor Jonathan Brown of the central office of the International Car Distribution Programme. Finally, he would like to thank students at the Universities of Eindhoven and Groningen who wrote cases applying lean thinking to diverse manufacturing and service organizations for the master classes given by Dan during 1993 and 1994.

Jim Womack would like to thank colleagues in the MIT Japan Program, especially Managing Director Pat Gercik, Professor Richard Samuels, and Dori DeGenti, for providing a continuing "home base" within the university world.

Finally, we must thank Carrie and Katherine Copeland Womack and Mike, Kate, and Simon Jones for tolerating their fathers' distraction and absences during the four years of this project. Shigeo Shingo once remarked that the Toyota Production System (and, by extension, lean thinking) should be implemented everywhere *except* at home. We're not so sure about this—indeed, our wives often ask why we can't apply our lean knowledge to become more efficient with our chores around the house! However, we do know that devoting years of nights and weekends to writing about lean thinking, plus weeks cumulating to months away from home on research trips, imposes a burden on the next generation. We hope that Katherine and Carrie and Kate, Simon, and Mike will someday feel that this completed effort compensates in a small way for their sacrifices.

Glossary

(For a more thorough listing of lean terms, with examples and illustrations, please consult *The Lean Lexicon: A Graphical Glossary for Lean Thinkers*. Brookline, Mass.: The Lean Enterprise Institute, 2003.)

activity-based costing—A management accounting system that assigns costs to products based on the amount of resources used (including floor space, raw materials, machine hours, and human effort) in order to design, order, or make a product. Contrast with **standard costing.**

andon **board**—A visual control device in a production area, typically a lighted overhead display, giving the current status of the production system and alerting team members to emerging problems.

autonomation—Transferring human intelligence to automated machinery so machines are able to detect the production of a single defective part and immediately stop themselves while asking for help. This concept, also known as *jidoka*, was pioneered by Sakichi Toyoda at the turn of the twentieth century when he invented automatic looms that stopped instantly when any thread broke. This permitted one operator to oversee many machines with no risk of producing vast amounts of defective cloth.

batch-and-queue—The mass-production practice of making large lots of a part and then sending the batch to wait in the queue before the next operation in the production process. Contrast with **single-piece flow.**

brownfield—An established design or production facility operating with mass-production methods and systems of social organization. Contrast with **greenfield.**

cells—The layout of machines of different types performing different operations in a tight sequence, typically in a U-shape, to permit single-piece flow and flexible deployment of human effort by means of **multi-machine working.** Contrast with **process villages.**

chaku-chaku—A method of conducting single-piece flow in which the operator proceeds from machine to machine, taking a part from the previous operation and loading it in the next machine, then taking the part just removed from that machine and loading it in the following machine, etcetera. Literally means "load-load" in Japanese.

changeover—The installation of a new type of tool in a metal working machine, a different paint in a painting system, a new plastic resin and a new mold in an injection molding machine, new software in a computer, and so on. The term applies whenever a production device is assigned to perform a different operation.

cycle time—The time required to complete one cycle of an operation. If cycle time for every operation in a complete process can be reduced to equal *takt* **time,** products can be made in **single-piece flow.**

five Ss—Five terms beginning with S utilized to create a workplace suited for visual control and lean production. *Seiri* means to separate needed tools, parts, and instructions from unneeded materials and to remove the latter. *Seiton* means to neatly arrange and identify parts and tools for ease of use. *Seiso* means to conduct a cleanup campaign. *Seiketsu* means to conduct *seiri, seiton,* and *seiso* at frequent, indeed daily, intervals to maintain a workplace in perfect condition. *Shitsuke* means to form the habit of always following the first four Ss.

five whys—Taiichi Ohno's practice of asking "why" five times whenever a problem was encountered, in order to identify the root cause of the problem so that effective countermeasures could be developed and implemented.

flow—The progressive achievement of tasks along the value stream so that a product proceeds from design to launch, order to delivery, and raw materials into the hands of the customer with no stoppages, scrap, or backflows.

greenfield—A new design or production facility where best-practice, lean methods can be put in place from the outset. Contrast with **brownfield.**

heijunka—The creation of a "level schedule" by sequencing orders in a repetitive pattern and smoothing the day-to-day variations in total orders to correspond to longer-term demand. For example, if customers during a week order 200 of Product A, 200 of Product B, and 400 of Product C in batches of 200, 200, and 400 respectively, level scheduling would sequence these products to run in the progression A, C, B, C, A, C, B, C, A, C. . . . Similarly, if customer orders totaling 1,000 products per week arrive in batches of 200 products on day one, 400 on day two, zero on day three, 100 on day four, and 100 on day five, the level schedule would produce 100 per day, and in the sequence A, C, A, B. . . . Some type of level scheduling is unavoidable at every producer, mass or lean, unless the firm and all of its suppliers have infinite capacity and zero changeover times. However, lean producers tend to create excess capacity over time as they free up resources and to work steadily at reducing changeover times so the short-term discrepancy between the *heijunka* schedule and actual demand is steadily minimized, aided by level selling.

hoshin kanri—A strategic decision-making tool for a firm's executive team that focuses resources on the critical initiatives necessary to accomplish the business objectives of the firm. By using visual matrix diagrams similar to those employed for **quality function deployment,** three to five key objectives are selected while all others are clearly deselected. The selected objectives are translated into specific projects and deployed down to the implementation level in the firm. **Hoshin kanri** unifies and aligns resources and establishes clearly measurable targets against which progress toward the key objectives is measured on a regular basis. Also called **policy-deployment.**

jidoka—See **autonomation**.

Just-in-Time—A system for producing and delivering the right items at the right time in the right amounts. Just-in-Time approaches **just-on-time** when upstream activities occur minutes or seconds before downstream activities, so single-piece flow is possible. The key elements of Just-in-Time are **flow, pull, standard work** (with standard in-process inventories), and *takt* **time.**

kaikaku—Radical improvement of an activity to eliminate *muda,* for example by reorganizing processing operations for a product so that instead of traveling to and from isolated "process villages," the product proceeds through the operations in single-piece flow in one short space. Also called **breakthrough** *kaizen,* **flow** *kaizen,* and **system** *kaizen.*

kaizen—Continuous, incremental improvement of an activity to create more **value** with less *muda.* Also called **point** *kaizen* and **process** *kaizen.*

kanban—A small card attached to boxes of parts that regulates **pull** in the Toyota Production System by signaling upstream production and delivery.

keiretsu—A grouping of Japanese firms through historic associations and equity interlocks such that each firm maintains its operational independence but establishes permanent relations with other firms in its group. Some *keiretsu,* such as Sumitomo and Mitsui, are horizontal, involving firms in different industries. Other *keiretsu,* such as the Toyota Group, are vertical, involving firms up- and downstream from a "system integrator" firm that is usually a final assembler.

lead time—The total time a customer must wait to receive a product after placing an order. When a scheduling and production system are running at or below capacity, lead time and **throughput time** are the same. When demand exceeds the capacity of a system, there is additional waiting time before the start of scheduling and production, and lead time exceeds throughput time. See **throughput time.**

level selling—A system of customer relations that attempts to eliminate surges in demand caused by the selling system itself (for example, due to quarterly or monthly sales targets) and that strives to create long-term relations with customers so that future purchases can be anticipated by the production system.

Material Requirements Planning (MRP)—A computerized system used to determine the quantity and timing requirements for materials used in a production operation. MRP systems use a master production schedule, a bill of materials listing every item needed for each product to be made, and information on current inventories of these items in order to schedule the production and delivery of the necessary items. **Manufacturing Resource Planning** (often called **MRP II**) expands MRP to include capacity planning tools, a financial interface to translate operations planning into financial terms, and a simulation tool to assess alternative production plans.

meister—A production group leader in a German manufacturing firm.

milk run—A routing of a supply or delivery vehicle to make multiple pickups or drop-offs at different locations.

mittelstand—Mid-sized and usually family-controlled German manufacturing firms that have been the backbone of the postwar export economy.

monument—Any design, scheduling, or production technology with scale requirements necessitating that designs, order, and products be brought to the machine to wait in a queue for processing. Contrast with **right-sized tool.**

muda—Any activity that consumes resources but creates no **value.**

multi-machine working—Training of employees to operate and maintain different types of production equipment. Multi-machine working is essential to creating production cells where each worker utilizes many machines.

open-book management—A situation in which all financial information relevant to design, scheduling, and production tasks is shared with all employees of the firm, and with suppliers and distributors up and down the value stream.

operation—An activity or activities performed on a product by a single machine. Contrast with **process.**

perfection—The complete elimination of **muda** so that all activities along a **value stream** create **value.**

poka-yoke—A mistake-proofing device or procedure to prevent a defect during order-taking or manufacture. An order-taking example is a screen for order input developed from traditional ordering patterns that questions orders falling outside the pattern. The suspect orders are then examined, often leading to discovery of inputting errors or buying based on misinformation. A manufacturing example is a set of photocells in parts containers along an assembly line to prevent components from progressing to the next stage with missing parts. The *poka-yoke* in this case is designed to stop the movement of the component to the next station if the light beam has not been broken by the operator's hand in each bin containing a part for the product under assembly at that moment. A *poka-yoke* is sometimes also called a *baka-yoke*.

policy deployment—See *hoshin kanri*.

process—A series of individual operations required to create a design, completed order, or product.

processing time—The time a product is actually being worked on in design or production and the time an order is actually being processed. Typically, processing time is a small fraction of **throughput time** and **lead time**.

process villages—The practice of grouping machines or activities by type of operation performed; for example, grinding machines or order-entry. Contrast with **cells**.

product family—A range of related products that can be produced interchangeably in a production cell. The term is often analogous to "platforms."

production smoothing—See *heijunka*.

pull—A system of cascading production and delivery instructions from downstream to upstream activities in which nothing is produced by the upstream supplier until the downstream customer signals a need. The opposite of **push**. See also **kanban**.

Quality Function Deployment (QFD)—A visual decision-making procedure for multi-skilled project teams which develops a common understanding of the voice of the customer and a consensus on the final engineering specifications of the product that has the commitment of the entire team. **QFD** integrates the perspectives of team members from different disciplines, ensures that their efforts are focused on resolving key trade-offs in a consistent manner against measurable performance targets for the product, and deploys these decisions through successive levels of detail. The use of **QFD** eliminates expensive backflows and rework as projects near launch.

queue time—The time a product spends in a line awaiting the next design, order-processing, or fabrication step.

right-sized tool—A design, scheduling, or production device that can be fitted directly into the flow of products within a product family so that production no longer requires unnecessary transport and waiting. Contrast with **monument**.

sensei—A personal teacher with a mastery of a body of knowledge, in this book lean thinking and techniques.

seven *muda*—Taiichi Ohno's original enumeration of the wastes commonly found in physical production. These are *overproduction* ahead of demand, *waiting* for the next processing step, unnecessary *transport* of materials (for example, between process villages or facilities), *overprocessing* of parts due to poor tool and product design, *inventories* more than the absolute minimum, unnecessary *movement* by employees during the course of their work (looking for parts, tools, prints, help, etcetera), and production of *defective parts*.

shusa—A strong team leader in the Toyota product development system. (Literally, however, a level of supervisor, like *katcho* or *honcho*.)

Single Minute Exchange of Dies (SMED)—A series of techniques pioneered by Shigeo Shingo for changeovers of production machinery in less than ten minutes. **One-touch setup** is the term applied when changeovers require less than a minute. Obviously, the long-term objective is always **zero setup,** in which changeovers are instantaneous and do not interfere in any way with continuous flow.

single-piece flow—A situation in which products proceed, one complete product at a time, through various operations in design, order-taking, and production, without interruptions, backflows, or scrap. Contrast with **batch-and-queue.**

spaghetti chart—A map of the path taken by a specific product as it travels down the value stream in a mass-production organization, so-called because the product's route typically looks like a plate of spaghetti.

standard costing—A management accounting system which allocates costs to products based on the number of machine hours and labor hours available to a production department during a given period of time. Standard cost systems encourage managers to make unneeded products or the wrong mix of products in order to minimize their cost-per-product by fully utilizing machines and labor. Contrast with **activity-based costing.**

standard work—A precise description of each work activity specifying **cycle time,** *takt* **time,** the work sequence of specific tasks, and the minimum inventory of parts on hand needed to conduct the activity.

takt **time**—The available production time divided by the rate of customer demand. For example, if customers demand 240 widgets per day and the factory operates 480 minutes per day, *takt* time is two minutes; if customers want two new products designed per month, *takt* time is two weeks. *Takt* time sets the pace of production to match the rate of customer demand and becomes the heartbeat of any lean system.

target cost—The development and production cost which a product cannot exceed if the customer is to be satisfied with the value of the product while the manufacturer obtains an acceptable return on its investment.

throughput time—The time required for a product to proceed from concept to launch, order to delivery, or raw materials into the hands of the customer. This includes both processing and queue time. Contrast with **processing time** and **lead time.**

Total Productive Maintenance (TPM)—A series of methods, originally pioneered by Nippondenso (a member of the Toyota group), to ensure that every machine in a production process is always able to perform its required tasks so that production is never interrupted.

transparency—See **visual control.**

turn-back analysis—Examination of the flow of a product through a set of production operations to see how often it is sent backwards for rework or scrap.

value—A capability provided to a customer at the right time at an appropriate price, as defined in each case by the customer.

value stream—The specific activities required to design, order, and provide a specific product, from concept to launch, order to delivery, and raw materials into the hands of the customer.

value stream mapping—Identification of all the specific activities occurring along a value stream for a product or product family.

visual control—The placement in plain view of all tools, parts, production activities, and indicators of production system performance, so the status of the system can be understood at a glance by everyone involved. Used synonymously with **transparency.**

Notes

Preface: From Lean Production to Lean Enterprise

1. This volume is still available from Rawson Macmillan in hardcover and from HarperCollins in paperback.
2. The Bibliography provides a listing of the most important books available on lean techniques and philosophy.
3. Peter Drucker, *The Concept of the Corporation* (New York: John Day, 1946).
4. The only exception is Dan Jones's involvement with the Unipart Group in the U.K. as part-time principal of Unipart University, their pioneering attempt to create a "lean" education and training activity to help implement lean thinking throughout their sales, distribution, and manufacturing activities.

Introduction: Lean Thinking versus *Muda*

1. Ohno stated his *muda* list as follows: *defects* (in products), *overproduction* of goods not needed, *inventories* of goods awaiting further processing or consumption, unnecessary *processing*, unnecessary *movement* (of people), unnecessary *transport* (of goods), and *waiting* (by employees for process equipment to finish its work or on an upstream activity). (See Taiichi Ohno, *The Toyota Production System: Beyond Large Scale Production* [Portland, Oregon: Productivity Press, 1988], pp. 19–20.) We've added the design of goods and services which do not meet users' needs. Although Ohno originally formulated his *muda* list for physical production, his typology applies equally to product development and order-taking, the other basic activities of any business.
2. Readers in other countries may find a simple exercise very useful: Take a few minutes to list the distortions in the process of value definition introduced by your national industrial system. To make it more concrete, simply ask what's most important to you in your current job and to your firm, compared with what's most important to your ultimate customer.
3. Some readers may be confused initially about the difference between the value stream as described here and the concepts of the value chain employed by business strategists, following the work of Michael Porter. (See particularly Michael Porter, *Competitive Advantage* [New York: Free Press, 1985], Chapter 2, "The Value Chain and Competitive Advantage.") The differences are very

simple. We apply the term "value stream" to the entire set of activities running from raw material to finished product *for a specific product* and we seek to optimize the whole from the standpoint of the *final customer* (the ultimate consumer of the good or service). The typical strategic analysis of the value chain aggregates activities like "production," "marketing," and "sales" for a range of products and asks which a firm can do to maximize its profits and how it can orchestrate the activities performed by other firms up and down the value chain to that firm's best advantage. For example, there is much discussion of how to "extract profits" from upstream and downstream players.

Readers may also wonder if the value stream concept is the same for services as for physical goods. Contrasting airline services with personal computers makes it clear that it is: The *problem-solving task* for the computer company is the design of the product and its operating system to a cost target while for the airline it's decisions on where to fly using what type of equipment at what frequency with what accompanying passenger services; the *information management task* for the computer company consists of taking orders and following them through to delivery while for the airline it's the reservation system and the operating schedule; and the *physical transformation task* for the computer company consists of physically making the product and writing the code for the operating system, which has its analogue at the airline in flying specific airplanes over specific routes while performing specific maintenance activities to support daily operations.

4. Taiichi Ohno, *Workplace Management* (Portland, Oregon: Productivity Press, 1988), p. 47.
5. For Shingo's classic statement of Toyota's conclusions see Shigeo Shingo, *A Study of the Toyota Production System from an Industrial Engineering Viewpoint* (Portland, Oregon: Productivity Press, 1989).
6. Michael Hammer and James Champy, *Reengineering the Corporation* (New York: Harper Business, 1993), is the classic statement. See also Michael Hammer and Steven A. Stanton, *The Reengineering Revolution: A Handbook* (New York: Harper Business, 1995), for methods of conducting reengineering.
7. The two basic texts are Jack Stack, *The Great Game of Business* (New York: Harper Business, 1993), and John Case, *Open Book Management* (New York: Harper Business, 1995).

1: Value

1. Carl Sewell and Paul B. Brown, *Customers for Life* (New York: Pocket Books, 1991).
2. That Doyle Wilson Homebuilder has started down the lean path does not mean implementation is easy. Skilled trades in the construction industry are quite possibly the most resistant group in society to the idea of "standard work" and only the most forceful leadership by Doyle Wilson has persuaded them to try the new system.
3. This figure was about typical of Jones's experience more generally during the second half of 1995, whenever he needed to pass through a large hub airport.

His proportion of door-to-door travel time actually spent moving on eighteen trips was as follows:

Flying via a hub in Europe (4 trips)	55%
Flying direct in Europe from Birmingham airport (10 trips)	65%
Flying intercontinental via a hub (2 trips)	69%
Flying intercontinental direct (2 trips)	78%

4. Those familiar with the origins of lean thinking will know that Taiichi Ohno thought of target cost in a different way in the late 1940s. He was trying to break into the world motor vehicle industry with low production volume, a tiny capital budget for production tools, and a need to produce a variety of cars and trucks with the same tools in order to serve a small, fragmented domestic market in Japan. What was more, the depressed state of the postwar economy meant that there was a severe limit on how much Japanese customers could afford to pay for a car or truck.

Ohno therefore stated that the existing oligopolistic car companies in the West could price backward in the seller's market of that time by taking their costs and adding their profits to determine prices. (His famous formula was: Cost + Profits = Price.) He, however, had to price forward by taking both the need for minimum profits and an upper limit on prices as fixed, then to reduce his costs through the relentless application of lean techniques until he achieved a cost permitting both an acceptable price and adequate profits to fund new product development initiatives. This gave the alternative formula of: Price − Profits = Costs, where both Price and Profits were determined by external forces, leaving the "target cost" as the only item under the control of the producer.

By contrast, most enterprises adopting lean thinking today are roughly comparable in scale to their competitors and the opening of the global economy has made markets almost everywhere highly price competitive. Thus the real issue is how to take major whacks out of costs in comparison with competitors to gain competitive advantage.

2: The Value Stream

1. Actually, his vantage point was only imagined—in an American supermarket he had heard about but never seen. Ohno only made his first trip to America in 1956.
2. Tesco, with 1995 sales of about $15 billion, is one of the largest grocery chains in the world and one of the three major grocery retailers in the United Kingdom. The firm has been collaborating for several years with the Lean Enterprise Research Centre at the Cardiff Business School in the U.K. to think through aspects of its value streams. As will become clear to the reader, Tesco has been an energetic participant in this process because it has been the most aggressive grocery chain in the world in introducing point-of-sale computing systems and in rethinking its own warehouse and stock-replenishment system. It is precisely

because of the success of these initiatives in removing the top layers of *muda*, still present in most grocery retailing, that Tesco has been ready to take the next steps.

3. "Cartons," as we will use this term here, contain a varying number of cans—four, eight, twelve, or twenty-four. Note that a carton of cola bought in a grocery store and taken home to chill before drinking is really a different product providing different value from a single can of cola bought chilled in a convenience store for immediate consumption. The same is true, except even more so, for a keg of cola bought by a restaurant or pub for use in a dispensing machine. However, the value stream of cola for these different products is commingled over a considerable portion of its length. This commingling of different products is one of the greatest challenges of both physical production and order-taking systems.

4. The analysis presented here is at a high level, without many details. To uncover every instance of every type of *muda* requires a detailed analysis using a portfolio of tools drawn from industrial engineering, systems dynamics, operations management, quality management, time compression, and logistics. The most important of these are *process mapping* (to identify and categorize each step together with the time, distance, and effort involved), the *responsiveness matrix* (to analyze lead times and stock levels), the *quality filter* (to determine where product defects, service errors, and scrap occur along the value stream), and the *demand amplification map* (to assess the variability of orders extending back up the value stream). Peter Hines and Nick Rich describe how to select and use the appropriate tools in "The Seven Value Stream Mapping Tools," *International Journal of Operations and Production Management*, forthcoming, 1996.

5. For branded soft drinks, the firm whose name goes on the carton (for example, Coca-Cola or Pepsi) typically manufactures only the essence and only does this to protect its trade secrets. It supplies the essence to licensee bottlers and concentrates its own efforts on marketing the brand and developing new products.

6. Cans are also made of steel for some customers. For simplicity, we will examine only aluminum cans.

7. Indeed, the can itself accounts for more than half of total manufacturing costs.

8. For example, bar codes are painted on cans sold as single items in vending machines but are not painted on cans destined for packing in cartons. The bar code is deleted in the latter case for fear the bar-code scanner will glimpse a single can inside the carton and ring up the carton as a single can.

9. The only changeovers which can be made without purging the system are from lighter to darker beverages, so the normal sequence is to start with clear sodas and continue through colas before starting over again. This adds some flexibility to the system but the bottler still finds it most economic to run thousands of cans of each specification through at a time.

10. They've also been busy taking weight and materials out of the can. Today's aluminum can uses only 60 percent of the metal needed to contain the same amount of liquid ten years ago—a positive result of the continuing competition between the aluminum can and its steel and plastic rivals.

11. The bauxite miner, the smelter, the cold roller, the hot roller, the can maker, the filler (bottler), and Tesco.
12. In order to get the best price from its suppliers, Tesco must order a complete truckload for each RDC. In addition, Tesco has to build stocks ahead of predictable surges in demand, notably weekly selling peaks on the weekends and, especially for beverages, hot weekends in the summer. As a result of the minimum lot size requirement and periodic demand surges, Tesco on some days has almost zero stocks of beverages in its RDCs and at other times may have as much as a seven- to ten-day supply. The average is three days, as shown in Table 2.1.
13. For many items, Tesco currently places nightly orders for delivery to the RDC seventy-two hours later. (That is, shipments are arriving nightly at every RDC from every supplier, but in many cases with goods ordered three days earlier.) However, for all fresh products delivery is for the next night and for many long-shelf-life goods the delivery window has been moved forward to forty-eight or twenty-four hours. The ultimate goal is to get all suppliers to deliver every order within twenty-four hours of receipt.
14. For a few extremely slow moving or highly seasonal items, Tesco has created a centralized warehouse for all of the U.K. which supplies the RDCs as needed. The RDCs then supply the stores nightly even though the suppliers deliver to the central warehouse much less frequently.
15. In the past year, partly in response to this study, the bottler and the can maker have begun to rethink their methods and are now working on "quick-change" can fillers and painting systems to permit the production of smaller lots at short notice.
16. The estimate of average launch costs for new products is from Kurt Salmon Associates, Inc., *Efficient Consumer Response: Enhancing Consumer Value in the Grocery Industry*, compiled for the Food Marketing Institute, Washington, D.C., 1993.
17. Benchmarking may still be very useful to large mass-production organizations, simply to convince the management that the firm lags far behind competitor performance and to gain the motivation to understand lean thinking.

3: Flow

1. Gilbert Herbert, *The Dream of the Factory-Made House* (Cambridge, Mass.: MIT Press, 1986).
2. For the best summary of QFD and the techniques needed to use it see Don Clausing, *Total Quality Development: A Step-by-Step Guide to World-Class Concurrent Engineering* (New York: American Society of Mechanical Engineers Press, 1994).
3. This term is an interesting example of a word moving from region to region until it is now becoming standard in German, Japanese, and English. The word itself, meaning a precise interval of time, as in a musical meter, was first introduced in German industry as it embraced mass production in the 1930s. German aircraft firms moved aircraft fuselages ahead to the next workstation at

steady intervals determined by the *takt* time. Mitsubishi imported the term in its German form for its own aircraft production efforts in Japan and the term was later taken up by Toyota. It has only crept into English in the last decade as lean thinking has spread. For the historical details see Kazuo Wada, "The Emergence of the 'Flow Production' Method in Japan," in Haruhito Shiomi and Kazuo Wada, *Fordism Transformed: The Development of Production Methods in the Automobile Industry* (Oxford: Oxford University Press, 1995).

4. We use the term *transparency* as an alternative to *visual control*, particularly to indicate the need for everyone to see all of the activities occurring along a value stream flowing through many departments, functions, and firms. The more traditional term *visual control* is accurate in the context of physical production, but unfortunately carries the connotation of top-down *control* of employees and facilities, which is the antithesis of lean thinking.

5. Because this volume is not intended as a technical manual on lean manufacturing, we have not mentioned one additional concept critical to successfully running a lean system. This is *cycle time*, the actual amount of time needed to complete a given task and move it along to the next step in production. For example, to produce a high-volume bicycle in a *takt* time of sixty seconds, it follows that all tasks being conducted along the final assembly line must be completed in sixty seconds or less. In a typical operation being converted to lean production, most jobs will have an observed cycle time of considerably less than sixty seconds and a few may run longer. A key task for the work team and its technical advisers is to determine how to adjust every job so it takes exactly sixty seconds. This can often be done through careful development of *standard work*, in which every aspect of the task is carefully analyzed, optimized, and then performed in exactly the same way each time in accordance with a work standard. In the process of doing this it is generally possible for many workers to transfer to other tasks within the firm in what is sometimes called the "least person" approach (that is, by using the least number of people possible to run the activity within the constraint of the *takt* time). Then, if sales increase and *takt* time needs to fall, the work team will need to *kaizen* their tasks to see if it is possible to lower cycle times to the desired *takt* time. If they can't, more hours of production or additional production capacity may be needed.

6. Yet another problem with MRP was that it hid the parameters of batch sizes, throughput times, and capacity that managers should be seeking to improve on every day. And the internal logic of the production algorithms was so complex that it was impossible to tell intuitively and visually that production was offtrack until a crisis emerged.

7. A related concept is *jidoka* or, in Toyota-speak, "automation with a human touch." The idea is to design every piece of production hardware so that it immediately shuts down if it detects that an error-free part cannot be produced. In the early years of development of the Toyota production system, *jidoka* had particularly striking effects because it meant that workers no longer needed to watch machines in order to avoid producing large numbers of defective parts. The technology needed for *jidoka* is now widely available, but we still frequently visit operations where large numbers of employees are simply watching display

screens and instrument panels on individual machines, ready to react if something goes wrong. With proper use of *jidoka* they could instead be performing preventive maintenance and routine housekeeping or tending to logistics.
8. The term "5Ss" derives from the Japanese words for five practices leading to a clean and manageable work area: *seiri* (organization), *seiton* (tidiness), *seiso* (purity), *seiketsu* (cleanliness), and *shitsuke* (discipline). The reader may note that lean thinkers in Japan have a fondness for numbered lists—the seven forms of *muda*, the five whys, the 5Ss. In our experience the exact number of whys or Ss is less important than the idea that eliminating waste and creating value requires a systematic approach and endless attention to detail.
9. These techniques are usually known collectively as SMED (for "Single Minute Exchange of Dies").
10. Csikszentmihalyi's two reports on his findings are easily readable and highly provocative: *Flow:* The Psychology of Optimal Experience (New York: Harper Perennial, 1990), and *The Evolving Self: A Psychology for the Third Millennium* (New York: Harper Perennial, 1993).

4: Pull

1. In Japanese, *sensei* means teacher, but because of the reverence for teachers in a Confucian society the term "master" can be applied instead.
2. OMCD's general manager, Hiroshi Ginya (now a Toyota Motor Corporation director), launched the project in May 1990 with a weeklong visit to Flex-N-Gate to develop a plan of attack. OMCD's *sensei* were supported by Toyota Motor Sales U.S. Products Department, with the result that a dozen Toyota advisers were often at Bumper Works.
3. The reader will look in vain in business writing on mass customization and among authors promoting expanded product variety as a competitive tool to find any mention of how this plethora of products is going to be fixed when broken or damaged. In fact, the ability to supply replacement parts in a timely, cost-effective manner is a key determinant of how much customization and product variety can be provided and sustained.
4. The age of the average car on the road in the United States zoomed from 5.6 years in 1970 to 8.4 years in 1994, and it is steadily rising. See American Automobile Manufacturers Association, *Motor Vehicle Facts & Figures '95* (Detroit: American Automobile Manufacturers Association, 1995), p. 39.
5. To make the system itself incapable of creating peaks and troughs in orders unrelated to end customer demand, Toyota has installed a series of filters into each level of the ordering system that allow only those orders to be passed on that correspond to the normal ordering pattern for that dealer or PDC. Orders outside these limits must be explicitly authorized by headquarters before they are accepted, to eliminate both clerical mistakes and "panic" orders based, for example, on rumors of shortages or of imminent price increases. In this way Toyota has installed a *poka-yoke* device in the ordering system to filter out noise.
6. This approach works for new cars as well. The International Car Distribution Programme, of which Dan Jones is a director, has developed a simulation model

of what should happen in new car distribution in Europe if all finished inventory is removed one step from the dealer to a central stock area. Typical savings should be about $300 per car. (See International Car Distribution Programme, *European New Car Supply and Stocking Systems Performance*, 1995.) In addition, as Vauxhall (General Motors) and Rover (BMW) are confirming from implementing a central stocking system with no dealer stocks in the United Kingdom, the proportion of customers getting exactly the specification of vehicle they want rises from under 30 percent (usually as a result of a dealer-to-dealer stock swap) to over 80 percent. Conversely, the proportion of customers who had to be persuaded (typically by cutting the selling price) to accept a compromise vehicle fell from 70 to 20 percent. In addition, the number of customers who walked away without buying a car was cut in half. Remarkably, all of this was possible simply by intelligently managing finished-unit inventories without making the factories themselves any more flexible or capable of building cars to specific customer order. An additional benefit of removing stocks to a central location is a change in the role of the salesperson, from being a clever negotiator pushing unwanted vehicles on commission, to someone who can work with customers to fulfill their exact needs while helping to smooth the flow of orders to the factory.

7. James Gleick, *Chaos: Making a New Science* (New York: Viking, 1987).
8. We are grateful to Professor Denis Towill of Cardiff University for bringing to our attention that the pioneers of systems dynamics, Jay Forrester and John Burbridge, provide strong theoretical and empirical support for these observations from their simulation models of demand amplification running up the value stream. Their proposed remedy of shortening response times upstream almost exactly mirrors the path Ohno took in applying lean principles to Toyota's value stream. See Denis R. Towill, "1961 and All That: The Influence of Jay Forrester and John Burbridge on the Design of Modern Manufacturing Systems," *International Systems Dynamics Conference on Business Decision Making*, 1994, pp. 105–15; Denis R. Towill, "Supply Chain Dynamics—The Change Engineering Challenge of the Mid-1990s," *Proceedings of the Institute of Mechanical Engineers*, Vol. 206, 1992, pp. 233–45; and Denis R. Towill, "Time Compression and Supply Chain Management—A Guided Tour," *Supply Chain Management*, Vol. 1, No. 1, 1996, pp. 15–27.
9. Peter Senge, *The Fifth Discipline: The Art and Practice of the Learning Organization* (New York: Doubleday Currency, 1990).
10. See Alan Blinder, *Inventory Theory and Consumer Behavior* (Princeton, N.J.: Princeton University Press, 1990).
11. See Christina A. Romer, "The Prewar Business Cycle Reconsidered," *Journal of Political Economy*, Vol. 97, No. 1, February 1989, pp. 1–37.

5: Perfection

1. Freudenberg GMBH of Stuttgart, Germany, and NOK Ltd. of Nagoya, Japan. The two firms formed a general partnership in 1989 to consolidate all of their North American operations, consisting of thirteen Freudenberg production facilities, one NOK facility, and sales, engineering, and purchasing activities.

2. We are indebted to Pat Lancaster, who you'll meet in the next chapter, for this term and for his very thoughtful discussions with us about the problem of managing a conversion in an organization that will keep it moving ahead at the maximum sustainable pace without overextending.

7: A Harder Case

1. Koenigsaecker is now president of the Hon Company, a major furniture manufacturer headquartered in Muscatine, Iowa.
2. Pentland is now a principal of Moffitt Associates, a firm consulting on lean methods headquartered in Hilton Head, South Carolina.
3. Readers with a management accounting background will appreciate that the full transition from mass to lean accounting, while simple in concept, required careful execution over an extended period. Wiremold could not eliminate tracking of labor and machine hours under the old system until work-in-process (WIP) was largely eliminated. Similarly, Wiremold could not stop its traditional practice of tracking every part in the production system every day (by means of its MRP system) until the number of internal storage locations—what Art Byrne promptly labeled "parts hotels"—was sharply reduced (ultimately to only two—incoming receiving and outgoing finished goods). Therefore, the new profit-and-loss statement was developed and run on spreadsheets in parallel with the old system for nearly a year before the old system was decommissioned and assigned the residual task of calculating the value of WIP and finished goods for the financial statements.
4. See Philip Hauser and Don Clausing, "The House of Quality," *Harvard Business Review*, Vol. 66, No. 3, pp. 63–73, May–June 1988. For a truly complete description of how to conduct Quality Function Deployment and organize development teams, consult Don Clausing, *Total Quality Development* (New York: American Society of Mechanical Engineers, 1994).
5. The American Supplier Institute.
6. As often happens in departmentalized organizations, Wiremold's engineers had lost touch with reality, expending major resources on development programs involving ingenious technological innovations very appealing to the engineers themselves but unrelated to the firm's actual businesses or customer needs.
7. Steve Maynard and his colleagues have recently presented an excellent summary of their achievements and their methods. See S. Blondin, S. Cancellieri, D. Grace, and S. Maynard, "We Designed It with Our Ears," a paper prepared for the Sixth Symposium on Quality Function Deployment, 1994.

8: The Acid Test

1. Pratt's F100 engine powers the F-15 and F-16 fighter planes. The F119 engine will soon power the F-22.
2. Pratt's PW2000 commercial engine family powers the Boeing 757 while a militarized version powers the C-17. Pratt's PW4000 family of engines powers the Boeing 747, 767, and 777; the Airbus A300, A310, and A330; and the McDonnell-Douglas DC-10 and MD-11.

3. The title of this section is taken from a wonderful volume by David Hounshell, *From the American System to Mass Production, 1800–1932* (Baltimore: Johns Hopkins University Press, 1984, revised, expanded, and reissued, 1995). The progression he describes from one-off craft production to mass production with standardized parts is exactly that followed by Pratt & Whitney between 1860 and the start of high-volume aircraft engine production during World War II.
4. Colt's system did not totally eliminate handwork because his gauging system was not sufficiently precise and because Pratt & Whitney's machine tools could only work parts when they were "soft." When the parts were reheated after machining, to harden them and make a durable weapon, the parts warped in unpredictable ways. Some hand "fitting" was required to assemble them into a completed gun, and parts in the same series could not be interchanged once fitted. See Hounshell, pp. 46–50, for a summary of Colt's armory practice and organization.
5. This account of the creation of Pratt & Whitney is taken from an unpublished memoir, "The Saga of Pratt & Whitney Co.," prepared in typescript by Frederick Rentschler, May 1, 1950. The original is in the Archives of the United Technologies Corporation in Hartford, Connecticut.
6. This was the legendary engine which propelled Lindbergh's plane across the Atlantic in 1927. While it had proved the reliability of air-cooled engines, it was too small and its power-to-weight ratio too low to make large commercial aircraft and high-speed military planes a realistic possibility.
7. "Saga of Pratt & Whitney," p. 11, and "Statement of Frederick B. Rentschler Before the Temporary National Economic Committee," Washington, D.C., May 18, 1939, p. 3.
8. The company continued to operate under the legal name of Pratt & Whitney Aircraft Company until the 1970s when it was shortened to Pratt & Whitney. For simplicity, we call the firm "Pratt & Whitney" or "Pratt" throughout this account.
9. The Pratt engine used a forging rather than a casting for its aluminum crankshaft. The forged aluminum crank could be machined more easily than a cast crank to produce a crankshaft much lighter than the cast aluminum crank in the Wright Whirlwind. For a review of aircraft engine development in the piston era see Bill Gunston, *The Development of Piston Aero Engines* (Sparkford, Somerset: Patrick Stephens Limited, 1993), especially pp. 130–31 on Pratt & Whitney.
10. The tool company eventually moved to West Hartford and soldiered on as a conventional machine tool maker. It gradually fell behind in its technologies and production methods and was finally liquidated in 1991 after 131 years of operations. The Pratt & Whitney Aircraft Company was soon merged into the United Aircraft and Transport Corporation, which combined Boeing, Sikorsky (flying boats, then helicopters), Hamilton-Standard (propellers), Chance Vought (military aircraft), and the predecessor companies of United Airlines into a vertically integrated aircraft equipment and operating company. When the U.S. government prohibited such arrangements in 1934, the United Aircraft Corporation was created out of Pratt & Whitney, Sikorsky, Hamilton-Standard,

and Chance Vought, while Boeing and United Airlines became independent companies. United Aircraft changed its name to United Technologies in 1975. Rentschler was chairman of United Aircraft from 1934 until his death in 1956.
11. This section is based on a memorandum in the United Technologies Archives titled "The Project Engineer." It is from Leonard S. Hobbs, later P&W vice president, engineering, to Andrew Willgoos, Pratt & Whitney's vice president, engineering, at that time. The memorandum is dated December 6, 1939.
12. For typologies of program management in product development see Kim Clark and Takahiro Fujimoto, *Product Development Performance* (Boston: Harvard Business School Press, 1991), pp. 253–56, and Don Clausing, *Total Quality Development* (New York: American Society of Mechanical Engineers Press, 1994), pp. 39–44. However, Pratt's concept went much farther in giving the project engineer responsibility for a product line from concept all the way through production to installation in the customer's airplane.
13. This section is based on J. Carlton Ward, Jr., "Typical Plant Layout, Facilities, and Method for Production of Modern High-Powered Air-Cooled Radial Aircraft Engines," a paper presented to the National Aircraft Production Meeting of the Society of Automotive Engineers, Los Angeles, October 1936. Ward was the assistant general manager of Pratt & Whitney, in direct charge of production.
14. Ibid., pp. 3, 7.
15. Ibid., p. 5.
16. Ibid., p. 6. The testing procedure also met the requirements of the Federal Aviation Administration and of customers, who would only accept an engine once its performance as a completed unit was demonstrated.
17. These were the main product of the International Business Machines Company before it perfected electronic computing.
18. Ward, p. 5.
19. Hobbs memorandum, p. 1.
20. Pratt and several licensees produced 363,000 engines for the war effort. Pratt's payroll expanded from less than 3,000 in 1938 to nearly 40,000 in 1943, at which point the company had nearly 9 million square feet of plant space in use. (These figures are taken from *Pratt & Whitney: In the Company of Eagles*, pp. 19 and 22, a booklet prepared by the company in 1990 to commemorate the sixty-fifth anniversary of Pratt & Whitney.)
21. At the same time, the United Automobile Workers organized one major plant at Pratt. This facility was organized by the IAM in 1970, giving Pratt a single union for all of its operations. Information about Pratt's unions in this and subsequent sections is taken from an internal document, "A History of Industrial Relations at United Technologies Corporation," July 13, 1990, in the Pratt & Whitney Archives.
22. Its development effort reflects this. The original Wasp engine of 1925 could have required no more than 20,000 hours of engineering. There were only six engineers involved over a nine-month period and they could not very well have worked more than twelve hours a day seven days a week, suggesting an upper limit of 19,710 engineering hours. The Wasp Major, by contrast, required

730,000 hours of engineering. (This latter figure is from United Aircraft president H. Mansfield Horner, "Producing the Jet," a lecture delivered to the Industrial College of the Armed Forces, Production Branch, Washington, D.C., 1952, reprinted by the company and contained in the company archives.)

23. Pratt's last piston engine, the Wasp Major, required 730,000 engineering hours while its first major jet engine, the J-57, required 1,338,000. In addition, as Pratt president H. Mansfield Horner pointed out in 1952, the nature of the knowledge was now very different. "The piston engine, particularly the radial air-cooled type that gave us supremacy in World War II, had a fundamental character that was peculiarly its own. It was an engine where background experience, lore, and a `feel in the fingertips' were vital to its successful design and production. It did not yield readily to theory and analysis. It was, to a major degree, designed on experience, and you often learned from it by deliberately breaking it or its components to smithereens." Horner, p. 1.

24. From the standpoint of the engine makers, the "trouble" started in 1970 when Douglas chose the GE engine for its new DC-10 model and Pratt offered to underwrite the $100 million cost of certifying this airplane with the Pratt JT9D as an option. GE then countered by getting its CF6 certified as an option for the Boeing 747 (initially planned by Boeing to have only the Pratt engine) and Rolls certified the RB211-535 for the 747 as well. Airbus, just preparing its initial offering with the A300, adopted a "multiple engine choices per wing" policy from the beginning, and a new dynamic was in place in the engine industry, which steadily ratcheted new engine prices down. As two-engine designs replaced the previously dominant three- and four-engine jets, and the total number of engines ordered began to decline even as total airframes ordered increased, competition became even more intense. By 1995, a situation had been reached in which engine makers were under intense pressure to offer engines essentially free to large customers, with all potential for long-term cost recovery and profits coming from spares purchases.

25. The number of orders for replacement engines for existing aircraft is surprisingly small because modern jet engines will operate for up to five years "on the wing" before their first major maintenance and can be refurbished several times before their useful life is over. Thus, orders for new jet engines closely track orders for new aircraft.

26. For an account of this episode written by a U.S. Air Force officer, see Robert W. Drewes, *The Air Force and the Great Engine War* (Washington, D.C.: National Defense University Press, 1987).

27. Pratt fought back by forming a consortium (International Aero Engines) with Mitsubishi in Japan, Rolls-Royce in the U.K., MTU in Germany, and Alenia in Italy to produce the IAE V2500, but the engine arrived late and gained only a small share of the market. In addition, Pratt contributed only a quarter of the value-added in each V2500.

28. The categories were known as "charter parts."

29. Charter Part Councils in Pratt-speak.

30. The thrust reversers used on jet aircraft today utilize a series of heavy clam shells or side shunts toward the rear of the engine which divert the exhaust

around the outside of the engine and toward the front of the plane to brake it. However, the machinery in the engine itself continues to push air toward the rear before it is diverted.
31. If a fan blade of the size needed for this engine were to escape from the engine nacelle, it could damage the wing or fuselage to such an extent that the aircraft could be lost.
32. The Advanced Research Projects Agency in the U.S. Department of Defense has taken a strong interest in the composites technology and is currently co-funding a $100 million effort with Pratt & Whitney and the suppliers of composites to develop the fiber-composite nacelle needed to contain the fan blades.
33. These are Otis, the world's largest elevator company; Carrier, the world's largest air-conditioning manufacturer; Sikorsky, the leading producer of helicopters; United Technologies Automotive, a $2 billion producer of auto parts; and Hamilton-Standard, the industry leader in propellers and aircraft climate-control systems.
34. A jet engine has up to eight rows of whirling turbine blades immediately behind the combustion area. Between each row of blades is a row of stationary guide vanes which straighten out the swirling airflow emerging from the turbine blades and funnel it smoothly into the next turbine stage. Temperatures of the gases flowing past the blades and guide vanes closest to the combustor approach 3,000 degrees Fahrenheit. These items, therefore, present one of the most difficult manufacturing challenges in the world.

    Blades and vanes are fabricated by Pratt using the world's most complex precision castings (obtained from suppliers). These introduce a rabbit warren of air spaces inside each blade which are critical for pushing air through the interior of the blade to keep it cool. For the most complex blades, installed immediately behind the combustor in the hottest area of the engine, approximately 1,000 holes are laser-drilled in each blade to permit high-pressure cold air to be pushed through the blade from inside to outside to create a laminar boundary on the blade surface. This keeps the hot gases a few molecules away from the ceramically treated surface of the blade, a critical feat because the temperature of the gases is higher than the melting point of the blade.
35. This "unitizing" process consisted of putting pallets under the machines and deploying air and electrical lines from the ceiling every few feet so that any machine could be moved anywhere on the floor and hooked up immediately.
36. The machine we described in the Introduction, which could fill fifteen hundred cans of soda per minute but required several catchment warehouses to keep it fully utilized, is a comparable example.
37. Please do not make the common mistake of confusing "simple" with "low-tech." The new grinders employ a proprietary positioning system which makes it possible for the employee in the cell to place a part in a machine with total precision in less than two seconds. What's more, the machines hold the blade in such a way that damage to the blade surface from the grinding forces is totally eliminated. This technology is simple but extremely "high-tech."
38. Rather like a "Toyota warehouse," a "lean test cell" sounds oxymoronic. Surely a perfectly lean operation would not require any testing at the end. In theory

this is true, but the jet engine is a special product. Few of us would probably care to fly on an airplane whose engines had never been run before, even engines produced in the leanest factory.
39. Pratt has dramatically altered its approach to training. As Bob Weiner notes, "We now ask our work teams, 'What do you need to know to do your job better?' We then attempt to supply this knowledge just-in-time and to teach skills right on the shop floor." The centralized training department with off-site classrooms has been eliminated and the union has appointed a training director to help Pratt provide the necessary skills.
40. We will have more to say on this point in Chapter 10 on Japan.

9: Lean Thinking versus German Technik

1. This is not to say that no perfect Porsche had ever been delivered to a customer. As we will see, Porsche and its workforce were masters of rework and rectification, so the product finally reaching the consumer had a level of defects and problems in the same best-in-class range as Mercedes or Toyota Lexus. The problem was the cost to Porsche of its historic path to perfection.
2. Historic details on Porsche are taken from Professor Dr. Ing. h.c. Ferry Porsche with Gunther Molter, *Cars Are My Life* (Wellingborough, England: Patrick Stephens Limited, 1989).
3. The model designations were based on the number of design projects undertaken by Porsche since its founding in 1930. These included suspension systems, engine improvements, and many other tasks besides whole vehicles. The great bulk of Porsche's work has never been publicly attributed to the firm.
4. Porsche and Molter, p. 237.
5. In the terminology of Shigeo Shingo, one of the great innovators of lean methods, they understood *operations*—that is, individual activities performed on individual parts—perhaps better than any group of workers in the world. However, as we will see, their knowledge of *processes*—Shingo's term for the linking together of individual operations to introduce flow through a production system —was largely lacking, particularly when a product traveled across many work groups and through many departments on its way from raw material to finished item. See Shigeo Shingo, *A Study of the Toyota Production System from an Industrial Engineering Viewpoint* (Portland, Oregon: Productivity Press, 1989), Chapter 1, for a summary of Shingo's thinking about the relationship between individual operations and linked processes.
6. Porsche and Molter, p. 301.
7. This 450-base-horsepower, 200-mile-per-hour, $500,000 redo of the 911 was Porsche's effort to "out-Ferrari Ferrari" and was successful in terms of its tiny sales target.
8. Imai was instrumental in introducing the idea of *kaizen* to Western managers in his 1987 book *Kaizen* (New York: Free Press, 1987).
9. Nick Oliver, Daniel T. Jones, Rick Delbridge, Jim Lowe, Peter Roberts, and Betty Thayer, *Worldwide Manufacturing Competitiveness Study: The Second Lean Enterprise Report* (London: Andersen Consulting, 1994).
10. In a desperate but largely successful effort to sustain buyer interest until new

models could be introduced, Porsche began to launch a variant of the 911 every six months. This kept Porsche's name in the auto enthusiast magazines because journalists seemed incapable of resisting the offer to test-drive "the new Porsche," even if the newness consisted only of minor modifications such as a Targa top or a refined transmission.
11. Delivery of parts by suppliers directly to line-side was considered but rejected because of the nature of the facility. The Zuffenhausen plant has four floors and very limited delivery points due to the plant's location in a residential neighborhood. A central kitting area for all deliveries is the only procedure that meshes with the physical constraints of the site.
12. Most practitioners of lean thinking utilize some form of game or simulation exercise to show both senior management and operating employees what happens when flow and pull are introduced. The Toyota Supplier Support Center in the United States and Porsche have developed factory simulation games and Peter Senge at MIT has developed his "beer game" to illustrate the effects of batch thinking in distribution. We urge any management trying to implement lean thinking to devise some variant of these games to start people thinking about the world beyond batch-and-queue.
13. Porsche, as a niche producer, has until now gone far beyond Volkswagen in offering variety. The 911 model offers eighty types of exterior door mirrors, not counting six color options! The new Boxster by contrast will offer four basic mirror designs (in twelve colors) customized with a choice of five types of glass fitted to the mirror housing on the final assembly line. This amount of variety is judged by Porsche to be a more appropriate trade-off between variety and cost in an upmarket product.
14. See B. Joseph Pine II, *Mass Customization* (Boston: Harvard Business School Press, 1993), for the best statement of these ideas.
15. The Pratt & Whitney blade grinding system described in Chapter 8 was a classic example of complex German equipment which reduced direct labor but at the expense of more than offsetting technical support costs. Other German tool builders have pushed resolutely ahead with automated transfer lines to assemble high-volume goods with no direct labor, only to discover that the demand for goods made in these volumes simply doesn't exist. We will look at a Japanese instance of this same problem in the next chapter.
16. However, the arguments in the next chapter about Japanese production location also apply to many high-volume German industries. Lean thinking calls for location of production as near the customer as possible, with the qualification that some low-volume, highly niched goods—in fact, those at which German *Mittelstand* firms tend to specialize—can continue to be successfully made for the entire world market from one production and design location.

10: Mighty Toyota; Tiny Showa

1. Kawabe is now managing director and general manager of Showa's Air-conditioning Products Division. He retains the Production Research Department in his portfolio of responsibilities.
2. From an interview with Taiichi Ohno in Isao Shinohara's *New Production System:*

JIT Crossing Industry Boundaries (Cambridge, Mass.: Productivity Press, 1988), p. 152.

3. The others were Takeo Chiku, Tatsu Inagawa, and Tozo Yabuta. For details of the origins of the chief engineer at Toyota, see Toyota Motor Corporation, *Toyota: A History of the First 50 Years* (Toyota City: Toyota Motor Corporation, 1988), p. 115.
4. It turns out that even Toyota finds it hard to completely synchronize production with sales when demand suddenly plummets. The irresistible urge in the early 1990s was to cut prices and seek to retain market share and volume. Toyota soon had to face the reality that Japanese consumers were dropping out of the car market for an extended period and that extra cars, as Ohno had always claimed, were simply *muda*.
5. The unique Japanese registration system for new vehicles requires the buyer to submit evidence that an appropriate parking space is available for the new vehicle. Because this submission is filed only when the car is actually sold and then requires a week to process, Toyota has no incentive to deliver the car in less than one week.
6. Technical descriptions of how to evaluate jobs for fatigue and stress can be found in Atsushi Nimi, H. Kako, and Yoshinori Eri, "On the Development of TVAL (Toyota Verification of Assembly Line) and Its Applications" (Toyota City: Toyota Motor Corporation, 1994), and Yoshinori Eri, Atsushi Nimi, Satoshi Ogata, and Bungo Hayashi, "Development of Assembly Line Verification," Society of Automotive Engineers Technical Paper 940890, 1994. We recommend these papers to anyone implementing lean techniques, particularly in factory settings.
7. Hines, op. cit.
8. For a more detailed discussion of the diffusion of lean thinking through Toyota and far beyond see James P. Womack, "The Diffusion of Lean Production: Process and Prospects," Cambridge, Mass., MIT Japan Program Research Monograph, 1996.
9. Indeed, as we noted in the Introduction in referring to the recent research of Professor Kazuo Wada at the University of Tokyo, Mitsubishi may have actually experimented with some lean techniques first, such as *takt* time.
10. Ohno himself found the original American emphasis on statistical sampling to be completely wrong-minded. He decreed that Toyota would implement *jidoka* techniques and *poka-yokes* in all production steps so that it would effectively be doing 100 percent quality inspection at the exact moment of manufacture. Because the Occupation authorities were not ready for these concepts, Ohno often found himself in trouble with Occupation headquarters.
11. For a good history of Total Quality Control in Japan and the adoption of cross-functional management of quality at Toyota see Kenji Kurogane, ed., *Cross-Functional Management: Principles and Practical Applications* (Tokyo: Asian Productivity Organization, 1993). For the contrasting attitudes to production management and quality at Toyota and Nissan, see Michael A. Cusumano, *The Japanese Automobile Industry: Technology and Management at Nissan and Toyota* (Cambridge, Mass.: Harvard University Press, 1991). Cusumano reports that

Nissan's quality drive slackened after winning the Deming Prize while Toyota went from strength to strength after winning.
12. We have concluded from our interviews with scholars and Toyota executives of Ohno's generation that the adoption of Total Quality Control at Toyota after 1960 helped align the work of departments not directly involved in production with Ohno's initiatives in manufacturing.
13. See Shinohana, *New Production Systems*, for details on the activities of this organization.

11: An Action Plan

1. The Bibliography at the end of this volume provides a list of books we've found particularly helpful.
2. One word of caution: Technical skills are essential but so is force of character and the ability to impose order on chaos. North American and European transplant operations of the best Japanese firms would seem to be the ideal place to search for individuals with the necessary knowledge, and sometimes they are. However, we have watched a number of Americans and Europeans with several years' experience in these firms fail at the task of introducing lean ideas in subsequent brownfield assignments for American and European employers. In retrospect, it is clear that these individuals were well suited to introducing lean ideas in a greenfield setting with constant advice from Japanese *sensei*, but they were not up to the daunting task of introducing them in organizations where they lacked backup support and met organizational resistance. At the same time, we've met lean experts with much less impressive formal credentials—like Bob D'Amore at Pratt who never had a Japanese *sensei*—who have the force of personality to overcome strong resistance.
3. Perhaps the most telling statement of this reality is that 68 percent of the five hundred largest industrial corporations in the *Fortune* listing of 1955 no longer exist or have fallen out of the listing. "40 Years of the 500," *Fortune*, May 15, 1995, p. 184.
4. David Hurst, *Crisis and Renewal* (Boston: Harvard Business School Press, 1995), makes a strong case that firms need to "burn the forest" in parts of their organization in order to keep the whole organization from going up in smoke at a later point. Creative (lean) solutions to specific operations in crisis may be the best way to create "fire breaks" and eventually renew the whole forest.
5. See Peter Hines, *Creating World-Class Suppliers* (London: Pitman, 1994), for the most comprehensive account available of methods for creating supplier associations and improving supplier performance. Hines, of the Lean Enterprise Research Centre, set up the first supplier association outside Japan in September 1991 and to date he has helped established supplier associations for 25 companies (including Toyota, Rover, British Aerospace, Borg-Warner, Ford, and Volvo) involving 350 suppliers in the U.K., Belgium, and Sweden. These have proved a very useful complement to one-on-one supplier development by downstream firms, because horizontal associations of suppliers give them the opportunity to share experiences and learn from each other. Supplier associa-

tions also give the downstream customer the ability to align the efforts of all suppliers on the most critical areas for improvement, using a shared policy deployment process.

12: A Channel for the Stream; a Valley for the Channel

1. Many readers will recognize this as a Plan-Do-Check-Act (PDCA) cycle of the type first utilized by the Total Quality Control movement, except now applied to the whole value stream rather than individual activities.
2. Indeed, maximizing an individual firm's returns from a shared value stream has been the objective of "value chain" analysis taught as a core element of the strategy curriculum in American business schools.

13: Dreaming About Perfection

1. The Toyota Motor Corporation manufactures housing, but only offers its products in the Japanese domestic market. And even there the complexities of land acquisition and site preparation stretch out the time and effort needed to move a home from concept to completion. In America and Europe, by contrast, many efforts over several decades to streamline construction by building modular components in factories have failed. (See Gilbert Herbert, *The Dream of the Factory-Made House* [Cambridge, Mass.: MIT Press, 1986], for the details of a century of experimentation.) The mobile home industry has flourished in the United States, but by using standard batch-and-queue factory techniques (themselves candidates for a lean revolution) and by offering designs which are far removed from those of the traditional, build-to-order housing industry.
2. Some of the ideas in this section first appeared in James P. Womack, "The Real EV Challenge—Reinventing an Industry," in Scott A. Cronk, ed., *Building the E-Motive Industry* (Warrendale, Pa.: Society of Automotive Engineers, 1995), pp. 128–39. A similar presentation of these ideas is James P. Womack, "The Real EV Challenge: Reinventing an Industry," in *Transport Policy*, Vol. 1, No. 4, October 1994, pp. 266–70. The implications of these ideas for car distribution are explored in Daniel T. Jones, "Peering into a Lean Future," in R. Hunerberg, ed., *International Automobile Marketing*, Gaberler Verlag, 1995, and Daniel T. Jones, "Does Lean Selling Need Dealers?" International Car Distribution Programme Working Paper, 1995.
3. An intervening variable on the cost front is that appreciation of the yen has caused Japanese car makers to lose their cost advantage when selling into North America and Europe from their production base in Japan. This has relieved the domestic producers from price pressures. However, the Japanese firms are currently working rapidly to redeploy their production base to match their markets and to introduce lean principles in their North American and European supply bases. When this is largely achieved in North America, by around the year 2000, and in Europe slightly later, we expect to see fierce price competition. The customer will finally receive the pocketbook benefits of lean thinking.
4. This same concept could be applied in the aircraft industry where the long-term

trend in the number of passenger miles traveled is very smooth but the peak-to-base ratio in aircraft orders through the business cycle is five to one. If an "aircraft provider"—perhaps one of the existing airframe manufacturers—provided "hassle-free lift" to mobility providers rather than trying to sell them airplanes in one-off encounters, it would probably be possible to synchronize airframe construction with the long-term trend in passenger travel.

14: The Steady Advance of Lean Thinking

1. For a comprehensive examination of the means used by Art Byrne and his team to create wealth at Wiremold, see M. L. Emiliani et al., *Better Thinking, Better Results: Using the Power of Lean as a Total Business Solution* (Kensington, Conn.: Center for Lean Business Management, 2003).
2. Toyota Motor Corporation, "Toyota Puts Forth '2010 Global Vision,' " (press release dated April 1, 2002).
3. And even in these cases, bold action was taken largely due to the need to address significant weaknesses in Toyota's traditional product portfolio. The RX300 is an SUV built on a car platform (the Camry) rather than on a truck platform like the segment-leading Ford Explorer, a move necessitated by Toyota's lack of a suitable truck platform in this size class. Similarly, the Prius-gasoline/electric hybrid—while a brilliant technical achievement and remarkably mature in execution for a product with so many new technologies—was necessitated by Toyota's lack of small diesel motors that European producers were utilizing to achieve the same magnitude of fuel economy improvements.
4. See Alfred P. Sloan, Jr., *My Years with General Motors* (New York: Doubleday Currency, 1990) pp. 65–66, for the classic statement of the role of product technology and bold design initiatives in GM's product strategy: "the policy [formulated in 1921] . . . was valid if our cars were at least equal in design to the best of our competitors in a grade, so that it was not *necessary* to lead in design or run the risk of untried experiments." [Italics in the original.]
5. Porsche's production in 2002 was 55,000 units. The next smallest completely independent car company, BMW, produced 906,000 units. A number of fairly large companies like Suburu and Suzuki have had to accept equity participation by larger companies (GM in their case) and all the other companies with production volume below the BMW level—Volvo, Saab, Jaguar, Land Rover, Rolls-Royce, Aston Martin, Ferrari, Lamborghini—have now lost their independence.
6. Its operations were also expanded from the overcrowded Zuffenhausen facility in Stuttgart to a new company-owned assembly plant in Leipzig in eastern Germany and to a contract assembler in Finland.
7. Pratt has received the contract for the entire product development process for the F-35 engine and will produce the engines for the first three production lots of aircraft, currently scheduled to be completed by 2012. Other firms may be given a share of the program at that point.
8. Note that when we reported on page 152 that Pratt suffered a loss of $283 million in 1992, we were including a structural charge of $667 for discontinued activities and facilities. By contrast, the earnings data in Figure 14.8 are exclusive of

charges because we believe that earnings on continuing operations is a better indication of performance over the long term. (Thus Pratt is shown in Figure 14.8 to have a profit of $384 million in 1992.)

9. We have decided only to update the stories of the firms receiving chapter-length treatment in *Lean Thinking*. We could add many more. For example, Tesco, the company helping us develop the story of the humble can of cola in Chapter 2, has marched steadily ahead on its lean journey, as explained in Daniel Jones and Philip Clarke, "Creating a Customer-Driven Supply Chain" *ECR Journal: The International Commerce Review*, Vol. 2, No. 2, Winter 2002.

10. Readers familiar with the recent work of Richard Schonberger (*Let's Fix It!* [New York: Free Press, 2001]) may be a bit surprised at our optimism. This is because Schonberger reports, based on an analysis of inventory turns calculated from the annual reports of hundreds of manufacturing companies worldwide, that average performance has ceased to improve in recent years and may even be going backwards. The difference is not in the nature of reality, but in our two methods. We use government data on inventories manufacturers hold in the United States in relation to sales in the United States, while Schonberger uses corporate annual reports calculating inventories held worldwide in relation to sales worldwide. And it's the "worldwide" that we believe is the difference.

For example, Schonberger reports that Toyota's inventory turns have fallen substantially between the 1960s and the 1990s and takes this to mean that Toyota has stopped improving. However, from our visits to individual Toyota plants, we know that this cannot be the case at the plant level. What has happened instead is that Toyota has rapidly globalized both its markets and its manufacturing operations, with the result that large amounts of parts (including service parts) and whole vehicles are now being shipped long distances between continents. (What's more, because Toyota has bought out most of its regional distributors around the world, a much larger fraction of its finished vehicles now show up in its total inventory calculation.) This is bad in the sense that it increases global inventories—an important issue we return to in Chapter 15—but it should not be taken to mean that plant-level and country-level manufacturing performance is less lean. Indeed, we believe that just the opposite is the case.

15: Institutionalizing the Revolution

1. Two of the *sensei* we most respected and whose work we mentioned briefly in this book have died since the publication of the first edition of *Lean Thinking*. Yoshiki Iwata, who worked for many years with Wiremold, Pratt & Whitney, and Porsche, died in 2001. Yuzuru Ito, who instilled quality thinking at United Technologies (Pratt & Whitney), died in 2000. Both continued with their *kaizen* activities right up until their deaths, working long after their age and health suggested that they retire, like Taiichi Ohno and Shigeo Shingo before them.
2. For a detailed description of Value Stream Mapping, see Mike Rother and John Shook, *Learning to See* (Brookline, Mass.: Lean Enterprise Institute, 1998).
3. Readers with backgrounds in Six Sigma, Total Productive Maintenance, the Theory of Constraints, and the Toyota Production System will recognize that each of

these concerns is the starting point for one of the traditions. In the end, we believe that they are all seeking the same goal: a perfect process providing correctly specified value exactly when the customer wants it with no waste, no defects, no breakdowns, no bottlenecks, and no excess capacity.
4. The simplest evidence is that *Learning to See* has now sold more than 120,000 copies in English and has been translated into a dozen languages. When we walk through facilities in many countries, as we do constantly, we now almost always see value stream maps for the current state and the future state.
5. For example, we are often shown cellularized production and we are grateful that the cells are usually marked by large signs. Otherwise we might not know they are cells, because what we see instead of true cells is a group of adjacent machines with erratic output rather than smooth flow, poor utilization of operators, and piles of inventory between each machine. For an action plan for achieving truly continuous flow in cellularized operations see Mike Rother and Rick Harris, *Creating Continuous Flow* (Brookline, Mass.: Lean Enterprise Institute, 2002).
6. Recently we've tried to introduce some consistency in lean terminology by leading an effort to publish a lean dictionary. See *The Lean Lexicon: A Graphical Glossary for Lean Thinkers* (Brookline, Mass.: Lean Enterprise Institute, 2003).
7. See Mike Rother and Rick Harris, *Creating Continuous Flow*, for further insight on best-practice and model cells.
8. We are indebted to John Shook for this point.
9. Dan Jones and Jim Womack, *Seeing the Whole: Mapping the Extended Value Stream* (Brookline, Mass.: Lean Enterprise Institute, 2002). While the names of the firms sharing this value stream have been disguised, the data we present are precisely what we found on our walk and are completely typical of today's manufacturing practices around the world.
10. The simple test of value is to ask of a step: "Would the customer pay less or be less satisfied with the product if this step could somehow be left out?" In the example cited, only the eight stamping, painting, and assembly steps actually create value the customer would miss. No customer would complain if the 65 handoff, rework, transport, and storage steps could somehow be eliminated. Indeed, to the extent that these steps stretch out the elapsed time to make the product and thwart the customer's desire to got just what is wanted just when it is wanted, they actually destroy value.
11. As so often, we are grateful to John Shook for this point.

Bibliography

The following are books and articles we have found particularly helpful in understanding lean thinking and lean techniques.

Arnold, Horace, and Fay Faurote. *Ford Methods and the Ford Shops.* North Stratford, N.H.: Ayer, 1998 (a reprint of the *Engineering Magazine* edition of 1915).
Case, John. *Open Book Management.* New York: Harper Business, 1995.
Clark, Kim, and Takahiro Fujimoto. *Product Development Performance.* Boston: Harvard Business School Press, 1991.
Clausing, Don. *Total Quality Development: A Step-by-Step Guide to World-Class Concurrent Engineering.* New York: American Society of Mechanical Engineers Press, 1994.
Cooper, Robin. *When Lean Enterprises Collide: Competing Through Confrontation.* Boston: Harvard Business School Press, 1995.
Csikzentmihalyi, Mihaly. *Flow: The Psychology of Optimal Experience.* New York: HarperPerennial, 1990.
———. *The Evolving Self: A Psychology for the Third Millennium.* New York: Harper Perennial, 1993.
Cusumano, Michael. *The Japanese Automobile Industry: Technology and Management at Nissan and Toyota.* Cambridge, Mass.: Harvard University Press, 1985.
Fujimoto, Takahiro. *The Evolution of a Manufacturing System at Toyota.* New York: Oxford University Press, 1999.
Gleick, James. *Chaos: Making a New Science.* New York: Viking, 1987.
Jones, Dan, and Jim Womack. *Seeing the Whole: Mapping the Extended Value Stream.* Brookline, Mass.: Lean Enterprise Institute, 2002.
Philip Hauser and Don Clausing, "The House of Quality," *Harvard Business Review*, Vol. 66, No. 3, May–June 1988, pp. 63–73.
Hines, Peter. *Creating World-Class Suppliers.* London: Pitman, 1994.
Hounshell, David. *From the American System to Mass Production, 1800–1932.* Baltimore: Johns Hopkins University Press, 1984 (revised, expanded, and reissued, 1995).
Hurst, David. *Crisis and Renewal.* Boston: Harvard Business School Press, 1995.
Kurogane, Kenji, ed., *Cross-Functional Management: Principles and Practical Applications.* Tokyo: Asian Productivity Organization, 1993.
Lamming, Richard. *Beyond Partnership: Strategies for Innovation and Lean Supply.* New York: Prentice-Hall, 1993.

Mather, Hal. *Competitive Manufacturing.* New York: Prentice-Hall, 1991.
Monden, Yasuhiro. *The Toyota Production System.* Atlanta: Institute of Industrial Engineers, 1983.
———. *Cost Reduction Systems: Target Costing and Kaizen Costing.* Portland, Ore.: Productivity Press, 1995.
Nishiguchi, Toshihiro. *Strategic Industrial Sourcing: The Japanese Advantage.* Oxford: Oxford University Press, 1994.
Ohno, Taiichi. *The Toyota Production System: Beyond Large-Scale Production.* Portland, Oregon: Productivity Press, 1988.
———. *Workplace Management.* Portland, Oregon: Productivity Press, 1988.
Rother, Mike, and Rick Harris. *Creating Continuous Flow.* Brookline, Mass.: Lean Enterprise Institute, 2001.
Rother, Mike, and John Shook. *Learning to See.* Brookline, Mass.: Lean Enterprise Institute, 1998.
Schonberger, Richard J. *Japanese Manufacturing Techniques.* New York: Free Press, 1982.
———. *World Class Manufacturing: The Lessons of Simplicity Applied.* New York: Free Press, 1986.
———. *World Class Manufacturing: The Next Decade.* New York: Free Press, 1996.
———. *Let's Fix It.* New York: Free Press, 2001.
Sewell, Carl and Paul B. Brown. *Customers for Life.* New York: Pocket Books, 1991.
Shingo, Shigeo. *A Study of the Toyota Production System from an Industrial Engineering Viewpoint.* Portland, Oregon: Productivity Press, 1989.
Stack, Jack. *The Great Game of Business.* New York: Harper Business, 1993.
Suzaki, Kiyoshi. *The New Manufacturing Challenge.* New York: Free Press, 1987.
———. *The New Shopfloor Management.* New York: Free Press, 1993.
Toyota Motor Corporation. *The Toyota Production System.* Operations Management Consulting Division and International Public Affairs Division. Toyota City: Toyota Motor Corporation, 1995.
———. *Toyota: A History of the First 50 Years.* Toyota City: Toyota Motor Corporation, 1988.
Womack, James P., and Daniel T. Jones. *How the World Has Changed Since* The Machine That Changed the World. Brookline, Mass.: Lean Enterprise Institute, 2000.

Index

accounting systems, 60, 136, 262, 270, 347, 352
action plan, 247–71, 313–36, 374n–75n
  batch-and-queue mode vs., 257–58, 265, 267
  change agents for, 247–50, 253, 254, 256, 257, 260, 261, 268, 269–70, 313–14
  charts and tables for, 257, 317, 318, 319, 320, 321, 324–25, 328–32
  competition and, 250–51, 336
  cost reductions in, 250, 251, 252, 259, 266–67, 332–35
  creative crisis and, 250–51, 258, 315–16
  customers and, 248, 327–32
  for flow, 250, 254, 255, 258, 264
  global strategy in, 267–68, 270, 332–35
  grand strategy vs., 251–52
  growth strategy in, 258–59, 270
  immediate results for, 253–54
  initiation of, 247–55, 270
  for inventories, 250, 271
  kaikaku in, 247, 248, 254, 255, 262, 265, 270
  kaizen in, 248, 262, 268, 315, 318, 319
  knowledge in, 248–50, 314–15, 323
  layoffs and, 249, 258–59, 260
  lean promotion function in, 256–57, 322–23, 326, 336
  for management, 248, 250, 256, 257, 259–61, 264, 268–69, 313–14, 315–16, 336
  momentum in, 253, 254–55, 260–61
  muda eliminated in, 247, 249, 251, 252, 254, 255, 257, 263, 269, 314, 315, 323, 327, 328–31
  opposition to, 258, 259–60, 261
  for order processing, 254, 255, 256, 262, 268
  for perfection, 250, 260, 270, 322, 323–26
  policy deployment and, 261–62, 326, 336, 349
  for product development, 250, 251–52, 255, 256, 257, 268
  productivity and, 262–63
  for pull, 250, 253, 254, 255, 264, 314, 323–26, 328–31
  quality control and, 257, 267, 268
  reorganization in, 255–62, 265, 270, 320–22
  salaries and, 262–63, 268, 270
  for sales, 254, 256, 259, 262
  sensei for, 249–50, 253, 254, 256, 268, 269–70, 314–15
  for suppliers, 248, 249, 252, 265–67, 268, 270, 327–32, 371n–72n
  terminology of, 257
  time frame for, 269–70
  training in, 264, 270
  transparency and, 253, 261, 263–64, 268, 270
  value stream and, 252–53, 254, 255–56, 262, 264, 270, 271, 315, 316–22, 323, 327, 375n

Activity Based Costing, 136, 262, 347, 352
Advanced Ducted Propfan (ADP), 166
advertising, 48
AEG, 284
aggregated processes, 10, 23–24, 37, 44
Airbus, 18, 164
Airbus A3XX aircraft, 152
Airbus 320 aircraft, 164
aircraft industry, 18, 19, 28, 164, 217, 286–89, 305–9, 373n
airfoils, turbine, 165, 173
airline industry, 18–19, 20, 32–34, 50–51, 160, 161–62, 163, 166, 175, 182, 186, 244, 286–89, 305–6, 356n–57n, 373n
airports, 18–19, 32–34, 51, 175, 286–87, 288, 356n
Aisin Seiki, 235
aluminum, 38–41, 59, 156, 193, 241, 358n
andon boards, 56, 61, 234, 287, 347
assembly lines, 23, 56
Aston Martin, 373n
Audi, 191, 205, 211
automated guided vehicles (AGVs), 176, 177, 179
automated storage and retrieval system (ASRS), 176, 177, 179
automobile industry:
   batch-and-queue mode used in, 68–69, 70
   bicycle industry and, 57
   dealerships in, 29, 35, 67–68, 73, 74, 76, 81–86, 287, 293–94, 361n–62n
   German, 189–218, 302–4, 373n
   Japanese, 85–86, 197–98, 200, 211, 222, 242, 300–302, 336, 373n, 374n
   JIT system in, 70
   maintenance agreements in, 82–87, 93
   materials revolution in, 28
   parts distribution in, 67, 72–87, 302
   personal mobility and, 286, 293–94
   pull in, 67–87
   sales in, 29, 35, 67, 73, 74
   in U.S., 22–23, 218, 301
availability (uptime), 318–20, 322–23

backflow, 52, 54, 112, 119, 137, 148, 180, 182, 183, 202, 280
back orders, 143
backtracking, 107–8, 120
Baldrige Award, 29
bankruptcy, 19, 230, 231
Barnett, Richard, 71
bauxite, 38, 39, 42, 43, 44
benchmarking, 9, 10, 27, 48–49, 238, 253–54, 263
B-52 bomber, 160
bicycle industry, 20, 52–64, 339
   batch-and-queue mode used in, 53, 57, 58, 60
   departmentalization in, 53
   final assembly in, 53, 56–57, 62
   frames produced in, 55, 59, 62
   JIT in, 59
   order processing in, 54–56
   part fabrication in, 56–63
   product design in, 53–54, 58
   takt time in, 55–56
Bill of Materials (BOM), 105
blanking machines, 40, 70, 84
BMW, 211, 212, 373n
Boeing, 18
Boeing 707 aircraft, 160, 305
Boeing 727 aircraft, 160, 163
Boeing 737 aircraft, 160, 163–64
Boeing 757 aircraft, 163
Boeing 777 aircraft, 152
Bohn, Arno, 195
boilers, 219, 220, 222, 224, 226, 227
bonuses, 26, 56, 58, 263
bottlenecks, 58, 114, 265
bottlers, 39, 41–42, 46, 47, 48
box scores, 27, 121, 148–50, 212–13
Brooks, Gary, 126
Brooks Electronics, 126, 147
"brownfield" plants, 10–11, 28, 261, 347, 348
Bubble Economy, 80, 191, 238, 299
bumpers, automobile, 67–72, 73, 74, 75, 83
Bumper Works, 68–72, 74, 76, 84–85
"bumping-rights" system, 172

business cycles, 88, 109, 168, 336
Byrne, Art, 125, 127, 128, 129, 130–36, 139, 140, 142, 144, 145, 146, 147–48, 152, 168, 169, 171, 181, 299, 312, 373*n*

call-back rates, 181
Canada, 333, 335
cans, aluminum, 38–41, 358*n*
capability (first-time quality), 318–20, 322–23
careers, 245, 271, 275, 278–79, 284
Carrier, 170, 171
castings, ornamental, 220, 225, 226
CFM, 163–64
chaku-chaku (load-load) cells, 179, 232, 347–48
change agents, 97–98, 111–12, 115, 124, 127, 130–31, 133–34, 247–50, 253, 254, 256, 257, 260, 261, 268, 269–70, 313–14
chaos, 81, 87–88
Chericoni, Roger, 181, 182
Chicago Pneumatic Tool Company, 127
China, People's Republic of, 228, 230, 243, 333
chrome, 68, 70, 71
Chrome Craft, 71, 72, 84, 85
Chrysler, 238, 267, 278, 300
Chubu Industrial Engineering Association, 242
Claramunt, Dennis, 129, 130
Clarke, Philip, 374*n*
Clausing, Don, 141
cola, 38–48, 374*n*
Cold War, 17, 151, 164, 276–78, 280, 306
Colt, Samuel, 153, 364*n*
Comet, 305
computer-aided design (CAD), 30, 148, 283
computer industry, 21, 28, 252
Computer Integrated Manufacturing, 216, 283
computer systems, 30, 45–46, 100, 110–11, 117, 121, 148, 175, 177, 179, 226–27, 261, 283

Concept of the Corporation, The (Drucker), 12
"concrete heads," 112, 129, 130, 140, 269
Condeco, Joe, 135
construction industry, 28, 29–31, 51, 286, 291–92, 372*n*
Coran, Mark, 151, 152, 167, 168, 172, 173, 175, 184, 248, 260–61
corporations, virtual, 21, 87
Cosentino, John, 130
crash parts, 68, 69–71, 73, 75, 81, 83, 85, 93
"created demand," 72–73
credit cards, 287, 288
credit checks, 55, 117, 292
Csikszentmihalyi, Mihaly, 65
currency risks, 335
Current State, 316–20, 321, 323, 325, 327–32
Curtiss Liberty engine, 155
Curtiss-Wright, 159
customers:
   cancellations by, 58
   in global strategy, 332–35
   "for life," 29, 235
   passivity of, 51
   pull directed by, 10, 24, 27, 67, 68, 76, 77, 82, 83, 84, 88, 94
   satisfaction of, 9, 15, 26, 29, 105, 106, 107, 118, 121, 123, 126, 127, 137, 216, 235, 259
   value defined by, 16, 18, 28, 29–36, 93, 123, 217–18, 252–53, 262, 291–92
Customers for Life (Sewell), 29
cycle time, 348, 352, 360*n*

Daimler-Benz, 189, 217
D'Amore, Bob, 167–68, 169, 184, 248
Danaher Corporation, 111, 127, 128, 129, 130–31, 133, 134, 168, 171
Daniell, Bob, 151
data control, 110–11
David, George, 152, 168–69, 170, 171, 172–73, 181–82, 184, 249

Day, Joe, 90, 338
de-encapsulation, 176, 179
Deming, W. Edwards, 29, 126, 127, 242
Deming Prize, 242
deselection, project, 97, 119, 141, 262
Directly Responsible Individual (DRI), 119, 321, 322
Dodge Line, 233
Douglas DC-7 aircraft, 159
Douglas DC-8 aircraft, 160
Douglas DC-9 aircraft, 160
Doyle Wilson Homebuilder, 29–31, 32, 51, 276, 356*n*
Drucker, Peter, 12

"early adopters," 260
"economic order quantities," 73
efficiency, 15, 16, 18–19, 21–22, 34, 50–51, 52, 289
electrostatic discharge machines (EDMs), 178
employees:
  bonuses for, 26, 56, 58, 263
  concentration of, 65–66
  cooperation of, 129, 138, 168, 269, 278–79
  dress code for, 135
  fatigue and stress of, 240
  feedback for, 15, 26, 65, 122, 263, 295
  injuries of, 27, 149
  job security of, 17, 62, 77, 115–16, 122–23, 133, 134, 139–40, 168, 179, 253, 258, 260, 271, 275, 280
  layoffs of, 15, 16, 24, 28, 109, 131–33, 138, 140, 172–73, 175, 179, 180, 205–6, 220, 233, 234, 249, 258–59, 260
  movement of, 15, 182–83
  overtime by, 81
  productivity of, 26, 27, 28, 64–65, 80, 90, 118, 137, 148, 173, 175, 197, 198, 212–13, 222, 224, 239, 262–63, 270, 295
  relocation of, 59, 135–36
  rotation of, 122
  seniority of, 172, 179
  skills of, 116, 120, 122, 132, 135–36, 187, 207, 215, 216–17, 268, 279
  suggestions by, 199–200
  turnover of, 116
  wages of, 63, 64, 116, 125, 137, 144, 150, 262–63, 268, 270
encapsulation, 93, 176, 177, 179
engineering, 10, 17, 19, 31, 32, 154–55, 213–14, 279, 280, 284
engines, aircraft, 20, 26, 151–52, 154–88, 225, 305–9, 364*n*, 365*n*–66*n*, 367*n*
enterprise, lean, 241, 271, 275–85
  batch-and-queue mode vs., 278
  careers and, 275, 278–79, 284
  "cold war" in, 276–78, 280
  cost reduction in, 276, 277, 280, 281–82
  definition of, 276
  flow in, 276, 285
  functions in, 256–57, 279–80
  in German industry, 281, 282–83, 284
  in Japanese industry, 281, 283–84
  JIT system used in, 280
  job security and, 275, 280
  management in, 275, 276, 282
  muda eliminated in, 276, 277, 279, 280, 285
  as organizational mechanism, 20–21
  pull in, 276, 285
  quality control in, 280
  role of firm in, 280–81
  self-perpetuation of, 279
  suppliers in, 277, 280, 282
  transparency in, 276
  trust in, 277
  in U.S. industry, 281, 282
  value stream in, 275, 277, 278, 281, 283, 285
  see also lean thinking; production, lean
environmental issues, 176, 179

F-15 fighter plane, 160
F-16 fighter plane, 160, 306

F-22 fighter plane, 306
F-35 fighter plane, 306, 373*n*
F-100 engine, 160, 162
factories:
    automation in, 28, 56, 60, 217, 230–31, 232, 239–41, 243, 244, 245, 268, 283
    "focused," 63, 164
    location of, 63–64
Ferrari, 267, 373*n*
Ferro, Jose, 340
"fill rate," 74
financial statements, 136, 138
Finland, 373*n*
"fire fighting," 114
Fiume, Orrie, 126, 127, 136
five Ss, 61, 348, 361*n*
five whys, 348
flexibility (changeover time), 318–20, 323
Flex-N-Gate, 68, 71
flow, 50–66
    action plan for, 250, 254, 255, 258, 264, 316–22
    continuous, 10, 21–24, 25, 26, 27, 49, 50–66, 95, 103, 105, 106, 108, 111–12, 125, 127, 134, 146, 217, 242, 276, 285
    definition of, 348, 349
    departmentalization vs., 10, 21, 23, 24, 53, 56, 112
    general case of, 23, 281
    implementation of, 52–66, 126, 135–36, 139
    management and, 52, 53, 54, 60
    mapping of, 57, 60, 62, 315
    muda and, 21, 56, 58, 60, 61, 62, 66
    for order processing, 54–56, 58
    perfection and, 65–66, 94
    quality in, 60–61
    as single-piece flow, 60, 62, 64, 112, 115, 119, 128, 139, 148, 173, 222, 259, 304–5, 314, 347, 348, 352
    small-lot production in, 23, 24, 52, 69–71, 72, 145
    special case of, 22–23
    transparency in, 56, 61
    of work, 64–66, 78–79, 120, 122–23
food production and distribution, 37–49, 286, 290–91
Ford, Henry, 22–23, 51, 258
Ford Explorer, 373*n*
Ford Motor Company, 74, 213, 242, 301
Ford Taurus, 213
Ford Tri-motor transport, 155
Freudenberg-NOK General Partnership (FNGP), 90–91, 210, 223, 226, 248, 259, 338
    pursuing perfection at, 323–26
"From Lean Production to the Lean Enterprise" (Womack and Jones), 275*n*
Fukuoka Chamber of Commerce, 221
Future State, 318–20, 321, 323, 328–30

General Electric, 112, 127, 152, 159, 161, 162, 163, 169, 175, 180, 306
"generalist engineer" problem, 279
General Motors, 12, 49, 74, 162, 170, 171, 277, 300, 301, 302, 373*n*
General Motors Institute, 170
Germany:
    automobile industry in, 189–218, 302–4, 373*n*
    competition from, 214, 215, 216–17, 218
    industrial traditions of, 191, 192, 214–18
    labor unions in, 198, 199, 202, 206, 216–17, 283
    lean enterprise in, 281, 282–83, 284
    lean production in, 189–218
    lean thinking in, 16–17, 19, 101, 188
    living standards in, 217–18
    "technik" in, 178, 189, 214–18
Giannattasio, Frank, 132, 139
glass, 91–93, 94, 241, 259
Gleick, James, 87
glossary, 347–53
Glyco, 197
"greenfield" plants, 10, 28, 217, 347, 348

grinding systems, 26, 60, 176–80, 367*n*, 369*n*
gruppen meisters (work group leaders), 193, 199
guide vanes, 174, 175

Harley-Davidson, 167–68
Harris, Rick, 375*n*
Hauni-Blohm blade grinding centers, 176–78
"head of the fish" system, 180
health care, 50, 51, 286, 289–90
health maintenance organizations, 290
heijunka (level scheduling), 10, 58, 70, 81–82, 139, 186, 235, 254, 256, 259, 262, 319, 348, 351
Hennessy Industries, 111, 112, 130
Hetzer, Fred, 163
Hicks, Ron, 111–12, 115, 116, 130
Hines, Peter, 241, 371*n*–72*n*
Hitachi, 181
Hobbs, L. S., 157–58
Hollerith machines, 157
homebuilding industry, 29–31, 51, 291–92
Honda, 242, 251
Horner, H. Mansfield, 366*n*
Hornet engine, 155
hoshin kanri (policy deployment), 94–98, 261–62, 349, 351
hot lists, 75, 106–7, 220
House of Quality concept, 141
hubs, airline, 18–19, 20, 175, 287, 288, 356*n*
Hurst, David, 371*n*

IBM, 162, 250
Ideal State, 331–32
Imai, Masaaki, 128, 198
information management, value-stream mapping and, 316–20
information management task, 19
information technology, 310, 327
injuries, job-related, 27, 149
Integrated Product Development (IPD), 165, 166

International Association of Machinists, 158, 172–73
International Brotherhood of Electrical Workers, 125
Inter Turbine, 175
inventories:
    action plan for, 250, 271
    as assets, 60
    business cycles and, 88
    carrying costs for, 67, 76, 146
    cash flow and, 137–38, 143, 146–47
    computerized, 45–46
    forecasts for, 84
    in-process, 71, 136, 138, 183, 210, 222
    lean distribution of, 74–82
    muda in, 15, 146–47
    perpetual, 45
    production and, 57–58, 67–68, 72–74, 110, 114, 115, 138
    reduction of, 24, 27, 45, 86–87, 88, 114, 126, 137–40, 146–47, 150, 318
    shipping costs for, 68, 73, 74, 76, 81
    stocking systems for, 42, 45, 67–68, 72–82
    warehouses for, 39, 42, 43, 44, 64, 68, 72–87
inventors, 102–3, 108, 124
inventory turns, 310–12
investment:
    capital, 94, 152, 179, 222, 230, 252, 257–58, 295
    in equipment, 60, 61, 85, 121
    return on, 24, 270, 277
Ito, Yuzuru, 181–82, 183, 184, 249, 257, 374*n*
Iwata, Yoshiki, 128–30, 134, 169, 201, 221, 257, 338, 374*n*

Jacobs Brake Company, 111–12, 128–30, 171
Jacobs Chuck Company, 129, 169
Jaguar, 373*n*
Japan:
    automobile industry in, 85–86, 197–98, 200, 211, 222, 242, 300–302, 336, 373*n*, 374*n*

economy of, 27, 80, 191, 225, 229,
    238, 244, 245, 246, 331
lean enterprise in, 281, 283–84
lean production in, 219–46
lean thinking in, 9, 17, 64, 88, 218,
    230, 242, 245–46
U.S. occupation of, 233, 235
vertical integration in, 235, 284
jidoka (autonomation), 231, 347, 349,
    360*n*–61*n*
Jones, Daniel, 374*n*
Just-in-Time (JIT) system, 37, 47,
    58–59, 70, 88, 126–27, 139, 144,
    145, 149, 179, 207, 208–9, 223, 231,
    234, 236, 250
just-on-time concept, 349

kaikaku (radical improvement), 23, 27,
    35, 61, 91–93, 94, 112, 139, 142,
    168, 183, 202, 222, 226, 247, 248,
    254, 255, 262, 265, 270, 349
kaizen (continuous incremental
    improvement), 23, 35, 79, 85,
    90–91, 94, 116, 117, 119, 122,
    128–30, 134, 139, 140, 142,
    144–45, 169, 182, 183, 202, 205,
    207, 214, 226–27, 230, 240, 248,
    262, 268, 315, 318, 319, 349, 374*n*
Kaizen (Imai), 128
"kamikaze *kaizen*," 315
Kamiya, Shotaro, 235, 237
kanban (signal card) system, 70, 203–4,
    232, 236, 319, 349, 351
Kawabe, Takeshi, 219, 222–24, 226
Keiper Recaro, 208
keiretsu (vertical integration), 21, 150*n*,
    284, 349
Kessler, Manfred, 202–3, 208
Khan, Shahid, 68–72, 74
Koenigsaecker, George, 128, 129, 247*n*,
    249, 338
Korean War, 164, 234
Krapek, Karl, 152, 170–73, 184, 248, 313

Lamborghini, 373*n*
Lancaster, Jim, 123

Lancaster, Pat, 102–3, 106, 107, 108–9,
    110, 112, 115–16, 118–19, 123,
    124, 247, 304–5, 313, 322
Land Rover, 373*n*
Lantech, 102–24
    batch-and-queue mode used by,
        103–4, 106, 107, 108, 112, 115, 117,
        119, 120, 121, 123
    box score of, 121
    competition of, 103, 108–9, 119,
        267
    computerized scheduling used by,
        106, 110–11, 117, 121
    cost reductions by, 109, 117
    customer satisfaction with, 105, 106,
        107, 118, 121, 123
    customization by, 104–5, 106, 107,
        118
    delivery times for, 106–7, 108, 114,
        115, 117–18
    departments of, 103, 104, 105, 106,
        107, 110, 112, 155
    engineering in, 103, 105, 107–8, 110,
        120
    final assembly in, 103–4, 113
    H Line of, 115
    lean production in, 103, 111–24, 128,
        188, 217, 226, 261
    lean thinking in capital goods at,
        304–5
    management of, 109, 112, 210, 321
    muda eliminated by, 112, 122
    order processing by, 104–7, 112,
        113–14, 117–18, 122
    pricing by, 104–5, 109, 110, 111, 115,
        117
    product development by, 102, 110,
        112, 118–21, 228, 304–5
    production layout of, 104, 105, 108,
        113, 116, 118, 120
    Q Line of, 112–14
    quality control by, 108–9
    sales of, 104–5, 106, 110, 111, 115,
        117, 121, 259, 305
    single-piece-flow manufacturing of,
        304–5

Lantech (*cont.*)
   S Line of, 120
   value stream manager at, 321–22
lean enterprise, *see* enterprise, lean
Lean Enterprise Institute, 339–40
Lean Enterprise Research Centre, 47, 200, 241, 339, 357*n*
Lean Enterprise Summits, 297–98
"Lean Production—The Challenge of Multi-Dimensional Change" (Koenigsaecker), 247*n*
lean thinking:
   bottom-up approach to, 10, 268–69, 270
   competition and, 49
   as counterintuitive, 23, 28, 134, 233, 234
   economic impact of, 27–28
   efficiency and, 15, 16, 18–19, 21–22, 34, 50–51, 52, 289
   evidence of economy-wide embrace of, 309–12
   function for, 95–96, 139, 223, 256–57, 263, 270
   in Germany, 16–17, 19, 101, 188
   glossary for, 347–53
   hierarchical organization vs., 132–33
   inertia vs., 97–98
   in Japan, 9, 17, 64, 88, 218, 230, 242, 245–46
   management and, 10, 19, 94–98, 101, 132, 139, 141–42, 147–48, 168, 173–74
   network for, 338–39
   performance leaps and, 10–11, 27, 269–71
   principles of, 10, 15–98, 101
   research on, 11–12
   steady advance of, 299–312
   sudden insight into, 28, 111–12, 127, 130, 170, 181
   timetables for, 95, 270
   see also enterprise, lean; production, lean
Learning to See (Rother and Shook), 327, 374*n*, 375*n*

Legrand S.A., 299
Lockheed Super Constellation aircraft, 159
logistic innovations, 310
Lorenz, Edward, 87

machines:
   changeover of, 41, 44, 56–57, 58, 61, 69–70, 85, 106, 114, 126, 143, 149, 177, 178–79, 222, 232, 265, 348
   design of, 56, 141–42, 286
   disaggregation of, 112
   large vs. small, 62
   maintenance of, 115, 126, 232
   monitoring of, 44, 60–61, 168, 176, 177, 178, 206, 231–32, 350–51
   as "monuments," 175–76, 179, 215, 261, 265, 350, 351
   noise of, 59, 63
   processing by, 38–44
   relocation of, 112–15, 117, 128–30, 135, 168, 175–76, 183, 201–2, 260
   right-sized, 23, 25, 60, 93, 114, 123, 256, 261, 265, 270, 280, 350, 351
   spread of, 56, 63
Machine That Changed the World, The (Womack and Jones), 9–10, 48, 197, 238–39, 339
management:
   action plan for, 248, 250, 256, 257, 259–61, 264, 268–69, 314, 315, 323, 327, 328–31
   cross-functional, 155, 163, 165
   flow and, 52, 53, 54, 60
   as fractal, 322
   "heavyweight" program, 53–54
   information, 19
   in lean enterprise, 275, 276, 282
   lean thinking and, 10, 19, 94–98, 101, 132, 139, 141–42, 147–48, 168, 173–74
   in mass production, 10, 16, 17–18, 44, 53–54, 141–42, 147–48, 173–74
   mind-set of, 16, 17–18
   open-book, 26, 294, 350
   of product line, 321–22

program, 156
   of value stream, 321–22, 323
Manufacturing Resource Planning (MRP II), 350
margin squeezing, 327
market:
   change in, 122
   core, 150
   niche in, 147, 175, 195, 197, 198, 202, 211, 217, 267
   recovery of, 115
   regional, 17, 245–46, 372*n*
   segment retreats in, 211, 214
   share of, 47, 115, 121, 126, 149, 151, 259
   stagnation of, 87–88, 150
Material Requirements Planning (MRP), 57, 63, 85, 88, 106, 110–11, 117, 126, 135, 142, 143, 164, 182, 184, 232, 290, 317, 319, 350, 360*n*, 363*n*
math, lean, 334–35
Matsushita, 181–82, 249
Max-Flex production method, 110, 144
Maynard, Steve, 31–32, 140–42
Mazda, 242
meisters (foremen), 193, 199–200, 201, 215, 283, 350
Mercedes, 193, 205, 211
Mexico, 333, 335
Microsoft, 28, 284
milk run, 291, 350
Mitsubishi, 242, 360*n*
Mittelstand companies, 191, 192, 214, 350, 369*n*
Mizuguchi, Keiji, 226, 227, 228, 229
mobility, short-range personal, 286, 293–94
Model T Ford, 22–23
Moffitt, Bill, 339
molding machines, 92, 149
Motorola University, 264
muda (waste):
   definition of, 15, 350
   elimination of, 15, 25–26, 27, 28, 43, 49, 90–98, 134, 146–47, 193, 206, 210, 217–18, 247, 249, 251, 252, 254, 255, 257, 263, 269, 276, 277, 279, 280, 285, 295, 315, 323, 327, 328–31, 349, 350, 370*n*
   errors as, 15, 43
   flow and, 21, 56, 58, 60, 61, 62, 66
   information vs., 111
   in order processing, 44–47
   pull and, 82, 86, 90
   target costs and, 35–36
   type one, 38, 43, 48, 131
   types of, 38, 43, 351–52, 355*n*
   type three, 43, 48
   type two, 38, 43, 48, 86, 131
   value stream and, 19–21, 25, 37–38, 327–28
multi-machine working, 347–48, 350

Nakamura, Kenya, 235
Nakao, Chihiro, 128, 129–30, 134, 169, 171, 173, 180, 201–3, 205, 207, 210, 220, 221, 338
Nakayama, Kiyotaka, 339
Navy, U.S., 154, 155
NEC, 284
Neill, John, 251
New Economy, 327
New Production System (NPS), 221, 243
Nippondenso, 235–36, 244, 353
Nissan, 215, 236, 242–43, 267
Nissan Micra, 215–16
Nissan 300ZX, 197
Northern, Ed, 174–75, 177, 179, 180, 257
Northwest Airlines, 18
NUMMI, 74, 230

ober meisters (group foremen), 193, 199
Ohba, Hajime, 339
Ohno, Taiichi, 10, 15, 22, 23, 37, 58, 110, 111, 128, 219, 220–23, 230–33, 234, 236, 239, 242, 243, 249, 281, 348, 351, 355*n*, 357*n*, 370*n*, 374*n*
Opel Eisenach plant, 217

operation, 350, 368*n*
opportunities, 336–37
Otis Elevator, 171, 181–82
overhead, 136, 262
overproduction, 58, 255

packaging industry, 304–5
paint systems, 60, 61, 113, 194, 204, 205–6
palletizers, 305
parking carousels, 225, 252
partnerships, 327
patents, 103, 108, 109
Pentland, Bob, 128, 129
perfection, 90–98
   action plan for, 250, 260, 270
   definition of, 350
   dreaming about, 285, 286–95
   flow and, 65–66, 94
   incremental path to, *see kaizen*
   pull and, 85, 92, 94
   pursuit of, 10, 12, 25–26, 35, 37, 49, 109, 134, 139, 224
   radical path to, *see kaikaku*
pickers, 42, 73, 75, 76, 77–79, 82, 143
Plan-Do-Check-Act problem-solving cycle, 242
platforms, automobile, 237, 238, 278
"pogo stick" phenomenon, 81
Point-of-Sale (POS) system, 45
point-to-point services, 18, 19, 20
point velocity, 178, 288
poka-yoke process, 9, 61, 203, 228, 350–51, 361*n*, 370*n*
Poland, 333
Pontiac assembly plant, 170–71
Porsche, Ferdinand, 189, 190, 191, 193
Porsche AG, 199–218
   batch-and-queue mode used by, 192, 215
   box score of, 212–13
   change agents for, 197–98, 201–5, 214
   competition of, 192, 214, 215
   cost reductions in, 197, 200, 210
   craft culture of, 193–94, 201, 206, 207
   creative crisis in, 195–97
   delivery times for, 201
   departments of, 192, 215
   engine assembly in, 201–5, 213
   engineers of, 190, 192, 194, 195, 202, 206, 210, 212, 213–14, 215, 279
   expanded operations of, 373*n*
   family control of, 191, 195
   founding of, 189
   hierarchy of, 192, 193, 199–200, 201, 215
   history of, 189–94
   inventory of, 194, 201–3, 213, 215
   JIT system used by, 207, 208–10
   labor unions of, 198, 199, 202, 206–7
   layoffs by, 205–6
   lean production in, 189, 197–218, 226, 229, 258, 264, 302–4, 338, 373*n*
   legal name of, 192
   machines used by, 193, 201–2, 205, 206, 364*n*
   management of, 191–92, 194, 198–99, 202, 203, 207, 210–11, 214, 374*n*
   market niche of, 195, 197, 198, 202, 211, 267
   meister system of, 193, 199–200, 201, 215
   muda in, 193, 206, 210
   order processing by, 194
   performance standards of, 191, 193–94, 211, 212
   plant layout of, 203, 204
   POLE team of, 207–10
   Pre-Delivery Inspection Centers closed by, 303
   product development in, 191, 192, 193–94, 195, 198, 206, 211–12, 215, 276, 302–4
   productivity in, 197, 198, 212–13
   profits of, 191, 198, 213, 303, 304
   pull system used by, 208–9
   quality control in, 189, 193–94, 198, 199, 200, 202, 206, 208
   reorganization of, 198–200
   sales of, 195–97, 206, 213, 214, 303
   sensei for, 201–5

suppliers of, 192–93, 194, 203–4,
  207–10, 214, 215, 252, 266
value stream of, 195, 215
Works Council of, 198, 199, 202, 206
Porsche Boxster, 211, 302, 369*n*
Porsche Carrera, 189, 201
Porsche Consulting, 210
Porsche Improvement (*Verbesserungs*)
  Process (PVP), 200–201, 205,
  206
Porsche 356, 190
Porsche 911, 190, 191, 195, 196, 197,
  201, 211, 302, 368*n*–69*n*
Porsche 912, 196
Porsche 914, 190–91, 195, 196
Porsche 924, 191, 195, 196
Porsche 928, 191, 195, 196, 197, 211
Porsche 944, 191, 195, 196, 197
Porsche 959, 195
Porsche 968, 191, 196, 205, 211
Pratt, Francis, 153, 154
Pratt & Whitney, 151–88
  American Eagle logo of, 155
  batch-and-queue mode used by, 153,
    160, 165, 173, 175, 177, 180, 182
  cells used in, 156–57, 168, 169, 173,
    175, 179, 183
  change agents for, 168–73, 257
  commercial accounts of, 151–52, 155,
    160, 161, 162
  competition of, 151, 157, 159, 161–64
  Continuous Improvement Office of,
    168, 184, 223
  cost reductions by, 20, 26, 151, 152,
    179, 182, 183, 187
  creative crisis in, 166–86
  delivery times for, 164, 173, 174, 183,
    186
  departments of, 155, 159, 171–72,
    180–81
  in difficult environment, 305–9
  downsizing plan for, 166–67
  earnings of (1992–2002), 152, 309,
    373*n*–74*n*
  employees of, 158, 168, 172–73, 174,
    175, 187

engineers of, 154–58, 160–61,
  164–65, 166, 182–83, 184, 186
exit strategy for, 167, 183
final assembly in, 157, 160, 173, 174,
  180, 182, 232
flow in, 156–57, 164–65, 167–69, 173,
  175, 176–79, 180, 182, 187
founding of, 153
history of, 153–66
inventory of, 170–71, 175, 183
JIT system used by, 179
labor unions of, 158, 172–73, 187,
  365*n*
layoffs by, 162, 163, 172–73, 175, 179,
  180
lean production in, 150, 152–53,
  166–68, 217, 226, 229, 259, 338,
  367*n*–68*n*
machines used by, 153–54, 160, 165,
  168, 175–80, 183
management of, 155–56, 158, 163,
  164–66, 168, 173–74, 180, 182–83,
  184, 210, 260–61
market share of, 151, 160, 162, 164,
  169
mass production in, 157–62
Material Review Boards (MRBs) of,
  181, 183
military accounts of, 151, 155,
  158–59, 160, 162, 306, 373*n*
modular system used by, 180, 182, 186
order processing by, 158, 161, 167,
  174
plant layout of, 165, 166, 168, 172,
  177, 178, 182–83, 306–7
Product Centers of, 172, 184, 185
product development in, 152, 154,
  158–64, 167, 184–86, 276, 308,
  365*n*–66*n*, 373*n*
profits of, 170, 187
project engineer's role in, 155–58
pull in, 182
quality control in, 157, 163, 165, 175,
  179, 180–83, 184
reorganization of, 184–86
return on assets and sales of, 308

Pratt & Whitney (*cont.*)
  sales of, 161–62, 163, 169–70, 171, 186, 187, 306, 307, 308
  spare parts manufactured by, 151, 161, 162, 169, 174–75, 187, 308
  suppliers of, 166–67, 168, 172, 173, 179–80, 182, 183
  tools used by, 157, 158, 164, 168, 180, 183
  value stream of, 20, 48, 169, 172, 175, 178
Pratt PW4084 engines, 152
"Pratt Salute," 159
prices:
  competitive, 163, 251
  constant, 82
  control of, 17, 241
  as global strategy, 332–35
  reduction of, 35–36, 218
  return on assets and sales vs., 308
  supplier's, 327
  targets for, 10, 267
Prius, 373*n*
process:
  efficiency and, 50–51, 52
  technology for, 16–17, 26, 95
  as term, 350, 351, 368*n*
  time for, 62, 351, 352
  villages for, 128, 135, 220, 232, 243, 347, 351
Procter & Gamble, 282
production, lean:
  acid test of, 151–88
  action plan for, *see* action plan
  cellular assembly in, 10, 62, 63, 112–15, 117, 128–30, 156–57, 168, 169, 173, 175, 179, 183, 252, 314, 323–26, 347, 351, 375*n*
  conversion to, 10–11, 12, 101–246
  cost reductions in, 20, 26, 28, 43, 45, 63, 64, 80, 109, 117, 217, 244, 250, 251, 252, 259, 266–67, 268, 276, 277, 280, 281–82
  egalitarian nature of, 97, 111, 268
  German example of, 189–218, 302–4, 373*n*

  goals for, 96–97
  hard case for, 125–50
  Japanese examples of, 219–46, 300–302, 336, 373*n*
  job security and, 115–16, 122–23, 133, 134, 139–40, 168, 179, 258, 260
  "just do it" approach to, 12, 129, 134, 202, 261
  logistics and, 63–64
  matrix for, 96–97
  "mean" production vs., 16, 258, 278–79
  noise and, 59, 63
  order processing in, 24, 26, 35, 44–47, 52, 54–56, 58, 81, 194, 246, 254, 255, 256, 262, 268
  quality control in, 9, 27, 29, 51, 54, 60–61, 96, 109, 115, 121, 126, 134, 137, 140–41, 147, 149, 165, 242, 249, 257, 267, 268, 280, 349, 351
  resources in, 36, 47, 85, 88, 97, 144–47, 179, 255, 262
  scheduling in, 10, 58, 70, 81, 186, 235, 254, 256, 259, 262, 348–49, 351
  simple case for, 102–24
  transparency (visual control) in, 21, 26, 56, 61, 70, 97, 117, 122, 125, 139, 142, 149, 180, 200, 201, 217–18, 228, 253, 261, 263–64, 268, 270, 276, 353, 360*n*
  see also enterprise, lean; lean thinking
production, mass:
  automated, 28, 56, 60, 217, 230–31, 232, 239–41, 243, 244, 245, 268, 283
  batch-and-queue mode used in, 9, 21–22, 23, 27, 47, 53, 65, 88, 257–58, 265, 267, 278, 347, 352
  "brownfields" in, 10–11, 28, 261, 347, 348
  buffers in, 60, 61, 112, 113, 171
  departmentalization in, 10, 21, 23, 24, 53, 56, 112, 286
  errors in, 15, 27, 43, 61, 96, 115, 121, 137, 149

final assembly in, 20, 22, 23, 26, 56, 80, 93
"greenfields" in, 10, 28, 217, 347, 348
inventory in, 67–68, 72–74
in lean global strategy, 332–36
management in, 10, 16, 17–18, 44, 53–54, 141–42, 147–48, 173–74
quotas for, 114
scheduling in, 55
volume in, 22–23, 103, 104
products:
categories of, 335
customized, 104–5, 106, 107, 118, 216, 224, 225, 230
definition of, 32–34
design of, 16, 24, 30–31, 32, 40, 52, 53–54, 55, 60, 63, 93, 107–8, 118, 119, 154, 226–27
development of, 9, 10, 21, 26, 27, 31–32, 35, 37, 47, 48, 52, 53–54, 102, 110, 112, 118–21, 140–42, 147, 148, 150, 242, 245–46, 250, 251–52, 255, 256, 257, 259, 262, 266, 268, 301–2, 308
discounting of, 24
distribution of, 42, 55, 72–82, 85–87
duplication of, 245
end, 216
expedition of, 55, 58, 63, 67–68, 71, 73, 75, 83, 106–7, 110, 119, 140, 194, 220
families of, 23, 62, 63, 95, 111, 121, 135, 136, 146, 147, 225, 226, 238, 241, 250, 252, 254, 255, 256, 259, 261, 263, 270, 320–22, 351
fast-moving, 46
global strategy for, 332–35
"hit rate" of, 54
launching of, 16, 24, 47–48, 63, 120–21, 131
lead times for, 30, 38, 58, 85, 87, 107, 110, 114, 121, 165–66, 167, 186, 237, 251, 259, 266, 268, 349, 351, 352
margins for, 47
market trials for, 47

reengineering of, 53, 107–8, 120, 194, 216, 227
services vs., 36, 51, 187, 259, 286, 294
standardized, 232
target costs for, 10, 35–36, 141, 149, 236, 267, 277, 352, 357n
teams for, 10, 19, 25, 31–32, 53–54, 55, 60–61, 63, 95, 96, 109, 112, 114, 119–20, 135–36, 137, 139, 141–42, 143, 148, 184–86, 252, 278, 279, 280, 321, 322
throughput times for, 24, 27, 54, 60, 115, 121, 150, 210, 240, 349, 351, 352
time-to-market for, 27, 148, 165, 222, 238, 251, 268
variety of, 27, 31, 41, 119, 124, 140, 215, 226, 268
profits, 16, 35, 54, 109, 121, 125, 127, 133, 136–37, 138, 144, 149, 150, 161, 251, 258, 263, 276
profit sharing, 137, 144, 150
progress control boards, 78–79
promotions, special service, 73, 81, 82, 88
publishing industry, 25
pull, 67–89, 349
action plan for, 250, 253, 254, 255, 264, 314, 323–26, 328–31
customer as source of, 10, 24, 27, 67, 68, 76, 77, 82, 83, 84, 88, 94
definition of, 67, 351
implementation of, 24–25, 26, 66, 67–89, 126, 134, 139, 217, 276, 285
mapping of, 77, 78, 80
muda and, 82, 86, 90
perfection and, 85, 92, 94
punch presses, 135, 149
PW2037 engine, 163
PW4084 engine, 165
P&W J-57 engine, 160
P&W JT3 engine, 160
P&W JT8D engine, 160, 163, 164
P&W JT9D engine, 366n

Q-Plus Management, 165
Quality Circles, 242
Quality Function Deployment (QFD), 9, 54, 140–41, 147, 249, 349, 351
queue time, 351

Rales, Mitchell, 111, 130
Rales, Steve, 111, 130
rearview mirrors, 215–16
recessions, 305, 311, 327, 336–37
recycling, 38, 42, 43
reengineering movement, 23–24, 28, 55, 97, 249, 252
Regional Distribution Centers (RDCs), 45–47, 359n
rental car industry, 287, 293–94
Rentschler, Frederick, 154
retail formats, innovations in, 310
retirement, 140
retrofitting, 110
Reutter, 190
reverse auctions, 327
revolution, institutionalizing of, 313–37
rework, 51, 53, 54, 107, 120, 160, 193–94, 227, 292
Rich, Nick, 37n
"road warriors," 305
robotics, 28, 232, 243
roll carriages, 102–3
rolling mills, 40, 42–43, 44, 135, 149
Rolls-Royce, 152, 161, 180, 306, 373n
Rolls-Royce RB211-535 engine, 163
Rother, Mike, 316, 327, 374n, 375n
Ryerson, 145

Saab, 373n
sales:
    action plan for, 254, 256, 259, 262
    bonuses in, 56, 58
    commissions for, 29
    department for, 10
    forecasts of, 24, 252
    level selling in, 81–82, 235, 349–50
    order processing and, 54–56
    tracking of, 45–46
    volume of, 35–36

scale economies, 17, 44, 49, 106, 146, 232
Schonberger, Richard, 374n
Schrempp, Juergen, 217
Scott, Bob, 67–68, 72, 73, 75, 76, 83
scrap, 26, 27, 43, 52, 92–93, 137, 202, 244
Seeing the Whole: Mapping the Extended Value Stream (Jones and Womack), 327, 375n
Senge, Peter, 88, 369n
seniority, 172, 179
sensei, 69–71, 128–30, 169, 201–5, 234, 249–50, 253, 254, 256, 268, 269–70, 314–15, 322, 339, 351, 361n, 371n
services, 11, 36, 46, 51, 52, 187, 259, 286–87, 294
Sewell, Carl, 29
Seyler, Judy, 131, 132–33
shareholders, 16, 138, 144
Sharma, Anand, 115, 117, 338
Shingijutsu, 169, 182, 201, 221, 338
Shingo, Shigeo, 23, 243, 249, 368n, 374n
shipment dates, 55, 71, 73
shoe manufacturing, 332–33, 335
Shook, John, 316, 327, 374n, 375n
"shop hours," 151, 169
Showa Manufacturing Company, 219–30
    batch-and-queue mode used by, 220, 222, 225–26
    change agents for, 220–24
    Chinese subsidiary of, 228, 230
    cost reductions by, 226, 227
    creative crisis in, 219–21
    final assembly in, 222
    inventory of, 220, 222, 224, 229
    layoffs by, 220, 233
    lean production in, 221–30, 246, 338
    machines used by, 222
    management of, 222
    market share of, 224, 228, 229, 230
    order processing by, 227–28, 230

product development by, 222, 225–27, 230, 252, 259, 276
production layout of, 220, 223
Production Research Department of, 223, 226
productivity in, 222, 224, 229
product teams in, 225–28, 230
profits of, 229
reorganization of, 225–26, 230
sales of, 224, 225, 229
suppliers of, 244
value stream in, 228
shrink-wrapping, 102
shusa system, 234–35, 237–38, 352
Single Minute Exchange of Dies (SMED), 352, 361*n*
single-point billing, 287
Sloan, Alfred P., Jr., 302, 373*n*
smelters, 39, 41, 42, 43, 44
Snecma, 163
Southwest Airlines, 19, 288
Spaghetti Chart, 104, 352
specialization, 50, 54, 141–42
Srock, Rainer, 212
stagnation, economic, 27–28
stamping presses, 68, 69–70
standard-cost accounting, 60, 136, 352
steel, 59, 71, 84, 85, 145, 156, 193, 227, 241
stereolithography, 87
stockers, 72–73, 75, 82, 83
stock-outs, 45, 291
storage bins, 72, 75–76, 77, 79, 110
stretch-wrapping, 41, 102–3, 112, 121, 123
subcontractors, 26, 29
Suburu, 373*n*
supermarkets, 37–49
suppliers:
  action plan for, 248, 249, 252, 265–67, 268, 270, 327–32, 371*n*–72*n*
  first-tier, 26, 46–47, 59, 194, 214, 235–36, 237, 239, 241, 243, 267, 268
  in lean enterprise, 277, 280, 282
  marginal, 140

margins of, 16, 282
reduction of, 140, 143, 144–45, 173, 179–80, 244
second-tier, 82, 237, 239, 241, 267
third-tier, 241
surge protectors, 125, 126
SUVs, 301, 373*n*
Suzumura, Kikuo, 243
"systems integrator," 167

Takenaka, Akira, 128, 129–30
takt time, 55–56, 63, 70, 114, 117, 122, 139, 149, 227–28, 348, 349, 352, 359*n*–60*n*
TBM, 338
technology:
  appropriate, 81
  complex, 188
  democracy and, 111
  development of, 27–28, 270, 295
  information, 310, 327
  "key," 146, 225
  process, 16–17, 26, 95
Tele-Power Poles, 135, 136, 141, 142
Tesco, 37–49, 51, 94, 357*n*–58*n*, 359*n*, 374*n*
titanium, 20, 55, 59
"to do" lists, 29, 30, 292
tools, *see* machines
Total Productive Maintenance (TPM), 60, 149, 244, 322, 353, 374*n*
Total Quality Control (TQC), 242, 322
Total Quality Management (TQM), 29, 51, 109, 126, 134, 141, 165, 242, 322
Toyoda, Eiji, 234
Toyoda, Gosei, 219, 221, 235
Toyoda, Kiichiro, 231, 233, 236
Toyoda, Sakichi, 231, 347
Toyoda Spinning and Weaving, 219, 221
Toyota Corolla, 237
Toyota Corona, 72, 237
Toyota Crown, 235
Toyota Daily Ordering System (TDOS), 79, 80

Toyota Motor Corporation, 230–46
  automation at, 230–31, 239–41, 243, 244
  batch-and-queue mode used by, 231, 233, 237, 241
  cells used in, 232
  chief engineer at, 322
  competition of, 215, 217, 251
  cost reductions by, 236, 237, 241
  creative crisis in, 233
  customer relations of, 235, 238, 241, 244
  Daily Ordering System of, 302
  dealerships of, 67–68, 73, 74, 76, 81–86
  flow in, 240, 242
  Global 10 initiative of, 300
  homebuilding by, 372n
  inventory of, 72–87, 176, 232, 237, 255, 361n, 374n
  JIT implemented by, 58, 70, 127, 231, 234, 236
  labor unions of, 233
  layoffs by, 233, 234
  lean production developed by, 9–10, 49, 61, 69–71, 77, 82, 128, 168, 219, 220, 221, 230–46, 271, 370n
  lean thinking disseminated by, 69–71, 128–30, 242–44
  Local Distribution Centers (LDCs) of, 85–86
  management of, 231, 233, 234, 326, 336
  market share of, 237, 243, 300–301
  Miyata plant of, 240
  modular system used by, 51
  Motomachi plant of, 234, 240
  Operations Management Consulting Division (OMCD) of, 236–37, 268, 323, 361n
  order processing by, 231, 237
  Parts Distribution Center (PDCs) of, 72–82, 83, 84, 85, 86–87, 255, 302, 361n
  Parts Redistribution Center (PRC) of, 74, 79, 84, 85
  performance chart for, 239
  product development in, 197, 231, 234–35, 237–38, 301–2, 352
  productivity at, 239
  pull in, 67–68, 231, 232, 238, 339
  quality control in, 231, 238, 242
  sales of, 85, 233, 234, 235, 237, 241, 303
  sensei of, 69–71, 128–30, 234, 314–15
  shusa system of, 234–35, 237–38, 352
  steady advance of, 300–302, 373n, 374n
  suppliers of, 194, 221, 234, 235–37, 239, 241, 243–44, 255, 266–67, 302, 339
  Supplier Support Center (TSSC) of, 339
  Tahara plant of, 80, 239–40
  "2010 Global Vision" of, 300
  value specification in, 17
  value stream of, 232, 233, 239, 241, 321–22
Toyota Motor Sales (TMS), 85, 235, 237, 339
Toyota Production System (TPS), 72, 74, 128, 221, 231, 234, 236, 237, 240, 242–43, 322, 374n–75n
Toyota Publica, 237
Toyota RAV4 vehicle, 240–41
Toyota RX300, 373n
Toyota Supra, 197
trade protection, 335
transparency, 21, 26, 56, 61, 70, 97, 117, 122, 125, 139, 142, 149, 180, 200, 201, 217–18, 228, 253, 261, 263–64, 268, 270, 276, 353, 360n
travel industry, 15, 32–34, 43, 286–89, 293–94, 373n
"treasure hunts," 83, 180, 202
turbine blades, 161, 164–65, 174, 175
turn-back analysis, 182, 353
Twin Wasp engine, 155

Underwood, Bob, 109, 114, 116
unions, labor, 124, 125, 129, 139, 140, 150, 198, 199, 202, 206–7, 216

Unipart Group, 251, 264, 339
Unipart University, 264
United Technologies Corporation (UTC), 151, 152, 168, 170, 182, 249, 308, 338

value, 29–36
  cost and, 218
  creation of, 16, 20, 23–24, 25, 38, 43, 93, 131, 132, 133, 187, 253, 265–66, 276, 280, 327, 349, 350
  customer's definition of, 16, 18, 28, 29–36, 93, 123, 217–18, 252–53, 262, 291–92
  specification of, 10, 16–19, 25, 28, 29–36, 52, 54, 89, 94, 112, 217, 276, 277, 291–92, 293
  as term, 353
value stream, 37–49
  action plan and, 252–53, 254, 255–56, 262, 264, 270, 271, 315, 316–22
  application of, 48–49, 85
  control of, 47, 135–36
  created demand in, 72–73
  Current State and, 316–20, 321, 323, 325, 327–32
  definition of, 19, 353, 355n–56n
  extended, 327–31
  firm-to-firm relations in, 20–21, 93
  functional needs and, 54
  Future State and, 318–20, 321, 323, 328–30
  Ideal State and, 331–32
  identification of, 10, 11, 19–21, 25, 36, 37–49, 52, 89, 94, 112, 139, 217
  in lean enterprise, 275, 277, 278, 281, 283, 285
  management of, 321–22, 323
  mapping of, 37–38, 39, 42, 315, 316–20, 327–32, 353, 375n
  perfecting of, 319
  realignment of, 12, 25, 42–43, 85, 93, 94, 134–36, 292
  reorganization by, 320–23
variance analysis, 137
vehicle off road (VOR) system, 73, 75

Vietnam, 333
visual control, 21, 26, 56, 61, 70, 97, 117, 122, 125, 139, 142, 149, 180, 200, 201, 217–18, 228, 253, 261, 263–64, 268, 270, 276, 353, 360n
Volkswagen, 49, 191, 215, 216, 277
Volkswagen Beetle, 189, 190
Volkswagen Golf, 216
Volvo, 337n

wage costs, in global strategy, 332–34
Wal-Mart, 55, 282
Ward, Carlton, 164, 166
Wasp engine, 155, 156, 365n
Wasp Junior engine, 155
Wasp Major engine, 365n–66n
Weiner, Bob, 174, 180, 368n
welding, 20, 70, 113, 160, 227
Westinghouse, 159
Whitney, Amos, 153, 154
Wiedeking, Wendelin, 189, 197–201, 202–3, 205, 210–11, 214, 248, 313
Wilson, Doyle, 29–31, 51, 292, 356n
wire guides, 31–32, 51
Wiremold Company, 125–50, 373n, 374n
  acquisitions of, 126, 146, 147
  batch-and-queue mode used by, 126, 127, 131, 137, 142–43, 145, 146, 147
  box score of, 148–50
  buyout offer accepted by, 299
  change agent for, 125, 269
  cost reductions by, 32, 127, 136, 137–38, 145
  customer satisfaction and, 126, 127, 137
  "de-layering" of, 131–33, 135
  delivery times for, 137, 142, 143–44, 148
  departments of, 31, 131, 135, 139, 141–42
  employees of, 125, 131, 133, 134, 137, 144, 150, 263
  engineers of, 31, 32, 142, 146
  growth strategy of, 145–48, 149

Wiremold Company (*cont.*)
  inventories of, 137–40, 143, 146–47
  JIT Promotion Office (JPO) of, 139, 223
  JIT system used by, 126–27, 139, 144, 145, 149, 223
  labor unions of, 125, 139, 140, 150
  lean production in, 127–50, 153, 168–69, 217, 226, 363*n*
  management of, 131–32, 147
  market share of, 259
  muda eliminated by, 134, 146–47
  order processing by, 131, 142–44, 147, 148, 149
  product development in, 31–32, 51, 131, 135–36, 140–42, 147, 148, 149, 150
  production layout of, 132, 133, 135, 147
  sales of, 125, 127, 131, 137, 140, 146, 147, 149, 150
  scoreboards used by, 136–37
  space reductions by, 147, 149, 150
  steady advance of, 299
work:
  flow of, 64–66, 78–79, 120, 122–23
  rethinking of, 52
  standardization of, 54, 60, 113, 114, 115, 122, 139, 142, 180, 352, 360*n*
work-in-process (WIP), 363*n*
World War II, 158–59, 164
Wright Aeronautical Corporation, 154
Wright Whirlwind engine, 154, 155
www.lean.org, 340
www.leanuk.org, 340

Yamamoto, Tetsuo, 219, 220–21, 225
yen, 17, 225, 243, 372*n*

Zabaneh, Jose, 110–11, 115
zero setup, 352

About the Authors

JAMES P. WOMACK is president and founder of the Lean Enterprise Institute (www.lean.org), a nonprofit education and research organization based in Brookline, Massachusetts. LEI is devoted to promoting lean thinking by presenting lean knowledge in workbook formats and teaching this knowledge in a variety of venues.

DANIEL T. JONES is chairman and founder of the Lean Enterprise Academy (www.leanuk.org), a nonprofit education and research organization based in the U.K. The Academy shares the mission of the Lean Enterprise Institute in the U.S. of raising lean consciousness and making lean knowledge available in a variety of formats.